SOCIAL MEDIA AND ELECTRONIC COMMERCE LAW

SECOND EDITION

The ever-evolving nature of electronic commerce and social media continues to challenge the capacity of the courts to respond to privacy and security violations in 'cyberlaw'. *Social Media and Electronic Commerce Law* is designed to provide students and legal practitioners with a thorough and engaging exploration of the laws, regulations and grey areas of commerce via online platforms.

This new edition has been thoroughly revised to address changes in legislation and recent court judgments, and to reflect the dynamic sphere of social media. New chapters focus on internet and e-commerce law regarding social media, P2P file sharing, cloud computing and workplace issues, with an emphasis on data security made particularly relevant by the proliferation of hacking incidents.

Written in an accessible style, *Social Media and Electronic Commerce Law* investigates the challenges facing legal practitioners and commercial parties in this dynamic field, as well as the underlying legal theory that governs it.

Alan Davidson is Senior Lecturer in the School of Law, University of Queensland. He is a solicitor and barrister of the Supreme Court of New South Wales and the High Court of Australia, as well as a delegate on the Electronic Commerce Working Group of UNCITRAL.

SOCIAL MEDIA AND ELECTRONIC COMMERCE LAW

SECOND EDITION

Alan Davidson

CAMBRIDGE
UNIVERSITY PRESS

CAMBRIDGE
UNIVERSITY PRESS

University Printing House, Cambridge CB2 8BS, United Kingdom

One Liberty Plaza, 20th Floor, New York, NY 10006, USA

477 Williamstown Road, Port Melbourne, VIC 3207, Australia

314-321, 3rd Floor, Plot 3, Splendor Forum, Jasola District Centre, New Delhi - 110025, India

79 Anson Road, #06-04/06, Singapore 079906

Cambridge University Press is part of the University of Cambridge.

It furthers the University's mission by disseminating knowledge in the pursuit of education, learning and research at the highest international levels of excellence.

www.cambridge.org
Information on this title: www.cambridge.org/9781107500532

First published as *Law of Electronic Commerce* 2009
Reprinted 2012
Second edition 2016

Cover designed by Sardine Design
Typeset by Aptara Corp.

A catalogue record for this publication is available from the British Library

*A Cataloguing-in-Publication entry is available from the catalogue
of the National Library of Australia at* www.nla.gov.au

ISBN 978-1-107-50053-2 Paperback

Reproduction and communication for educational purposes

....

CONTENTS

ACKNOWLEDGEMENTS

We are in the midst of an 'Electronic Renaissance'. The access to the copious amounts of information and knowledge has never been so vast and so effortless. The result globally impacts communications, social interactions, commerce, entertainment and research. The law has been catching up, rationalising traditional principles in a new landscape. Nevertheless, from the avalanche of knowledge, information and technology, an order has emerged endogenously – a *rule of cyberspace*. John Perry Barlow, speaking about cyberspace, 'the new home of the mind', declared:

> Ours is a world that is both everywhere and nowhere, but it is not where bodies
> live … In our world, whatever the human mind may create can be reproduced and
> distributed infinitely at no cost. The global conveyance of thought no longer requires
> your factories to accomplish. We will create a civilization of the Mind in Cyberspace.
> May it be more humane and fair than the world your governments have made
> before.[1]

In the past two decades many of the legal challenges have been answered. The phenomena that is social media calls for an understanding of the development of laws relating to peer-to-peer file sharing, copyright and the attack on Internet Service Providers; the recent emergence of cloud computing; social media use and workplace law; defamation online; privacy law and the 2014 Australian Privacy Principles; digital personae online and online censorship. In the field of electronic commerce all Australian jurisdictions have adopted the terms of the UNCITRAL *Convention on the Use of Electronic Communications in International Contracts* (2006). Other areas include cybercrime, the regulation of spam, internet gambling, identity theft, cybersquatting, intellectual property issues and the evidence of electronic records.

My interest in this area arose some three decades ago when I undertook a degree in computing science while practising law. At the time the combination was most unusual, but the world of cyberspace and the regulation of that world have crystallised. The aim of this work is to define the law relating to social media and electronic commerce within Australia as determined by the legislature, judicial interpretations and the common law. It is intended for legal practitioners and students of what has broadly become known as cyberlaw. I have had the advantage of synthesising work in this field by being a delegate to the *Electronic Commerce Working Group* of UNCITRAL, working on new instruments.

---

1 John Perry Barlow, 'A Declaration of the Independence of Cyberspace' published as email to barlow@
eff.org on 9 February 1996.

I would like to thank my colleagues Russell Hinchy, Paul O'Shea and Matthew Floro for their feedback, suggestions and assistance. Finally I would thank my late father and my wonderful family Dianne, Taylor and Chelsea.

Dr Alan Davidson

Senior Lecturer, TC Beirne School of Law, University of Queensland

Solicitor and Barrister

July 2015

TABLE OF CASES

TABLE OF STATUTES

TABLE OF INTERNATIONAL INSTRUMENTS

PART 1

INTRODUCTION

1

AN 'ELECTRONIC RENAISSANCE' – DIGITAL *LEX MERCATORIA* AND DIGITAL PERSONA

The clichéd and now classic approach to introducing the digital revolution is to compare it to the invention of the printing press by Johannes Gutenberg in 1450.[1] The Renaissance of the Middle Ages emerged from dark and secretive times, and was contributed to by an explosion of books and the release of knowledge into the wider world. A neoteric intellectual spirit was fostered. Knowledge was power – a power formerly harnessed and monopolised by a relatively small number of abbey-bound monks who hand-copied rare and invaluable tomes and held them in monastic libraries unavailable to any but those the Church permitted. Mechanisation of the production process changed this situation dramatically, and within 50 years there were 20 million books published in Europe. 'Information wants to be free' may be the catch-cry of the internet age but it applies to the Middle Ages as well. Mass communication through the printed word became the vehicle that drove the Renaissance, enabling and fostering an exchange of knowledge and ideas. The 'Electronic Renaissance' takes advantage of global communications, high speeds, bulk transfers and massive data storage capacities to power a new global knowledge revolution. Individuals in modern society have their digital persona on multiple computers: in government databases, employer databases, as memberships, via social media participation, on criminal databases for some, and as more surreptitiously collected data when we browse the internet. Much of an individual's digital persona is available to those who know the language of computers. Commercial enterprises collate data and make serious commercial decisions on a macro and micro level.

This book hypothesises that order is endogenous. The structure of language, the systemisation of laws and the constitution of economic systems all emerge from unplanned, arbitrary chaos. The social order which emerges from this chaos is reliant on and will be largely framed by the available raw materials: the nature of any markets it operates within, the structures and the natural and constructed environments within which it must prove efficacious. Technology emerges in response to the experience of the marketplace with emergent technologies, access to the technology, and perceived utility in terms of opportunity costs. The order of any regulation that also emerges will depend upon the perspective of the players. The chapters that follow examine the creation of the law, each providing examples of endogenous order and the societal responses to the creation of that order. These societal responses emerge from three fundamental bases: technological, the legal and the pragmatic.[2] The heterogeneous expert would argue that substance is merely a function of form. Whether we call it Daoism, determinism, spontaneous

---

1 There are earlier inventions of the printing press in the East, but Gutenburg's invention sparked the Western Renaissance.
2 See, for example, Albert Loan, 'Institutional bases of the spontaneous order: Surety and assurance', *Humane Studies Review* (1991) 7(1).

order or an invisible hand,[3] the course of development, conscious or even inanimate, will invariably follow the path of best fit.

Aphorisms such as 'Information wants to be free', 'Good order results spontaneously' or 'That which is the result of human action but not of human design'[4] reflect the tensions and isomorphism in the order of law and technology. Each twist and turn takes a path of least resistance. This multiplicity provides the legal system's comfort and structure whilst retaining flexibility and adaptability.

This construct mirrors the development and use of *lex mercatoria*. In the absence of an operative legal framework, the players within the commercial environment resorted to practice, custom, fair play and repetition. Commercial actors independently sculptured norms, free from the clumsy, uninformed overlords whose purpose and directions would be shaped by other considerations. The traditional merchants moulded commercial law in a manner that was 'far reaching and remarkable'.[5] In the Electronic Renaissance, the pragmatists are the computer technicians, the commercial actors and the individuals interacting socially in a new world of electronic commerce and social media. The law of social media and of electronic commerce has emerged at a breakneck pace for lawyers and legislators. The common law system emerged from centuries of turmoil, as 'an amorphous and unruly thing'.[6] Even with its rapid advances, the law lags behind the Electronic Renaissance. Nevertheless, there are international bodies intent on filling the gaps.[7]

On one level, electronic commerce began in the mid-1800s, when the first contract was entered into using the telegraph, and later the telephone.[8] However, the expression 'electronic commerce' is typically used in connection with the expansion of commerce using computers and modern communications, most notably the internet and cyberspace. The word 'electronic' first appeared in 1902,[9] but the expression 'electronic commerce' did not emerge until the 1990s. The development of security protocols has aided the rapid expansion of electronic commerce by substantially reducing commercial risk factors.

The expression 'social media' is used to mean personal interaction between individuals using modern communications networks. Some argue that the first such

---

3   See, respectively, the works of Zhuangzi, 4th century BC; a philosophical concept running contrary to free will and choice; the works of Friedrich Hayek; and the works of Adam Smith, discussed in Chapter 2.

4   See Chapter 2, The rule of cyberspace.

5   Gilles Cuniberti, 'Three Theories of Lex Mercatoria', *Columbia Journal of Transnational Law* (2013) 52(1).

6   Frank Kitto, 'Foreword', in Meagher, Gummow and Lehane, *Equity, Doctrines and Remedies*, Butterworths, Sydney, 1975, v.

7   Ibid.

8   The first known 'electronic' contract was *Walsh v Ionides* (1853) 1 El & Bl 383; 118 E.R. 479, where the court acknowledged a contract of agency made in 1851 by telegraph.

9   Oxford English Dictionary, online edition, <www.oed.com>.

social interaction arose with the use of the telephone in the early or mid-20th century. However, the expression dates from 1994, when the internet began to mature.[10] The human penchant for communication was liberated. The cost of long-distance communication evaporated. Entrepreneurial types have provided a plethora of devices, programs and apps for social media interaction. Their reason for doing so is not altruistic. The greater the uptake, the greater the revenue from advertising, data collection and heuristic marketing. The advantages of electronic commerce to commercial parties include ease of access, anonymous browsing of products, larger choice, the convenience of shopping from the computer, and includes the social media explosion. The disadvantages include the potential for invasion of privacy and security risks. There are also questions regarding jurisdiction, standards, protection of intellectual property, taxation, trade law and other issues. Nevertheless, acceptance of electronic products and services has grown prodigiously.

Security is of paramount importance in electronic commerce. Public key cryptology was invented in response to security concerns and has revolutionised electronic commerce. Communications are now relatively secure: digital signatures or certificates permit the authentication of the sender of a message or of an electronic commerce product.

This book addresses legal issues relating to the introduction and adoption of various forms of social media and electronic commerce. Whether it is undertaking a commercial transaction on the World Wide Web, sending electronic communications to enter into commercial arrangements, social media, downloading material subject to copyright, or privacy concerns about our digital personas, there are legal considerations. Parties must consider the risks associated with social media and electronic commerce, whether or not electronic writing and signatures are equivalent to paper writing or wet ink signatures, and which jurisdiction and which law governs a dispute between parties if the parties are in different countries from the servers. This book addresses intellectual property, cybercrime, surveillance, privacy, defamation, evidence of records and domain name usage and disputes.

Social media and electronic commerce law

An examination of social media law and the law of electronic commerce must begin with a fundamental understanding of the law and its role in society as it has evolved over the centuries. It necessitates understanding terrestrial norms, social

---

10 According to the Oxford English Dictionary, the expression 'social media' was coined in 2004. See above n 9.

behaviour and the application of the rule of law. These principles must be applied to new circumstances, infrastructure and contexts, even if these challenge such foundations of society as sovereignty and human rights. It is an exciting time to be charting the course and watching as legislators, courts, merchants and the populace wrestle with this new epoch. In the 18th and 19th centuries there may have been a similar opportunity to observe principles evolving, as there were new developments in relation to consideration (in contract law) and the postal acceptance rule (also in contract law), and as principles of equity matured. But such development was at a snail's pace compared with the eruption of the law of social media and electronic commerce over the last three decades.

The majority of legal problems arising through the use of social media and electronic commerce can be answered satisfactorily by the application of standard legal principles. Contract law, commercial law, defamation and consumer law, for example, all apply to the internet, email communications, electronic banking and cyberspace generally. However, cyberspace gives rise to unique and unusual circumstances, rights, privileges and relationships that are not adequately dealt with by traditional law. This has necessitated legislation, international agreements and a plethora of cases before the courts.

Electronic commerce law

The expression 'electronic commerce law' is used to describe all changes and additions to the law that are a result of the electronic age. Justice Fryberg,[11] in an address to the Australian Conference on the Law of Electronic Commerce, asked, 'Is there such a thing as Electronic Commerce Law? I suggest there is not',[12] although he acknowledged that he had completed a keynote address on precisely that topic. Joseph Sommer[13] argued that 'cyberlaw' was nonexistent as a separate body of law, and that cyberspace 'is a delightful new playground for old games':

> [N]ot only is 'cyberlaw' nonexistent, it is dangerous to pretend that it exists. A lust to define the future can be very dangerous, especially when we cannot even agree on the present. A lust to define the law of the future is even worse, since law tends to evolve through an inductive accretion of experience. It is much safer to extract first principles from a mature body of law than to extract a dynamic body of law from timeless first principles. An overly technological focus can create bad taxonomy and bad legal analysis, at least.

---

11 Former Justice of the Supreme Court of Queensland.
12 HG Fryberg, 'The Impact of Electronic Commerce on Litigation' 28 March 2003. Available at <archive.sclqld.org.au/judgepub/2003/fry070403.pdf>.
13 'Against cyberlaw', (2000) 15 *Berkeley Tech LJ* 1145.

At worst, it can lock us into bad law, crystallizing someone's idea of a future that will never be.[14]

Judge Frank Easterbrook[15] initiated the debate with his article 'Cyberspace and the law of the horse'. Easterbrook argued that cyberlaw is unimportant because it invokes no first principles.[16] He made reference to the comment of a former Dean of the University of Chicago Law School that a course in the law of the horse was not offered: 'Lots of cases deal with sales of horses; others deal with people kicked by horses; still more deal with the licensing and racing of horses, or with the care veterinarians give to horses, or with prizes at horse shows' – nevertheless there is no discrete body of horse law.[17] Judge Easterbrook argued that there was no reason to teach the 'law of cyberspace', any more than there was reason to teach the 'law of the horse', because neither, he suggested, would 'illuminate the entire law'. By analogy he proclaimed that cyberlaw did not exist.[18]

In his article 'The law of the horse: What cyberlaw might teach', Lawrence Lessig[19] responded to Easterbrook's assertions. Through a series of examples he demonstrated that cyberlaw or electronic commerce law, however described, forms a unique area of legal discourse. Lessig referred to privacy and spam in cyberspace. He argued that any lesson about cyberspace requires an understanding of the role of law, and that in creating a presence in cyberspace, we must all make choices about whether the values we embed there will be the same values we espouse in our real-space experience. Understanding how the law applies in cyberspace in conjunction with demands, social norms and mores, and the rule of cyberspace, will be valuable in understanding and assessing the role of law everywhere.

Easterbrook and Lessig's disquisitions are now dated in a field which has advanced more quickly than any other field of law. The law of electronic commerce has increasingly become a distinct study, with legal specialists, texts and courses in every law school. Legislation has been deemed necessary for several cyber issues. Those who scorned words such as 'cyberlaw' and 'cybercrime' perhaps winced at the introduction of the Australian *Cybercrime Act 2001* (Cth). Traditional laws had proven inadequate, necessitating legislation on computer-related crime, credit card fraud, bank card fraud, computer forgery, computer sabotage, unauthorised access to computer systems, unauthorised copying or distribution of computer programs, cyberstalking, theft of intellectual property and identity theft.

---

14 Ibid.
15 Judge of the US Court of Appeals for the Seventh Circuit.
16 'Cyberspace and the law of the horse', (1996) *University of Chicago Legal Forum* 207.
17 Interestingly, the US law firm of Miller, Griffin and Marks advertises that it specialises in 'commercial, corporate and equine matters'.
18 See also James Boyle, 'Foucault in cyberspace: Surveillance, sovereignty, and hard-wired censors', (1997) 66 *University of Cincinnati Law Review* 177.
19 'The law of the horse: What cyberlaw might teach', (1999) 113 *Harvard Law Review* 501.

Spam has become a real economic waste for virtually all business, resulting in legislation and international agreements.[20] The digitisation of data results in real privacy concerns. In response to this the Australian *Privacy Act 1988* (Cth) was overhauled in 2000 to make the private sector accountable, and was revitalised in 2013. The Australian Law Reform Commission (ALRC) has undertaken a further review, with recommendations to expand privacy laws so that they deal with technological developments.

Domain names are valuable business identifiers, traded in the millions of dollars and subject to numerous disputes. Most national domain name administrators have introduced dispute resolution procedures. The courts have dramatically expanded the tort of passing off, in a manner not contemplated until recently, in an attempt to provide remedies.

Conflict of laws principles in cyberspace have been inadequately served by traditional principles established over centuries. The courts have formed new approaches. Online defamation, for instance, is unlike the static occurrences. Now, a defamation statement can be published continuously worldwide 24 hours a day. The courts have had to reconsider the single publication rule, and the applicability of local laws to a website that was intended for another jurisdiction but has global reach.

Child pornography, terrorism, suicide materials, spyware and censorship are issues on which laws vary dramatically internationally, and yet each website is typically available globally. Nations have different ages at which a person is no longer regarded as a child, and freedom of speech issues arise with terrorism issues (plans to make a bomb) and suicide information. The law must address the easy reach of such material in the digital age in ways that in other contexts may be considered draconian. Censorship laws for print and television are ineffective for online materials. What is electronic writing, and an electronic signature? The range of issues related to electronic contracting has resulted in international Electronic Transactions Acts. Evidentiary issues arise in relation to digitising paper documents and printing out electronic documents. The internet raises a range of intellectual property issues, such as peer-to-peer file sharing (music and videos in particular), digital rights management, time-shifting and format-shifting. Electronic commerce by its nature does not recognise borders, and it raises questions regarding security of transactions, standards and protection, legally and otherwise, in an international context.

Many international organisations have spent considerable time and resources on resolving legal issues and difficulties in electronic commerce: the UN Commission on International Trade Law (UNCITRAL), the International Chamber of

---

20 For example, the *Spam Act 2003* (Cth) and the Memoranda of Understanding between Australia, South Korea and the US.

Commerce (ICC), the Asia-Pacific Economic Cooperation (APEC), the Organisation for Economic Cooperation and Development (OECD) and the World Trade Organization (WTO) are some examples.[21]

The law of electronic commerce (or cyberlaw) has emerged as a new, disparate and coherent body of law.

Internet use in Australia

Internationally there are more than 3 billion internet users, and more than 1 billion websites. Each day we send 250 billion emails, make 600 million contributions to Twitter, and view 8 billion videos on YouTube. There are 1.3 billion Facebook users.

The following figures are for the year 2012–13 from the Australian Bureau of Statistics (ABS): 83 per cent of Australians were internet users, and there were 12.397 million active internet subscribers, of which 78 per cent were household subscribers and 22 per cent were business and government. Those aged 15–17 had the highest proportion of use, at 97 per cent, compared to those aged 65 or over (46 per cent). The most popular online activities were paying bills and banking online (72 per cent), social networking (66 per cent), listening to music or watching videos or movies (58 per cent) and accessing government services (also 58 per cent). Those aged 15–17 most commonly used the internet for educational purposes (93 per cent) and those aged 18–24 used it for social networking (92 per cent).[22]

The vast majority (97 per cent) of internet users accessed the internet from home, with the next most popular being the user's place of employment (49 per cent) and a neighbour's, friend's or relative's house (41 per cent). Most internet users (76 per cent) purchased goods or services via the internet. The three most common types of goods or services purchased were travel, accommodation, memberships or tickets of any kind (74 per cent); CDs, music, DVDs, videos, books or magazines (50 per cent); and clothes, cosmetics or jewellery (49 per cent). Although the proportion of households with internet access is higher in capital cities, at 85 per cent, the percentage outside capital cities has increased significantly recently, to 79 per cent. Finally, 81 per cent accessed the internet at home every day.

The ABS report also found that income and education were key factors in people's internet access: 97 per cent of those earning $120,000 or more were internet users, compared to 77 per cent of those earning less than $40,000. Of those with a Bachelor degree or higher, 96 per cent were internet users, whereas of persons educated to Year 12 or below, 75 per cent were internet users.

---

21 See Chapter 19.
22 In 2013 the ACT had the highest connection rate, with 89 per cent of all homes connected, with Tasmania the lowest at 78 per cent.

Judicial consideration in Australia

The High Court of Australia has had few opportunities to consider the impact of electronic commerce, cyberspace and the operation of the internet. In *Roadshow Films Pty Ltd v iiNet Limited* the majority stated: 'the internet can be used for diverse purposes, including viewing websites, downloading or streaming non-infringing content, sending and receiving emails, social networking, accessing online media and games, and making voice over IP telephone calls'.[23] In *Dow Jones v Gutnick*[24] the court considered defamation on the World Wide Web and whether or not it was appropriate for the Supreme Court of Victoria to exercise jurisdiction over a US-based website. This was the first real opportunity for the court to consider its role in law making and the common law in the context of cyberspace and electronic commerce.

The nature and essence of the common law makes it amenable to development, subject to the *Constitution* and statute.[25] The judiciary, scholars and commentators debate the length and breadth of acceptable developments using various forms of legal reasoning to justify their approaches. Whether the approach is principle-based, a coherence-based incremental method or policy-based, development is an integral part of the common law and of our socio-legal structure.[26]

In a joint majority judgement, Gleeson CJ, McHugh, Gummow and Hayne JJ accepted the evidence before the judge at first instance, Hedigan J, regarding 'the unusual features of publication on the internet and the World Wide Web'. The majority accepted that the internet is:

> a telecommunications network that links other telecommunication networks
> ... [that] enables inter-communication using multiple data-formats ... among
> an unprecedented number of people using an unprecedented number of
> devices [and] among people and devices without geographic limitation.[27]

The majority expressed concern regarding the lack of evidence adduced to reveal what electronic impulses pass or what electronic events happen in the course of

---

23 [2012] HCA 16, para 64 per French CJ, Crennan and Kiefel JJ.
24 *Dow Jones v Gutnick* [2002] HCA 56.
25 See *Theophanous v Herald and Weekly Times Limited* [1994] HCA 46, especially Brennan J at para 4. See also *D'Orta-Ekenaike v Victorian Legal Aid* [2005] HCA 12; (2005) 223 CLR 1 and *Arthur J S Hall & Co v Simmons* [2000] UKHL 38; [2002] 1 AC 615.
26 For a considered and valuable discourse see Russell Hinchy, *The Australian legal system: History, institutions and method*, Pearson Education Australia, Sydney, 2008, in particular, Part Three.
27 *Dow Jones v Gutnick* [2002] HCA 56, para 13.

passing or storing information on the internet. Nevertheless the majority took the opportunity to define a broad range of internet terms:

15. The World Wide Web is but one particular service available over the Internet. It enables a document to be stored in such a way on one computer connected to the Internet that a person using another computer connected to the Internet can request and receive a copy of the document ... the terms conventionally used to refer to the materials that are transmitted in this way are a 'document' or a 'web page' and a collection of web pages is usually referred to as a 'web site'. A computer that makes documents available runs software that is referred to as a 'web server'; a computer that requests and receives documents runs software that is referred to as a 'web browser'.

16. The originator of a document wishing to make it available on the World Wide Web arranges for it to be placed in a storage area managed by a web server. This process is conventionally referred to as 'uploading'. A person wishing to have access to that document must issue a request to the relevant server nominating the location of the web page identified by its 'uniform resource locator (URL)'. When the server delivers the document in response to the request the process is conventionally referred to as 'downloading'.[28]

In the same case Kirby J was more philosophical in discussing the ramifications of technological developments, quoting Lord Bingham of Cornhill, who said that the impact of the internet on the law of defamation will require 'almost every concept and rule in the field ... to be reconsidered in the light of this unique medium of instant worldwide communication'.[29] Kirby J added that the appeal before the High Court 'enlivens such a reconsideration'.[30]

In any reformulation of the common law, Kirby J continued, many factors would need to be balanced: the economic implications of any change, valid applicable legislation, the pros and cons of imposing retrospective liability on persons, and social data and public consultation.[31] Most significantly, reform is the purview of government; it is not the primary role of the courts. Nevertheless, as Kirby J pointed out, courts have reversed long-held notions of common law principle when 'stimulated by contemporary perceptions of the requirements of fundamental human rights'.[32]

---

28 Ibid., paras 15, 16.
29 Matthew Collins, *The law of defamation and the internet*, Oxford University Press, Oxford, 2001.
30 *Dow Jones v Gutnick* [2002] HCA 56, para 66.
31 Ibid., paras 75 and 76.
32 Ibid., para 77.

As they have recognised the enormity of the impact of the internet as a revolutionary communications giant, courts all over the world have been forced to reconsider basic principles. Kirby J appropriately quoted noted US jurist Billings Learned Hand:

> The respect all men feel in some measure for customary law lies deep in their nature; we accept the verdict of the past until the need for change cries out loudly enough to force upon us a choice between the comforts of further inertia and the irksomeness of action.[33]

Of this passage Brennan J, in *Theophanous v Herald and Weekly Times Limited*,[34] remarked, 'Other judges find the call to reform more urgent.'[35] To varying degrees the judiciary acknowledges its role in the law-making process, balancing consistency, cohesion and precedent in an analytical ballet of deductive, inductive and abductive reasoning. On the one hand, the common law is the rock and the foundation of modern English and colonial law (including Australia's law). On the other hand, it has remained sufficiently flexible to adapt to modern developments. And so it should. With the advent of novel factual circumstances the judiciary must find solutions for the benefit, stability and protection of society and commerce. This has been described as the 'genius of the common law': that the courts may adapt principles of past decisions, by analogical reasoning, 'to the resolution of entirely new and unforeseen problems'.[36] When the new problem is as novel, complex and global as Gutnick's case, an opportunity – indeed a duty – arises to fashion and build the common law.[37]

Two examples illustrate the best and worst of judicial malleability. The common law crime of larceny dictates that the prosecution must prove certain elements of the crime to elicit a conviction. One key element is to prove that the accused intended to deprive another of property. This is problematic for intangibles. Where a person accesses a computer and 'steals' a computer file a curious thing happens: the information is both stolen and left behind. The development of common law larceny failed to predict or consider this. Attempts at prosecution failed. The courts could not or would not modify the well-established common law offence of larceny to accommodate this development. It was left to the legislature to enact cybercrime legislation to encompass offences that could not be imagined only a

---

33 BL Hand, 'The contribution of an independent judiciary to civilisation', in Irving Dillard (ed.), *The spirit of liberty: Papers and addresses of Learned Hand*, 3rd edn, Alfred A Knopf, New York, 1960.
34 [1994] HCA 46.
35 Ibid., para 5.
36 *Dow Jones v Gutnick* [2002] HCA 56, para 91, per Kirby J.
37 For a view of the role and limitations of the judiciary see the judgement of Brennan J in *Mabo v Queensland (No. 2)* [1992] HCA 23; (1992) 175 CLR 1.

matter of years earlier.[38] A reading of the US Supreme Court decision of *Reno v American Civil Liberties Union*[39] provides a similar missed opportunity in the US context. On the other hand, the English Court of Appeal, in the domain name case *Marks & Spencer v One in a Million*,[40] moulded, twisted and interpreted the five established elements of the tort of passing off to provide a remedy where one previously did not exist. The result is such a departure from traditional passing off that it is referred to as 'domain name passing off'.[41]

This extension of principle when faced with domain name piracy is to be applauded. In the words of Kirby J, 'When a radically new situation is presented to the law it is sometimes necessary to think outside the square.'[42] Kirby J reflected on the specific issue of defamation in the Dow Jones appeal and theorised a re-evaluation and formation of a new 'paradigm', and a 'common sense' approach to change. His Honour questioned the wisdom of refusing to find a new remedy in new circumstances, describing it as 'self-evidently unacceptable'.[43] Change is not new. The *lex mercatoria,* for example, emerged from the customs and practices of merchants from the Middle Ages. Rules governing bills of exchange and letters of credit were crafted by commercial parties long before the law makers had the opportunity to legislate. Their aim was commerce, but the result was that commercial customs and practice became recognised by the courts and then the legislature, both institutions responding to commercial realities.

In the context of reconceptualisation, Kirby J (in Gutnick's case) dabbles with new rules for a 'unique technology' and the 'urgency' of considering such changes:

> To wait for legislatures or multilateral international agreement to provide solutions to the legal problems presented by the Internet would abandon those problems to 'agonizingly slow' processes of lawmaking. Accordingly, courts throughout the world are urged to address the immediate need to piece together gradually a coherent transnational law appropriate to the 'digital millennium'. The alternative, in practice, could be an institutional failure to provide effective laws in harmony, as the Internet itself is, with contemporary civil society – national and international. The new laws would need to respect the entitlement of each legal regime not to enforce foreign legal rules contrary to binding local law or important elements of local public policy. But within such constraints, the common law would adapt itself to the central features of the Internet, namely its global, ubiquitous and reactive

---

38 See Chapter 16.
39 521 US 844 (1997). See also *American Civil Liberties Union v Reno* 929 F. Supp 824 (1996), particularly the joint judgement of Sloviter CJ, Buckwalter and Dalzell JJ.
40 [1999] 1 WLR 903; [1998] EWCA Civ 1272.
41 See Chapter 9.
42 *Dow Jones v Gutnick* [2002] HCA 56, para 112.
43 Ibid., para 115.

characteristics. In the face of such characteristics, simply to apply old rules, created on the assumptions of geographical boundaries, would encourage an inappropriate and usually ineffective grab for extra-territorial jurisdiction …

Generally speaking, it is undesirable to express a rule of the common law in terms of a particular technology. Doing so presents problems where that technology is itself overtaken by fresh developments. It can scarcely be supposed that the full potential of the Internet has yet been realised. The next phase in the global distribution of information cannot be predicted. A legal rule expressed in terms of the Internet might very soon be out of date.[44]

In some instances, such as electronic banking and finance, commercial parties have embraced electronic commerce, forging new paths and boldly leading the way, even in the absence of any adequate laws. In other instances the law makers have taken the initiative: the UN Commission on International Trade Law (UNCITRAL) in 1996, with the Model Law on Electronic Commerce, is an important example.[45]

There are many pitfalls, warnings and surprises in the regulation of social media and electronic commerce, both practical and legal. These voyages are examined in this book. The law relating to social media, electronic commerce, the internet and cyberspace requires careful management by legislators and structured application and development of existing legal principles by the courts.

FURTHER READING

Justice George Fryberg, Keynote Address to the Australian Conference on the Law of Electronic Commerce, Brisbane 2003. See Supreme Court of Queensland publications: <archive.sclqld.org.au/judgepub/2003/fry070403.pdf>.

Billings Learned Hand, 'The contribution of an independent judiciary to civilisation', in Irving Dillard (ed.), *The Spirit of Liberty: Papers and addresses of Learned Hand*, 3rd edn, Alfred A Knopf, New York, 1960.

Russell Hinchy, *The Australian Legal System: History, institutions and method*, 2nd edn, Thomson Reuters, 2015, Part Three.

Neil MacCormick, *Legal Reasoning and Legal Theory*, Clarendon Law Series, Oxford University Press, Oxford, 1979.

---

44 Ibid., paras 119 and 125.
45 See Chapter 3.

2

THE RULE OF CYBERSPACE

This chapter examines and contemplates law and culture in cyberspace. The role of law and indeed the rule of law have different dynamics in cyberspace as a consequence of the architecture of cyberspace and its anonymous, pseudonymous and borderless features. The resultant structural balance among technology, law and culture may be expressed as the 'rule of cyberspace'. This spatial dimension, economic influence on human culture and the role of law and regulation together form a subculture which both impacts on and moulds electronic commerce.

First, the nature of cyberspace is examined. This is followed by consideration of theoretical bases for law and order in cyberspace. The rule of cyberspace emerges, by processes known as 'spontaneous order', from the environmental factors fashioning cyberspace. It is spontaneous order which best describes – and to a limited extent predicts – regulation for electronic commerce.

This chapter examines the juxtaposition of culture and cyberspace, a modern application of spontaneous order, and then uses a discussion of libertarian and classical approaches to predict the future of cyberspace.

Cultural and environmental juxtaposition with cyberspace

Human interaction tends towards order and has an aversion to chaos. Culture brings about communities, law, order and stability. And so it is for cyberspace and the rule of cyberspace.[1]

Cyberspace is infused with a kind of spontaneous order, and has thus evolved protocols through public participation. No one controls cyberspace. There are many stakeholders and users, all with their own agendas, impacts and influences. Customs, usages and structure have emerged from human action and interaction, but not human command. Organising bodies do not know the diverse predilections and demands of the participants. The size, direction, extent and use of cyberspace have challenged forecasters. By incalculable actions and inputs – spontaneous order – cyberspace has gained structure and presence.

Through a process of exploration and learning, humankind has begun to understand the limits of its physical world. With curiosity and wonder we develop an appreciation of real space as a home and vessel for life. Similarly, cyberspace is a mystery ... at least initially. Some dip their toe in and play in this new universe. To many, cyberspace is a nebulous, unsafe and ungoverned place.[2] Cyberspace

---

1 See Sir Edward Burnett Tylor, *Primitive culture: Researches into the development of mythology, philosophy, religion, language, art and custom*, Gordon Press, London, (1871) 1974.
2 Tom Bell, *The internet: Heavily regulated by no one in particular*, (1997), <www.tomwbell.com/writings/InterReg.html>.

poses problems and challenges to visitors, and to owners, regulators, consumers, merchants and tourists.

The legend of King Canute[3] is of a king believed to be so powerful that he could command the tides to stop. Concerned that his subjects believed him to be almighty, to the point of immortality, Canute undertook a practical demonstration at Thorney Island and ordered the tide to stop. This was of course futile, and the tide proceeded to disobey him. The demonstration merely confirmed the limits of his sovereignty. The sea was beyond mere human governance. Many have drawn a parallel with cyberspace: any attempt to regulate it would be equally futile.[4]

Cyberspace

Cyberspace is an illusion. It has no physical presence. Yet its users visit it, send messages and transact business through it. Electrical, magnetic and optical forces with storage facilities permit users to carry out actions that produce results in real space. Whether users find information or goods and services via Google, listen online to radio from around the world, or send and receive email, every step is carefully planned and choreographed. This is not new. Technology has fooled human senses for years. The dot matrices on newspaper photographs give the illusion of people and places. Tiny pixels on a television or computer screen give the illusion of words, drawings and movement. Flashing still pictures 24 times a second gives the illusion of movement. Users become as immersed in cyberspace as they are in the narrative of television and movies. The illusion is powerful, and it takes on an ethereal quality and allows escape from terrestrial shackles. In the end, though, it is all real people dealing with real people, and sometimes their relationships and actions become convoluted and conflicted enough for them to look to the law for resolution, to regulation or a form of rule in cyberspace.

In *Reno v American Civil Liberties Union* the US Supreme Court defined 'the internet' and 'cyberspace' in the following terms:

> The Internet is an international network of interconnected computers ...
> [which] now enable[s] tens of millions of people to communicate with one
> another and to access vast amounts of information from around the world
> ... 'cyberspace' – [is] located in no particular geographical location but [is]
> available to anyone, anywhere in the world, with access to the Internet ...
> Cyberspace undeniably reflects some form of geography; chat rooms and

---

3 Canute (994–1035AD) was king of England, Denmark and Norway and overlord of Schleswig
   and Pomerania.
4 See, for example, Michael Kirby, 'Privacy in cyberspace', (1998) *UNSW Law Journal* 47 and
   Graham Greenleaf, 'An endnote on regulating cyberspace: Architecture vs law?', (1998)
   UNSWLJ 52.

Web sites, for example, exist at fixed 'locations' on the Internet. Since users can transmit and receive messages on the Internet without revealing anything about their identities or ages … cyberspace is malleable. Thus, it is possible to construct barriers in cyberspace and use them to screen for identity, making cyberspace more like the physical world and, consequently, more amenable to zoning laws. This transformation of cyberspace is already underway.[5]

The High Court of Australia described the described the internet and cyberspace in the following terms:

[It is a] decentralised, self-maintained telecommunications network. It is made up of interlinking small networks from all parts of the world. It is ubiquitous, borderless, global and ambient in its nature. Hence the term 'cyberspace'. This is a word that recognises that the interrelationships created by the Internet exist outside conventional geographic boundaries and comprise a single interconnected body of data, potentially amounting to a single body of knowledge. The Internet is accessible in virtually all places on Earth where access can be obtained either by wire connection or by wireless (including satellite) links. Effectively, the only constraint on access to the Internet is possession of the means of securing connection to a telecommunications system and possession of the basic hardware.[6]

Science fiction author William Gibson coined the term 'cyberspace' in his 1982 novelette *Burning Chrome*, published in *Omni* magazine.[7] He depicts cyberspace as a 'consensual hallucination experienced daily by billions of legitimate operators'.[8] Michael Benedikt describes cyberspace as:

A new universe, a parallel universe created and sustained by the world's computers and communication lines … The tablet becomes a page becomes a screen becomes a world, a virtual world … Its corridors form wherever electricity runs with intelligence … The realm of pure information.[9]

He believes that cyberspace, 'like cityspace, can be inhabited, explored, and designed'.[10] Benedikt puts forward the notion that we drift into cyberspace every time we speak on the telephone or become absorbed in a book.

5 521 US 844 (1997).

6 *Dow Jones v Gutnick* [2002] HCA 56, para 80 per Kirby J.

7 The concept was expanded and popularised in his 1984 novel *Neuromancer* (Ace Books, New York). Many sources incorrectly cite Gibson's 1984 book as the first use of the word 'cyberspace'. Gibson has stated, 'When I came up with the term [cyberspace] in *Burning Chrome*, I used it to define a kind of navigable, iconic, three-dimensional representation of data.'

8 William Gibson, *Neuromancer*, Ace Books, New York, 1984.

9 Michael Benedikt, *Cyberspace: First steps*, MIT Press, Cambridge MA, 1991.

10 Michael Benedikt, *Cityspace, cyberspace, and the spatiology of information*, University of Texas at Austin, 1993: Available at <www.utexas.edu/architecture/center/benedikt/articles/cityspace.html>.

It is not a precondition for living, working and engaging in commerce in real space that its participants understand real space's underlying physics. And so it is for cyberspace. Users, vendors and consumers embrace cyberspace however it is defined. The law of cyberspace emerges as a consequence of their actions. Yet real space norms remain a starting point. Appreciating the difference gives meaning to the application of law and regulation. The conservative approach is to apply all real space laws, rules and behavioural norms in cyberspace. The libertarian view is to remove the shackles of real space and create a utopia, free from any form of regulation or encumbrance.

Author and artist John Perry Barlow falls into the latter group. He describes the action of visiting cyberspace as 'like having had your everything amputated'.[11] Physical existence in cyberspace remains impossible. Nevertheless consciousness becomes meshed and even lost in computer depictions. Barlow was an early advocate of freedom of expression and freedom from regulation in cyberspace. His response to the US *Telecom Reform Act* of 1996 was to write and issue a 'Declaration of the Independence of Cyberspace',[12] in which he colourfully proclaims that cyberspace cannot be ruled by terrestrial norms, legal or otherwise. This declaration galvanised the growing anxiety regarding rights and liberties within the cyberspace community:

A Declaration of the Independence of Cyberspace

Governments of the Industrial World, you weary giants of flesh and steel, I come from Cyberspace, the new home of Mind. On behalf of the future, I ask you of the past to leave us alone. You are not welcome among us. You have no sovereignty where we gather.

We have no elected government, nor are we likely to have one, so I address you with no greater authority than that with which liberty itself always speaks. I declare the global social space we are building to be naturally independent of the tyrannies you seek to impose on us. You have no moral right to rule us nor do you possess any methods of enforcement we have true reason to fear.

Governments derive their just powers from the consent of the governed. You have neither solicited nor received ours. We did not invite you. You do not know us, nor do you know our world. Cyberspace does not lie within your borders. Do not think that you can build it, as though it were a public

---

11 Michael E Doherty Jr, 'Marshall McLuhan meets William Gibson in "Cyberspace"', (1995) *Computer-Mediated Communication Magazine*. Available at <www.ibiblio.org/cmc/mag/1995/sep/doherty.html>.

12 Available at <projects.eff.org/~barlow/Declaration-Final.html>.

construction project. You cannot. It is an act of nature and it grows itself through our collective actions.

You have not engaged in our great and gathering conversation, nor did you create the wealth of our marketplaces. You do not know our culture, our ethics, or the unwritten codes that already provide our society more order than could be obtained by any of your impositions.

You claim there are problems among us that you need to solve. You use this claim as an excuse to invade our precincts. Many of these problems don't exist. Where there are real conflicts, where there are wrongs, we will identify them and address them by our means. We are forming our own Social Contract. This governance will arise according to the conditions of our world, not yours. Our world is different.

Cyberspace consists of transactions, relationships, and thought itself, arrayed like a standing wave in the web of our communications. Ours is a world that is both everywhere and nowhere, but it is not where bodies live.

We are creating a world that all may enter without privilege or prejudice accorded by race, economic power, military force, or station of birth.

We are creating a world where anyone, anywhere may express his or her beliefs, no matter how singular, without fear of being coerced into silence or conformity.

Your legal concepts of property, expression, identity, movement, and context do not apply to us. They are based on matter. There is no matter here.

Our identities have no bodies, so, unlike you, we cannot obtain order by physical coercion. We believe that from ethics, enlightened self-interest, and the commonweal, our governance will emerge. Our identities may be distributed across many of your jurisdictions. The only law that all our constituent cultures would generally recognize is the Golden Rule. We hope we will be able to build our particular solutions on that basis. But we cannot accept the solutions you are attempting to impose.

In the United States, you have today created a law, the Telecommunications Reform Act, which repudiates your own Constitution and insults the dreams of Jefferson, Washington, Mill, Madison, De Toqueville, and Brandeis. These dreams must now be born anew in us.

You are terrified of your own children, since they are natives in a world where you will always be immigrants. Because you fear them, you entrust your bureaucracies with the parental responsibilities you are too cowardly to confront yourselves. In our world, all the sentiments and expressions of humanity, from the debasing to the angelic, are parts of a seamless whole, the global conversation of bits. We cannot separate the air that chokes from the air upon which wings beat.

In China, Germany, France, Russia, Singapore, Italy and the United States, you are trying to ward off the virus of liberty by erecting guard posts at the frontiers of Cyberspace. These may keep out the contagion for a small time, but they will not work in a world that will soon be blanketed in bit-bearing media.

Your increasingly obsolete information industries would perpetuate themselves by proposing laws, in America and elsewhere, that claim to own speech itself throughout the world. These laws would declare ideas to be another industrial product, no more noble than pig iron. In our world, whatever the human mind may create can be reproduced and distributed infinitely at no cost. The global conveyance of thought no longer requires your factories to accomplish.

These increasingly hostile and colonial measures place us in the same position as those previous lovers of freedom and self-determination who had to reject the authorities of distant, uninformed powers. We must declare our virtual selves immune to your sovereignty, even as we continue to consent to your rule over our bodies. We will spread ourselves across the Planet so that no one can arrest our thoughts.

We will create a civilization of the Mind in Cyberspace. May it be more humane and fair than the world your governments have made before.

John Perry Barlow Cognitive Dissident, Co-Founder,

Electronic Frontier Foundation

Barlow co-founded the Electronic Frontier Foundation, an apt name, as cyberspace genuinely is a frontier. Some compare the electronic frontier with the Western frontier of North America in the 1800s, and see similarities in its openness and initial lawlessness. David Post[13] is one such who saw the potential of the new

---

13 See David G Post, 'Napster, Jefferson's Moose, and the law of Cyberspace', (8 June 2009) www.temple.edu/lawschool/dpost/Napster.html; David G Post, 'What Larry doesn't get: Code, Law, and Liberty in Cyberspace' (1999) <www.temple.edu/lawschool/dpost/Code. pdf>; David G Post, '"The free use of our faculties": Jefferson, cyberspace, and the languages of social life' (2001) 49 *Drake Law Review* 407, <papers.ssrn.com/sol3/papers.cfm?abstract_id=264201>.

frontier, as did his role model, Thomas Jefferson, in relation to that earlier frontier. Post advocates unfettered movement in cyberspace, arguing that the internet 'should be a free-flowing cauldron of creative energy unencumbered by copyright, trademark, jurisdictional, and other concerns'.[14] Andrew Morriss continues the analogy in his article 'The Wild West meets cyberspace'.[15] However, the social norm of netiquette, a form of etiquette on the internet, has been judicially recognised.[16]

The rule of law and the rule of cyberspace

The 'rule of law' is a basic precept of legal systems. It is enshrined in the common law tradition, and in continental Europe is known as Rechtsstaat. The concept of impartial rule of law is found in the Chinese political philosophy of legalism. The rule of cyberspace is not and cannot be based on the rule of law. Nevertheless there are parallels between the development of the rule of law and the emergence and adoption of the rule of cyberspace. Order and regulation emerge from varied parties, unplanned and unexpected. The rule of cyberspace morphs, melds and moulds in response to its own inherent dynamic forces. An understanding of the rule of law allows the cyber user to appreciate the rule of cyberspace.

The rule of law

The rule of law ordains that all people come before the law equally. No one is above the law. Many writers have espoused subsets of legal principles in an attempt to define this concept. Aristotle posited the rule of law as a system of rules inherent in the natural order of things. More than 2000 years ago Aristotle wrote, 'The rule of law is preferable … to that of any individual.'[17] It ensures fairness for all, the right to be heard by an unbiased authority, and similar outcomes in similar circumstances.

---

14 Elizabeth Greene, 'David Post: Freeing cyberspace from the rule of law', (2000) *The Chronicle*, 20 October.
15 Andrew Morriss, 'The Wild West meets cyberspace', (1998) 48 *The Freeman: Ideas on liberty* 427. See below, Spontaneous (or endogenous) order.
16 *Ontario Inc. v Nexx Online Inc.* [1999] OJ No. 2246 (Sup Ct), dealing with bulk emailing at a time when such practices were not legislatively prohibited.
17 Aristotle, *The Politics*, Book Three, Part XVI, trans. Benjamin Jowett, <classics.mit.edu/Aristotle/politics.3.three.html>.

In the British common law tradition, Albert Venn Dicey, in his treatise *Law of the Constitution* in 1895, explained the rule of law thus:

> [E]very official, from the Prime Minister down to a constable or a collector of taxes, is under the same responsibility for every act done without legal justification as any other citizen. The Reports abound with cases in which officials have been brought before the courts, and made, in their personal capacity, liable to punishment, or to the payment of damages, for acts done in their official character but in excess of their lawful authority. [Appointed government officials and politicians alike] ... and all subordinates, though carrying out the commands of their official superiors, are as responsible for any act which the law does not authorise as is any private and unofficial person.[18]

> [The 'rule of law' ensures] ... the absolute supremacy or predominance of regular law as opposed to the influence of arbitrary power ... Englishmen are ruled by the law, and by the law alone; a man may with us be punished for a breach of law, but he can be punished for nothing else. It means, again, equality before the law or the equal subjection of all classes to the ordinary law of the land administered by the ordinary law courts; the 'rule of law' in this sense excludes the idea of any exemption of officials or others from the duty of obedience to the law which governs other citizens or from the jurisdiction of the ordinary tribunals.[19]

As part of the Scottish Enlightenment, Adam Ferguson provided an early exposition of the spontaneous order concept, regarding it as a coherent and realistic result stemming from the uncoordinated actions of many individuals. Ferguson has been described as the 'father of modern sociology'. His 'Essay on the History of Civil Society'[20] espoused a theory of social interaction, progress and the pursuit of perfection, based on the belief that commercial growth was achieved through individual self-interest, and paradoxically believing that such growth might result in a Romanesque collapse. Ferguson resolved this paradox in part through his Christian faith in the divine and its interaction with human free will. He expressed a concern that social chaos would lead to despotism, and theorised that social laws emerged from the chaos to both restrict liberty and simultaneously regulate society and justice.

In a similar vein, John Adams, in a draft of the constitution of the Commonwealth of Massachusetts, in justification and enunciation of the principle of

---

18 AV Dicey, *Law of the Constitution*, 9th edn, Macmillan, London, 1950, p. 194.
19 AV Dicey, *Introduction to the study of the Law of the Constitution*, 10th edn, Macmillan, London, 1959, pp. 202–03.
20 Adam Ferguson, *An Essay on the History of Civil Society*, 1767. In addition to Adam Ferguson, the Scottish Enlightenment included philosophers and scientists such as Francis Hutcheson, David Hume, Alison Rutherford, Adam Smith, James Watt, Thomas Reid, Robert Burns, Joseph Black and James Hutton.

separation of powers, wrote: 'to the end it may be a government of laws and not of men'.[21] The concept of rule of law does not relate to morality, justice or efficacy of laws, but to how the legal system upholds the law. It is often perceived as a prerequisite for democracies, though non-democratic nations and dictatorships can also be said to adhere to the rule of law.

Dicey outlined the three 'kindred conceptions' underpinning the English *Constitution*:

> No man could be punished or lawfully interfered with by the authorities except for breaches of law.

> No man is above the law and everyone, regardless of rank, is subject to the ordinary laws of the land.

> There is no need for a bill of rights because the general principles of the constitution are the result of judicial decisions determining the rights of the private person.[22]

Bradford Smith describes the internet as a third industrial revolution, based on the joint and corresponding technological advances in software, hardware and telecommunications.[23] He examines the characteristics of the rule of law in real space and compares them with the rule of law in cyberspace.

The rule of cyberspace

Cyberspace is crammed with data, text, images, sounds and videos, from priceless gems of information, knowledge and reasoning to abhorrent rubbish and trivia. This data is not stored or presented with any order or structure. There are no global editors, data checkers or barriers. While certain nation states do control and restrict access and there are laws which address certain materials and behaviour, neither directly impacts the ability of a user to place any data online, nor attempts any structural control. Cyberspace is chaos.

However, powerful search engines give order and structure to the data. Forms of etiquette emerge in social and commercial situations. Order spontaneously results from such chaos. The rule of cyberspace is the natural, emergent order arising from data chaos. Demand yields an effective order.

---

21 *Massachusetts Constitution 1780*, First Part, article XXX. The quote has been cited with approval by the US Supreme Court and every State Supreme Court in the United States.
22 Dicey, above n 19, 175–84.
23 Bradford Smith, 'The third industrial revolution: Policymaking for the internet', (2001) 3 *Columbia Science and Technology Law Review* 1.

Spontaneous (or endogenous) order

> Good order results spontaneously when things are let alone.
>
> Zhuangzi, 4th century BCE

The concept of spontaneous order has been used to explain the development of language, science and technology, markets and economies, agriculture and eco-systems. It is a natural mechanism, operating without any specific intent or design: given an environment with rules, multiple behaviours and structures, a coherent order emerges. In all human culture, language emerged without design. Given human relations, emerging intelligence, multiple behavioural inputs and a commu-nity, language became ordered. A rainforest has a particular hierarchical order and structure because of laws of science and physical attributes (gravity, light, energy transference, water flow, soil nutrients, air composition and so forth). This order and stability may have evolved over eons. And yet, should any factor alter, count-less other things alter as well, and a new order emerges with such speed that it is said to be effectively spontaneous. Cyberspace, like the rainforest, is complex, with a multitude of independent factors.

However, the expression 'spontaneous' is misleading. On one level, order in cyberspace is developing continuously. Rather than arising 'spontaneously', order arises naturally, even automatically. An alternative expression might be 'endog-enous order': that is, order which originates naturally from within.

Friedrich Hayek was a Nobel Laureate economist whose theories and principles relating to spontaneous order have been applied to the rule of law. For Hayek, the rule of law meant that government is bound by rules fixed in advance, with the result that those in command of the rules will use (or abuse) their coercive powers in given foreseeable situations of fact. He saw problems with this: 'To act on the belief that we possess the knowledge and the power which enable us to shape the processes of society entirely to our liking, knowledge which in fact we do not pos-sess, is likely to make us do much harm.'[24] Hayek defined 'order' as a reaction to given stimuli and circumstances. He contrasted 'cosmos' and 'taxis' types of order, the former being spontaneous and self-generating, the latter forced or engineered, and argued that human beings lived within a social order that was more 'taxis' than 'cosmos'. He believed that the rule of law could not arise artificially, but was instead a spontaneous development for societies, structured around a belief in the virtues of the free market.

---

24 Friedrich Hayek and Gunnar Myrdal, 'Prize Lecture: The Pretence of Knowledge', The Sveriges Riksbank Prize in Economic Sciences in Memory of Alfred Nobel (1974).

For example, Hayek recognised and accepted that language emerged not as a conscious human phenomenon; it emerged as an ordered form, but spontaneously. Equally, he regarded the economic concept of a 'price mechanism' as a spontaneous form of order rather than a conscious human invention. He discussed and theorised about evolved behaviour. Hayek used the expression 'constructivistic rationalism'[25] to describe and rationalise existing doctrines which evoke an appropriate sense of order retrospectively. His was a conjectural reconstruction of societal realism, with a sense of liberalism. In later years he attributed the birth of civilisation to private property:[26]

> the spontaneous interaction of a number of people, each possessing only bits of knowledge, brings about a state of affairs in which prices correspond to costs, etc., and which could be brought about by deliberate direction only by somebody who possessed the combined knowledge of all those individuals.[27]

Morriss[28] argues that the regulation of the internet component of cyberspace arose spontaneously in the same manner as did regulation in the Wild West of the United States, which was 'far away from government because there [we]re no centralised control mechanisms'.[29] Nevertheless, the miners and cattlemen in the West established protocols and developed norms of behaviour. In both the internet and the Wild West, acceptable behaviour is maintained by rules which have appeared and then developed spontaneously. There is not necessarily any law-making authority to determine and enforce appropriate rules. Morriss provides a range of insights into natural order in the Wild West and parallels this to examples in cyberspace. He argues that cyberspace, through the mechanism of spontaneous order, is well equipped to govern and rule itself.

An alternative approach to the concepts of spontaneous order and natural order is Adam Smith's 'invisible hand' theory:

> Every individual ... generally, indeed, neither intends to promote the public interest, nor knows how much he is promoting it ... he intends only his own gain, and he is in this, as in many other cases, led by an invisible hand to promote an end which was no part of his intention.[30]

25 Friedrich Hayek, *Law, Legislation and Liberty*: Vol. I: Rules and Order, (1973) University of Chicago Press, 8–11; Vol. III: The Political Order of a Free People, (1979), xii.
26 Friedrich Hayek, *The Fatal Conceit*, University of Chicago Press, Chicago IL, 1988.
27 Friedrich Hayek, 'Economics and knowledge', (1937) IV *Economica* (New Series), 33.
28 See Morriss, 'The Wild West meets cyberspace' (1998) 48 *The Freeman: Ideas on liberty* 427.
29 Ibid.
30 Adam Smith, *The Wealth of Nations*, Book IV Chapter II, Bantam Classic, [1776] 2003. Smith was a contemporary of Adam Ferguson and was also a part of the Scottish Enlightenment.

Smith's *Theory of Moral Sentiments*,[31] an early work, contains the philosophical underpinnings and statements of methodology that underlie his later broader works on political economics, such as *The Wealth of Nations*.[32] It commences with the following declaration regarding human existence and natural influences:

> *How selfish soever man may be supposed, there are evidently some principles in his nature,* which interest him in the fortunes of others, and render their happiness necessary to him, though he derives nothing from it, except the pleasure of seeing it. Of this kind is pity or compassion, the emotion we feel for the misery of others, when we either see it, or are made to conceive it in a very lively manner. That we often derive sorrow from the sorrows of others, is a matter of fact too obvious to require any instances to prove it; for this sentiment, like all the other original passions of human nature, is by no means confined to the virtuous or the humane, though they perhaps may feel it with the most exquisite sensibility. The greatest ruffian, *the most hardened violator of the laws of society, is not altogether without it.*[33]

> The natural effort of every individual to better his own condition, when suffered to exert itself with freedom and security is so powerful a principle that it is alone, and without any assistance, not only capable of carrying on the society to wealth and prosperity, but of surmounting a hundred impertinent obstructions with which the folly of human laws too often incumbers its operations.[34]

Notwithstanding the philosophical differences between Smith's early and later writings, each can be extended to human existence in cyberspace. *The Theory of Moral Sentiments* accentuates the union of human intention and behaviour in a benevolent sense. *The Wealth of Nations* argues that an organised economic society results from the individual acting selfishly in a capitalistic manner, as if guided by an 'invisible hand', which results in an overall good for the community.

Spontaneous order is a process akin to evolution, with no planned direction or apparent purpose. Such a process is reflected in the phrase 'information wants to be free', taken from a hackers conference in 1984:

> On the one hand information wants to be expensive, because it's so valuable. The right information in the right place just changes your life. On the other hand, *information wants to be free,* because the cost of getting it out is

---

31 Adam Smith published *The Theory of Moral Sentiments* in 1759.
32 Adam Smith published *The Wealth of Nations* in 1776, at the beginning of the Industrial Revolution.
33 Smith, *The Theory of Moral Sentiments*, emphasis added.
34 Smith, *The Wealth Of Nations*: Book IV, Chapter V, (1776).

getting lower and lower all the time. So you have these two fighting against each other.[35]

Bruce Benson, a noted American economist, believes that cyberspace evolves towards self-regulation through spontaneous order. Benson sees 'spontaneous development' in the emergence of the culture of online social ostracism, eBay reputation and online wealth. He postulates:

> these rules evolve spontaneously from the bottom up rather than being intentionally designed by a legislator, and they are voluntarily accepted rather than being imposed. No central 'authority' with coercive powers is necessary to produce the resulting cooperative social order, as obligations are largely self-enforcing: it pays for each party to behave as expected in order to be able to expand wealth over the long run through mutually beneficial interaction.[36]

Cyberspace structure, organisation and continuation can be successfully explained by such spontaneous order notions, and by moral and capitalistic principles. Cyberspace, like real space, operates on multiple levels: social, commercial, domestic, educational and entertainment. Each section of the community, by investing time and effort into cyberspace, builds on the tools and structure laid down by predecessors. Cyberspace is dynamically evolving, pulsating with checks and balances, and subject to the vicissitudes of human behaviour.

A code of cyberspace

Lawrence Lessig espouses a new and separate code applicable in cyberspace; a version of the rule of cyberspace. Lessig is an academic who has theorised about the nature of cyberspace from its infancy. In response to the remark by Judge Frank Easterbrook that there was no more a 'law of cyberspace' than there was a 'law of the horse',[37] Lessig published a rebuttal: 'The law of the horse: What cyberlaw might teach'.[38] He began by considering particular problems

---

35 Stewart Brand, *Whole Earth Review,* Point Foundation, San Diego CA, 1984, p. 49, emphasis added.
36 Bruce Benson, 'The spontaneous evolution of cyber law: Norms, property rights, contracting, dispute resolution, and enforcement without state involvement', (2005) *Journal of Law, Economics & Policy* 269–348.
37 'Cyberspace and the law of the horse', 1996 *University of Chicago Legal Forum* 207. Judge Easterbrook's reference is to an argument by Gerhard Casper, a former Law Dean at University of Chicago, who boasted that the law school did not offer a course in 'the law of the horse'.
38 Lawrence Lessig, 'The law of the horse: What cyberlaw might teach', (1999) 113 *Harvard Law Review* 501.

of regulation that cyberspace might present. He expanded these examples to propose models for applying regulation in cyberspace and real space, then examined how law in real space can regulate cyberspace, and finally proposed that cyberspace could in turn regulate law. At heart, he claimed, there is a systematic competition between cyberspace and real space which 'illuminate[s] the entire law'.

Lessig believed that cyberspace has a parallel 'architecture' to real space.[39] He describes the rule of cyberspace as a code. The code of cyberspace comprises components real and ethereal, 'the software and hardware that makes this part of cyberspace as it is':[40]

> Once it is plain that code can replace law, the pedigree of the codewriters becomes central. Code in essence becomes an alternative sovereign – since it is in essence an alternative structure of regulation. But who authors this sovereign authority? And with what legitimacy?[41]

One of Lessig's examples relates to copying. Cyberspace has impacted on the technology of copying and on the power of law to protect against illegal copying.[42] Lessig explores the notion that computer code may regulate conduct in much the same way that legal codes regulate real space. He argues that computer code in cyberspace supplants copyright law in real space, and that such intellectual property concepts are inappropriate in the new medium.

Lessig proposes four factors which regulate real space and cyberspace: law, norms, markets and code.[43] In real space, law demands and requires that citizens behave in a certain community-minded manner, with sanctions for non-compliance. Social norms involve the threat of punishment (for breaches) by fellow citizens. Markets restrain behaviour fiscally. Code establishes, or is the foundation for, regulation of individual and of collective (resulting) behaviour by the architecture of the physical world. These four factors apply equally to the dynamic architecture of cyberspace. But we may be surprised by the manner in which they are manifested. Lessig gives this example: 'Talk about democratic politics in the *alt.knitting* newsgroup, and you open yourself to flaming; "spoof" someone's identity in a MUD, and you might find yourself toaded.'[44] Understanding the forces inherent in the rule of

---

39 Lawrence Lessig, *Code: The future of ideas*, Basic Books, New York, 2002. See Lawrence Lessig's website <code-is-law.org>. For example, in *Code: The future of ideas*, Lessig argues that too much long-term copyright protection hampers the creation of new ideas, and he advocates the importance of existing works entering the public domain quickly.

40 Lessig, above n 38, 502.

41 Lawrence Lessig, *Code, and other laws of cyberspace*, Basic Books, New York, 1999.

42 Lessig, above n 39, 125–7.

43 See also Lawrence Lessig, 'The new Chicago School' (1998) 27(2) *Journal of Legal Studies* 661.

44 Ibid.

cyberspace assists in an appreciation of the rule of law in real space by providing a new and unexpected perspective.

Lessig does not support Smith's 'invisible hand' approach:

> Constitutions in this sense are built; they are not found. Foundations are laid; they don't magically appear. Just as the founders of our nation learned from the anarchy that followed the revolution (remember: our first constitution, the Articles of Confederation, was a miserable failure of do-nothingness), so too are we beginning to see in cyberspace that this building is *not the work of an invisible hand*. There is *no reason to believe that the grounding for liberty in cyberspace will simply emerge*. In fact, quite the opposite is the case. As our framers learned, and as the Russians saw, we have reason to believe that cyberspace, left to itself, will not fulfill the promise of freedom. Left to itself, cyberspace will become a perfect tool of control.

> Control. Not necessarily control by government, and not necessarily control for some evil, fascist end. The invisible hand of cyberspace is building an architecture that's quite the opposite of what it was at cyberspace's birth. The invisible hand, through commerce, is constructing an architecture that perfects control – an architecture that makes possible highly efficient regulation.[45]

Lessig's libertarian writings stem from a deep concern and passion for the protection of the growth of cyberspace as a new and significant medium. He does not want the future of the internet to be left to the 'invisible hand' or some natural or spontaneous ethereal force.

David Post submits an impressive rebuttal in his article 'What Larry doesn't get'.[46] Post argues that Lessig's calls for collective action are unlikely to entice libertarians into action. Collective action, in Post's view, is another way of using coercive force to achieve directed change for the common good. Post questions any structured direction, expressing concern at who makes such determinations and at what expense. Post states that the 'conscientious libertarian recognizes that there are times when collective action is required to promote the common welfare', but the 'architectures of liberty are of fundamental importance'. He concludes that while cyberspace needs architecture, there remains disagreement about the extent to which the coercive power of the state needs to be invoked to get those communities built and to get people to live there.[47]

---

45 Ibid., emphasis added.
46 'What Larry doesn't get: Code and other laws of cyberspace', (2000) 52 *Stanford Law Review* 1439.
47 Ibid., 1439, 1458–9.

Information wants to be free

The dynamics of cyberspace and the resultant order give the impression that an overall design and structure was planned, much like Smith's 'invisible hand' concept.

'Information', of itself, has no mind or direction. Subjectively, to human users certain information may be considered valuable, and other information may be regarded as rubbish. But it is of different value to each individual. And yet, in cyberspace, where multiple access and the copying of digital data (information) has virtually no cost, information appears to have a life of its own, as it is copied, sent, read, posted and downloaded. The infrastructure of cyberspace provides both order and freedom given the demands of its human users.

Conclusion

Spontaneous order facilitates diversity and flexibility and arises in many and varied ways: online protocols, hypertext mark-up language, the commercial presence of the private sector, intellectual property tensions, business identifiers, and speedy communications are just a few of the factors that shape and contribute to – and equally are shaped and developed by – the rich fabric of cyberspace.

The architecture of the internet interprets attempts at censorship as damage and routes around it.[48] This is a by-product of the utilisation of mass networks, which include in their initial design a way to route around damage, should there be, for example, massive actual damage from blackouts, war or even a nuclear catastrophe. Cyberspace has become a medium beyond the control of terrestrial jurisdictions. The behaviour of individuals in real space can be targeted, but the control of cyberspace globally is beyond reach.[49]

Spontaneous or endogenous order is not regulation and it is not control. It is a process. The cyberspace community is impacted first by the human condition and human use, and our penchant for information and entertainment; second by legislation and regulation, the human predilection to control for particular purposes (this targets aspects of cyberspace such as child pornography, defamation and crime); third by protocols, either innate in the architecture or in the form of etiquette, netiquette and rules of human interaction. These factors coexist and coalesce. A variation in any one aspect may result in a change in cyberspace, but

---

48 John Gilmore, *The Electronic Frontier Foundation quotes collection*, 2001, <www.chemie.fu-berlin.de/outerspace/internet-article.html>.

49 See J Goldsmith, 'Regulation of the internet: Three persistent fallacies', (1998) 73 *Chicago-Kent Law Review* 1112.

the process engenders order. Those who attempt control will cause shifts in the structure of cyberspace and fluctuations in the order, but control of cyberspace is not possible. Local communities may filter or restrict access: parents and schools may utilise filters, for instance, and North Korea and China may severely regulate their population's use of and entry into cyberspace. However, the rule of cyberspace has evolved to a point where it cannot be regulated by any person, body or government. Behavioural traits and social norms inhibit abhorrent behaviour to a substantial degree, but no less so than in real space. Cyberspace and the internet are exquisite examples of spontaneous or endogenous order.

The rule of cyberspace is not simply the rule of law in cyberspace; it is the amalgamation and the fraternity of factors that produce spontaneous endogenous order. The rule of cyberspace is a combination of the juxtaposition of hardware and structure with verisimilitude, and human behaviour within the cyberspace environment.

The backbone of a democratic society is the concept of the rule of law. The backbone of a robust community in cyberspace is the rule of cyberspace.

FURTHER READING

Michael Benedikt, *Cyberspace: First steps*, MIT Press, Cambridge MA, 1991.

James Boyle, 'Foucault in cyberspace: Surveillance, sovereignty, and hardwired censors', (1997) 66 *University of Cincinnati Law Review* 177.

AV Dicey, *Introduction to the study of the Law of the Constitution*, Macmillan, London, 1885.

William Gibson, *Neuromancer*, Ace Books, New York, 1984.

Graham Greenleaf, 'An endnote on regulating cyberspace: Architecture vs law?' (1998) *UNSW Law Journal* 52.

Friedrich Hayek, *Law, Legislation and Liberty*, Vol. 1: Rules and Order, Routledge & Kegan Paul, London, 1973.

Friedrich Hayek, *Law, Legislation and Liberty*, Vol. III: The Political Order of a Free People, University of Chicago Press, 1979.

David R Johnson and David Post, 'Law and borders – The rise of law in cyberspace', (1996) 48 *Stanford Law Review* 1367.

Lawrence Lessig, *Code: The future of ideas – the fate of the commons in a connected world*, First Vintage Books, 2002.

Lawrence Lessig, *Code, and other laws of cyberspace*, Basic Books, 1999.

Lawrence Lessig, 'The law of the horse: What cyberlaw might teach', (1999) 113 *Harvard Law Review* 501.

Lawrence Lessig, 'Reading the Constitution in cyberspace', (1996) 45 *Emory LJ* 869.

AP Morriss, 'The Wild West meets cyberspace', (1998) 48 *The Freeman: Ideas on Liberty* 427.

David Post, 'What Larry doesn't get: Code and other laws of cyberspace' (2000) 52 *Stanford Law Review* 1439.

Adam Smith, *The Wealth of Nations*, Book IV, Chapter II, Bantam Classics, [1776] 2003.

PART 2

SOCIAL MEDIA

3

SOCIAL MEDIA LAW

In Chapter 1 it was proposed that we are living through an Electronic Renaissance, with the global acceptance of modern communications, increased data storage and transfer capacities enabling interaction on an unprecedented level. It's not just big business and governments with this communications capacity; individuals have been quick to take up computer use and now use the basic mobile phone as a mass communication instrument. Each incremental advance follows principles of endogenous order. Out of the chaos of vast technological capacity, entrepreneurial players and a willing and eager global market comes an embracement of media for social and entertainment purposes by a substantial proportion of the world's population.

Social media gives individuals, as well as large and small businesses, a direct way to interact, and to have access to and promote products and services. Businesses using social media channels such as Facebook, Twitter, LinkedIn and YouTube have a responsibility to ensure that content on their pages is accurate and legally compliant, irrespective of who put it there.

Social media has become the next stage of communications, bypassing post and telephone and becoming truly international. Social media may be briefly defined as online networking facilitating social interaction amongst individuals.

More broadly, social media refers to the numerous online applications which permit the creation and exchange of personal information such as text, photos and videos. Social media differs from standard forms of media, such as newspapers, television and radio. Social media facilitates mass individual communications to the global community. As a corollary, social media is community-based for individuals, allowing communications around particular interests, personal content sharing, collaborations, networking and exposure.

Many websites facilitate social media to permit forums, blogging, microblogging, the release of personal comments, photos and videos, social networking, chats, conferences and wikis. Some forms are instantaneous. Social media changes as the user base expands, the availability of connection increases, and the principle of endogenous order weighs in. As a consequence, the definition of social media shifts. The content expands, the types of content increase and the number of interactions becomes ever higher.

Individuals interact in a virtual community or communications portal to share thoughts, ideas and messages in various forms such as text, images and videos. Such participation may identify the individual or be anonymous or pseudonymous. Social media permits individuals to engage in social networking with family, friends and strangers with ease. The facilities may be public or closed to select membership or groups. Ultimately the range and type of social media is as diverse as the individuals who use it and the enterprising hosts who set up such facilities. Social media can be traced back to forum sites and blogging sites, which led to services which allowed users to set up personal details, post opinions and materials and permit other friends or the general public to access them. The number of mobile devices now exceeds the number of personal computers; this allows more and more people the experience of being continuously engaged in many forms of networked communications. Social media outlets are taking over traditional media, such as newspapers and television, with online information flow becoming the norm. News is posted on Twitter, Facebook, YouTube and many blogs as well as on news outlet websites.

Critics of social media express concerns about the trustworthiness of the information on such sites, the possibility of monopolies, the misuse and misflow of information by special interest groups, reliability and privacy. In Australia complaints can be made to the Australian Competition and Consumer Commission (ACCC), which has the power and responsibility to enforce the Australian Consumer Law. The ACCC can require persons to substantiate statements made on social media, and can take enforcement action in certain circumstances. The ACCC is particularly concerned about 'widespread public detriment' and conduct which infringes consumer laws.

This Part is not intended to provide a discourse on social media; instead it examines legal issues which arise from the use and misuse of social media. The following chapters deal with a range of legal issues emerging from this phenomenon. Chapter 4 deals with peer-to-peer file sharing, which has posed challenges, in particular for copyright holders. In the past 15 years there have been numerous legal challenges as hosts and users have exploited existing and developing technologies to share and disseminate music, movies and files. Chapter 5 addresses cloud computing, which refers to a virtual place used to store information and to facilitate communications. The legal risks and privacy issues of such a development are examined. Chapter 6 deals with social media and the workplace. There are numerous cases where social media has been used injudiciously, most typically by employees who have made statements and posted comments and photos which breach their contract of employment or fall foul of their employer's code of conduct. Chapter 7 deals with defamation in cyberspace, most particularly imprudent and impulsive comments made on social media. Chapter 8 broaches the issue of privacy within social media. The often impetuous and careless way in which digital data is shared on social media results in the potential for many privacy breaches. Chapter 9 deals with legal issues arising from the use of electronic mail and one's online presence. Finally, Chapter 10 addresses online censorship and the current state of law in Australia.

There are many lessons to be learnt from the mistakes, legal and otherwise, of others on social media.

Axioms – use of social media

- Do not defame – that is, do not say anything in social media which you would not be prepared to print on the front page of a newspaper.
- Do not make misleading statements.
- Do not engage in conduct which can be legally regarded as deceptive.
- Do not repost statements which you would not be prepared to make for yourself or defend.
- Minimise your exposure.
- Do not makes statements about work colleagues, your employer or employees which you would not make to them personally.
- Remember, texting or typing, posting an image or video will be available to others for evidentiary purposes should the need arise; this is akin to making a statement on your own permanent records.
- Business should take the same care with social media promotions as they would with any other form of advertising.
- Consumer protection law applies equally to social media, where made within jurisdiction.

FURTHER READING

Sarah Evans, 'Technology: Courted by social media', (2014) 52(4) *Law Society Journal* 51.

P George et al., *Social Media and the Law*, Lexis Nexis Butterworths, 2014.

JH Lipschultz, *Social Media Communication: Concepts, practices, data, law and ethics*, Taylor & Francis, 2015.

Alessandro Mantelero, 'Social control, tranparency, and participation in the big data world', (2014) 17(10) *Journal of Internet Law* 23.

PEER-TO-PEER
FILE SHARING

A prime example of the uptake of technology and the resulting order from the disorder has arisen through the availability of music and video files. In the 1990s the compression of files and increasing speed of the internet permitted the downloading of music files such as individual songs. In the 21st century the compression and speed have increased so dramatically that entire music albums, television shows and movies (of any length) are downloaded with ease. Internet users relish the technology. In the words of the High Court of Australia:

> Access to the internet can be used for diverse purposes, including viewing websites, downloading or streaming non-infringing content, sending and receiving emails, social networking, accessing online media and games, and making voice over IP telephone calls.[1]

The downloading of music, video and other files online is prolific, if not epidemic. The transfer of copyright material – material that would have cost several billion dollars in total to buy – is a source of considerable concern for the music industry, in particular. The fact that a substantial number of such files are subject to copyright, and that the right to copy is one of the many exclusive rights provided by the *Copyright Act*, is typically disregarded by internet users.[2] Notwithstanding the popularity of micropayment through the iTunes store, the Google Play store and the Microsoft store, to name a few, peer-to-peer (P2P) transfers have facilitated the majority of the downloads. There have been numerous cases brought before the courts aimed at stopping or at least discouraging these downloads. Yet sites providing access, most of them indirectly, on a P2P basis continue to flourish. This is a question of supply attempting to meet demand notwithstanding legal and perhaps moral concerns.

The US decision of *A & M Records Inc. v Napster Inc.*[3] was the first significant case challenging P2P transfers of copyright material online. Copyright law in the United States is governed by the *United States Copyright Act 1976*. The Ninth Circuit Court rejected Napster's claim that the online service and alleged infringements were exempted by the 'fair use' defence. (This claim was based on the fact that international copyright law is generally more lenient on personal file sharing where fair use is involved.) The transfer of files without copyright protection is uncontroversial, of course, and there is considerable legitimate benefit to be gained by using P2P in these circumstances. Australia and New Zealand do not have a general fair use defence; instead they have a relatively narrow range of 'fair dealing' defences for specific circumstances. Napster argued that each transfer was in fact a personal transfer within the meaning of the fair use principle.

---

1 *Roadshow Films Pty Ltd v iiNet Ltd* [2012] HCA 16, para 64 per French CJ, Crennan and Kiefel JJ.
2 *Copyright Act 1968* (Cth) s31.
3 239 F. 3d 1004 (9th Cir 2001).

'Fair use' is defined in the US copyright statute thus:

> the fair use of a copyrighted work, including such use by reproduction in copies or phono-records or by any other means specified by that section, for purposes such as criticism, comment, news reporting, teaching (including multiple copies for classroom use), scholar-ship, or research, is not an infringement of copyright. In determining whether the use made of a work in any particular case is a fair use the factors to be considered shall include –
>
> 1. the purpose and character of the use, including whether such use is of a commercial nature or is for nonprofit educational purposes;
> 2. the nature of the copyrighted work;
> 3. the amount and substantiality of the portion used in relation to the copyrighted work as a whole; and
> 4. the effect of the use upon the potential market for or value of the copyrighted work.[4]

The US courts, applying these four determining factors, have permitted the sharing of material with family or friends. Posting material to a website can be in breach even if the host's intention is not commercial. In *LA Times v Free Republic*[5] the court found that the posting of material with no commercial motive or intent neverthe-less allowed others to avoid paying the customary price charged for the works, and was thus an infringement.

In the Napster case, the court determined that Napster had played an integral role in the transfer process and could have blocked access to infringing material had it chosen to do so. The court rejected the defence that the fair use of the end users protected Napster. It questioned whether sampling and space-shifting were protected in any event.

Subsequent online file sharing programs took note of the Napster case and at-tempted to respond to the court's concerns by decentralising their databases and removing their direct ability to control or track transfers.

Attempts have been made by file sharing site proprietors to rely on the princi-ple enunciated in *Sony Corp. v Universal City Studios*.[6] This pre-internet case held that making recordings of television programs to be viewed later, known as time-shifting, was fair use. Universal Studios and other joint applicants argued that the manufacturers of Betamax and VCR devices and of the corresponding blank tapes authorised infringing copies by the purchasers of the tapes or, alternatively, were liable for contributory infringement. The US Supreme Court, by a majority of 5–4, held that there must be a balance between a copyright holder's legitimate demand for effective protection of the statutory monopoly and the rights of others freely to engage in substantially unrelated areas of commerce. The court ruled that:

---

4 *United States Copyright Act 1976*, §107.
5 54 USPQ 2d 1453 (2000).
6 464 US 417 (1984).

the sale of copying equipment, like the sale of other articles of commerce, does not constitute contributory infringement if the product is widely used for legitimate, unobjectionable purposes. Indeed, it need merely be capable of substantial noninfringing uses.[7]

However, in 2005, in *MGM v Grokster*, in line with the Napster case, the US Supreme Court unanimously held file sharing site proprietors Grokster and Streamcast liable for authorising others to infringe copyright:

We hold that one who distributes a device with the object of promoting its use to infringe copyright, as shown by clear expression or other affirmative steps taken to foster infringement, is liable for the resulting acts of infringement by third parties.[8]

Grokster was ordered to pay US$50 million to the music and recording industries. It also announced that it would no longer offer P2P file sharing, citing the Supreme Court case as the reason.

The issues of thumbnails, inline linking and fair use were considered in *Kelly v Arriba Soft Corporation*.[9] The defendant used online thumbnail images of copyright material which linked to further information and data. The Ninth Circuit Court of Appeals applied the four factors for fair use, and held that creating the thumbnail images as previews was 'transformative' only. The images were not intended to be viewed at high resolution, as the original artwork was. It was questionable whether the low-resolution images could be regarded as a full replication, as a significant amount of detail was, by necessity, lacking. The court regarded their use as reasonable and necessary. Finally, the court held that the market for the original photographs was not substantially diminished, and in fact that the thumbnails may increase demand.

Australian copyright law includes fair dealing defences for research and study, criticism and review, parody or satire, reporting the news, and professional legal advice, but does include the four factors found in the US legislation permitting fair use. In the Federal Court of Australia in *Universal Music Australia Pty Ltd v Sharman License Holdings Ltd*,[10] Wilcox J considered the P2P file sharing system known as Kazaa. Despite the fact that the Kazaa website contained warnings against the sharing of copyright files, and an end user licence agreement under which users agreed not to infringe copyright, it had 'long been obvious' that those measures were ineffective to prevent, or even to substantially curtail, copyright infringements by users. It had 'long been known', said Wilcox J, that Kazaa was widely used for

---

7 Ibid., at 442.
8 545 US 913 (2005).
9 336 F. 3d 811 (CA9 2003).
10 [2005] FCA 1242.

the sharing of copyright files. In granting relief, Wilcox J ordered a complex series of arrangements, including declarations and an order restraining future violations. Wilcox J stated that he was 'anxious' not to make an order which the respondents would not be able to obey except at the unacceptable cost of preventing the sharing even of files which did not infringe the applicants' copyright. The infringing respondents were restrained from authorising Kazaa users to do any of the infringing acts in relation to any sound recording of which any of the applicants were the copyright owners.

Most significantly, Wilcox J ordered that a comprehensive filtering system and update process be put in place. His Honour stated that Kazaa may continue if a protocol which included detailed filter technology, and which was updated regularly, were put in place.

In *Cooper v Universal Music Australia Pty Ltd*[11] the Full Federal Court considered the position of the website www.mp3s4free.net and relevant provisions of the *Copyright Act 1968* (Cth). The action included more than 40 parties. The decision of the Full Federal Court – French, Branson and Kenny JJ – particularly considered the meaning of 'authorising' an infringement of copyright in the context of websites, and concluded that website hosts may be liable for authorising copyright infringement, and that in certain circumstances, so may Internet Service Providers (ISPs).

The website included links to music files on websites which were independent of the registrant (Cooper). The links facilitated the transmission of music files, typically in MP3 format, to the user. Several copyright holders commenced proceedings against Cooper and others for copyright infringement. The Federal Court at first instance[12] found that Cooper had 'authorised' the making of copies.

The appeal to the Full Federal Court helped clarify two important issues: first, the meaning of 'authorisation' of copyright infringement in a sound recording, and second, the application of section 112E of the *Copyright Act* in relation to the protection of the carrier.

Authorisation

Section 13(2) provides, in part, that:

> the exclusive right to do an act in relation to a work, an adaptation of a work or any other subject-matter includes the exclusive right to authorize a person to do that act in relation to that work, adaptation or other subject-matter.

---

11 [2006] FCAFC 187.
12 *Universal Music Australia Pty Ltd v Cooper* [2005] FCA 1878 ('*Cooper's* case').

Section 101 deals with infringement by doing acts comprised in copyright:

(1)   … a copyright subsisting by virtue of this Part is infringed by a person who, not being the owner of the copyright, and without the licence of the owner of the copyright, does in Australia, or authorizes the doing in Australia of, any act comprised in the copyright.

(1A) In determining … whether or not a person has authorised the doing in Australia of any act comprised in a copyright … without the licence of the owner of the copyright, the matters that must be taken into account include the following:

   (a)   the extent (if any) of the person's power to prevent the doing of the act concerned;
   (b)   the nature of any relationship existing between the person and the person who did the act concerned;
   (c)   whether the person took any other reasonable steps to prevent or avoid the doing of the act, including whether the person complied with any relevant industry codes of practice.[13]

Pivotal to the reasoning in *Cooper's* case was the application of section 101(1A). The court reasoned that Cooper had the power to prevent the infringement of copyright, as he could determine not to make his website available, as he knew it was designed to permit downloading of music files. The hyperlinks could be automatically added to the mp3s4free website. Cooper argued that once the website was established, he did not have any relevant power to control its use or prevent users from accessing and using the site for the purpose of copying music.

In relation to section 101(1A)(a), the court rejected the contention that unless Cooper had power, at the time of the doing of each relevant act comprised in a copyright, to prevent its being done, he had no relevant power within the meaning of paragraph.[14] Cooper was responsible for creating and maintaining the mp3s4free website. The court's conclusion was that:

> a person's power to prevent the doing of an act comprised in a copyright includes the person's power not to facilitate the doing of that act by, for example, making available to the public a technical capacity calculated to lead to the doing of that act.[15]

The 'inexorable inference' is that Cooper made a deliberate choice to establish and maintain this website in a form which did not give him the power to immediately prevent, or restrict, internet users from using links to copy sound recordings in which copyright subsisted.

---

13 The two spellings of 'authorise' are faithfully replicated for the provision.
14 [2006] FCAFC 187, para 41.
15 Ibid.

The principal content of the website was links to other websites and files on other servers, the overwhelming majority of which were the subject of copyright. It was the intentional choice of Cooper to establish his website in a way which allowed the automatic addition of hyperlinks. The court concluded that within the meaning of section 101(1A)(a), Cooper did have power to prevent the communication of copyright sound recordings to the public in Australia via the website.[16]

Section 101(1A)(b) deals with the nature of the relationship between, in this case, Cooper and the person who downloaded the music. Cooper submitted that he did not have any relationship with people who made MP3 files generally accessible over the internet or with people who downloaded such files. However, the court considered that an aspect of the relationship was the deliberate attraction of the user-friendly website for downloading. The court considered that Cooper benefited financially from sponsorship and advertisements on the website:

> that is ... the relationship between Mr Cooper and the users of his website had a commercial aspect. Mr Cooper's benefits from advertising and sponsorship may be assumed to have been related to the actual or expected exposure of the website to internet users. As a consequence Mr Cooper had a commercial interest in attracting users to his website for the purpose of copying digital music files.[17]

Section 101(1A)(c) deals with whether the person took any other reasonable steps to prevent or avoid the doing of the act, including complying with relevant industry codes of practice. Cooper submitted that disclaimers on the website amounted to reasonable steps within the meaning of the paragraph. However, the court considered that the disclaimers misstated Australian copyright law in a material way and the inclusion did not constitute a reasonable step to prevent or avoid the infringement of copyright. Tamberlin J, at first instance, attributed little weight to them, as he found their intended purpose was 'merely cosmetic'.[18] The disclaimer stated, in part:

> When you download a song, you take full responsibility for doing so. None of the files on this site are stored on our servers. We are just providing links to remote files ... This site only provides links to the according (sic) sites and no songs are located on our servers ... We are not responsible for any damage caused by downloading these files, or any content posted on this website or linked websites.[19]

Indeed, Tamberlin J considered that the disclaimers indicated Cooper's knowledge of the existence of illegal MP3s on the internet and the likelihood that some of the

16 See, generally, ibid., paras 41–45.
17 Ibid., para 48.
18 Ibid., para 49.
19 Ibid., para 100.

MP3s downloaded were infringing copies of copyright music and sound record-ings.[20] The Full Federal Court concluded that Cooper did not establish that he took any reasonable steps to prevent or avoid the use of his website for copying copyright sound recordings or for communicating such recordings to the public.

Cooper, the ISP and the directors all claimed protection under section 112E of the *Copyright Act*, which provides that:

> a carrier ... who provides facilities for making, or facilitating the making of, a communication is not taken to have authorised any infringement of copyright ... merely because another person uses the facilities so provided to do something the right to do which is included in the copyright.

The court ruled out Cooper's claim relatively perfunctorily. The director, Mr Bal, was also held liable, as on the facts he was the 'controlling mind' of the company.[21] In relation to the ISPs, the court found that:

> As all of the relevant acts of copyright infringement took place via Mr Coop-er's website, I conclude that E-Talk (the internet service provider) had power to prevent the doing of the acts concerned because ... it had the power to withdraw the hosting of Mr Cooper's website.[22]

The Full Federal Court considered the High Court decision in *University of New South Wales v Moorhouse*.[23] The High Court held 'authorise' to mean to 'sanction, approve or countenance'.[24] Gibbs J stated that a person who has control of the means by which an infringement of copyright could be committed, in that case a photocopier, and who permitted it to be used for a copyright infringement know-ingly, or with reasonable suspicion that it is likely to be used for infringement, has authorised the breach, unless reasonable steps were taken to limit such use. The Full Federal Court applied the *Moorhouse* case by analogy.[25]

The cases indicate that setting up a website which facilitates the file sharing of copyrighted materials will fall foul of copyright law. With the paucity of websites from which to download such material, users have turned to BitTorrent technol-ogy. Created in 2001, the BitTorrent protocol is an effective mechanism to distrib-ute large quantities of data. Users no longer rely on direct file sharing. BitTorrent

---

20 *Universal Music Australia Pty Ltd v Cooper* [2005] FCA 972, para 87.
21 See also *Roadshow Films Pty Ltd v iiNet Ltd* [2012] HCA 16, paras 26, 69 and 112–116.
22 [2006] FCAFC 187, para 62.
23 (1975) 133 CLR 1 ('*Moorhouse* case').
24 Ibid., para 10. The word 'authorise' 'has been held judicially to have its dictionary meaning of 'sanction, approve, countenance': *Falcon v Famous Players Film Co.* (1926) 2 KB 474, at 491; *Adelaide Corporation v Australasian Performing Right Association Ltd* [1928] HCA 10; (1928) 40 CLR 481, at 489, 497.
25 The Full Federal Court drew a distinction between Cooper and other parties who, unlike him, did not have the ability to take reasonable steps to prevent the copyright infringement.

allows users to join smaller parts from a larger number of hosts and thus reconstruct a desired file from multiple sources. Although originally designed to improve the efficiency of movement on the internet, the protocol has been utilised by individuals seeking copyrighted material. In these circumstances, copyright holders cannot target any host who could be said to have authorised the copying. The users will breach section 86 of the *Copyright Act*, but multiple actions against individuals is impractical. Instead, copyright holders have targeted ISPs.

The issue came before the Federal Court and in due course the High Court of Australia in *Roadshow Films Pty Ltd v iiNet Ltd*.[26] Thirty-four applicants[27] commenced action against iiNet Limited (iiNet), Australia's third largest ISP, claiming that iiNet had authorised copyright infringements. Australian Federation Against Copyright Theft (AFACT) had established that iiNet customers used the BitTorrent protocol to download films belonging to the applicants. AFACT served notices on iiNet with information that its users were using BitTorrent to infringe copyright. The notices did not specify the method used to determine the information.[28] iiNet was asked to '[p]revent the Identified iiNet Customers from continuing to infringe' by warning, suspending or terminating the internet service of those users.[29] iiNet did not take any action, claiming that it had no obligation to respond to or take heed of notices from AFACT.

The question of authorisation was pivotal to determining liability. In the view of the High Court, iiNet had no technical power to prevent its customers from using BitTorrent.[30] The only relationship was through its ISP agreement with customers, which empowered iiNet to terminate accounts for a breach of conditions, including use for illegal purpose or infringing another person's rights. The applicants argued that iiNet should have acted on the AFACT notices. However, by acting on the notices, wrongful termination could have exposed iiNet to the risk of liability.[31] Gummow and Hayne JJ expressed concern about the effectiveness of the notices, in particular the fact that the notices gave no statement of foundation. The High Court observed that the termination of accounts would be futile because customers would join up with other ISPs rather than do without internet access. The High Court concluded it was 'not unreasonable for iiNet to take the view that it need not act upon the incomplete allegations of primary infringements in the AFACT Notices without further investigation'.[32]

---

26 [2010] FCA 24 and [2012] HCA 16 respectively ('*iiNet* case').
27 Including some of the world's leading movie copyright holders, such as Universal Pictures, Paramount, Warner Bros, Disney, Columbia, Twentieth Century Fox, Village Roadshow, NBC and DreamWorks.
28 *Roadshow Films Pty Ltd v iiNet Ltd* [2012] HCA 16, para 75.
29 Ibid., para 32.
30 Ibid., para 69.
31 Ibid., para 75.
32 Ibid., para 146.

The conclusion from *Cooper's* case and the *tiNet* case is that, in effect, anyone hosting a website which is known to be used to infringe copyright by downloading will be regarded as 'authorising' the breach and will incur liability. ISPs will not be liable by acting merely in their role as ISPs. However, the High Court has left the door open should, for example, a body such as AFACT provide not only a list of infringing customers but, more importantly, conclusive evidence of the breach and the methodology used to compile the information.

FURTHER READING

Australian Copyright Council: <www.copyright.org.au>.

Intellectual Property Society of Australia and New Zealand: <www.ipsanz.com.au>.

IP Australia: <www.ipaustralia.gov.au>.

A Strowel, *Peer-to-peer file sharing and secondary liability in copyright law*, Edward Elgar Publishing, 2009.

CLOUD COMPUTING

Knowledge, information and electronic data of all forms are stored by the majority of the world's population on complex range of devices and storage facilities. From large computer servers to personal tablets and mobile devices, storage has expanded in direct proportion to the advances in the capability and capacity in computing.[1] In 2014 the number of mobile devices exceeded the number of desktop and laptop computers worldwide. Users are relying less and less on fixed storage devices and individual computer capacity. Entrepreneurs have quickly recognised the individual's proclivity for gadgets, communications, photographic and video devices, as well as text and internet connections and communications, and have taken advantage of the spontaneous order which can arise from the chaotic juxtaposition of new technology, social media and the human spirit. The inevitable next step has been the creation of central storage facilities and computer resources to provide a reliable rapid use facility for all individuals.

Cloud computing promises fast, efficient and convenient storage and access networks and resources that are permanently at the fingertips of users. The promise may be premature as users evaluate the security and privacy risks. A reasonable and considered definition of cloud computing is:

> Cloud computing is a model for enabling ubiquitous, convenient, on-demand network access to a shared pool of configurable computing resources that can be rapidly provisioned and released with minimal management effort or service provider interaction.[2]

The National Institute of Standards and Technology (NIST) lists five essential characteristics of cloud computing:

1. on-demand self-service
2. broad network access
3. resource pooling
4. rapid elasticity or expansion, and
5. measured service.[3]

The uptake of these centralised facilities has been described as a:

> sea change – a deep and permanent shift in how computing power is generated and consumed. It's as inevitable and irreversible as the shift from steam to electric power in manufacturing.[4]

---

1 That is to say, following Moore's Law: the perpetual increase of computer speed and capacity.
2 National Institute of Standards and Technology (NIST), an agency of the US Department of Commerce <www.nist.gov/itl/csd/cloud-102511.cfm>.
3 Ibid.
4 Andrew McAfee, 'What every CEO needs to know about the cloud' (2011) 89 *Harvard Business Review* 125, 126.

For many businesses, government departments and service providers, this means substantial infrastructure costs, maintenance, updating, virus protection and hence the employment of a computing technician, or a team of technicians. Some organisations have abandoned in-house email facilities and now use global providers, such as Gmail. Others take advantage of various global storage facilities that promise permanent access and impeccable security.[5] Online banking, social media chat rooms and blogs and webmail email accounts all utilise cloud computing technology.[6] Their arguments are persuasive. The average downtime for in-house computing services may average two or three days a year, taking into consideration updates, services, maintenance and outages. Cloud computing services boast a downtime of no more than 5 minutes per year. The need for resources and maintenance is reduced. The appeal is clear: they offer financial benefits, enhanced computing resources which remain state of the art, economies of scale and remote access at all times.

For the individual, cloud computing is a place to store, swap and share social media. The individual is not tied to a central home computer or work computer, but is connected online by devices that can connect to the cloud.

Origin

The expression 'cloud computing' dates back less than two decades, but its implementation and uptake has been much more recent. However, there were visions of global connections permitting a vast network for sharing as far back as the 1960s. This prediction came true. The internet became a reality; however, until recently, internet connections to data and information came about by using specific addresses to access information that was stored on private computers with public access. Cloud computing facilities would have proved impossible in the late 20th century, when computer speeds and capacity were limited and relatively expensive. True cloud computing has emerged endogenously in an environment where capacity and speed can provide cost-effective and user-friendly facilities.

The Oxford English Dictionary defines cloud computing as 'the use of networked facilities for the storage and processing of data rather than a user's local computer, access to data or services typically being via the Internet', and credits its first use to an internal document of Compaq Computer Corporation in 1996.[7]

---

5 Statistics on security breaches are largely unreliable. First, the media will report specific instances of security breaches in clouds, giving the public the impression of a greater concern than the facts suggest. Second, most businesses do not report security breaches for in-house reasons, thwarting accurate comparison.

6 H Dixon, 'Cloud computing' (2012) 51 *The Judges' Journal* 36.

7 The expression used was: 'Cloud computing: The cloud has no borders' (2011) *Technology Rev* 31 October.

However, the first public use of the expression is typically credited to Google CEO Eric Schmidt in 2006.

The majority of internet users use cloud facilities, often without knowing it. Social media is cloud based. Users effectively add to the cloud when they enter and contribute to Facebook, Twitter, YouTube, Flickr and so forth. When search engines such as Google are used, the user is accessing a cloud comprising, effectively, a database of the internet, cross-referenced and indexed for easy access. Even Wikipedia is effectively a public cloud made up of millions of contributions and updates.

Cloud providers

Google, Microsoft, IBM, Apple, Dell and Amazon are putting resources into the research and development of cloud computing.[8] Public clouds are available to the general public. Private clouds are also available, depending on the needs and budget of the organisation.

Cloud providers typically form one of three groups: Software-as-a-service (SaaS), Infrastructure-as-a-service (IaaS) and Platform-as-a-service (PaaS).

The SaaS model is the most used model. Under this model the cloud providers supply a service which users would otherwise be required to download and set up. The organisation's users can thus access emails from any place that has an online connection. The two most popular cloud email services are Gmail and Outlook. com (formerly Hotmail). Gmail is well established and has proved its reliability. Outlook.com is a vast step up from Hotmail, providing business users in particular with services that work efficiently and securely. Many other services may be used through an SaaS model, including human resources management, social media monitoring and client tracking management. The SaaS model is typically a 'take it or leave it' service, with little opportunity to personalise the service.

The IaaS model is intended to provide users with control over the infrastructure and computing services. The approach permits the transfer of an organisation's entire computing services to the cloud provider so that the organisation's operations can be truly online and available to the organisation's members and authorised users. Amazon Web Services, for example, offers computing, storage, database, analytics, application, and deployment services described as reliable, scalable, and inexpensive.[9]

In their simplest form, cloud providers merely offer a location for storing files, such as Dropbox and Amazon Cloud Drive. Amazon, Google, Apple and Microsoft

---

8 H Dixon, 'Cloud computing' (2012) 51 *The Judges' Journal* 36.
9 Amazon Web Services: <aws.amazon.com>.

have been the largest providers in this market. Amazon offers a user-pays service for data storage. It also offers SimpleDB, a database web service; CloudFront, for content; and Simple Queue Service, for storing messages. Amazon was one of the first into the marketplace. Amazon's Elastic Compute Cloud provided users with direct computing capacity.

Google provides a set of online office productivity tools including email, calendaring, word processing and a simple website creation tool. Google Apps (formerly Postini) is a set of email and web security services. The Google App Engine is a Platform-as-a-service (PaaS) offering that lets developers build applications and host them on Google's infrastructure. Microsoft offers Azure, a Windows-as-a-service platform. The Microsoft Cloud is located in data centres 'sprinkled across the world' and connected by the fastest networks. The data services support Microsoft's One-Drive, Bing, Azure and Office 365. No single person knows where data is stored – it is stored optimally by the operating system, in multiple locations, for backup, redundancy and efficiency purposes.

Other prominent cloud providers include Enomaly, GoGrid, NetSuite, Rackspace, RightScale and Salesforce.com. Many such providers do not use the expression 'cloud' or 'cloud computing', but nevertheless offer cloud services.

Legal concerns

By necessity, a great deal of trust and control is placed in the hands of cloud computing providers. It is this control that is central to the legal analysis of the relationship between the provider and the user. The overarching position is that a cloud provider must comply with the local laws – anti-terrorism, copyright, defamation and privacy, for example. This requirement is exacerbated by the actual location of the storage facilities, which may be one or more jurisdictions.

Legal and practical issues

The underlying legal principles and security issues for mobile devices and for cloud use are largely the same for online users. As with all contracts, users need to consider online contracts carefully. However, the evidence is that users tend to bypass complex legal jargon and click the 'I agree' icon and proceed.[10] For cloud usage, users are often placing private, and sometimes sensitive, information in the hands of a third party, and the fine print of these contracts will exclude all liability and responsibility for that third party. Google excludes liability for any lost

10 See Chapter 12.

data: 'use of Google Services is at your sole risk. Google Services are provided on an "as is" and "as available" basis'.[11] Electronic contract terms and conditions are often lengthy, and written in language that seems more like Middle English than everyday language. No assumptions should be made about continuous service or about recovery for loss of time or for loss of data. Cloud providers are generally not prepared to assume commercial, corporate or personal risk. Many agreements provide for a maximum liability to be the equivalent of the 12 month fee.

From the users' perspective, the first step should be to investigate user reports and media reviews, and perhaps to contact the local consumer protection agency. Users should consider separate insurance for loss of information and downtime. On one view, users' agreements with cloud providers:

> will necessitate a review, as a minimum, of provisions relating to privacy, security, confidentiality, records management requirements, audit, compensation for data loss/misuse, subcontractor obligations, intellectual property rights in relation to the data, limitations on liability, indemnity, service levels, termination rights and dispute resolution options.[12]

The first two on this extensive list, privacy and security, are real issues that have sparked media attention, because hackers have broken into clouds to retrieve compromising images of celebrities.[13] Hackers may simply trick a user into providing a password through well-known methods such as phishing, fraud, illegal surveillance or non-electronic means, such as trash picking, burglary, theft or infiltration.[14] Issues around password access are not new, and have been dealt with by the banking industry in relation to credit and debit cards. Through the Australian ePayments Code of Conduct (formerly the Electronic Funds Code of Conduct),[15] financial institutions have willingly agreed to accept liability where there is loss through fraud or negligence by the bank's employee, by hacking into the system, or by use of a pass code that was forged, faulty, expired or cancelled. The user will be liable where the user contributed to the loss, for example by inappropriately sharing the username and pass code, or contributed to the fraud or negligence, or failed to report a breach in a timely manner. This Australian ePayments Code has worked well because it is within a single jurisdiction, because of the goodwill of

---

11 See Google Apps Terms of Service: <www.google.com/apps/intl/en/terms/user_terms.html>. See also Microsoft terms: <www.microsoft.com/en-us/legal/intellectualproperty/copyright/default.aspx>.

12 Ben Allen, 'Managing disputes in the cloud', (2012) 50 *Law Society Journal* 74.

13 See Chapter 8.

14 Nicholas Hoover, 'Compliance in the Ether: Cloud Computing, Data Security and Business Regulation', (2013) 8 *Journal of Business and Technology Law* 255.

15 Available through ASIC: <www.asic.gov.au/asic/asic.nsf/byheadline/EFT-code-amendments>.

Australian banks and because there is a concern that without voluntary compliance legislative intervention may be necessary.

For cloud computing users, the problems are apparent. Clouds operate across multiple jurisdictions and legislative intervention is not universally applicable. Nevertheless, as the industry matures it can be anticipated that users will act on reports of misuse and mishandling and that an order will emerge, from leaders in the market and consumer use and consumer demand.

Interference from law enforcement

All cloud providers are subject to applicable local law. A court may order access to a cloud or database provided the data is within the reach of the jurisdiction. Microsoft's CEO confirmed at the launch of the Microsoft cloud that Microsoft would comply with any lawful order under the US *PATRIOT Act*.[16] In addition to police powers under criminal legislation, Australia has enacted the *Anti-terrorism Act 2004* (Cth) and the *Anti-Terrorism Act (No. 2) 2005* (Cth) and made substantial amendments more recently with the *National Security Legislation Amendment Act (No. 1) 2014* (Cth) and the *Counter-Terrorism Legislation Amendment (Foreign Fighters) Act 2014* (Cth). Similar provisions have been enacted internationally, including the *Council of Europe Convention on Cybercrime*,[17] which Australia has ratified. Article 29 of the Convention requires its 45 members to honour requests by other members for access to information in cybercrime databases. Article 19 requires signatories to adopt legislation that empowers the 'competent authorities' of other signatories to search and access computer systems and computer data within their own territory.

Legal practitioners have been reluctant to place information in the cloud.[18] There are concerns that placing information in a cloud waives or even breaches a lawyer's duty to confidentiality and legal privilege.[19] This should be distinguished from Virtual Data Rooms (VDRs). A VDR is a secure online repository of data. These[20] have been used to provide confidential access to select parties – they

---

16 The US *PATRIOT Act* was drafted debated and enacted within 7 weeks of the attacks on the World Trade centre in September 2001. The response was to give security agencies and law enforcement broad and extensive powers *inter alia* to search electronic databases. See Chapter 18.

17 Council of Europe, *Council of Europe Convention on Cybercrime* (2001): <www.coe.int/cybercrime>.

18 Ben Allen, above n 12.

19 Ibid.

20 The term originated in the US *Security Act 1933* to protect brokers.

have been used, for commercial or legal reasons, for mergers and acquisitions, for example. VDRs have become popular among law firms for the release and inspection of confidential information, including in the discovery process. Where the site remains outside the cloud, the issues associated with cloud computing do not arise. However, where access is provided via the cloud, parties should be appropriately vigilant and consider the ramifications.

Conclusion

With the increase in use of mobile technology and its increasing economies of scale for business, cloud storage and computing facilities have a bright future. However, it is still the dawn of the technology. Until the types of systems stabilise – or diversify into new technology – the law will continue to have problems catching up. The problem is not one of applicable law, as the law of contract will provide the initial basis for determining the relationship between cloud provider and user. The problem has become a question of sustainability and security with respect to interference by external parties, by both lawful and unlawful means. Blanket exclusion clauses by cloud providers may be the norm, but an unforgiving market may shift allegiances to cloud providers who provide reasonable terms with evidence of a commercial and acceptable track record.

FURTHER READING

Ben Allen, 'Managing disputes in the cloud', (2012) 50 *Law Society Journal* 74.

H Dixon, 'Cloud computing', (2012) 51 *The Judges' Journal* 36

Nicholas Hoover, 'Compliance in the ether: Cloud computing, data security and business regulation,' (2013) 8 *Journal of Business and Technology Law* 255.

Andrew McAfee, 'What every CEO needs to know about the cloud', (2011) 89 *Harvard Business Review* 125.

SOCIAL MEDIA AND THE WORKPLACE

Because of the very architecture of personal space in the offline world, social interactions used to be relatively private. The retelling of anecdotes and questionable behaviour in a social environment would, until the last decade or two, be taken with a grain of salt and with some expectation of embellishment or exaggeration. Rarely would an employer or others be faced with hard evidence, such as photographs, statements of admission by the employee or digital logs. Today, however, social media allows, if not encourages, such actions. In the words of the NSW Industrial Relations Commissioner, there exists:

> greater risk of private exchanges over the Internet becoming public than was ever the case with private spoken conversations. Exchanges over 'Facebook' and other social media appear to have an increasing likelihood of surfacing publicly at some later time.[1]

And of a Fair Work Australia Commissioner:

> What might previously have been a grumble about their employer over a coffee or drinks with friends has turned into a posting on a website that, in some cases, may be seen by an unlimited number of people. Posting comments about an employer on a website (Facebook) that can be seen by an uncontrollable number of people is no longer a private matter but a public comment.

It is well accepted that behaviour outside working hours may have an impact on employment.[2]

The underlying relationship in the workplace between the employer and employee has not changed, but the use and misuse of social media facilitates the free flow of information to a wider audience, potentially harming the interests of the employer (and, indeed, of the employee). A ban on the use of such devices might be a sledgehammer reaction, and in many businesses would be impossible, particularly where social interaction is encouraged for the benefit of the business. Restricting use after hours has its own problems. In *Stutsel v Linfox Australia Pty Ltd* the Commissioner commented that Facebook communication was of the nature 'of a group of friends letting off steam and trying to outdo one another in being outrageous ... [and] has much of the favour (sic) of a conversation in a pub or cafe, although conducted in an electronic format'.[3] However, on appeal the Full Bench reconsidered this statement, commenting:

1 *McDiarmid v Commissioner of Police* [2012] NSWIRComm 100, para 136.
2 *Fitzgerald v Dianna Smith trading as Escape Hair Design* [2010] FWA 7358, paras 50–51, Commissioner Bissett.
3 [2011] FWA 8444, para 81.

> The fact that the conversations were conducted in electronic form and on Facebook gave the comments a different characteristic and a potentially wider circulation than a pub discussion ... Unlike conversations in a pub or cafe, the Facebook conversations leave a permanent written record of statements and comments made by the participants, which can be read at any time into the future until they are taken down by the page owner.[4]

As with privacy, it is the construct of cyberspace that makes the transfer of information – information which is digital and thus faithfully reproduced – easy. Social media involves engaging in a social environment which is shared at the speed of light with limited chances to redact. Social media users have become enmeshed in seeking an increased presence, a greater number of hits, and more 'friends' and readers. In response to the chaos of the internet, such order has been achieved through structured sites and search engines. In the social media context, however, a huge number of programs and applications have been developed to cater to the worldwide demand for online social interaction, with its immediate gratification and sharing of information. Millions share thoughts, images and video moments. Such developments have revolutionised the traditional media.

From an employer's point of view there are legitimate concerns where employees demonstrate, with statements and photographs, behaviour which tarnishes a corporate image or may amount to a breach of contract conditions or policy. It may not even be the actions or statements which are recorded, but simply the actual or perceived impact.

According to the Fair Work Commission:[5]

> It was *inevitable with the seismic shift to the phenomenon of social media* as a means of widespread instantaneous communication, that it would lead to new issues in the workplace. These include the extent of the use of social media while at work, the content of such communications and whether they be work or non-work related. Employers have had to *respond to the new phenomenon with appropriate policies and codes of conduct* – just as they had to respond to employees using work provided computers to receive, store or distribute inappropriate or non-work-related material.[6]

---

4 *Linfox Australia Pty Ltd v Stutsel* [2012] FWAFB7097, para 26; for further details see the case analysis below.
5 In 2013 the Fair Work Commission took over from the body known as Fair Work Australia (2009–2013), which had replaced the Australian Industrial Relations Commission (1983 to 2009).
6 *Little v Credit Corp Group Limited* [2013] FWC 9642, at para 67, Deputy President Sams, emphasis added.

Social media usage is rampant. Facebook has 1.32 billion active users, Instagram 200 million, Twitter 271 million and LinkedIn 300 million.[7] YouTube has passed 1 billion hours viewed per month[8] and Twitter has more than 284 million tweets per day.[9]

While much of the discussion below deals with specific instances under the *Fair Work Act 2009* (Cth), the states have varying approaches, including in relation to which employees are covered. For example, the *Fair Work Act 2009* (Cth) applies only to employees who have completed the 'minimum employment period' and where there is a modern award, or an enterprise agreement, or the remuneration is less than the 'high income threshold' (currently $133,000).[10]

Status quo – employer's directions

The employee has a common law duty to act in the best interests of the employer and to carry out faithfully the employment contract. In addition the employee is obligated to obey reasonable directions of the employer, provided such directions are lawful, reasonable and related to the employment. Obeying lawful directions and complying with an employer's policy are not new requirements. In 1938, in *R v Darling Island Stevedoring and Lighterage Co. Limited*,[11] Dixon J, in the High Court of Australia, stated the common law position thus:

> If a command relates to the subject matter of the employment and involves no illegality, the obligation of the servant to obey it depends at common law upon its being reasonable. In other words, the lawful commands of an employer which an employee must obey are those which fall within the scope of the contract of service and are reasonable.[12]

In 1924, in *Adami v Maison de Luxe Ltd*, Isaacs ACJ commented that in an employment relationship 'obedience to lawful orders is, if not expressly, then impliedly, contemplated by the contract creating the relation, and mere disobedience of such

---

7 <www.linkedin.com/pulse/20141118182103–28964915-social-media-user-statistics-age-demographics-for-2014>.
8 <www.youtube.com/yt/press/statistics.html>.
9 <about.twitter.com/company>.
10 See section 382 *Fair Work Act 2009* (Cth). The high income threshold is regularly indexed. See also *Miller v WesTrac Pty Ltd* [2014] FWC 9310.
11 [1938] HCA 44; (1938) 60 CLR 601.
12 (1938) 60 CLR 601, 621.

orders is a breach of the bargain'.[13] Isaacs ACJ examined circumstances where a breach may or may not justify 'dissolution' of the employment contract. His Honour considered that the disobedience must be a 'radical breach' which is 'inconsistent' with the contract of employment. His Honour noted that where an employer's order is unclear, a benefit of doubt arises:

> It is incontestable that any conduct of an employee which is not merely in-consistent with some particular obligation involved, and possibly not striking at the root of the matter, but which is inconsistent with the relation estab-lished, is a just cause for the employer's termination of that relation. Habitual neglect or a definite refusal of a general kind to pursue the employer's lawful policy of business would afford such justification.[14]

Breaching an employer's policy will not of itself be sufficient to terminate employ-ment. According to the Full Bench of the Australian Industrial Relations Commis-sion, the policy must be both lawful and reasonable, and regard must be had to 'the character of the policy and the nature of the breach'.[15] For example, in *Atfield v Jupiters Ltd* the Full Bench regarded a breach of policy – a strict prohibition on employees of a casino gambling on the casino premises – as a breach of the em-ployment contract and a valid reason for termination in that the reason was 'sound, defensible or well-founded'.[16] However, the Full Bench accepted as mitigating fac-tors: that the employee was unaware that the prohibition applied to hotel premises adjoining the main casino premises; that he had withdrawn his bet as soon as it was suggested his bet may be in breach of policy; that the employee had an un-blemished record; and the impact in gaining employment in the industry in the future in circumstances where the employee had made a significant investment in self-funded training. The Full Bench determined that the Commissioner was enti-tled to conclude that the termination was harsh.[17]

In *Woolworths (Trading as Safeway) v Brown*, the Australian Industrial Rela-tions Commission suggested that it is a defence to refuse to comply with a policy or direction if it is illegal, unreasonable or the policy 'does not relate to the subject matter of the employment or matters affecting the work of the employee'.[18] The meaning of 'unreasonable' gives the courts great flexibility, but lacks clarity for employers and employees alike. It will depend upon the circumstances: the nature

---

13 [1924] HCA 45; (1924) 35 CLR 143, 151.
14 (1924) 35 CLR 143, 153.
15 *Potter v Workcover Corporation* (2004) 133 IR 458, at para 67.
16 (2003) 124 IR 217, para 11.
17 The expression 'sound, defensible or well-founded' comes from *Selvachandran v Peteron Plastics Pty Ltd* (1995) 62 IR 371 at 373 per Northrop J.
18 (2005) 145 IR 285, para 34. See also *Adidem Pty Ltd v Suckling* [2014] FWCFB 3611 and *Mayberry v Kijani Investments Pty Ltd* ATF [2011] FWA 3496.

of the employment and of the policy, the timing of the infraction and established practices and usages. In addition, the employee may establish ignorance of the policy. For example, see *Atfield v Jupiters Ltd* above. Also, in *R v Darling Island Stevedoring and Lighterage Co. Limited* Dixon J stated:

> what is reasonable is not to be determined, so to speak, *in vacuo*. The nature of the employment, the established usages affecting it, the common practices which exist and the general provisions of the instrument ... governing the relationship, supply considerations by which the determination of what is reasonable must be controlled.[19]

The termination of employment may be a disproportionate response in the circumstances after taking into consideration such factors as the length of employment and prior conduct. The employee may demonstrate prior non-enforcement or inconsistent application of the policy, which may in the circumstances render termination harsh, unjust or unreasonable. Alternatively, the employee may demonstrate that the policy was applied in a discriminatory manner or used as a pretence to disguise a hidden agenda.[20]

The danger for the employee, in a social media context, is misunderstanding the division between private and personal posts, and where bad taste becomes a work-related issue. For example, Yarra Trams terminated the employment of a tram driver who was a long-term blogger and poster, in particular for posting photographs with captions which insulted crash victims and taunted commuters, and so became work related. A photograph of a car accident had the caption, 'LOL girl drivers'; a photograph taken from the tram driver's view, showing a stop ahead, had the caption, 'Hanging back so everyone has to wait in the cold'; and a photograph of a tram accident had the caption, 'The best collision I ever had. Also serves as a nice reminder to stay out of the way.'[21]

Legislation

Employment and the workplace have been traditionally governed by common law principles, with a *laissez-faire* approach to applying the law of contract. More recently there have been steps, particularly at the federal level, to regulate the employment relationship. Within Australia the states have referred significant powers to the federal government, culminating in the *Fair Work Act 2009* (Cth) ('the Act'). The Act has been heavily amended with changes in government. The

---

19 [1938] HCA 44; (1938) 60 CLR 601, 622.
20 See *Woolworths (Trading as Safeway) v Brown* (2005) 145 IR 285, para 36.
21 *Herald Sun*, 18 August 2011.

Act replaced the Australian Industrial Relations Commission with Fair Work Australia, which itself was renamed – and restructured – in 2013 into the Fair Work Commission.[22]

In the context of the interaction between social media and employment, it is relevant to be cognisant of the relevant privacy and discrimination laws:

- *Privacy Act 1988* (Cth) (the new Australian Privacy Principles replaced the former National Privacy Principles in 2014);
- *Racial Discrimination Act 1975* (Cth);
- *Sex Discrimination Act 1984* (Cth);
- *Age Discrimination Act 2004* (Cth);
- *Australian Human Rights Commission Act 1986* (Cth); and
- *Disability Discrimination Act 1992* (Cth).[23]

Unfair dismissal

The *Fair Work Act 2009* (Cth) defines an unfair dismissal in the following terms. A person has been unfairly dismissed if the Fair Work Commission is satisfied that:

(a) the person has been dismissed; and
(b) the dismissal was harsh, unjust or unreasonable; and
(c) the dismissal was not consistent with the Small Business Fair Dismissal Code; and
(d) the dismissal was not a case of genuine redundancy.[24]

The Act also sets out the criteria for considering harshness of a dismissal.

387 Criteria for considering harshness etc.

In considering whether it is satisfied that a dismissal was harsh, unjust or unreasonable, the FWC must take into account:

(a) whether there was a valid reason for the dismissal related to the person's capacity or conduct (including its effect on the safety and welfare of other employees); and
(b) whether the person was notified of that reason; and
(c) whether the person was given an opportunity to respond to any reason related to the capacity or conduct of the person; and
(d) any unreasonable refusal by the employer to allow the person to have a support person present to assist at any discussions relating to dismissal; and

---

22 In relation to unfair dismissal see *Fair Work Act 2009* (Cth), Part 3.2.
23 The states and territories have similar legislation to varying degrees in relation to non-federal matters.
24 *Fair Work Act 2009* (Cth), s385.

(e) if the dismissal related to unsatisfactory performance by the person – whether the person had been warned about that unsatisfactory performance before the dismissal; and

(f) the degree to which the size of the employer's enterprise would be likely to impact on the procedures followed in effecting the dismissal; and

(g) the degree to which the absence of dedicated human resource management specialists or expertise in the enterprise would be likely to impact on the procedures followed in effecting the dismissal; and

(h) any other matters that the FWC considers relevant.[25]

In their judgements, the Commissioners of the Fair Work Commission often include a written consideration of each of those paragraphs.[26]

The Act permits the Fair Work Commission to reinstate a person unfairly dismissed or to award compensation.[27]

Grounds for dismissal but still harsh

The nature and degree of disciplinary action, up to and including dismissal, will depend on many factors. There may be cases where there are distinct grounds for dismissal, but taking into account all the circumstances, such a dismissal would be regarded as harsh. Such factors include:

- the seriousness of the transgression;
- whether the terms of the contract expressly or impliedly applied;
- the existence and applicability of any code of conduct or policy and the notice given to the employee;
- the damage and potential damage to the employer;
- whether the conduct of the employee is not consistent with the employee's obligation as employee;

---

25 *Fair Work Act 2009* (Cth), s387.

26 For examples of deliberations of s387 see *O'Keefe v Williams Muir's Pty Ltd trading as Troy Williams The Good Guys* [2011] FWA 5311, paras 46–56; *O'Connor v Outdoor Creations Pty Ltd* [2011] FWA 3081, paras 41–55; *Fitzgerald v Dianna Smith t/as Escape Hair Design* [2010] FWA 7358, paras 60–70; *Stutsel v Linfox Australia Pty Ltd* [2011] FWA 8444, paras 89–96; and *Faulkner v BHP Coal Pty Ltd* [2014] FWC 9330, paras 74–79.

27 Sections 390–92. For New Zealand examples, see generally *Wellington Free Ambulance v Adams* [2010] NZEmpC 59 (a Facebook exchange between employees) and *Hohaia v New Zealand Post Limited* [2010] NZERA 670 (blog damaged employer's reputation, and denigrated and humiliated a fellow employee).

- the extent to which the transgression and conduct identifies the employer;
- specifically for social media, the extent of public access to information posted.

In *Qantas Airways Limited v Carter*,[28] the Full Bench of the Fair Work Commission determined that although there was a valid reason for termination, as provided by section 385 of the *Fair Work Act 2009* (Cth), the termination could nonetheless be regarded as harsh, unjust or unreasonable, within the meaning of section 387 of the Act. Similar conclusions were reached in a number of recent cases. In *Mayberry v Kijani Investments Pty Ltd*,[29] notwithstanding cause, the dismissal was regarded as unfair because there was no evidence of damage to the employer. In *Faulkner v BHP Coal Pty Ltd*,[30] despite the strictness of the published policy prohibiting mobile devices on the work site, the Commissioner accepted a number of mitigating factors to determine that the dismissal was excessive.[31] In *Woolworths (Trading as Safeway) v Brown*,[32] there was a strict policy against jewellery in the workplace where the employee was a butcher and safety was a factor. The policy clearly prohibited piercing, such as the employee's eyebrow piercings, with instant dismissal the consequence. The employee had received several directions to remove the piercing. He had covered the piercing with tape, which was only permitting for wedding rings. The Commission discussed circumstances where it may be appropriate to order reinstatement, such as ignorance of the policy and that the dismissal may be a 'disproportionate response' having regard to its nature and the employee's length of service and prior history.[33] However, in this case, the Commission upheld the dismissal.

Relevance of policy – use of policy

Once a social media policy is in place, a decision should be made as to whether or not the social media sites of employees should be monitored. Postings to such sites as Twitter and YouTube are available to the public at large. Employers should be aware that account holders may act anonymously or pseudonymously. Some social media sites are closed to the public. Sites such as Facebook have a range of privacy settings limiting public access. It is suggested that any monitoring policy be open and transparent. Other actions may be appropriate once a complaint is lodged.

---

28 [2012] FWAFB 5776.
29 [2011] FWA 3496.
30 [2014] FWC 9330.
31 See Mitigating Factors below.
32 (2005) 145 IR 285.
33 Ibid., para 36.

In *Pearson v Linfox Australia Pty Ltd*,[34] Linfox had in place workplace policies with respect to absenteeism, mobile phone use, social media and safe work procedures. Pearson had been an employee of five years standing when in July 2013 Linfox issued several warnings for breaches of policies and for refusing to sign the required acknowledgement forms, which stated that the signor had 'read and understood' the policy; for example 'I ... have read and understood the content of this social media policy brochure.' Linfox terminated his employment and Pearson challenged the dismissal. Pearson stated that he 'refused to sign the social media policy because it intends to apply outside of working hours' and 'as Linfox do not pay me or control my life outside of my working hours, they cannot tell me what to do or say outside of work, that is *basic human rights on freedom of speech*'.[35] The Commissioner stated that he 'understood' Linfox's desire to have a social media policy in place. Indeed, the Commissioner noted evidence that Linfox had been criticised in other proceedings for not having such a policy. The Commissioner stated:

> Further, in an employment context the establishment of a social media policy is clearly a legitimate exercise in acting to protect the reputation and security of a business. It also serves a useful purpose by making clear to employees what is expected of them. Gone is the time (if it ever existed) where an employee might claim posts on social media are intended to be for private consumption only. An employer is also entitled to have a policy in place making clear excessive use of social media at work may have consequences for employees.[36]

In relation to Pearson's argument that the policy constrains his rights outside work hours, the Commissioner commented (whilst not deciding the matter) that:

> it is difficult to see how a social media policy designed to protect an employer's reputation and the security of the business could operate in an 'at work' context only. I accept that there are many situations in which an employer has no right to seek to restrict or regulate an employee's activities away from work. However, in the context of the use of social media, and a policy intended to protect the reputation and security of a business, it is difficult to see how such a policy could operate in this constrained way.

> I am satisfied in all the circumstances that what Linfox was asking of Mr Pearson in terms of his acknowledgement of its social media policy was neither unlawful or unreasonable. It was accordingly entitled to take the action it did in response to his refusal to do so.[37]

---

34 [2014] FWC 446.
35 Ibid., para 15, emphasis added.
36 Ibid., para 46.
37 Ibid., paras 47 and 48.

It is the employer's role, and indeed right, to protect the business, and in the case of employees it ought to have in place workplace policies appropriate for the type of business. The social media policy should be directed at preserving the legitimate interests of the employer, such as reputation, security and confidentiality. The policy must be lawful and reasonable, and provide for the opportunity to respond with varying and appropriate options of action, from warnings to dismissal.

In *McDiarmid v Commissioner of Police* the Commissioner noted that a social media policy is not about the employer 'seeking to prevent or stultify ... "gossip" or the ordinary day-to-day banter ... regarding what occurs at work'.[38] It is about legitimate workplace considerations.

In *Stutsel v Linfox Australia Pty Ltd*,[39] Commissioner Roberts strongly warned employers of the necessity to publish their social media policies. The Commissioner noted that the employer, Linfox, did not have any policy relating to the use of social media by employees. Instead the employer relied on its induction training and a handbook as the basis for its action against the employee, Mr Stutsel:

> In the current electronic age, this is not sufficient and many large companies have published detailed social media policies and taken pains to acquaint their employees with those policies. Linfox did not.[40]

On the other hand, in *Little v Credit Corp Group Limited*, a case where the employee, *inter alia*, made sexually suggestive Facebook postings about a new employee in breach the employer's policy, Deputy President Sams commented:

> Even if the respondent had no policies or a Code of Conduct directly addressing the applicant's actions, it would be of no consequence. One hardly needs written policies or codes of conduct to understand and appreciate that, firstly, the kind of sexual comments made about the new employee were grossly offensive and disgusting and were more than likely to cause hurt and humiliation.[41]

Outside work hours

Employees may be subject to disciplinary action for conduct and behaviour outside work hours where such conduct or behaviour breaches the terms of the employment contract, lawful directions or policies and codes of conduct of the employer.

---

38 [2012] NSWIRComm 100, para 137.
39 [2011] FWA 8444 ('*Stutsel's* case').
40 Ibid., para 87.
41 [2013] FWC 9642, para 69.

For example, employees will be liable for defamatory statements; for bullying, harassing and victimisation actions; and for the disclosure of confidential information – whether online or not. Where the employee's conduct has 'significant and adverse effects on the workplace', the employer may legitimately monitor or investigate the employee's after-hours activities.[42] For example, in *Fitzgerald v Dianna Smith trading as Escape Hair Design* the Tribunal stated:

> A Facebook posting, while initially undertaken outside working hours, does not stop once work recommences. It remains on Facebook until removed, for anyone with permission to access the site to see.[43]

In *Rose v Telstra* the Industrial Relations Commission noted that an employment may be validly terminated for out-of-hours conduct in limited circumstances. However, such circumstances are limited:

- the conduct must be such that, viewed objectively, it is likely to cause serious damage to the relationship between the employer and employee; or
- the conduct damages the employer's interests; or
- the conduct is incompatible with the employee's duty as an employee.[44]

In *O'Keefe v Williams Muir's Pty Ltd trading as Troy Williams The Good Guys*, the employee posted strong offensive language directed at certain female colleagues. The Tribunal confirmed the dismissal of the employee in circumstances where the Facebook posts were on the employee's home computer outside work hours:

> Even in the absence of the respondent's Handbook warning employees of the respondent's views on matters such as this, common sense would dictate that one could not write and therefore publish insulting and threatening comments about another employee in the manner in which this occurred.
>
> *The fact that the comments were made on the applicant's home computer, out of work hours, does not make any difference.*[45]

---

42 *McManus v Scott-Charlton* [1996] FCA 1820, para 56. See *Michael King v Catholic Education Office Diocese of Parramatta T/A Catholic Education Diocese of Parramatta* [2014] FWCFB 2194, which gives specific examples such as the police, public servants and teachers; and also *Cooper v Australian Taxation Office* [2014] FWC 7551, which addresses dismissal for criminal actions with 'no link to the employment relationship'.

43 [2010] FWA 7358, para 52. See generally *Rose v Telstra* [1998] AIRC 1592 where the Commission stated: 'An employee's behaviour outside of working hours will only have an impact on their employment to the extent that it can be said to breach an express or implied term of his or her contract of employment'.

44 [1998] AIRC 1592. See also *Applicant v ACT Department of Education and Training* [2012] FWA 2562.

45 [2011] FWA 5311, paras 42–3, emphasis added (*O'Keefe's* case). These comments were approved in *Little v Credit Corporation Group* [2013] FWA 9642.

The Full Bench of the Fair Work Commission has described 'at work' as encompassing the performance of work, at any time or location, and when engaged in some other activity which is authorised or permitted by the employer. This may include accessing social media while performing work, such as being on a break. However, the use of social media to engage in, for example, bullying, may arise outside work, for example through Facebook posts: 'Conceptually there is little doubt that using social media to repeatedly behave unreasonably towards a worker constitutes bullying behaviour.'[46]

Public accessibility

Mitigating factors in challenging a dismissal case include the level of damage to the employer, including harm to the employer's reputation. Evidence that the employee's social media transgressions were limited to a small group of people and unavailable to the public or to work colleagues would favour the employee.

Being able to access an employee's blog through a Google search is a significant factor in determining public accessibility. In *Dover-Ray v Real Insurance Pty Ltd*,[47] the employee argued that only online friends could access the offending MySpace blog. However, the blog was accessible through a Google search and her MySpace friends included work colleagues. The Commission stated: 'It is enough that her "friends" included other employees of [the employer] because (even if it had such a restriction) it could reasonably be expected that a document of such controversy would be circulated within the workplace.'[48] The comments described the management at the workplace as 'nothing but witch hunters'; referred to their values as 'absolute lies' and 'absolute mockeries'; and described workplace processes as 'corrupt' and 'biased'.[49] The Commission confirmed the dismissal. Similarly in *O'Keefe's* case, although the employee's Facebook posts made no mention of the employer and only 70 people, including some fellow employees, had access to the offending comments, the Commission confirmed the termination.

Damages – lack of evidence

Many cases before the Fair Work Commission and its predecessor have accepted the employee's argument that the dismissal was excessive in the circumstances and

---

46 *Bowker v DP World Melbourne Limited* [2014] FWCFB 9227, para 54. See *Fair Work Act 2009* (Cth), Part 6.8B 'Workers Bullied at Work', in particular s789FD.
47 [2010] FWA 8544.
48 Ibid., para 51.
49 Ibid., para 49.

that even where breach or misconduct occurred, it did not justify dismissal. The Fair Work Commission is required by section 387 of the *Fair Work Act 2009* (Cth) to consider specific criteria to determine whether the dismissal was harsh, unjust or unreasonable.[50] On occasion there is insufficient evidence of damage to the employer by the actions and posting of the employee.

In *O'Connor v Outdoor Creations Pty Ltd* the employer summarily dismissed the employee for, among other matters, 'over 3000 transactions on a chat line during work time' over a three month period, claiming this to be 'theft of hundreds, if not thousands of dollars worth of paid time from this office'.[51] The Tribunal accepted that employer found what he considered to be 'serious misconduct', however:

- there was no evidence of the time spent for each visit to the chat room, or the time spent on breaks or lunch time (the employee was known to have worked through lunch);
- the categorisation of the use of the chat line as 'theft' was questionable;
- even with an allegation of theft, the applicable Code provided for warnings and an opportunity to respond, and this was an appropriate case to request a response;
- there had been no evidence of any impact on his work;
- the investigation occurred only after the employee had submitted a letter of resignation, and the employer sought to end the employment early; and
- the allegations were not put to the employee and there was no opportunity to respond.[52]

In these circumstances the Tribunal did not consider the employer had reasonable grounds to believe the employee was guilty of misconduct.[53] The Tribunal found that the termination was 'harsh, unjust or unreasonable'.[54]

An employee making rash, or perhaps 'silly' comments on Facebook which do not name the employer nor result in any damage to the business may well still affect 'trust and confidence' in the employee, but not justify termination.[55] The relevant comments made in this case were: 'Xmas "bonus" alongside a job warning, followed by no holiday pay!!! Whooooooo! The Hairdressing Industry rocks man!!! AWSOME!!! [sic]'[56]

---

50 For a list of cases on s387, see above n 26.
51 [2011] FWA 3081, para 16.
52 Ibid., paras 31–39
53 Ibid., para 33.
54 Ibid., para 57.
55 See *Fitzgerald v Dianna Smith trading as Escape Hair Design* [2010] FWA 7358, paras 56–7. (The decision was confirmed on appeal: *Dianna Smith trading as Escape Hair Design v Fitzgerald* [2011] FWAFB 1422).
56 Ibid., para 21.

Mitigating factors

In *O'Keefe*, the Commission acknowledged, as mitigating factors, that the employee was angry at not being paid commissions due to him and that there was no intention for the subject of the Facebook comments to ever see the comments. However, on all the facts, the dismissal of the employee was confirmed.

Mitigating factors in *Stutsel* included the employee's 22 years of service; his senior age; his minimal knowledge of Facebook technology (he had arranged for his daughter to set up the account); his belief that he had the highest privacy settings; the fact that the conduct occurred outside the workplace and outside working hours; the fact that no action was taken against other employees; and the employee's remorse.[57]

In *Faulkner v BHP Coal Pty Ltd*,[58] the employer ran an open-cut coal mine and introduced a policy prohibiting mobile electronic devices on the worksite for safety reasons. The employee brought his mobile phone on site and posted a comment on Facebook. When this was reported he was dismissed. The employer described the breach as serious. Citing the Full Bench decision of *Qantas v Carter*,[59] Commissioner Spencer noted that even where was a valid reason for dismissal it may still be regarded as harsh in the circumstances. The Commissioner noted that in contemporary society there is reliance on communication devices, particularly mobile phones. The employer may legitimately prohibit such devices for safety reasons. The employer in this case allowed phone access during breaks, and placed telephones in the field crib rooms for employees free of charge.[60]

However, the employer's policy was not stated to be a zero tolerance policy with dismissal as the only outcome. In mitigation, the Commissioner found that there was cooperation, remorse, 6 years of service, good performance ratings and recent approval to train further. Upon considering the factors under section 387 of the *Fair Work Act 2009* (Cth), the Commissioner determined that the termination of the applicant's employment was harsh, unjust and unreasonable, and ordered reinstatement.

---

57 *Stutsel v Linfox Australia Pty Ltd* [2011] FWA 8444; for the facts and a detailed analysis see below.
58 [2014] FWC 9330.
59 [2012] FWAFB 5776.
60 [2014] FWC 9330, para 92.

Freedom of political communication

The Federal Circuit Court of Australia has held that an employee has no unfettered right of political communication. In *Banerji v Bowles*,[61] an employee of the Department of Immigration and Citizenship used her Twitter account to make comments which were 'sometimes mocking, sometimes critical' of practices and policies at immigration detention centres, the immigration policies of the Australian Government, information and comment by the Opposition spokesman on immigration, the Minister for Foreign Affairs, the Prime Minister, the Leader of the Opposition, and employees of the Department.[62] The employee claimed that a right of political expression was a constitutionally protected right which operated to prevent her dismissal.

The employee was subject to the Australian Public Service Code of Conduct and *Guidelines on Use of Social Media by DIAC Employees*. In addition, employees were provided with a fact sheet entitled 'What is Public Comment? Workplace Relations Conduct Section Fact Sheet'. The *Guidelines* provided that it is inappropriate for employees to make 'unofficial public comment that is, or is perceived to be, harsh or extreme in its criticism of the Government, a member of parliament or other political party and their respective policies'.[63] It was also considered inappropriate to make an unofficial public comment that is a 'strong criticism of the Department's administration that could disrupt the workplace'.[64] The employee claimed the enforcement of the Code would breach her implied right of political communication. Interestingly, the employee was not dismissed, but herself instigated the proceedings, initially for an injunction and later for declaratory orders to the effect that she could not be dismissed or be threatened with dismissal by reason of her 'implied freedom of political communication' under the *Australian Constitution*. His Honour Judge Neville found that there is no unfettered implied right of political communication, and even if there was, it would not support a breach a contract of employment. In any event, His Honour considered the right asserted was not a personal right, but one which operated as a restriction on legislative power.[65] Hence the employee's Twitter comments were not protected and she was subject to the Code of Conduct and Guidelines on Use of Social Media.

---

61 [2013] FCCA 1052.
62 Ibid., para 18.
63 Ibid., para 79.
64 Ibid.
65 Ibid., paras 101–02.

CASE STUDY 1: LINFOX AUSTRALIA PTY LTD V FAIR WORK COMMISSION [2013] FCAFC 157

Linfox Australia Pty Ltd (Linfox) employed Stutsel in April 1989. From February 2011 until May 2011 Stutsel made a number of Facebook posts about Linfox, the staff generally, and two specific managers. Comments were made by some of Stutsel's Facebook friends, and these comments were not removed. The Facebook privacy settings permitted any Facebook account holder to view the posts and comments. One manager viewed the site on 13 May 2011, and immediately complained formally to Linfox. The Group Manager Workplace Relations met with Stutsel on 20 May 2011 and on 31 May 2011 Linfox sent a letter of termination, noting the following:

1. on your Facebook profile page, which was open to the public, you made a number of statements about one of your managers, Mick Assaf, that amounted to racially derogatory remarks;

2. on your Facebook profile page, which was open to the public, you made a statement about one of your managers, Ms Nina Russell, which amounted to sexual discrimination and harassment; and

3. you made extremely derogatory comments about your managers, Mr Assaf and Ms Russell.

Stutsel applied for relief under section 394 of the *Fair Work Act 2009* (Cth) alleging unfair dismissal. The matter came before Fair Work Australia in December 2011.[66] FWA reinstated Stutsel, finding that the dismissal was 'harsh, unjust and unreasonable'.[67] The reinstatement was stayed on 20 December 2011 pending an appeal to the Full Bench of Fair Work Australia. The appeal was dismissed in October 2012.[68] Linfox then sought judicial review and the matter came before the Full Court of the Federal Court.[69]

Commissioner Roberts, at first instance, made the following findings of fact:

- Stutsel's Facebook account was set up by his wife and daughter with the belief that he had the highest privacy settings;
- Stutsel believed posts on his page could only be viewed by his Facebook friends;
- Stutsel had 170 Facebook friends, many of whom were work colleagues;

66 *Stutsel v Linfox Australia Pty Ltd* [2011] FWA 8444.
67 Ibid., para 100.
68 *Linfox Australia Pty Ltd v Stutsel* [2012] FWAFB 7097.
69 *Linfox Australia Pty Ltd v Fair Work Commission* [2013] FCAFC 157.

- Stutsel was unaware that he could delete comments from his Facebook page;
- Stutsel's posted comments about terrorism and the death of a terrorist were an expression of his private views, which he later came to regret;
- Stutsel's reference to 'bacon hater' was directed at one of the managers, Mr Assaf; 'the remark was not intended to be hurtful', although Mr Assaf was entitled to be offended by the comment;
- Mr Assaf only became aware of the remark through the action of the other manager, Ms Russell;
- No Facebook friend objected to the remark, finding the comments 'unexceptional';
- Comments of a sexual nature were made by Stutsel's Facebook friends about Ms Russell, and Ms Russell was 'entitled to be outraged by those comments and to complain';[70]
- Stutsel was unaware that he could delete comments once made, and could have disassociated himself from the comments.

On the issue of Stutsel's stated regret for the postings, the Commissioner added that whether the contrition was genuine did not concern him, as the comments were 'within his right to free speech' although the Commissioner personally regarded the discourse as 'distasteful'. Commissioner Roberts stated:

> It is a bridge too far in my opinion to make a connection between those comments and any personal attack on Mr Assaf. The Applicant's Facebook page was not a web blog, intended to be on public display. It was not a public forum.[71]

Commissioner Roberts regarded the expression 'bacon hater' as 'clearly in poor taste', but felt that it fell short of being a 'racially derogatory remark intended, or acting to, vilify Mr Assaf on racial grounds'.[72] The overall impression was that of 'a group of friends letting off steam'.[73] The Commissioner took a real world approach, stating: 'The fact that some of the material is not complimentary towards Linfox managers is unsurprising. This always has been, and always will be the fate of those holding managerial positions.'[74]

In relation to comments made by Stutsel's Facebook friends about Ms Russell, the fact that Linfox took action against Mr Stutsel, instead of the authors, 'strikes

---

70 Ibid., paras 77–81.
71 Ibid., para 79.
72 Ibid., para 80.
73 Ibid., para 81. See also the introduction to this chapter.
74 Ibid., para 82.

me [the Commissioner] as being more than passing strange'. The Commissioner did not regard the comments as a serious attack, but:

> as an attempt at humour ... and did not contain any credible threat ... The material was metaphorical and hyperbolic but certainly not hortatory. It might be ... 'disgusting' but it was in no way threatening.[75]

The Commissioner found that Stutsel was not guilty of serious misconduct and that the dismissal was 'harsh, unjust or unreasonable' within the meaning of section 387 of the *Fair Work Act 2009* (Cth). He ordered Stutsel's reinstatement pursuant to sections 390 and 391.[76]

On appeal under section 604 of the *Fair Work Act 2009* (Cth), the Full Bench of Fair Work Australia agreed with Commissioner Roberts. An appeal under section 604 is by way of a rehearing, and can occur only if there is thought to be error on the part of the Commissioner. Section 400 appeals relate to the public interest, and can occur only 'on the ground that the decision involved a significant error of fact'.[77] The Full Bench analysed the various facts and mitigating factors and rejected the arguments that the Commissioner failed to grasp the seriousness of the conduct, concluding that there was no error of fact.[78]

The case then went on appeal to the Federal Court, which could only address issues of jurisdiction error. The Federal Court regarded the findings of the Commissioner as significant, including mitigating factors such as the Facebook page being set up by his wife and daughter and that he believed it was on the highest privacy settings. Ultimately, the court dismissed the appeal, finding that 'no error [had] been exposed in the reasons for decision of the Full Bench, let alone a jurisdictional error'.[79]

As a final comment, while each case depends on its own facts, this case raises questions about the acceptance of mitigating factors. The precise state of knowledge of the employee, including knowledge of the very medium on which the employee is posting, becomes a very real problem for employers. With time and experience, courts may become more reluctant to accept ignorance as a factor. The Full Bench of Fair Work Australia expressed this view:

---

75 Ibid., paras 83–84.
76 Sections 390 and 391 deal respectively with when an order remedy for unfair dismissal may be made, and the remedy of reinstatement. See *Linfox Australia Pty Ltd v Fair Work Commission* [2013] FCAFC 157, para 11.
77 See *Coal and Allied Operations Pty Limited v Australian Industrial Relations Commission* [2000] HCA 47.
78 *Linfox Australia Pty Ltd v Stutsel* [2012] FWAFB 7097, paras 37–43.
79 *Linfox Australia Pty Ltd v Fair Work Commission* [2013] FCAFC 157, para 91, per Dowsett, Flick and Griffiths JJ.

> [W]ith increased use and understanding about Facebook in the community and the adoption by more employers of social networking policies, some of these factors may be given less weight in future cases. The claim of ignorance on the part of an older worker, who has enthusiastically embraced the new social networking media but without fully understanding the implications of its use, might be viewed differently in the future.[80]

The Full Bench also placed emphasis on the employer's lack of a social media policy. The adoption of such policies will mean a reduction in the argument regarding the use of such media by employees. Employers should be strongly encouraged to adopt a social media policy, not only to maximise protection, but also for the benefit and goodwill of all concerned.

CASE STUDY 2: LITTLE V CREDIT CORP GROUP LIMITED [2013] FWC 9642

The employee in this case made inappropriate use of his Facebook account to criticise an organisation with which his employer had professional dealings, and made sexually suggestive comments regarding a new employee. The employee had access to the employer's Employee Handbook and the Employee Code of Conduct and had attended an induction at the commencement of his employment three years earlier. Clause 7.9 of the Employee Handbook provided:

7.9 Social Media Website Usage

Use of social media websites should be limited to work purposes. Social media websites are sites based on user participation and user-generated content. These include social networking sites such as LinkedIn, Facebook, MySpace and Twitter.

Misuse of these sites will not be tolerated. Misusage [sic] includes, but is not limited to:

- Using these sites for personal use during work hours (accessing these sites via mobile phone will also not be tolerated during work hours);
- Posting confidential or proprietary Company information online, making disparaging or harassing comments about co-workers, managers, customers or the Company online; and
- Blogging about problems at work or posting inappropriate photographs online during or after work hours.

---

80 *Linfox Australia Pty Ltd v Stutsel* [2012] FWAFB 7097, para 34.

We also recommend that you remain aware of your personal reputation and safety online at all times.

Failure to comply with this policy may result in disciplinary action being taken against you, up to and including termination of employment.

The employee had made the following two comments on the Christians Against Poverty (CAP) Facebook page:

For reals bro, you should put a little more of funding into educating consumers on how the world works rather than just weaseling them out of debt, blah blahblah, give a man a fish/teach a man to fish.

No thanks, just take my advice and try to educate people about things like 'interest' and 'liability' rather than just weasel them out of contracts. #simple

One post claimed to be on behalf of the employer, although the employee later conceded at the hearing that he had no such authority. Deputy President Sams found that the comments about CAP were likely to adversely impact the employer's relationship with that organisation and damage the employer's wider reputation.[81] The employee was terminated the day after it came to their notice.

The employee raised several 'gratuitous, self-serving excuses' which were insufficient to constitute a defence, according to the Deputy President:

1   he had 'masked' his identity and he had never consented to the respondent releasing or confirming his personal details to third parties (CAP);

2   his Facebook profile was 'private';

3   he was entitled to his personal opinions;

4   he had made the comments in his own time outside of work hours;

5   Mr Hoye was not an employee at the time he posted the comment about him;

6   (an) earlier warning was about use of an internet site during work hours, not comments made outside of work;

7   the meeting with the Company was deliberately timed for 4:30pm when all the other employees had left work.[82]

The Deputy President upheld the dismissal, referring to the following factors:

• The employer had issued an Employee Handbook and the Employee Code of Conduct.

---

81 Ibid., para 69.
82 Ibid., para 71.

- The employee was made aware of the Handbook and Code, having attended an induction on the commencement of his employment and a 'working together' module in 2012.
- The employment contract provided that employer's policies and procedures constitute directions by the employer.
- The employee had the ability to access and change the privacy settings for his Facebook page.
- Because the employee maintained that he was entitled to express his opinion outside of work hours, it was reasonable to assume that if he were to be reinstated, there would be a repeat of this behaviour.
- The employee had received a previous warning about posting an inappropriate comment online for which he received a written warning.[83]

This case reaffirms the importance of a social media policy, of contractual terms requiring the employees to adhere to the employer's code, policies and directions, and of the wisdom of induction processes and staff seminars.

Lessons, contracts and policies

There are risks in any business enterprise. The employment of personnel is a necessary circumstance, with its own concerns and perils. The risks include impact on productivity; equal opportunity; breach of intellectual property and confidential information rights; vicarious liability for defamation; bullying, harassment and reputation damage. Within the past two decades employers have typically embraced online technology and provided access for employees in particular circumstances. Employers and their advisors are learning many lessons about how to address and combat social media misuse, both within the workplace and outside. It may often be appropriate to include express terms in the employment contract. Alternatively, employers should create a social media policy which sets out expectations around the use of social media. This policy should cover employee obligations, the use of specific media, such as Facebook and Twitter, use of photographs and videos, bullying and harassment and confidentiality.

For example, in some workplaces it may be appropriate to provide for a complete ban on the use of mobile devices for safety reasons.

---

83 Ibid., paras 9, 10, 16 and 43.

In *O'Connor v Outdoor Creations Pty Ltd*,[84] the employer raised allegations against the employee at the hearing that were not in the letter of dismissal. Even if the new allegations were sufficiently serious to warrant dismissal, the employer failed to follow the correct procedure, which would have permitted the employee to respond. The employer believed the stated grounds in the letter to be enough. Lesson: include all allegations of misconduct in formal documentation for dismissal.

Professional advice can be sought to draft a social media policy from groups such as Chambers of Commerce. There are many policies available for comparative purposes. Policies will vary, of course, according to the work involved, the level of the employee, safety factors, and business and commercial factors. However, all such policies should include:

- definitions of social media, to distinguish (where applicable) between social networking sites, video and photo sharing sites, blogs (public and closed), collaborations (such as Wikipedia), forums and bulletin boards, podcasts, online gaming and instant messaging;
- a statement of policy;
- a definition of appropriate and inappropriate use, with examples of reasonable use and unreasonable conduct;
- the employer's requirements and fair use requirements in the workplace;
- notification that social media action outside work hours may be in breach of the employment contract, the policy or even other lawful and reasonable directions and may have a sufficient workplace nexus;
- a statement regarding the level of monitoring that may be undertaken at the workplace and on workplace property and equipment;
- a statement of the contractual obligations with respect to confidential information; and
- statement about potential disciplinary actions, from warnings to dismissal.

Additionally a tribunal or court should look favourably upon employers who maintain the currency of the policy, taking into account recent cases and changes in technology. Employers should also provide information sessions and materials on the employer's policies.

There will be an initial increase in social media and workplace cases, as both employers and employees come to grips with the technology, communication expectations, appropriate standards and expectations. From this juxtaposition of employees' use of social media technology and the employers' interests, a new balance structure, an almost spontaneous order – which in the words of Hayek

---

84 [2011] FWA 3081.

results in a constructionist rationalism – will emerge.[85] Employees must understand that letting off steam in a medium that is accessible, searchable and subject to discovery will have consequences that should be reasonably foreseeable. Employers must plan their responses in terms of policies and enforcement carefully. These developments will find a natural path to order and structure. Courts and tribunals will be less willing to accept an employee's ignorance of the privacy settings or consequences as social media constructs become the norm within the workplace and the community.

FURTHER READING

N Constant and M Han, 'When the workplace and social media collide', (2013) May *Australasian Law Management Journal.*

P George *et al., Social media and the law,* Lexis Nexis Butterworths, 2014.

---

85 Friedrich Hayek, *Law, Legislation and Liberty* Vol. I: Rules and Order, (1973), 8–11; Vol. III: The Political Order of a Free People, (1979) xii, Chapter 2.

7

DEFAMATION IN CYBERSPACE

Social media permits people to engage in social discourse with hundreds of friends and associates. Online, everyone is a publisher. People use handheld devices to communicate to individuals, small and large groups and the world at large at any time – while waiting in queues, on public transport, whilst walking and indeed whilst driving. One modern danger is that users are not circumspect when texting off-the-cuff remarks or tweeting immediate and spontaneous responses. Each day users send 250 billion emails and make 600 million contributions to Twitter. Defamation is a real issue because of the audience which can access such discourses. When written, rather than spoken, words take on a sterner and more deliberate meaning than may have been intended, and injudicious replies may be sent in the heat of the moment.

From the beginning, the boundaries of appropriate and acceptable behaviour on the internet have been challenged. The notion that the internet is the last bastion of free speech has produced a general mindset that the laws that bind and regulate social behaviour should not apply in cyberspace. There has developed a sense that anything written in a digital forum should somehow be immune from oversight and censure. Courts internationally have disagreed with this view and have applied defamation laws to social media.

There is no universal definition of defamation, and so no one set of common elements that need to be satisfied in all jurisdictions. Articles 17 and 19 of the UN *International Covenant on Civil and Political Rights* (ICCPR)[1] provide for both freedom of expression and the right to hold opinions, but balance these rights and freedoms with considerations of unlawful interference, privacy and the protection of honour and reputation. Arguably, these provisions reflect international customary law:

Article 17

1 No one shall be subjected to arbitrary or unlawful interference with his privacy, family, home or correspondence, nor to unlawful attacks on his honour and reputation.
2 Everyone has the right to the protection of the law against such interference or attacks.

Article 19

1 Everyone shall have the right to hold opinions without interference.
2 Everyone shall have the right to freedom of expression; this right shall include freedom to seek, receive and impart information and ideas of all kinds, regardless of frontiers, either orally, in writing or in print, in the form of art, or through any other media of his choice.

---

1 Available at <www.ohchr.org/EN/ProfessionalInterest/Pages/CCPR.aspx>.

3   The exercise of the rights provided for in paragraph 2 of this article carries
    with it special duties and responsibilities. It may therefore be subject to
    certain restrictions, but these shall only be such as are provided by law
    and are necessary:
    (a)   For respect of the rights or reputations of others;
    (b)   For the protection of national security or of public order (*ordre
          public*), or of public health or morals.

These articles were considered and applied by Kirby J in the internet defamation
case *Dow Jones v Gutnick*.[2] According to Kirby J:

> any development of the common law of Australia, consistent with such prin-
> ciples, should provide effective legal protection for the honour, reputation
> and personal privacy of individuals. To the extent that our law does not do
> so, Australia, like other nations so obliged, is rendered accountable to the
> relevant treaty body for such default.[3]

The laws dealing with defamation have always struggled, in a philosophical sense,
with freedom of speech, freedom of the press, the framing of political debate, and
the public disclosure of malfeasance, as these have all in some ways always inherently contradicted the rights of protection afforded by the principles of defamation.

The opportunity for a significant body of 'e-defamation' case law to develop has
been limited. Many jurisdictions are struggling with content-specific cyberspace issues and have yet to address the implications of content, such as its effect on reputation. Defamation law in cyberspace will be tested in the courts and the interface
between the law and the internet will continue to be built.[4]

Any discussion of the law of defamation in cyberspace must be conducted in
conjunction with a discussion of jurisdictional issues in cyberspace.[5] This chapter
will provide an overview of the legal position regarding online defamation in Australia and, to some extent, in the North American and UK jurisdictions.

Defamation principles

Kirby J, in *Dow Jones v Gutnick*,[6] restated defamation principles in the following terms:

> First, a starting point for the consideration of the submission must be an
> acceptance that the principles of defamation law invoked by the respondent
> are settled and of long standing. Those principles are:

---

2 [2002] HCA 56, paras 115 and 116.
3 Ibid., para 116. See also *Chakravarti v Advertiser Newspapers Ltd* [1998] HCA 37, para 134.
4 See *Tamiz v Google Inc* [2012] EWHC 449 (QB).
5 See Chapter 17, Jurisdiction in cyberspace.
6 [2002] HCA 56.

1) that damage to reputation is essential for the existence of the tort of defamation;

2) that mere composition and writing of words is not enough to constitute the tort; those words must be communicated to a third party who comprehends them;

3) that each time there is such a communication, the plaintiff has a new cause of action; and

4) that a publisher is liable for publication in a particular jurisdiction where that is the intended or natural and probable consequence of its acts.[7]

Defamation legislation

The law of defamation in Australia is provided by state and territory legislation. Until 2005 it had differed quite significantly between jurisdictions, particularly in terms of the elements that need to be satisfied to establish an action for defamation, but in 2005 each state and territory enacted uniform legislation.[8] The term 'defamation' has historically been an expression of a composite tort encompassing both slander and libel, each of these being separate torts for verbal and written defamation respectively, and this distinction persists in some jurisdictions. All state and territory jurisdictions reformed their statutes in order 'to ensure the law of defamation within the State(s) ... is uniform in substance with the law of defamation in all Australian jurisdictions'.[9] The objects of the states and territories uniform defamation legislation are:

- to ensure that the law of defamation does not place unreasonable limits on freedom of expression and, in particular, on the publication and discussion of matters of public interest and importance;
- to provide effective and fair remedies for persons whose reputations are harmed by the publication of defamatory matter; and
- to promote speedy and non-litigious methods of resolving disputes about the publication of defamatory matter.

The Uniform Defamation Acts do not form a code, so the common law principles of defamation are to be read in conjunction with the Acts.

---

7 Ibid., para 124.

8 *Defamation Act 2005* (Qld), *Defamation Act 2005* (NSW), *Defamation Act 2005* (Vic), *Defamation Act 2005* (Tas), *Defamation Act 2005* (WA), *Defamation Act 2005* (SA), *Defamation Act 2006* (NT), *Civil Law (Wrongs) Act 2002* (ACT).

9 New South Wales, Standing Committee of Attorneys-General (SCAG) Working Group of State and Territory Officers, Legislation and Policy Division of the NSW Attorney General's Department, (2004) *Proposal for Uniform Defamation Laws*.

While the 'truth' of defamatory remarks has generally been held to be a defence to defamation suits, the burden of proof for establishing truth has occasionally been shown to be so onerous as to destroy any protection afforded by this defence.

It is a defence to the publication of defamatory matter if the defendant proves that:

a. the matter carried, in addition to the defamatory imputations of which the plaintiff complains, one or more other imputations (contextual imputations) that are substantially true; and

b. the defamatory imputations do not further harm the reputation of the plaintiff because of the substantial truth of the contextual imputations.[10]

One of the reforms provides for the abolition of the distinction between spoken and published defamation. None dealt specifically with online defamation. The Working Group of State and Territory Officers that created the reform proposals did, however, highlight the need for the defence of 'innocent dissemination' to be drafted in such a way as to 'ensure that the defence takes proper account of modern means of mass communication and the problems associated with its monitoring'.[11] This has been reflected in the legislation by provisions that exempt from the definition of 'primary distributor' those who provide services for:

the processing, copying, distributing or selling of any electronic medium in or on which the matter is recorded or the operation of, or the provision of, any equipment, system or service, by means of which the matter is retrieved, copied, distributed or made available in electronic form.[12]

These reforms were specifically aimed at standardising the legislative response to the case law across all state and territory jurisdictions, not at codifying the existing case law. The revised statutes do not affect the operation of the precedents already in law except to the extent that the statutes specifically provide.

---

10 *Defamation Act 2005* (Qld) s26, *Defamation Act 2005* (NSW) s26, *Defamation Act 2005* (Vic) s26, *Defamation Act 2005* (Tas) s26, *Defamation Act 2005* (WA) s26, *Defamation Act 2005* (SA) s24, *Defamation Act 2006* (NT) s23, *Civil Law (Wrongs) Act 2002* (ACT) s136.

11 Recommendation 12: The common law defence of innocent dissemination should apply, with careful drafting to ensure that the defence takes proper account of modern means of mass communication and the problems associated with its monitoring.

12 *Defamation Act 2005* (Qld) s32(3)(f)(i) and (ii), *Defamation Act 2005* (NSW) s32(3)(f)(i) and (ii), *Defamation Act 2005* (Vic) s32(3)(f)(i) and (ii), *Defamation Act 2005* (Tas) s32(3)(f)(i) and (ii), *Defamation Act 2005* (WA) s32(3)(f)(i) and (ii), *Defamation Act 2005* (SA) s30(3)(f)(i) and (ii), *Defamation Act 2006* (NT) s29(3)(f)(i) and (ii), *Civil Law (Wrongs) Act 2002* (ACT) s139C(3)(f)(i) and (ii).

Defamation in cyberspace – actions and issues

It has been established by both Australian courts and courts in other jurisdictions that a person may be defamed in an online forum and that damages may be awarded. The decision of the Supreme Court of Western Australia in 1993 in *Rindos v Hardwick*[13] was the first internet-based defamation determination in any jurisdiction. The decision did not advance principles of online defamation but the award of $40,000 in damages for untrue allegations of paedophilia demonstrated that a person can be held liable for statements made in the public space of the internet.

There have been few defamation actions related to online publication to date.[14] In the Australian context, this is likely to remain so given that the defamation reforms of 2006 specifically provide for an 'offer of amends' process that must precede formal litigation.[15] Historically, the introduction of such alternative dispute resolution mechanisms has resulted in a reduction in litigation; the impact on defamation actions is likely to be the same.

Electronic publication using the internet increases the scope of defamation actions in three ways. First, it is an additional mode of communication: many newspapers, magazines and media outlets republish their material online, and radio and television stations also place videos, sound files or transcripts online. Second, online publication of new material, including material that is otherwise intended to be relatively private, has a broad reach. Third, the broader reach can affect the amount of damages. Publication can occur through:

- the sending and redistribution of emails;
- postings to bulletin boards, news groups or discussion lists;
- chat rooms;
- information placed on web pages, including text, sound and video; and
- files that are made available for downloading.

These actions can occur easily and unintentionally, and can reach a large and indeterminate audience. In Australia, a separate cause of action arises each time defamatory material is published (see Single publication rule, below). This means

---

13 Unreported, Supreme Court of Western Australia, case 1994 of 1993.
14 See *The Buddhist Society of Western Australia Inc. v Bristile Ltd* [2000] WASCA 210.
15 *Defamation Act 2005* (Qld) Part 3, *Defamation Act 2005* (NSW) Part 3, *Defamation Act 2005* (Vic) Part 3, *Defamation Act 2005* (Tas) Part 3, *Defamation Act 2005* (WA) Part 3, *Defamation Act 2005* (SA) Part 3, *Defamation Act 2006* (NT) Part 3, *Civil Law (Wrongs) Act 2002* (ACT) Part 9.3.

that when defamatory material on the internet is downloaded and read, a new cause of action arises. If a person merely repeats another's defamatory statement, a new and separate cause of action arises,[16] so employees who forward defamatory emails may also be liable.

It is often the case that the authors of defamatory statements are protected from legal proceedings by their impecuniosity; those damaged may then seek out a party more likely to be able to meet any damages awards. This is often unsuccessful, because the law in many jurisdictions allows a publisher or disseminator protection through the principle of 'innocent dissemination'. Such 'innocence' is greatly qualified, however, and defendants using this defence have a high evidentiary burden in many jurisdictions. In Australia, the innocent dissemination defence appears in every state and territory jurisdiction:

Defence of innocent dissemination

(1) It is a defence to the publication of defamatory matter if the defendant proves that:
   (a) the defendant published the matter merely in the capacity, or as an employee or agent, of a subordinate distributor, and
   (b) the defendant neither knew, nor ought reasonably to have known, that the matter was defamatory, and
   (c) the defendant's lack of knowledge was not due to any negligence on the part of the defendant.

(2) For the purposes of subsection (1), a person is a "**subordinate distributor**" of defamatory matter if the person:
   (a) was not the first or primary distributor of the matter, and
   (b) was not the author or originator of the matter, and
   (c) did not have any capacity to exercise editorial control over the content of the matter (or over the publication of the matter) before it was first published.

(3) Without limiting subsection (2)(a), a person is not the first or primary distributor of matter merely because the person was involved in the publication of the matter in the capacity of:
   (a) a bookseller, newsagent or news-vendor, or
   (b) a librarian, or
   (c) a wholesaler or retailer of the matter, or
   (d) a provider of postal or similar services by means of which the matter is published, or
   (e) a broadcaster of a live programme (whether on television, radio or otherwise) containing the matter in circumstances in which the broadcaster has no effective control over the person who makes the statements that comprise the matter, or

16 See *McLean v David Syme & Co. Limited* (1970) 72 SR (NSW) 513.

(f)   a provider of services consisting of:

    (i)   the processing, copying, distributing or selling of any electronic medium in or on which the matter is recorded, or

    (ii)   the operation of, or the provision of any equipment, system or service, by means of which the matter is retrieved, copied, distributed or made available in electronic form, or

(g)   an operator of, or a provider of access to, a communications system by means of which the matter is transmitted, or made available, by another person over whom the operator or provider has no effective control, or

(h)   a person who, on the instructions or at the direction of another person, prints or produces, reprints or reproduces or distributes the matter for or on behalf of that other person.[17]

In *Stratton Oakmont Inc. v Prodigy Services Co.*,[18] the innocent dissemination defence was disallowed in the Supreme Court of New York. Prodigy Services Co. (Prodigy) was an online provider of a website that offered internet forum services to subscribers. Unlike most providers, Prodigy sought to differentiate itself in the market by providing a degree of censorship on the site. This censorship was minimal, comprising only a software-driven review of content for a preset range of specific words, mostly profanities. Prodigy did not advertise the limitations of its censorship role. When one of Prodigy's site users posted defamatory material in a forum about Stratton Oakmont Inc., the court was asked to determine the extent to which Prodigy's limited censorship program constituted editorial control. The court determined that while Prodigy in fact had no specific knowledge of the defamatory content, the fact that they practised some editorial control and informed users of that meant that they were liable for the defamation and could not claim innocent dissemination.

There was some initial misinformation regarding the Prodigy decision. One interpretation appeared to be that any control over the content to be disseminated would make the administrator liable. Administrators and Internet Service Providers (ISPs) thus often chose not to censor sites, to avoid liability. In the United States, section 230(c)(1) of the *Communications Decency Act 1996* (US) effectively overturned this restrictive interpretation of the Prodigy decision:

> No provider or user of an interactive computer service shall be treated as the publisher or speaker of any information provided by another information content provider.

---

17   *Defamation Act 2005* (Qld) s32; *Defamation Act 2005* (NSW) s32; *Defamation Act 2005* (Vic) s32; *Defamation Act 2005* (Tas) s32; *Defamation Act 2005* (WA) s32; *Defamation Act 2005* (SA) s30; *Defamation Act 2006* (NT) s29; *Civil Law (Wrongs) Act 2002* (ACT) s139C; *Defamation Act* (NZ) s8.

18   1995 WL 323710 (NY Sup Ct 1995).

This section excludes administrators, ISPs and other service providers from liability for defamatory statements made by users of public systems unless they know of the defamatory material and fail to take action on it, or are themselves involved in either the creation or development of the material.[19] Critics of the section claim that it is too broad, but it is yet to be repealed or modified. In *Barrett v Rosenthal* the court stated (in obiter):

> We conclude that section 230 prohibits 'distributor' liability for Internet pub-
> lications. We further hold that section 230(c)(1) immunizes individual 'users'
> of interactive computer services, and that no practical or principled distinc-
> tion can be drawn between active and passive use. We acknowledge that
> recognizing broad immunity for defamatory republications on the Internet
> has some troubling consequences. Until Congress chooses to revise the set-
> tled law in this area, however, plaintiffs who contend they were defamed in
> an Internet posting may only seek recovery from the original source of the
> statement.[20]

In *Cubby v CompuServe*, Compuserve was the administrator for an online forum. However, unlike Prodigy, CompuServe did not exercise any editorial control over the online forum content. The court intimated, but did not specifically find, that electronic publishers ought not be found liable for content on sites hosted on their servers in these circumstances:

> [the] requirement that a distributor must have knowledge of the contents of a
> publication before liability can be imposed for distributing that publication is
> deeply rooted in the First Amendment, made applicable to the states through
> the Fourteenth Amendment.[21]

CompuServe's defence was aided by the fact that the system operators for their online forums were independent entrepreneurs who were contracted to 'manage, review, create, delete, edit and otherwise control the contents'[22] of the forum on which the offensive material appeared. Cubby also sought to hold CompuServe vicariously liable for the libel, but the court held there to be no agency between the defendant and the other parties to the libel.

---

19 Ken S Myers, 'Wikimmunity: Fitting the Communications Decency Act to Wikipedia', (2006)
    20 *Harvard Journal of Law and Technology* 163.
20 (2006) 40 Cal 4th 33; 146 P. 3d 510.
21 776 F. Supp. 135 (SDNY 1991), 136.
22 Ibid.

CASE STUDY :   MICKLE V FARLEY [2013] NSWDC 295

Mickle v Farley[23] was the first Twitter defamation case to proceed to trial in Australia. Former Orange High School student Andrew Farley was ordered to pay $105,000 compensation for defamatory remarks made on Twitter and Facebook.

At the time of the publications Farley was one year out of high school. Mickle was a 58-year-old music teacher, married with three children. Judge Elkaim of the NSW District Court found that Mickle had 'established a widespread reputation … through a wide country area regarding her capacity as a teacher, her concern for her students and her devotion to the pursuit of excellence in teaching'. Students had even approached the Principal to ask for the music centre to be renamed the 'Mrs Mickle Music Centre'.[24]

Farley's father, who had been a teacher at the high school and had been head teacher from 2000 in the music and arts department, left the school in 2008 for personal reasons. Judge Elkaim stated that it seemed that Farley had a 'grudge' against Mickle, apparently believing that she had something to do with his father's leaving. However, there was 'absolutely no evidence' to support such a belief. In November 2012 Farley made defamatory comments on Twitter and Facebook about Mickle. His Honour described the effect of the publications as 'devastating': Mickle immediately took sick leave and only returned to work on a 'limited basis'. The court stated: 'But for the publications, her evidence was that she would have continued in the manner that she was teaching in 2012 until she reached the age of 65, which is in about seven years' time.'[25]

General damages

The court described general damages to reputation as 'the natural and probable consequence of a defamatory publication … intended to vindicate the person's reputation in the eyes of the general community and compensate the person for the distress and insult felt'. The general damages should be a signal to the public that the plaintiff is vindicated, so that the public knows the statements made have no truth whatsoever. The court awarded Mickle $85,000 in general damages.[26]

---

23 [2013] NSWDC 295.
24 Ibid., paras 5 and 6.
25 Ibid., paras 7 and 12.
26 Ibid., paras 13–16.

Aggravated damages

Aggravated damages are an augmentation of damages for conduct which increases the injury to the plaintiff for distress, embarrassment or humiliation. Judge Elkaim noted that Farley did not reply to Mickle's solicitor's initial correspondence. Farley's reply to later correspondence offered an unreserved apology for 'any hurt or upset' and stated that the comments had been removed from the social media pages. However, the court regarded the apology as insincere because Farley filed a spurious defence claiming the statements made were true. The court awarded $20,000 in aggravated damages.

Final comments

Judge Elkaim concluded with a warning about social media use:

> [W]hen defamatory publications are made on social media it is common knowledge that they spread. They are spread easily by the simple manipulation of mobile phones and computers. Their evil lies in the grapevine effect that stems from the use of this type of communication. I have taken that into account in the assessment of damages.[27]

Statute of limitations

The question of precisely when a defamatory tort occurs (for the purposes of deciding when a statute of limitation commences) was addressed by the New York Court of Appeals in *Firth v State of New York*[28] and considered by the High Court of Australia in *Dow Jones v Gutnick*.[29] The difficulty in relation to online publications is that, unlike other forms of publication, internet publication is continuous: 24 hours a day, seven days a week. Also, material placed online two years ago may only come to the attention of the general public after some form of publicity or report in the news. In Australia the limitation for commencing legal proceedings is one year from publication, with extensions of up to three years in limited circumstances.[30]

---

27 Ibid., para 21.
28 706 NYS 2d 835.
29 [2002] 210 CLR 575 at 602–603.
30 *Limitation Act 1969* (NSW) ss14B and 56A, *Limitations of Actions Act 1974* (Qld) ss10AA and 32A, *Limitation of Actions Act 1936* (SA) s37(1) and (2), *Defamation Act 2005* (Tas) s20A(1) and (2), *Limitation of Actions Act 1958* (Vic) s23B, *Limitation Act 2005* (WA) ss15 and 40(3), *Limitations Act 2005* (NT) ss12(2)(b) and 44A(2), *Limitations Act 1985* (ACT) s21B(1) and (2). *Limitation Act 1950* (NZ) s4 provides for a two year limitation period with a maximum extension to four years.

The US court held that the statute runs from the first posting of the defamatory article onto an internet site. In Australia the question has not been decided.

The single publication rule

Strictly speaking, a defamatory utterance or publication arises each time a newspaper or book is sold or read, separately in the homes of each person who hears or views a radio or television broadcast. A rule of convenience has developed to treat these multiple actions as one. The rule has been described as 'a legal fiction which deems a widely disseminated communication ... to be a single communication regardless of the number of people to whom, or the number of states in which, it is circulated'.[31]

Applying this principle to internet web pages is a minefield. As a continuous publication, the defamatory statement may be read, heard or viewed at different times, perhaps over a number of years, in locations all over the world.

In their joint judgement in *Dow Jones v Gutnick*, Gleeson CJ, McHugh, Gummow and Hayne JJ considered the single publication rule in relation to the place of publication:

> To trace, comprehensively, the origins of the so-called single publication rule ... may neither be possible nor productive. It is, however, useful to notice some of the more important steps that have been taken in its development. Treating each sale of a defamatory book or newspaper as a separate publication giving rise to a separate cause of action might be thought to present difficulties of pleading and proof. Following early English authority holding that separate counts alleging each sale need not be pleaded in the declaration, American courts accepted that, where the defamatory matter was published in a book or newspaper, each publication need not be pleaded separately. Similarly, proof of general distribution of a newspaper was accepted as sufficient proof of there having been a number of separate publications. It was against this background that there emerged, at least in some American States by the late nineteenth century, the rule that a plaintiff could bring only one action against a defendant to recover damages for all the publications that had by then been made of an offending publication. The expression 'one publication' or, later, 'single publication' was first commonly used in this context.
>
> In the early decades of the twentieth century, the single publication rule came to be coupled with statements to the effect that the place of that single publication was the place where the newspaper or magazine was published.

---

31 Debra Cohen, 'The single publication rule: One action, not one law', (1966) 62 *Brooklyn Law Review* 921, 924.

The source of this added proposition was given as a case of prosecution for criminal libel where the question was that raised by the Sixth Amendment to the United States Constitution and its reference to the 'state or district wherein the crime shall have been committed.' Despite this difference in the context in which the question of location arose, the statement that the place of publication was where the newspaper or magazine was published was sometimes taken as stating an element of (or at least a consequence of) the single publication rule applied to civil defamation suits.[32]

In *Firth v State of New York*[33] the court noted that the rationale behind the single publication rule was even more applicable to the internet, as there is greater potential there for multiple triggerings of the statute of limitations as well as for multiple suits and vexatious actions. The court regarded unrelated modifications to the website as insufficient to restart the one-year limitation period. This is to be distinguished from the issue of a new edition of a book, which is sold to a new and different readership.

The principle of the single publication rule is codified in legislation only in the United States. It has not found favour in United Kingdom or Australasian jurisdictions. The *Uniform Single Publication Act* (US) provides that multistate defamation must be dealt with in one jurisdiction and that the findings of the court in that jurisdiction are binding on the plaintiff in all other jurisdictions for any single defamatory publication. The *Uniform Single Publication Act* is legislation that has become law when a state enacts it. Its aim is to create a template. It has been widely adopted across the United States with very similar wording to this:

> No person shall have more than one (1) cause of action for damages for libel, slander or invasion of privacy or any other tort founded upon a single publication or exhibition or utterance, such as any one (1) edition of a newspaper or book or magazine, any one (1) presentation to an audience, any one (1) broadcast over radio or television or any one (1) exhibition of a motion picture. Recovery in any action shall include all damages for any such tort suffered by the plaintiff in all jurisdictions.[34]

In the United Kingdom the House of Lords was called upon to deal with the single publication rule in the defamation case of *Berezovsky v Michaels*.[35] An article published online was alleged to have defamed two Russian businessmen residing in Britain. The article was published by the Forbes Corporation in hardcopy and on their website. Their Lordships held that 'The *Uniform Single Publication Act* does not assist in selecting the most suitable court for the trial: it merely prevents

---

32 [2002] 210 CLR 575, paras 33–34 ('*Dow Jones* case').
33 706 NYS 2d 835.
34 State of Idaho Legislature, *Title 6: Actions in Particular Cases, Chapter 7: Libel and Slander*, 6-702. Avaiable at: <www.legislature.idaho.gov/idstat/Title6/T6CH7SECT6-702.htm>.
35 [2000] UKHL 28.

a multiplicity of suits.' The court stated that English law could find 'no support for this argument' (the single publication rule), but then reiterated its support for the long-established legal principle that 'each publication is a separate tort'.[36]

In the *Dow Jones* case, Dow Jones sought to persuade the court that as they were incorporated in the United States, and the server upon which the defamatory material was published was also physically located in that country, the most appropriate forum was the United States. The High Court disagreed on a number of grounds, including that Victoria was not a 'clearly inappropriate forum' in which to hear the action. The court expressed concerns that applying a single publication rule for internet-based defamation (in Australia) would in effect differentiate such defamation from all other types of defamation.

Kirby J gave a number of reasons for 'declining an Internet-specific single publication rule'. First, he concluded that the court could not justify changing the rules of Australian common law merely as a response to the Dow Jones submission. Second, he added:

> Where rules such as these are deeply entrenched in the common law and
> relate to the basic features of the cause of action propounded, their altera-
> tion risks taking the judge beyond the proper limits of the judicial function.[37]

Third, he expressed concern about a separate rule for the internet, stating that 'Rules should be technology-neutral.'[38] Fourth, he noted that there would be 'special difficulties' in achieving judicial reform of the multiple publication rule in Australian law, even if such reform were warranted.[39]

In the absence of a specific single publication rule, Australian courts have estopped parties from raising the same issue in subsequent litigation. It was said in *Henderson v Henderson* that:

> where a given matter becomes the subject of litigation in, and of adjudication
> by, a Court of competent jurisdiction, the Court requires the parties to that
> litigation to bring forward their whole case, and will not (except under special
> circumstances) permit the same parties to open the same subject of litigation in
> respect of matter which might have been brought forward as part of the subject
> in contest, but which was not brought forward, only because they have, from
> negligence, inadvertence, or even accident, omitted part of their case.[40]

36 [2000] UKHL 28.
37 [2002] HCA 56, para 124.
38 [2002] HCA 56, para 125.
39 See *Australian Broadcasting Corporation v Waterhouse* (1991) 25 NSWLR 519 at 537. See also Australian Law Reform Commission, *Unfair publication: Defamation and privacy*, Report No. 11, (1979), 60–61; Australian Law Reform Commission, *Choice of law*, Report No. 58, (1992), 57 paras 6.53–54.
40 [1843] 3 Hare 100, 115; 67 ER 313, 319.

The single controversy principle

Australian courts have *de facto* adopted a 'single controversy' principle. Where there are multiple publications of the same defamatory matter there exists only a 'single controversy' to be litigated. That controversy must include all separate utterances of the defamatory allegation, in order to properly determine breach and damages. The cases to date have not adequately addressed the issues of timing and place, particularly where internet publication is concerned.

The single cause rule

The single publication rule is not to be confused with the 'single cause' provision in the uniform Defamation Acts across Australia, which provides that:

> A person has a single cause of action for defamation in relation to the publication of defamatory matter about the person even if more than one defamatory imputation about the person is carried by the matter.[41]

Adventitious or opportunistic conduct

In *Dow Jones*, both parties raised the issue of adventitious or opportunistic conduct.[42] Dow Jones claimed that permitting jurisdiction in Victoria – that is, at the place of download rather than the place of upload – would encourage plaintiffs to commence actions in jurisdictions with favourable defamation laws. Gutnick's response was that should a plaintiff improperly attempt to take such an advantage, the courts should consider rejecting jurisdiction. He claimed that his choice of venue was not adventitious or opportunistic: Victoria was the place of his residence and his prime business interests.

Gutnick claimed that permitting jurisdiction in New Jersey – that is, at the place of upload rather than the place of download – would encourage defendants to move their servers to jurisdictions with weak defamation laws. Dow Jones'

---

41 *Defamation Act 2005* (Qld) s8, *Defamation Act 2005* (NSW) s8, *Defamation Act 2005* (Vic) s8, *Defamation Act 2005* (Tas) s8, *Defamation Act 2005* (WA) s8, *Defamation Act 2005* (SA) s8, *Defamation Act 2006* (NT) s7, *Civil Law (Wrongs) Act 2002* (ACT) s120; *Defamation Act* (NZ) s7 is a similar provision.
42 See para 131ff.

response was a copy of Gutnick's: should a defendant improperly attempt to take such an advantage, the courts should consider rejecting jurisdiction. Equally, Dow Jones claimed that its choice of location for the server was not adventitious or opportunistic.

Conclusion

While much of the law dealing with online defamation and other torts committed on the internet is still in its earliest days of development and interpretation, some general principles have already emerged. The first is that it would appear that for the purposes of mitigating risk, it is wiser for forum providers to not provide any editorial control whatsoever – and to advertise this fact widely.

Next, employers would be well advised to ensure that there are rigorous and effective systems in place to prevent employees from putting the firm into a defensive position. These might include a staff training régime, a compulsory Code of Conduct, and clear guidelines on the roles and responsibilities of every employee who is exposed to the internet as part of their work duties.

As the law develops, and both governments and industry groups better understand their rights and responsibilities in this domain, the law will be amended to provide direction and protection for those most at risk.

FURTHER READING

Australian Law Reform Commission, *Unfair publication: Defamation and privacy*, Report No. 11 (1979).

Australian Law Reform Commission, *Choice of law*, Report No. 58 (1992).

Debra Cohen, 'The single publication rule: One action, not one law', (1966) 62 *Brooklyn Law Review* 921.

Uta Kohl, 'Defamation on the internet – A duty free zone after all? Macquarie Bank Ltd & Anor v Berg', (2000) 22 *Sydney Law Review*.

Lyrissa Barnett Lidsky, 'Silencing John Doe: Defamation & discourse in cyberspace', (2000) 49 *Duke Law Journal* 855.

Ken S Myers, 'Wikimmunity: Fitting the Communications Decency Act to Wikipedia', (2006) 20 *Harvard Journal of Law and Technology* 163.

David Rolph, 'Before the High Court – the message, not the medium: Defamation, publication and the internet in *Dow Jones & Co Inc. v Gutnick*', (2002) 24 *Sydney Law Review* 263.

PRIVACY IN CYBERSPACE

Information in cyberspace is eternal. The very architecture of cyberspace facilitates information flow, the antithesis of privacy. Digital files reproduce faithfully, permitting an avalanche of material to be viewed, shared and stored. Social media allows millions to share thoughts, images and videos of brilliant quality and (sometimes) questionable taste. Never has information been so available at our fingertips. The expression 'going viral' has entered the vocabulary to describe this phenomenon. It is insidious. It is glorious. In any event it encroaches at a galloping pace on many individuals' privacy.

'Privacy' has numerous meanings, and its importance varies greatly among individuals, communities, organisations and governments. It is an aspect of freedom and human rights. Civil libertarians may believe that our actions and behaviour should not be subject to public or governmental scrutiny; protectionists may accept such erosions for the greater good in the name of law and order.

Historically, governments seem to have pursued increasing and systemic invasions of privacy in the name of law and order, fighting crime and terrorism. However, their role is in fact to ensure and balance security issues and the proper protection of the privacy rights of the individual. In the 1990s the Clipper Chip was proposed by the US Government, ostensibly for the purpose of allowing the government to override individual encryption to protect society from 'gangsters, terrorists and drug users'.[1] Such a process would have allowed the government to access and decipher all encrypted files. The proposal was unsuccessful. In Australia in 1984, an attempt to pass a Privacy Act failed because it set in place an anti-privacy provision: a central national identification card.[2]

Search engines such as Google use sophisticated programs called spiders, robots and wanderers to trawl the internet gathering data on several billion websites, creating an index that handles several trillion inquiries per year. Individuals are often surprised by the digital persona visible when their name is searched. This challenges notions of privacy as a fundamental human right. False, distorted and damaging information may be compiled. A consequence of this massive index on the internet is dataveillance. Privacy is one of the established values challenged by the internet. Other areas challenged include organised crime, terrorism, intellectual property rights, pornography, the integrity of financial markets and tax systems, and cultural diversity.

In 2001 the NSW Supreme Court[3] expressed its view on the expectation of privacy or confidentiality when information is placed on the internet:

---

1 See Mark Berthold, 'Regulating surveillance: Hong Kong's proposals', (1996) *Privacy Law and Policy Reporter* 443 and Graham Greenleaf, 'OECD searches for crypto-consensus', (1996) *Privacy Law and Policy Reporter* 22.
2 Michael Kirby, 'Privacy in cyberspace', (1998) 21 (2) *UNSW Law Journal*.
3 *EPP v Levy* [2001] NSWSC 482, per Barrett J.

It must be said at the outset that part of the information that the defendants have used is in the public domain. I regard everything which is accessible through resort to the internet as being in the public domain. It is true that someone can obtain that information only if they have access to a computer which has a modem which connects to an internet service provider who, for a fee, provides a connection to the internet. But those barriers are, in my view, no more challenging or significant in today's Australia, complete with internet cafes, than those involved in access to a newspaper or television content, both of which should, according to precedent, be seen as involving the public domain.[4]

Information wants to be free

This is the catchcry of the digital age.[5] The absence of a controlling and enforceable law facilitates free expression, the communication of ideas and notions of individual liberty (all of which are themselves important human rights). Such values are not the only human rights.[6] There are other fundamental human rights which compete, or conflict, with the right to free expression. The right to privacy and to reputation and honour, and the confidentiality of communications, must also be protected. In the world of the internet, technological capacity tends to favour the spread of information.

Electronic communication and storage of data have a real impact on issues of privacy and censorship. Previously, many of the safeguards of our privacy were in fact only the costs of retrieving personal information. Retrieving data stored in hardcopy form involved time and expense. Data could be lost, destroyed or misfiled. Hardcopies could deteriorate. Many data collections were incompatible. Considerable time could be spent gaining access. Our privacy was protected only by the fact that methods of data storage were impractical and inconvenient.

These so-called safeguards have evaporated in the digital age. One body, less cognisant of privacy issues and more concerned about costs and time, may respond to another body's request for information by transmitting its entire database, the password or the entire record of an individual rather than the response

---

4 Ibid., para 22. See also *Duchess of Argyle v Duke of Argyle* [1967] Ch 302 and *G v Day* [1982] 1 NSWLR 24.
5 An aphorism attributed to Stewart Brand from the First Hackers Conference in 1984. The full quote is: 'On the one hand, information wants to be expensive, because it's so valuable. The right information in the right place just changes your life. On the other hand, information wants to be free because the cost of getting it out is getting lower and lower all the time. So you have these two fighting against each other.'
6 See the Universal Declaration of Human Rights, adopted and proclaimed by the UN General Assembly Resolution 217A (III) of 10 December 1948.

to the specific request. Data is now stored in compatible operating systems. Due to the ease of storage, bodies both public and private are collecting and amassing a greater amount of personal material than ever before. This is a side of globalisation that is both irreversible and inevitable. Privacy dilemmas in the digital world are a Pandora's Box. Individuals now have a virtual existence in cyberspace, a digital persona made up of a collection of otherwise unconnected and previously unconnectable data, and the quantity of personal information in cyberspace is likely to increase.

Privacy and regulation

Privacy can be divided into two broad categories: information privacy and personal privacy. Information privacy refers to the ways in which information is gathered, recorded, accessed and released. In the digital age there are multitudes of records of individuals on databases. Only since the advent of electronic recording has information privacy become a serious matter for regulation and control. The most significant step towards regulation began with the drafting of privacy principles by the Organisation for Economic Co-operation and Development (OECD) in the 1970s.

Personal privacy relates to privacy of the person, of an individual's personal space: it can be 'invaded' by those seeking to photograph, film and record in public and private places. Media outlets pay substantial amounts for even blurred long-distance photographs of celebrities. Australian laws permit surveillance cameras in shops, malls, service stations, railway stations and many other places.

Information privacy

As law and society evolved, pressing issues such as lawful behaviour – in both criminal and civil senses – and the enforcement of commercial agreements and promises were the priority of law makers. Philosophical concepts such as privacy were insignificant in comparison with survival against warring neighbours and the enforcement of property rights. The courts and legislatures failed to recognise the concepts of isolation, seclusion and the protection of personal information. In the Middle Ages only the few who were literate could access written information. With mass literacy came dissemination. With government came secrets: national security secrets as well as personal ones. Although crude methods of encryption were developed during World War II, it was the Cold War and the perceived need to protect state secrets that pushed cryptography into the limelight as a science.

The modern concept of information privacy emerged in the late 1970s, and the OECD set up an International Experts Group to draft *Guidelines on the Protection of Privacy and Transborder Flows of Personal Data* (the *OECD Guidelines*). The Experts Group was chaired by the Hon Mr Justice Michael Kirby,[7] then Chairman of the Australian Law Reform Commission (ALRC). The *OECD Guidelines* were formally adopted and disseminated in September 1980. They included these recommendations:

- that Member countries take into account in their domestic legislation the principles concerning the protection of privacy and individual liberties set forth in the Guidelines contained in the Annex to this Recommendation which is an integral part thereof;
- that Member countries endeavour to remove or avoid creating, in the name of privacy protection, unjustified obstacles to transborder flows of personal data;
- that Member countries co-operate in the implementation of the Guidelines set forth in the Annex;
- that Member countries agree as soon as possible on specific procedures of consultation and co-operation for the application of these Guidelines.

The OECD supplemented these *Guidelines* with the *Declaration on Transborder Data Flows* (1985) and the *Ministerial Declaration on the Protection of Privacy on Global Networks* (1998).

Electronic commerce law developed as a result of the need to find solutions for novel circumstances. The OECD Guidelines noted that it was the increase in international data transmission that had made it necessary to address privacy protection in relation to personal data. The OECD observed that privacy protection laws were at that time being contemplated or introduced in many OECD countries – Austria, Belgium, Canada, Denmark, France, Germany, Iceland, Luxembourg, Norway, the Netherlands, Spain, Sweden, Switzerland and the United States – and expressed its concern about new 'violation[s] of fundamental human rights',[8] including the unlawful storage of personal data, the storage of inaccurate personal data, and the abuse or unauthorised disclosure of such data.

Even in the late 1970s the rapid growth of digital communication was foreseen: automatic data processes that would result in the transmission of vast quantities of data across national boundaries was already being developed. The OECD's major concern was that disparities in national legislation could lead to interruptions in international flows of data and hamper the free flow of personal data across frontiers; restrictions on these flows, the OECD noted, 'could cause

---

7 Former Justice of the High Court of Australia.
8 OECD, *OECD Guidelines on the Protection of Privacy and Transborder Flows of Personal Data*, Preface (2013) <www.oecd.org/sti/ieconomy/oecdguidelinesontheprotectionofprivacyandtrans borderflowsofpersonaldata.htm>.

serious disruption in important sectors of the economy, such as banking and insurance'.[9]

The *OECD Guidelines* require that personal information not be collected unless the person concerned either consents to its collection or is informed as to why it is being collected, is informed as to who will use it, and is aware of their right to, and how to, access and correct it. The Guidelines state, in part:

> Member countries have a common interest in protecting privacy and individual liberties, and in reconciling fundamental but competing values such as privacy and the free flow of information; that automatic processing and transborder flows of personal data create new forms of relationships among countries and require the development of compatible rules and practices; That transborder flows of personal data contribute to economic and social development

> That domestic legislation concerning privacy protection and transborder flows of personal data may hinder such transborder flows.

Part Two of the Guidelines sets out the key principles:

> **Part Two – Basic Principles of National Application**
> **Collection Limitation Principle**
> 7. There should be limits to the collection of personal data and any such data should be obtained by lawful and fair means and, where appropriate, with the knowledge or consent of the data subject.
>
> **Data Quality Principle**
> 8. Personal data should be relevant to the purposes for which they are to be used, and, to the extent necessary for those purposes, should be accurate, complete and kept up-to-date.
>
> **Purpose Specification Principle**
> 9. The purposes for which personal data are collected should be specified not later than at the time of data collection and the subsequent use limited to the fulfilment of those purposes or such others as are not incompatible with those purposes and as are specified on each occasion of change of purpose.
>
> **Use Limitation Principle**
> 10. Personal data should not be disclosed, made available or otherwise used for purposes other than those specified in accordance with Paragraph 9 except:
>
> a) with the consent of the data subject; or
> b) by the authority of law.

9 Ibid.

Security Safeguards Principle

11. Personal data should be protected by reasonable security safeguards against such risks as loss or unauthorised access, destruction, use, modification or disclosure of data.

Openness Principle

12. There should be a general policy of openness about developments, practices and policies with respect to personal data. Means should be readily available of establishing the existence and nature of personal data, and the main purposes of their use, as well as the identity and usual residence of the data controller.

Individual Participation Principle

13. An individual should have the right:

a) to obtain from a data controller, or otherwise, confirmation of whether or not the data controller has data relating to him;

b) to have communicated to him, data relating to him
   - within a reasonable time;
   - at a charge, if any, that is not excessive;
   - in a reasonable manner; and
   - in a form that is readily intelligible to him;

c) to be given reasons if a request made under subparagraphs (a) and (b) is denied, and to be able to challenge such denial; and

d) to challenge data relating to him and, if the challenge is successful to have the data erased, rectified, completed or amended.

Accountability Principle

14. A data controller should be accountable for complying with measures which give effect to the principles stated above.[10]

Australia

In Australia there is no specific right to privacy at common law.[11] Privacy was not a significant issue for legislators in the immediate postwar period. However, it began to attract attention in Europe and North America, and in 1969 Zelman Cowen (later Governor General), in his ABC Boyer Lecture Series, discussed the real

---

10 Other Parts of the *OECD Guidelines* are: Part 1 – General Definitions; Part 3 – Basic principles of international application: Free flow and legitimate restrictions; Part 4 – National implementation; Part 5 – International co-operation.

11 See Personal privacy, below.

privacy concerns faced by Australians. In 1972, the NSW Attorney-General, John Madison, commissioned a report into the law of privacy by Professor Morison of the University of Sydney. Morison concluded that privacy was an interest, not a right. Concerned at possible legislative overreaction, the Australian Computer Society lobbied the government to prevent the perceived imposition of excessive or inappropriate regulation.

While the *Australian Constitution* makes no direct reference to a privacy right or power, it contains sufficient powers, in section 51, to justify such legislation. The relevant heads of power in that section include:

- trade and commerce [s51(i)];
- postal, telegraphic and telephonic [s51(v)];
- banking [s51(xiii)];
- insurance [s51(xiv)];
- foreign corporations and trading or financial corporations [s51(xx)];
- marriage [s51(xxi)];
- divorce and matrimonial causes [s51(xxii)];
- invalid and old-age pensions [s51(xxiii)];
- social security and other allowances [s51(xxiiiA)];
- external affairs [s51(xxix)];
- matters referred by states [s51(xxxvii)];
- incidental matters [s51(xxxix)]; as well as
- public service [s52(ii)]; and
- financial assistance to the states [s96].

New South Wales enacted the *Privacy Committee Act 1975*, pre-dating the *OECD Guidelines*. The Act created a complaints-driven investigative process and a research organisation. The work of the latter contributed to establishing information privacy principles for organisations using computers.

In April 1976, the Commonwealth government gave the ALRC a reference to study interferences with privacy arising under the laws of the Commonwealth. The report, which was handed down in 1983, took into account the OECD Guidelines. In 1986 the government introduced a Privacy Bill which included a controversial national identification card. Many argued that this was in fact an anti-privacy move. The Bill was defeated by a hostile Senate. In 1988 the government set out to enhance the Tax File Number (TFN) scheme used by the Australian Tax Office. This was intended in part as a replacement of the defeated Australia Card scheme.

The *Privacy Act 1988* (Cth) was passed in December 1988. Australia's first Privacy Commissioner was immediately appointed. The Act applied to the public sector, not to the populace at large. In 1989 the *Privacy Act* was amended to protect consumers from adverse consumer credit reporting. Subsequent amendments extended coverage to 'spent' criminal convictions[12] and to data matching.[13] In 1994 New South Wales introduced the Privacy and Data Protection Bill, but it was withdrawn after heavy criticism.

In 1996, the NSW Health Commission issued a consolidation of privacy law, policy and practice for health care workers. In 1997, the Asia Pacific Smart Cards Forum Code of Conduct included privacy principles for members. In 1998, the Australian Privacy Commissioner released a document entitled *National Principles for the Fair Handling of Personal Information* (FHPI). This was intended to be a way to apply the OECD Guidelines to the wider community.

The *Privacy Act 1988* (Cth) currently includes 13 Australian Privacy Principles, which replace both the Information Privacy Principles (IPP) and National Privacy Principles (NPP). The former applied to Commonwealth government departments and agencies, and the latter to the private sector. The Act also imposes restrictions on how credit providers and credit reporting agencies may handle personal information, together with rules applicable to the entire community in relation to the handling of tax file number information. The Act implements the OECD Privacy Principles and observes Australia's obligations under Article 17 of the *ICCPR*.[14] The Privacy Act provides that the IPP be treated as law.[15]

All firms and businesses need to monitor the changing Australian and international legal environment to ensure that the risk of data protection breaches is minimised.

Australian Privacy Principles (APP)

The APP became operative in March 2014, taking over from the NPP, which had operated since 2001 with respect to the private sector.

Schedule 1 of the Act sets out 13 Australian Privacy Principles:

APP 1 – open and transparent management of personal information

APP 2 – anonymity and pseudonymity

APP 3 – collection of solicited personal information

APP 4 – dealing with unsolicited personal information

---

12 By way of an amendment to Part VIIC of the *Crimes Act 1914* (Cth).
13 *Data-matching Program (Assistance and Tax) Act 1990* (Cth).
14 1. No one shall be subjected to arbitrary or unlawful interference with his privacy, family, home or correspondence, nor to unlawful attacks on his honour and reputation.
   2. Everyone has the right to the protection of the law against such interference or attacks.
15 *Privacy Act 1988* (Cth) s13.

APP 5 – notification of the collection of personal information

APP 6 – use or disclosure of personal information

APP 7 – direct marketing

APP 8 – cross-border disclosure of personal information

APP 9 – adoption, use or disclosure of government related identifiers

APP 10 – quality of personal information

APP 11 – security of personal information

APP 12 – access to personal information

APP 13 – correction of personal information

In a social media context, these provisions require, for example, a website operator or social media provider that is classified as an organisation and that collects personal information online to take reasonable steps to ensure that internet users know who is collecting their information and how it is used, stored and disclosed. A breach of the APP amounts to an interference with the privacy of an individual, and gives rise to a right to complain to the Privacy Commissioner and a right to seek compensation.

Under the *Privacy Act 1988* (Cth), individuals have the right to know why an organisation is collecting their personal information, what information it holds about them, how the information will be used and who else may receive the information. Generally, individuals have the right to access this information and correct it if it is wrong. Individuals can also make a complaint to the Privacy Commissioner if they believe their information is not being handled properly. Alternatively, they can apply to the Federal Court or the Federal Circuit Court for an order to restrain an organisation from engaging in conduct that breaches the APP. The individual's rights arise where an 'act or practice' results in an 'interference with the privacy of an individual'. Section 7 comprehensively defines an 'act or practice'; sections 13–13F provide that an act or practice of an APP entity is an 'interference with the privacy of an individual' if the act or practice breaches the APP or a registered APP code. An APP entity is defined as an agency or an organisation.[16] The definition of 'agency' is designed to include Commonwealth public bodies such as a Minister, a government department, a federal court and the federal police. An 'organisation' refers to the private sector and is defined below. Special provisions apply with respect to credit reporting, contracted service providers, tax file numbers, data-matching programs and health.[17]

---

16 See *Privacy Act 1988* (Cth) s6.
17 Respectively see *Privacy Act 1988* (Cth) s13(2), (3), (4), (5)(a) and (5)(b).

The Act broadly defines an organisation as an individual, a body corporate, a partnership, any other unincorporated association or a trust that is not a small business operator, a registered political party, an agency or instrumentality.[18] A small business operator is defined as a business which:

- has an annual turnover of three million dollars or less;
- is not related to a business with an annual turnover of greater than three million dollars;
- does not provide a health service and hold health records;
- does not disclose personal information about an individual for a benefit, service or advantage;
- does not provide a benefit, service or advantage to collect personal information;
- is not a contracted service provider for a Commonwealth contract (even if the entity is not a party to the contract); and
- is not a credit reporting agency.[19]

Employee records are exempt if the organisation is or has been an employer of the individual and the act or practice is directly related to the employment relationship.[20] Acts and practices engaged in by a media organisation in the course of journalism are exempt.[21] Registered political parties are exempted by being excluded from the definition of organisation.[22] Certain acts or practices of members of parliament, local government councillors and their contractors, for any purpose in connection with an election under an electoral law, a referendum, or in connection with participation of the member or councillor in an aspect of the political process, are exempt.[23]

Data protection

In relation to data protection in Australia, a limited form of privacy protection was introduced by the *Telecommunications Act 1997* (Cth). Part 13 prohibits the disclosure by carriers, carriage service providers and others, of certain information acquired as a result of their normal business activities. However, the same Act requires carriers to have wiretapping capabilities in place for 'lawful' surveillance. The *Crimes Act 1914* (Cth), Part VIIC, Division 5 affords some protection for past criminal convictions. The *Data-matching Program (Assistance and Tax) Act 1990* (Cth) provides protection for specific major data-matching.

---

18 *Privacy Act 1988* (Cth) s6C.
19 *Privacy Act 1988* (Cth) s6D.
20 *Privacy Act 1988* (Cth) s7B(3).
21 *Privacy Act 1988* (Cth) s7B(4).
22 *Privacy Act 1988* (Cth) s6C.
23 *Privacy Act 1988* (Cth) s7C.

Victoria

There are several Victorian Acts related to privacy. The *Surveillance Devices Act 1999* (Vic) aims to regulate the use of surveillance devices, to restrict the communication and publication of records of private conversations and to establish procedures for law enforcement officers to obtain warrants or emergency authorisations. The Act imposes requirements for the secure storage – and destruction – of records obtained by police through the use of surveillance devices.

The *Information Privacy Act 2000* (Vic) aims to:

- establish a regime for the responsible collection and handling of personal information;
- provide individuals with rights of access to information about them held by organisations; and
- provide individuals with the right to require an organisation to correct errors.

The Act covers the handling of all personal information except health information in the public sector in Victoria. It adopts 10 Information Privacy Principles which are similar to the APP.[24]

The *Health Records Act 2001* (Vic) covers the handling of all personal information held by health service providers in the state's public sector and also seeks to govern acts or practices in the Victorian private health sector. The Act contains a set of principles adapted from the NPP and similar to the APP.[25]

Other relevant Victorian laws include: *Freedom of Information Act 1982*; *Public Records Act 1973*; *Surveillance Devices Act 1999*; and *Telecommunications (Interception) (State Provisions) Act 1988*.

New South Wales

The *Privacy and Personal Information Protection Act 1998* (NSW) regulates the management of personal information within NSW public sector agencies. It also sets out the role of the Information and Privacy Commissioner. New South Wales has also developed statutory guidelines in the form of legally binding documents that define the scope of particular exemptions in the health privacy principles.

Other relevant NSW laws include: *Health Records and Information Privacy Act 2002*; *Freedom of Information Act 1989*; *State Records Act 1998*; *Criminal Records Act 1991* (spent convictions); *Workplace Surveillance Act 2005*; *Telecommunications (Interception) (New South Wales) Act 1987*; *Terrorism (Police Powers) Act 2002*; and *Access to Neighbouring Land Act 2000*.

---

24 Office of the Victorian Privacy Commissioner: <www.privacy.vic.gov.au>.
25 Office of the Health Services Commissioner: <www.health.vic.gov.au/hsc/>.

Queensland

The *Information Privacy Act 2009* (Qld) aims to provide for the fair collection and handling in the public sector environment of personal information, and a right of access to personal information in the government's possession. It contains privacy principles that govern how government agencies collect, store, use and disclose personal information. An individual may lodge a complaint about an agency's breach. The Act also requires Queensland Health to comply with the stated NPP, which mirror the former provisions of the federal legislation. The Queensland Health Rights Commission provides an inquiry service and a health complaints system which covers privacy-related complaints involving the state public health sector.[26]

Other relevant Queensland laws include: *Public Records Act 2002*; *Criminal Law (Rehabilitation of Offenders) Act 1986* (spent convictions); *Invasion of Privacy Act 1971* (listening devices, invasion of privacy of the home); *Invasion of Privacy Act 1971*; and *Police Powers and Responsibilities Act 2000* (Chapter 4 of the Act deals with covert evidence-gathering powers).

Western Australia

The public sector in Western Australia does not have a privacy regime. However, the *Freedom of Information Act 1992* (WA) includes some privacy principles and its confidentiality provisions cover government.

Other relevant WA laws include: *State Records Act 2000*; *Spent Convictions Act 1988*; *Surveillance Devices Act 1998*; and *Telecommunications (Interception) Western Australia Act 1996*.

South Australia

South Australia has issued Information Privacy Principle Instructions that government agencies must comply with. South Australia has a Code of Fair Information Practice, based on the former NPP, which is applicable to the SA Department of Health, its funded service providers and others with access to the Department's personal information.

Other relevant SA laws include: *Freedom of Information Act 1991*; *State Records Act 1997*; *Listening and Surveillance Devices Act 1972*; and *Telecommunications (Interception) Act 1988*.

Tasmania

In Tasmania the *Personal Information Protection Act 2004* (Tas) implements Personal Information Protection Principles (PIPP) applicable to 'personal information

---

26 Office of the Information Commissioner Queensland: <www.oic.qld.gov.au>.

custodians' such as public and local government sectors and the University of Tasmania. The PIPP are based on the federal NPP. The Act is administered by the Department of Justice and complaints may be made to the Tasmanian Ombudsman.

Other relevant Tasmanian laws include: *Personal Information Protection Act 2004*; *Right to Information Act 2009*; *Archives Act 1983*; *Annulled Convictions Act 2003* (spent convictions); *Listening Devices Act 1991*; and *Telecommunications (Interception) Tasmania Act 1999*.

Northern Territory

The Information Commissioner for the Northern Territory is the independent authority responsible for overseeing the freedom of information and privacy provisions of the *Information Act 2002* (NT). The Act deals with the protection of personal information, record keeping and archive management in the public sector and incorporates freedom of information and privacy principles. The Health Information Privacy website provides information and links to health privacy-related matters in the Territory, and includes a Code of Conduct. A discussion paper on protecting the privacy of health information in the Territory was issued in March 2002.[27]

Other relevant NT laws include: *Information Act 2002* (privacy, FOI and public records); *Criminal Records (Spent Convictions) Act 1992*; *Surveillance Devices Act 2007*; and *Telecommunications (Interception) Northern Territory Act 2001*.

Australian Capital Territory

The *Privacy Act* applies to ACT government agencies and is administered by the federal Privacy Commissioner on behalf of the ACT Government. The *Health Records (Privacy and Access) Act 1997* covers health records held in the public sector in the ACT and also seeks to apply to acts or practices in the private sector that are not covered by the *Privacy Act*. It contains privacy principles based on the federal legislation but modified to suit the requirements of health records. The ACT Community and Health Services Complaints Commissioner handles health record privacy complaints.

Abuses

There have already been many early warning signs of the potential for privacy abuse. Naval officer Timothy R McVeigh was discharged from the US Navy after he came under investigation following details of his use of the internet which revealed

---

27 Office of the Information Commissioner Northern Territory: <www.privacy.nt.gov.au>.

the use of the word 'gay' on his Internet America Online (AOL) profile. AOL agreed to pay damages to McVeigh for having improperly disclosed his identity.[28] While the US Senate considered the nomination of Judge Robert Bork to the Supreme Court, a journalist retrieved and reported the record of the judge's 146 video rentals as itemised by computer from his local video store.

The increase in the amount of data being collected and kept also leads to an increase in mistakes. A brother who had made a few payments of rent for his sister was blacklisted when the sister later defaulted. Records that show that a particular computer or network was used to access or download 'undesirable material' do not identify the actual individual using the facility.

Cookies

Normal use of the internet typically causes information from personal computers to be sent to the hosts of sites visited. One such process uses 'cookies'. A cookie, in an internet context, is a small text file placed on the user's hard drive, often unknown to the user, by the host of the website visited. The cookie can act like an identification card, but cannot be executed as code or deliver viruses. It can only be read by the host that presented it to the user. Internet browsers are designed to facilitate cookies.

A positive example of a cookie may be accessing a website of a particular cinema chain. The user typically must click through several links and pages, choosing the state, city and suburb of the local cinema. However, such a website may allow the user to customise the page so that the web page showing the local cinema appears immediately on access. A cookie is created and is stored on the user's computer. It is read by the cinema website, which automatically responds by customising the information to be displayed.

Cookies are automatically created by such sites as Wikipedia, the *New York Times* and Google. Cookies are used to identify users and track their movements through the site. A particular website may be made up of several web pages. One web page may include graphics and links from a range of outside sources. Some of these may be advertising banners. Indeed the owner of the page may not know which advertisement will be displayed. A user in Europe may call up a web page based in Canada, but the advertising banner, text and material may be automatically accessed from a location in the United States. It may be that both the host in Canada and the advertising owner place cookies on the user's page. Their purposes may be entirely different: the web host may want information in order to

---

28 *Timothy R McVeigh v William Cohen* 983 F. Supp. 215 (DDC January 1998). (Not to be confused with the infamous criminal, Timothy J McVeigh.)

provide a more functional site, and the advertiser may be collecting information for marketing purposes.[29]

Web hosts may systematically share information for identification or tracking. Typically, the main purpose of sharing is identification. Where the user voluntarily supplies these details, they can be placed in a cookie that lets the host take a shortcut to supplying unique information. The host may register each visit, and the time and number of pages visited within its site. The host may also track the visit: this means using cookies to trace usage and status from page to page. For example, where a user accesses an online shopping basket, each time the basket is filled with items to purchase from separate web pages within a service, the cookies verify that the user is the person requesting those items. When a user is at the 'checkout', the details of all the items can be retrieved using the cookie file.[30]

A website cannot uncover your email address, for example, without its being specifically disclosed. However, many sites require an email address as part of their operation; when it is provided, it may be placed or referenced in a cookie. This information can then be shared. As a result of cookie technology, a user can be tracked.

In the most usual situation, when a user visits a particular web page, the web browser usually makes a request for http code to be displayed and for the graphics that appear on the screen. The graphics may come from various locations, and the user will be unaware of their origin. There may be, for example, banner advertisements from two companies. Any information provided by the user can go to each of these companies. With this information the advertising companies may develop a database for future marketing. Many advertising banners on search engine web pages can record the search engine inquiries. Depending on the information in the cookie, next time you visit a site with that advertiser, a personal banner that reflects your profile may appear. For many people, all this raises serious privacy concerns.

One view is that a cookie is a unique identifier, like a serial number, that is used to retrieve your records from databases. Cookies may have an expiry date, but many last for years. Cookies are stored on users' hard drives and may be viewed. Microsoft Internet Explorer[31] has a dedicated directory for this purpose. Each individual cookie may be viewed or deleted.

Cookies operate in a surreptitious manner. The majority of users are unaware of their existence and of those who are, few appreciate the extent of their operation. Cookies make use of the user's computer without the user having given express consent to either the writing or the reading of them. The default setting for most

29 Sharon Nye, 'Internet privacy – Regulating cookies and web bugs', (2002) 9(2) *Privacy Law and Policy Reporter* 21.

30 Morris Averill, 'The spiders stratagem on the Web: Hunting and collecting web users', (2004) 5(1) *Digital Technology Law Journal* 1.

31 Microsoft Internet Explorer, version 7.

web browsers is to permit the use of cookies. The latest version of the Microsoft Internet Explorer browser has six options in relation to cookies, from accept all to reject all.

While cookies provide significant benefits for users of the internet, their operation has been largely clandestine, and in certain situations they will stretch privacy rules to the limit, if not break them. Users must take care with the type of response they make to questions asked of them on websites; but this applies to all sites, not just those with cookies.[32]

Web bugs

Web bugs are objects embedded in web pages or email, and are used to monitor use. Originally web bugs were actually tiny invisible or virtually invisible images – one pixel in size – on a computer screen. A web bug is sometimes referred to as 'clear gif': it is invisible and is usually a 'gif' file (image). The image need not be invisible and can be any size, but invisibility of course assists surreptitious use.

Web bugs may initiate contact with another server.[33] When a web bug is loaded unknowingly by a user, it will yield the IP address of the computer that fetched the web bug, the URL of the web page with the web bug, the URL of the web bug image, the time and date the web bug was viewed, the type and version of the browser that fetched the web bug image and cookie information related to the website the bug is on.

As with cookies, web bugs may be used nefariously by advertising agencies to gather information for marketing purposes. This includes the personal profile of the users. This information may be used in conjunction with cookies to provide statistics, such as the number of visitors to a website, and other information.

In emails, web bugs can be used to determine whether the email was read, and when it was read, the IP address of the recipient and how often a message is being forwarded and read. This can give an indication of the success of, for example, junk email, and thus on whether or not the person should be sent future emails. Web bug programmers can synchronise the web bug with a cookie to a particular email address. This connects the identity of the user to future access to websites. Web bug detectors are freely available, but web bugs cannot be removed.

Most privacy laws require disclosure of when information is being collected. This is a standard privacy principle and appears in the OECD principles and the APP. Anecdotally, the majority of web-based privacy policies do not disclose the

---

32 See Australia Law Reform Commission (ALRC), 'Review of Australian privacy law', Discussion Paper No. 72 (2007), paras 11.9–11.11.
33 See Kaman Tsoi, 'Web bugs and internet advertising', (2001) *PLPR* 21.

use of web bugs. This is either in ignorance of the applicable law or is deliberate, so as not to alert potential users. The minimum disclosure standard typically requires there to be a privacy policy on the web page's site. For email, either disclosure within the email or a link to the privacy policy would be required.[34]

International Covenant on Civil and Political Rights (ICCPR)

The ICCPR, which is based on the Universal Declaration of Human Rights, provides for privacy protection. More than 170 state parties have ratified it, and several are soon to ratify it. Article 17 provides:

> No one shall be subjected to arbitrary or unlawful interference with his privacy, family, home or correspondence, nor to unlawful attacks on his honour and reputation.
>
> Everyone has the right to the protection of the law against such interference or attacks.

The Universal Declaration of Human Rights, in Article 12, states:

> No one shall be subjected to arbitrary interference with his privacy, family, home or correspondence, nor to attacks upon his honour and reputation. Everyone has the right to the protection of the law against such interference or attacks.

Many nations have enshrined the right of privacy in their constitutions and laws. The *Constitution of France*, for instance, includes the 'Declaration of the Rights of Man and of the Citizen'. However, in many nations there is an absence of a controlling and enforceable law to facilitate free expression, privacy, reputation and honour, and the confidentiality of communications. The United Nations has a role to play in enunciating such issues and encouraging adoption and enforcement.

The US Senate has declared that acceptance of the ICCPR 'will not create a private cause of action in US Courts'.[35] The treaty binds the United States as a matter of international law, but does not form part of its domestic law. The US Supreme Court has stated that the *Constitution of the United States* includes 'penumbras' that guarantee the right to privacy against government intrusion. For example, in *Griswold v Connecticut*[36] the state legislature in Connecticut prohibited the use of

---

34 See ALRC, above n 32, paras 11.12–11.13.
35 S Exec. Rep., No. 102–23, 15 (1992).
36 381 US 479 (1965) (*'Griswold's'* case).

contraceptives. The US Supreme Court, by a majority of 7 to 2, invalidated the law on the grounds that it violated the 'right to marital privacy'. The court used the first nine amendments to the Bill of Rights (the *US Constitution*), in particular the Ninth Amendment,[37] in reaching its decision. The US Supreme Court has used the right to privacy in several decisions since *Griswold's* case, particularly in relation to healthcare. In *Roe v Wade*[38] the Supreme Court stated that a woman's choice to have an abortion was protected as a private decision between her and her medical practitioner.

Data protection

Data privacy (or data protection) is an issue in electronic commerce. The term 'data' refers to electronic symbols typically stored on some form of disk for computers or transmitted from computer to computer. Australian Freedom of Information legislation[39] deals with documents, data and records, but not with the much larger concept of information. There is a view that data has now become so freely available and accessible that privacy has largely disappeared – every individual has some personal data recorded on computer databases, and so has a kind of digital persona. Some of this data is freely available online. The technology has, in a sense, released data, making it now relatively easy to locate, copy and transfer.

Internationally, legislation has focused on data protection. This means that the laws protect the data directly rather than the people who are the subject of the data.

At common law, the tort of passing off and the principles relating to confidentiality and trade secrets provide indirect protection. The main protection for privacy in the past arose from the sheer cost of retrieving personal information, itself a result of the tangible nature of the forms in which that information was stored and the inconvenience of procuring access (assuming that the existence of the data was known). Privacy was further protected by the incompatibility of collections with available indexes and the difficulty in ascertaining the existence of most personal data. These practical safeguards for privacy have largely disappeared.

---

37 The Ninth Amendment is: The enumeration in the Constitution, of certain rights, shall not be construed to deny or disparage others retained by the people.
38 410 US 113 (1973).
39 *Freedom of Information Act 1982* (Cth), *Freedom of Information Act 1989* (NSW), *Freedom of Information Act 1982* (Vic), *Freedom of Information Act 1992* (Qld), *Freedom of Information Act 1991* (SA), *Freedom of Information Act 1992* (WA), *Freedom of Information Act 1991* (Tas), *Freedom of Information Act 1989* (ACT); *Information Act 2006* (NT); *Right to Information Act 2005* (India); *Official Information Act 1982* (NZ); *Freedom of Information Act 2000* (UK); *Freedom of Information (Scotland) Act 2002; Freedom of Information Act 1966* (US) and *Privacy Act 1974* (US).

Personal privacy

Personal privacy involves 'invasion of the person'. This may take the form of surveillance cameras, stalking, and the media following people, such as politicians and celebrities.

In 1937, in *Victoria Park Racing v Taylor*,[40] the High Court of Australia determined, in a majority verdict, that there was no right to privacy at common law. The case was about a prominent Sydney radio station setting up a platform adjacent to a horseracing track for the purpose of calling the races live on the radio. They did not have the permission of the racetrack authorities. The High Court ruled that the racetrack authorities could not prevent a party viewing or broadcasting from an adjacent private property.

Whether or not Australian law recognises a tort of invasion of privacy was raised in the High Court case *Australian Broadcasting Corporation v Lenah Game Meats Pty Ltd*.[41] In particular, the question was whether or not such a right might attach to a corporation. The facts were that unidentified trespassers gained access to the abattoirs and filmed the slaughtering and processing of possum meat for the export market. The ABC intended to broadcast excerpts on a television current affairs program in Tasmania.

Most of the High Court held that whether or not a tort of 'invasion of privacy' might develop under Australian law was still an open issue. Callinan J gave tentative approval for such a development in several paragraphs of his judgement. He did so first by arguing for a property right in a spectacle:

> It may be that the time is approaching, indeed it may already have arrived, for the recognition of a form of property in a spectacle. There is no reason why the law[s] should not, as they emerge, or their value becomes evident, recognise new forms of property.[42]

His Honour went on:

> It seems to me that, having regard to current conditions in this country, and developments of the law in other common law jurisdictions, the time is ripe for consideration whether a tort of invasion of privacy should be recognised in this country, or whether the legislatures should be left to determine whether provisions for a remedy for it should be made. Any consideration of that matter should be undertaken with regard to the separation of the roles of the judiciary and the legislature ...[43]

---

40 (1937) 58 CLR 479.
41 [2001] HCA 63 (*Lenah Game Meats* case).
42 [2001] HCA 63, para 316.
43 Ibid., para 335.

The High Court's decision in *Lenah Game Meats* was based on the law of trespass, but the observations and statements made in obiter revived the issue of a possible tort of invasion of privacy to the person.

Gummow and Hayne JJ referred to the case of *Church of Scientology v Woodward*,[44] in which Murphy J identified 'unjustified invasion of privacy' as one of the 'developing torts'.[45] Kirby J stated that 'cheque-book journalism', intrusive telephoto lenses, surreptitious surveillance, gross invasions of personal privacy, deliberately deceptive 'stings' and trespass onto land 'with cameras rolling' are mainly phenomena of recent times.[46] Such phenomena have produced applications to the courts for relief, including injunctive relief. Adapting the words of Cardozo J used in another context, '[t]he cry of distress is the summons to relief'.[47] In Australia, generally, 'courts exercising equitable jurisdiction have upheld the entitlement to relief where to turn their backs would be seriously offensive to conscience'.[48]

While the Supreme Court of New South Wales,[49] the Supreme Court of Victoria,[50] the South Australian Court of Appeal[51] and the Federal Court of Australia have questioned this development, the Supreme Court of Queensland,[52] the District Court of New South Wales,[53] the County Court of Victoria[54] and the Federal Court[55] have availed themselves of opportunities to develop the principles of invasion of personal privacy. The UK courts have been more positive in accepting and implementing a tort of privacy. However, in the United Kingdom it is based on principles of confidentiality.[56]

In *Grosse v Purvis*[57] the District Court of Queensland recognised a separate common law cause of action for invasion of privacy. The plaintiff, Ms Grosse, a prominent Queensland political figure, sued the defendant for, among other things,

---

44 [1982] HCA 78.

45 Ibid., para 13.

46 *Australian Broadcasting Corporation v Lenah Game Meats Pty Ltd* [2001] HCA 63, para 172.

47 *Wagner v International Ry Co.* 133 NE 437 at 437 (NY 1921).

48 [2001] HCA 63, para 172.

49 *NRMA v John Fairfax* [2002] NSWSC 563, *Chan v Sellwood* [2009] NSWSC 1335, *Gee v Burger* [2009] NSWSC 149 and *Maynes v Casey* [2011] NSWCA 156.

50 *Giller v Procopets* [2004] VSC 113.

51 *Sands v State of South Australia* [2013] SASC 44.

52 *Gramotnev v Queensland University of Technology* [2013] QSC 158.

53 *Grosse v Purvis* [2003] QDC 151. Also see *Doe v Yahoo!7 Pty Ltd; Wright v Pagett* [2013] QDC 181.

54 *Jane Doe v ABC* [2007] VCC 281.

55 *Dye v Commonwealth Securities Limited* [2010] FCA 720 and [2012] FCA 242.

56 See *Campbell v Mirror General Newspapers Ltd* [2004] 2 AC 457 and *Douglas v Hello!* [2008] 1 AC 1 [2007] UKHL 21, based on *Coco v AN Clark* [1969] RPC 41. In New Zealand see *P v D* [2000] 2 NZLR 591 and *Hosking v Runting* [2005] 1 NZLR 1.

57 [2003] QDC 151.

damages for invasion of privacy. The conduct of the defendant included instances of loitering, spying, unlawful entry to her home, unwelcomed physical contact, repetitious phone calls and use of offensive language and behaviour towards the plaintiff over an extended period of time. The judge was satisfied on the evidence that the defendant had developed an extraordinary and active infatuation with the plaintiff.

As a result of the defendant's stalking behaviour, the plaintiff suffered post-traumatic stress disorder (PTSD). The plaintiff's condition was held to seriously and adversely affect her enjoyment of life and ability to function, including in her elected position. The plaintiff was successful and was awarded $178000 in compensatory, aggravated and exemplary damages – for invasion of privacy and other causes of action.

Skoien SDCJ stated:

> It is not my task nor my intent to state the limits of the cause of action nor any special defences other than [are] necessary for the purposes of this case. In my view the essential elements would be:
>
> - a willed act by the defendant,
> - which intrudes upon the privacy or seclusion of the plaintiff,
> - in a manner which would be considered highly offensive to a reasonable person of ordinary sensibilities, [and]
> - … which causes the plaintiff detriment in the form of mental, psychological or emotional harm or distress or which prevents or hinders the plaintiff from doing an act which she is lawfully entitled to do.[58]

In *Jane Doe v Australian Broadcasting Commission*,[59] Hampel J of the Victorian County Court awarded a rape victim $234190 in damages, based in part on invasion of her privacy. Despite a court order, the ABC broadcast in its news bulletins the name of the rapist, who was the husband of the victim, the name of the victim, and her suburb. Without formulating an exhaustive definition, her Honour held that it was wrong to publish this personal information where there was no corresponding public interest and where there was a prohibition on publishing.

Surveillance cameras have become a part of modern life. They are largely taken for granted. In petrol stations, supermarkets, hotels and malls surveillance cameras record our movements. The community as a whole has come to accept the underlying rationale: the need to protect personal safety and to reduce theft.

---

58 [2003] QDC 151, para 444.
59 [2007] VCC 281.

The cost of surveillance equipment has reduced dramatically, making increased digital scrutiny within the reach of nearly all businesses. Walls of TV screens allow authorities in control rooms in major cities to monitor major roads. Concerned parents have set up cameras which record actions by their babysitters. Some link the cameras to the internet for remote surveillance. Internet cameras are commonplace, and are used for a variety of purposes: there are now more than 40 million cameras linked online.

More employers are using surveillance cameras and connecting them to the internet for remote surveillance. Cameras are being placed not only in places the public may frequent, but also in employee-only areas. The areas in which employees have the greatest sensitivity in relation to the use of video surveillance are toilets, showers and areas where employees may change clothing. However, employees also express concern about surveillance in areas set aside for employees when they not engaged in actual employment, such as dining areas, recreational areas, places to practise regular religious observances; and also about surveillance of personal behaviour such as flirting and other general behaviour where there is an assumption of privacy. The employers' concerns may also relate to areas with expensive furnishings or recreational equipment and other 'vulnerable' assets (such as vending machines).

It is clear that employers have a legitimate interest in placing cameras in positions frequented by members of the public. However, this has the secondary effect of keeping an eye on employees. Misuse is not unknown. One US advocate has documented police parties where 'best of' videos are shown. In call centres, where there are high levels of monitoring of employees, studies have shown that workers experience greater health problems – such as depression, tension, anxiety – than the average and have lower productivity levels. Employers must consider these effects of surveillance on productivity. The employer has the right to manage the workplace, but also an obligation to protect employees and the company from unlawful activities.[60]

In an effort to address these competing interests, the NSW Government introduced the *Workplace Video Surveillance Act 1998* (now replaced by the *Workplace Surveillance Act 2005*), which was designed to restrict and regulate the use of video surveillance equipment in the workplace. Under the 2005 Act, a court may order surveillance only where 'reasonable grounds exist to justify its issue ... [having] regard to the seriousness of the unlawful activity with which the application is concerned'[61] and only under the following conditions:

---

60 See *Griffith v Rose* [2011] FCA 30.
61 *Workplace Surveillance Act 2005* (NSW) s25.

(2) The notice must be given at least 14 days before the surveillance commences. ...

(4) The notice must indicate:

   (a) the kind of surveillance to be carried out (camera, computer or tracking), and

   (b) how the surveillance will be carried out, and

   (c) when the surveillance will start, and

   (d) whether the surveillance will be continuous or intermittent, and

   (e) whether the surveillance will be for a specified limited period or ongoing.[62]

The two Acts prohibit 'covert' surveillance unless an 'authority' has been issued by a magistrate. When the 1998 Act came into effect, the then Attorney-General and Minister for Industrial Relations, Jeff Shaw, stated: 'the secret filming of workers in the workplace will be illegal unless there are reasonable grounds to suspect an employee is committing an unlawful act and a court authority is obtained'. There is still no specific legislation dealing with workplace surveillance in other Australian states. However, there are provisions which relate to general surveillance activities by 'authorities', which provide some protection.

In an unfair dismissal case in the Australian Industrial Relations Commission, Commissioner Larkin considered videotape of an employee removing a bag of coins from a weighing scale and placing the bag between the scales and her till.[63] The Commissioner expressed concern that the applicant did not have access to the surveillance videotape and had not been shown the videotape at any point during the investigation. However, the Commissioner still accepted the surveillance, stating: 'I am not satisfied that the applicant made an honest mistake on the night in question. In my view, the videotape is clear on its face'.[64] The Commissioner ruled that the termination was not harsh, unjust or unreasonable.

Disclosure in the contract of employment clarifies the position for all parties. New employees have the 'choice' of refusing employment under such conditions. However, imposing conditions on existing employees may prove problematic. It is advisable for employers to disclose the use of surveillance cameras. Indeed, one may argue that the surveillance, if its purpose is to deter thieving, is ineffective unless its use is known. The employer needs to decide whether the priority is to prevent theft or to catch a thief.

Formulating a policy may prove useful. The policy would presumably note that public areas are subject to surveillance and that personal areas such as toilets and changing areas are not. As for the middle ground, a more circumspect policy may state that surveillance will only be undertaken if a legitimate concern regarding an employee's actions has arisen. Even if the policy is not initially disclosed to the

---

62 *Workplace Surveillance Act 2005* (NSW) s10.
63 *Y Liu v Star City Pty Limited* PR903625 [2001] AIRC 394.
64 Ibid., para 30.

employees, its release in the event of a complaint or other action would demonstrate a considered and judicious approach to surveillance.

Mobile phone cameras provide a clandestine method for taking photographs and videos. If someone photographs a bather in a change room and posts the image on the internet, clearly the bather's privacy has been violated. The YMCA and the Royal Life Saving Society of Australia have banned camera phones because of their concerns about inappropriate pictures being taken surreptitiously.

In *Grosse v Purvis*,[65] Senior Judge Skoien stated, 'there can be a civil action for damages based on the actionable right of an individual person to privacy'.[66] The elements of the cause of action proposed for personal privacy are most appropriate for camera surveillance situations.[67]

Reasonable use surveillance would be unlikely to be regarded as an invasion of privacy. However, misuse, such as for voyeurism or to eavesdrop for negotiation purposes, may cross the line.

New Zealand

The *Privacy Act 1993* (NZ) came into effect on 1 July 1993. It followed the *Privacy Commissioner Act 1991* (NZ), which had established the office of Privacy Commissioner.

The *Privacy Act 1993* uses the 1980 OECD Guidelines on the Protection of Privacy and Transborder Flows of Personal Data as its template. Generally, the Act applies to both the public and private sectors. Its underlying aim is the promotion and protection of individual privacy. The Act contains twelve IPP, dealing with collecting, holding, use and disclosure of personal information and assigning unique identifiers. The privacy principles give individuals the right to access personal information and to request correction of it. Like the Australian Act, the New Zealand *Privacy Act* gives the Privacy Commissioner the power to issue codes of practice that become part of the law. In certain circumstances the Privacy Commissioner may authorise agencies to collect, use or disclose information even though that would otherwise breach information privacy principles.[68]

---

65 [2003] QDC 151 (based on the High Court Justices' comments in *ABC v Lenah Game Meats* (2001) HCA 63).

66 Ibid., para 442.

67 Ibid., para 444.

68 See, generally, the New Zealand Privacy Commissioner: <www.privacy.org.nz/>. For a judicial consideration of the *Privacy Act 1993* (NZ) see *Harris v Selectrix Appliances* (Complaints Review Tribunal, Decision No. 12/2001, 2001), *L v L* (Complaints Review Tribunal, Decision No. 15/2001, 2001), *Commissioner of Inland Revenue v B* [2001] 2 NZLR 566.

United States

In the United States, the right of freedom of speech granted in the First Amendment has limited the effects of lawsuits for breach of privacy.

The US *Privacy Act 1974* was passed during the administration of President Nixon. The Act provides that:

> no agency shall disclose any record which is contained in a system of records by any means of communication to any person, or to another agency, except pursuant to a written request by, or with the prior written consent of, the individual to whom the record pertains.[69]

There are a number of specific exceptions. They include for statistical purposes by the Census Bureau and the Bureau of Labor Statistics, for archival purposes, for law enforcement purposes, and for congressional investigations and other administrative purposes. Every US federal government agency must put in place an administrative and physical security system to prevent the unauthorised release of personal records.[70]

All government agencies are required to maintain a system permitting access upon request by any individual to permit the review and copying of their own record, and to allow the individual to request amendments of their record.

The US *Computer Matching and Privacy Protection Act 1988* amended the *Privacy Act* to include protections for the subjects of *Privacy Act* records whose records are used in automated matching programs. These protections are designed to ensure procedural uniformity in carrying out matching, due process, and oversight of matching programs through the establishment of Data Integrity Boards at each agency engaging in matching to monitor the agency's matching activity.

The full name of the *USA PATRIOT Act* is the *Uniting and Strengthening America by Providing Appropriate Tools Required to Intercept and Obstruct Terrorism Act 2001*.[71] This Act was in response to the attacks of 11 September 2001 and was conceived, written, debated and passed within 45 days.

The Act significantly expands the authority of US law enforcement agencies for the purpose of fighting terrorism. It has many provisions that affect the lives of Americans in the US. It affects their privacy by arming authorities with a range of rights to access and gather information about communications, health and finances. The Act permits 'sneak and peek' searches: law enforcement officers may search a home or business without the owner's or the occupant's permission or knowl-

---

69 *Privacy Act 1974*, 5 USC § 552a.
70 See also the US *Computer Matching and Privacy Protection Act*.
71 Public Law 107–56, also known as the *USA PATRIOT Act*.

edge. 'National Security Letters' allow the Federal Bureau of Investigation to search telephone, email and financial records without a court order. At a time when the right to privacy was solidifying in the US courts and Congress, this Act single-handedly set information privacy rights back decades.

Final comment

Law makers and businesses need to monitor the changing national and international legal environments to ensure that the risk of privacy breaches in the future is minimised. Regulations in cyberspace must evolve in a way that includes fundamental human rights and national governance, and reflects global values and human diversity. The rule of cyberspace encompasses law, practice, procedure and presence in cyberspace. The internet should develop in a way that demonstrates respect for fundamental and universal human rights and democratic governance. Its expansion should reflect global values and human diversity.

FURTHER READING

Australia Law Reform Commission (ALRC), *Review of Australian privacy law*, Discussion Paper 72 (2007).

Alan Davidson, 'Privacy in a brave new world: ALRC proposals for privacy and technology', (2007) *Privacy Law Bulletin* 61.

Alan Davidson, 'Privacy reforms: Technological considerations in the age of the internet', (2008) *Internet Law Bulletin* 21.

Mark Davison, *The legal protection of databases*, Cambridge University Press, Cambridge, 2003.

Sharon Nye, 'Internet privacy – Regulating cookies and web bugs', (2002) 9(2) *Privacy Law and Policy Reporter* 21.

ELECTRONIC MAIL
AND ONLINE
PRESENCE

The changes that have occurred as a result of the availability of electronic mail (email) and digital communications go well beyond those wrought by the introduction of postal systems, the telephone, telexes and facsimile. Verbal communication can take place with greater ease and clarity online than over the telephone. Additionally, users can now digitally save conversations in a similar way to the way in which they can save email messages. The tools used to access and navigate between systems are steadily becoming cheaper, more powerful and easier to use. The internet allows us all to maximise our engagement in discourse, study and recreation in a manner previously unimaginable.

Email is now required by many government departments and courts for the lodging of materials and for correspondence. Email is a fast and efficient worldwide communication portal. This chapter deals with legal and practical issues relating to the use of electronic mail.

Email

Email is one of the most popular applications of the internet. It allows users to send messages created on the computer to any other internet computer in a matter of seconds. Data files such as photographs, sound clips and, more usually, word-processed document files, can be attached to an email message. In fact any file which can be stored digitally can be transferred by email. It is usually cheaper and quicker, and more reliable, than the ordinary post. Email is becoming integrated with other communication technologies, such as faxes, pagers and mobile devices. Email messages can be accessed on smartphones and tablets.

The internet's use for recreation and business is newer. The integration of the telephone into the office, now almost before living memory, had a significant effect on business and communication. Many can recall similar effects when the telex, the facsimile and the photocopier were introduced to offices.[1]

In cyberspace, the address for each person, each computer and each internet page is unique. Unlike names, no two email addresses may be the same. Many individuals have several email addresses.

When a person writes a letter, puts it in a stamped, addressed envelope and drops it in a post box, they do not have to understand the processes conducted by the mail carrier to know that the letter will be delivered. Email is the same. Users do not need to understand that the email facility creates text, typically using standard protocol (ASCII, HTML or Rich Text files), for transmission, or that the protocol

---

1 This is known as Innovation Diffusion Theory. For discussions of it, see Everett M Rogers, *Diffusion of Innovations*, 5th edn, Simon & Schuster, 2003 and Myles McGregor-Lowndes and Alan Davidson, *The Internet for Lawyers*, LBC Information Services, Sydney, 1997, Chapter 2.

used on the internet to standardise the transfer of mail is called SMTP (Simple Mail Transfer Protocol). SMTP is activated when mail is sent.

The interface with the internet mail protocol allows incoming messages to be read, deleted or saved, and new messages to be created. Users can use more than one email program on their computer. Several companies have produced software applications that aim to maximise ease of use and offer attractive additional features, such as folders for filing mail, feature buttons, checks on delivery and receipt of mail sent, encryption for security, preparation of group lists, and forwarding on to others.

Attachments

Like normal mail, emails are generally text based. Although it is impossible to email hard copies of photographs, plans, documents for signature and so forth, it is possible to attach data files to email.

Depending upon the intention of the sender, the attachment may constitute an electronic record, proof of which may be determined by inherent metadata. It may also be the intention of the sender that the attachment be printed and the printout be the original document. In this situation the email is regarded as a courier, much like an envelope. Depending upon the requirements of the sender, it is prudent to make an express statement of this intention either within the accompanying email or in the attachment itself.[2]

Authentication

Authentication of electronic messages will become increasingly important for evidentiary purposes. Australian Evidence Acts do not address all aspects of email communication. Section 71–6 of the Evidence Acts of the Commonwealth, New South Wales, Tasmania and the ACT make presumptions regarding the sending and receipt of postal articles, telexes, lettergrams and telegrams. There is no similar presumption regarding email. However, they do provide that:

> The hearsay rule does not apply to a representation contained in a document recording a message that has been transmitted by electronic mail or by a fax, telegram, lettergram or telex so far as the representation is a representation as to:
> • the identity of the person from whom or on whose behalf the message was sent; or
> • the date on which or the time at which the message was sent; or
> • the message's destination or the identity of the person to whom the message was addressed.

2 See Chapter 19.

Recently section 161, dealing with the facilitation of proof, was expanded to apply to electronic communications – this includes all modern electronic technologies as well as more outmoded ones such as facsimile and telex. The exception to the hearsay rule in section 71 was similarly expanded.[3] Courts increasingly need to be satisfied regarding the authenticity of transmissions. The Electronic Transactions Acts in the Commonwealth, states and territories were enacted to facilitate admission of electronic communications where they are functionally equivalent to traditional paper-based communications.[4]

Language

Several texts that discuss electronic communications emphasise the need to keep language formal. Grammar, syntax and an appreciation of the form of the medium involve customs which many of us take for granted. The use of language without careful consideration may have unintended and potentially disastrous consequences. However, email can be handled with such relative ease and speed that communications tend to become less formal, perhaps more akin to speaking in person or on the telephone. The parties may soon be involved in a conversation that involves an exchange of a dozen or so emails within a few minutes. The likelihood of carelessly making a glib or sarcastic or angry comment increases. Irony and sarcasm do not translate well on email; nor do they on any other form of written communications. Some people take care to make their intentions clear by writing the obvious '(just kidding)'. Others use smiley faces or other specialised images (called emoticons).

In any event, for all writing, it is important to be aware of the context and to consider how the written communication will appear when read by other parties, including a court.

Viruses

There are many myths and rumours about the dangers of catching a computer virus from email, particularly unsolicited email. Several of these rumours have been hoaxes. Most users have a rudimentary understanding of how data is transmitted by email and how it is read, interpreted and converted into meaningful text and files. Many have nonetheless decided to err on the side of caution.

The reality is that a virus cannot be contracted by simply opening an email message. However, they can be transmitted by attachments. As a general rule,

---

3 See *Evidence Amendment Act 2008* (Cth).
4 See Chapter 11 and Chapter 19.

users should only open attachments from persons they know, or sources which are regarded are secure.

Disclaimers

Disclaimers often appear at the end of emails. They are much more routinely included in emails than in standard mail. The reasons suggested for this vary. One is that the nature of email means that writers are often less formal and more unguarded than they would be with hardcopy mail. They reply and send without taking sufficient time to reflect, and they may not have as good a system of checks and balances as they have with standard mail. Another could be the fact that Norwich Union paid out £450000 to a competitor, Western Provident, for defamatory emails circulated by an employee. Defamation, unintended contract formation, misdirected emails, confidentiality, legal privilege, infringement of copyright, plus viruses, sexual and racial discrimination and harassment are just a few issues of concern addressed in disclaimers. Many are ignored by recipients, however, indicating their lack of effectiveness.[5]

Thus the value of these disclaimers is questionable. First, the courts will typically attach more weight to the substantive content of the email. There are occasions where a standard disclaimer is clearly inappropriate in relation to the actual content of the email. This occurs where the sender includes a standard, all-purpose disclaimer but does not address the reasons for its inclusion in the email in question.

Second, courts will look to the surrounding circumstances. This may include such factors as prior communications, the nature of the relationship (for example, whether or not it is contractual) and how prior disagreements were resolved. The High Court has expressed a 'commercial reality' view in relation to the balance between an attempt to limit proper warnings and to 'seduce consumers with attractive communications, unembarrassed by messages of restraint'.[6] Courts require written disclaimers to be 'clear, detailed and prominent':

> For centuries, lawyers have lamented the disinclination of their clients to read the fine print of documents. For a long time they have realised that it usually takes binding obligations of professional duty, a peculiar turn of mind and strong spectacles to combine in that result. Whatever they *should* do in theory, ordinary people cannot be converted to reading hidden messages contained in tiny print. It requires a large measure of judicial self-deception to say that the purchasers should have read the written disclaimers.[7]

5 *Hedley Byrne v Heller* [1964] AC 465 is a precedent on negligent misstatement. However, the judgment on that issue is strictly obiter as the defendant succeeded because of the inclusion of an effective disclaimer.
6 *Butcher v Lachlan Elder Realty Pty Ltd* [2004] HCA 60, para 216.
7 Ibid.

Importantly, the disclaimer may ward off legal action. A person contemplating legal action may think twice if an appropriately worded disclaimer was included in the transmission. The disclaimer may provide a useful argument in negotiations to resolve a dispute early and for a lower sum.

Generally, if in doubt, a disclaimer should be included, even though one of the greatest problems with disclaimers is the use of inappropriate ones. The writer should consider the purpose for which the email is sent and which areas require protection. There is a vast difference, for example, between commercial and personal emails. In a commercial context, there is a variety of concerns regarding legal liability: contractual or defamatory concerns, concerns regarding confidentiality, and concerns regarding accidental delivery to the wrong address.

Confidentiality

An express statement that a communication is confidential may well make the difference between its being treated as confidential or not. It could be argued that the notice may be ineffectual if it is in small print or placed after the sign-off at the end of the message. Prepending such notices (putting them at the start of a message) rather than appending them (at the end) may be useful.

Viruses

Many email writers include a disclaimer that they take no responsibility for checking for viruses: that responsibility falls on the recipient. Whether these disclaimers would be effective in court is questionable, but they may discourage disgruntled recipients from initiating a dispute.

Defamation

Employers have been held liable for defamatory statements made in emails by employees. A disclaimer will most likely not excuse the act where it is made in the ordinary course of business. Where it is not made in the ordinary course of business the disclaimer would not be needed. Nevertheless, adding a disclaimer may be a useful negotiation tactic in appropriate circumstances.

Copyright

A disclaimer would be unlikely to serve as a defence to a charge of breach of copyright. However, an appropriately worded disclaimer may indicate the level of care taken and the intention behind the transmission. Additionally, the disclaimer may resolve internal responsibilities and liabilities between employee and employer.

Negligent misstatement

By law, a person is obliged to take care when giving advice that a third party relies on. If an employee were to give professional advice in an email, the company will be liable for the effect of the advice that the recipient, or even a third party, reasonably relies upon. A suitably worded disclaimer could protect the sender and the sender's organisation from this kind of liability.

Accidental contract formation

A disclaimer could clearly set out the extent to which personnel have actual authority to bind the company or employer. The company should establish procedures to guard against such situations. However, the nature of email is that an immediate reply is more likely. Such a disclaimer may state: 'No employee or agent is authorised to conclude any binding agreement on behalf of this firm/company without the express written confirmation by a partner/director of the firm/company.'

Sexual and racial discrimination and harassment

Internal emails may give rise to claims of discrimination or harassment. Employees should be informed of the employer's policy and expected practice. Liability will depend upon whether the act was or was not in the course of business, and on factors such as the level of supervision and position and authority of the offending employee. A disclaimer on internal emails may put all parties on notice about the employer's policy and concerns.

Risk audit

Each organisation and individual should consider undertaking a risk audit on its email procedures and policies. The audit should determine who sends emails, their authority, how often emails are sent, whether there is a supervisory process or checking process, and how much time is allowed or available for reflection, thought and consideration before replying. Many employers may be surprised and disturbed at the use and misuse of email by employees. Once a risk audit has been completed, the organisation is in a much better position to prepare a policy or code of conduct and to determine the extent to which disclaimers ought to be used in their email system.

Service of documents by email

In the NSW Supreme Court case of *Macquarie Bank v Berg*[8] the plaintiff sought an order restraining the defendant, Berg, from publishing certain material on the

8 [1999] NSWSC 526, 1.

internet. The summons first came before BM James J, who abridged the time for service and directed that service be effected by delivering a copy of the documentation on the solicitors acting for the defendant in other proceedings between the parties, and by sending copies of the documents, marked for the attention of the defendant, to a specified email address.

Since that case New South Wales has amended its *Electronic Transactions Act 2000* by inserting Part 2A Court Administration. This Part established an Electronic Case Management (ECM) system to enable documents with respect to legal proceedings to be created, filed, issued, used and served in electronic form. For example, section 14M provides that any document filed in or issued by an ECM court by means of the ECM system may be served electronically. Other states and territories have made similar provisions in their equivalent statutes and regulations.

Time and place of dispatch and receipt

All nine jurisdictions in Australia have enacted an Electronic Transactions Act that includes a provision regarding the time and place of dispatch and receipt of electronic communications.[9] Electronic communication includes emails, facsimiles, SMS and instant messaging.[10]

Time of dispatch

Unless otherwise agreed, the dispatch of the electronic communication occurs when it leaves the control of the originator, or, if it has not left the control of the originator, when it is received.[11]

Time of receipt

If the recipient of an electronic communication has designated an information system for the purpose of receiving electronic communications then, unless otherwise agreed, the time of receipt is the time when it is capable of being retrieved. The designation of an information system may be by prior conduct, prior email use, or by including the email address in correspondence, such as a letterhead or a business card. If the recipient has not designated such an information system then, unless otherwise agreed, the time of receipt is the time when the electronic communication has become capable of being retrieved and the addressee becomes aware that it has been sent to that address.[12]

---

9 The provisions are examined in detail in Chapter 12.
10 Electronic Transactions Acts – NSW s13; Cth – s14; Qld – s23; SA – s13; Tas – s11; Vic – s13; WA – s13; ACT – s13; NT – s13.
11 Ibid.
12 Ibid., NSW s13A; Cth – s14A; Qld – s24; SA – s13A; Tas – s11A; Vic – s13A; WA – s14; ACT – s13A; NT – s13A.

Place of dispatch and receipt

Unless otherwise agreed, the electronic communication is taken to have been dispatched at the place where the sender has its place of business, and is taken to have been received at the place where the recipient has its place of business. If the sender or recipient has more than one place of business, and one of those places has a closer relationship to the underlying transaction, it is to be assumed that that place of business is the only place of business. If the sender or recipient has more than one place of business, but it cannot be determined which has a closer relationship to the underlying transaction, then it is assumed that the principal place of business is the only place of business. If the sender or recipient does not have a place of business, it is assumed that the place of business is the place where the sender or recipient ordinarily resides.[13]

Web page presence

All forms of business have taken hold of internet technology, many just in order to have simpler and speedier communication. Others have created web pages. Some use the pages in a simple static way. That is, they provide a simple electronic brochure. This form of advertising is cheap and continuous. For a modest fee, often included in the price of connection, the user may have allocated internet space to place a number of web pages with text, graphics and links. The pages may be updated at any time, and the material is available to all 24 hours a day.

Alternatively, the business may produce dynamic web pages. These are pages where potential consumers may interact with the host by placing orders and making inquiries; the pages can act as an online store.

Some issues faced by the host in the design of the website are technical and practical. However, there are many legal concerns as well.

As most of those who want a website lack the expertise to develop one, they generally seek the services of a web developer. A contract with a web designer should include provisions dealing with:

- intellectual property aspects of the content, structure, graphics, domain names and computer and web code;
- the product delivered – the content, plus information on compatibility, and functionality and performance criteria;
- the degree of subcontracting, including rights between the head contractor and the subcontractors;

---

13 Ibid., NSW s13B; Cth – s14B; Qld – s25; SA – s13B; Tas – s11B; Vic – s13B; WA – s15; ACT – s13B; NT – s13B.

- the marketing strategy – including the steps to be taken to place the page/s on the most appropriate search engines and the strategy for indexing by search engines, such as the placement of key terms in the web pages and in meta tags (HTML is searched and indexed by the search engines – called Search Engine Optimisation);
- maintenance and future amendments; and
- indemnities.

Liability for online material

Misleading and deceptive conduct

Online businesses are liable for material and information that is misleading and deceptive within the meaning of laws such as the Australian Consumer Law (ACL) and the Fair Trading Acts of the states and territories. These laws apply to statements and representations made on web pages just as they do to hardcopy advertisements and brochures. The nature of a web page means that it is a continuing publication.[14] Steps should be taken to ensure that information remains current, accurate and correct. In particular, note the application of ACL sections 18 and 29:

18 Misleading or deceptive conduct

(1) A person must not, in trade or commerce, engage in conduct that is misleading or deceptive or is likely to mislead or deceive.

29 False or misleading representations about goods or services

A person must not, in trade or commerce, in connection with the supply or possible supply of goods or services or in connection with the promotion by any means of the supply or use of goods or services:

(a) make a false or misleading representation that goods are of a particular standard, quality, value, grade, composition, style or model or have had a particular history or particular previous use; or

(b) make a false or misleading representation that services are of a particular standard, quality, value or grade; or

(c) make a false or misleading representation that goods are new; or

---

14 For example, in 2000 the Dow Chemical Co. audited their employees' usage. This led to the dismissal of 24 employees and the disciplining of 230 others for engaging in inappropriate email messaging: <archives.cnn.com/2000/TECH/computing/09/19/dow.firing.idg/index.html>.

(d) make a false or misleading representation that a particular person has agreed to acquire goods or services; or

(e) make a false or misleading representation that purports to be a testimonial by any person relating to goods or services; or

(f) make a false or misleading representation concerning:

    (i) a testimonial by any person; or

    (ii) a representation that purports to be such a testimonial; relating to goods or services; or

(g) make a false or misleading representation that goods or services have sponsorship, approval, performance characteristics, accessories, uses or benefits; or

(h) make a false or misleading representation that the person making the representation has a sponsorship, approval or affiliation; or

(i) make a false or misleading representation with respect to the price of goods or services; or

(j) make a false or misleading representation concerning the availability of facilities for the repair of goods or of spare parts for goods; or

(k) make a false or misleading representation concerning the place of origin of goods; or

(l) make a false or misleading representation concerning the need for any goods or services; or

(m) make a false or misleading representation concerning the existence, exclusion or effect of any condition, warranty, guarantee, right or remedy (including a guarantee under Division 1 of Part 3–2); or

(n) make a false or misleading representation concerning a requirement to pay for a contractual right that:

    (i) is wholly or partly equivalent to any condition, warranty, guarantee, right or remedy (including a guarantee under Division 1 of Part 3–2); and

    (ii) a person has under a law of the Commonwealth, a State or a Territory (other than an unwritten law).[15]

Where a person becomes aware that information, such as testimonials, posted on social media is in fact misleading and deceptive, liability attaches. In an action commenced by the Australian Competition and Consumer Commission (ACCC), the Federal Court accepted a company's undertaking to remedy its breaches, and subsequently found the respondent guilty of contempt for its failure to comply.[16]

The High Court noted in *Google v ACCC* that the displaying of an advertisement online is capable of being misleading or deceptive:

---

15 Australian Consumer Law.
16 *ACCC v Allergy Pathway Pty Ltd* [2011] FCA 74.

Displaying the advertisement to those people may lead them into error. Whether it is likely to mislead or deceive depends upon how the ordinary or reasonable member of the class of persons to whom the publication was directed would understand what was published.[17]

Defamation

Statements made online – by web pages or email – are of course subject to defamation laws. Indeed, web pages often have a great potential for being viewed than hardcopy material, as they are continuing publications.[18]

Disclaimers – conditions of use

Before proceeding to the main pages, some sites require the user to click a button titled 'I agree' which follows 'terms and conditions of use'. The courts have held that users are bound by such 'agreements'.[19] Some sites place less obvious links to their terms and disclaimers.[20] All users (including website designers and administrators) need to understand the significance of such notices and to balance legal considerations with practical and aesthetic considerations.

Linking and framing

Some US actions have been taken where the host site includes an 'unauthorised' link to another website. The plaintiffs' concerns have included the fact that links sometimes bypass the 'home page', thus avoiding security, implementation of cookies, tracking techniques and stated terms and disclaimers. Some sites place a 'frame' around other sites, giving the appearance that the 'framed' site is the creation of the host site.[21] The liability for such framing is yet to be ironed out by the courts. However, misleading and deceptive conduct provisions such as ACL section 18 have been applied broadly. Many websites are directed to the general public, which the courts have described as 'the knowledgeable and those who are not, the superficial reader ... as well as the profound, the gullible as well as the cautious'.[22] Actions may also be based on the tort of passing off.

17 [2013] HCA 1, para 118, per Hayne J.
18 See Chapter 7.
19 See Chapter 12.
20 See Disclaimers, above.
21 See Chapters 14 and 15.
22 See *World Series Cricket Pty Ltd v Parish* (1977) 16 ALR 181.

Information to be placed on pages for practical and legal purposes

Other sites may link not to the host's opening page but to some interesting feature in the middle of the pages. Users need to find their way out of this situation. Consideration should be given to placing certain essential information on every web page as part of the page template. Design considerations should be not only aesthetically pleasing, for marketing purposes, but also practical in terms of liability. The use of headers, footers and frames is a way to provide fundamental information, such as a privacy policy and disclaimers, on every page of a website. Including the date of revision in such features tells users how current the information on the web pages is. Although one of the advantages of websites is that they can be updated quickly, one of the dangers is that users rely on them for current information when the page may not in fact have been altered recently. Many legal researchers cite the date they visited web pages for this very reason. Many law firms provide online legal bulletins to the general public. A statement placed online regarding the law may quickly be obsolete. With a time stamp, members of the public can be sure that they may rely on the advice; in the end, this will be an advantage to the host.

Backup copies

Before photocopying, carbon copies were often kept. For electronic documents and records, legal offices must have in place a system of creating and maintaining backup copies. In many jurisdictions it is vital to retain the electronic version: evidentiary rules may exclude a printout of an email, or a scanned copy of paper documents.[23]

Maintain supervisory checks

Some organisations have procedures for the checking of all forms of mail by supervisors before sending. It is too easy to write emails and press the send button, so electronic gateways may need to be put in place by systems programmers.

Confidentiality

Email has a range of potential security problems. Confidentiality is often extremely important. As a parallel, when facsimiles are used, it is usually prudent to ask the

---

23 For example, the secondary evidence rule applies in Queensland, South Australia and Western Australia; see Chapter 19.

recipient in advance if sensitive information may be sent by that medium. In certain cases the recipient may wish to know when the facsimile is being sent so that he or she may be on hand to receive it to ensure privacy and confidentiality. It would be prudent to prepare a standard message regarding the risks of email and obtain the recipient's written consent before sending sensitive information electronically. Where appropriate, the recipient may agree to the use of an encryption program as added security.[24]

Confirmation of sending

One continuing problem with email is determining whether a particular email has been delivered and read. This problem existed with standard mail and facsimiles as well. Some email programs claim to have a facility that will send a message to the sender when the email was received, and again when it has been read. However, such facilities are dependent on the mail systems and protocols used by the other party or the mail path. The most certain method of reassurance is to ask the recipient – even insist, in appropriate situations – to send a reply that is as short as 'Received', and that includes a copy of the original email. Most email systems allow the user to reply, either with or without the body of the received message in the reply. It may be worthwhile to adopt a policy of sending confirmations and requesting confirmations from recipients.

Conclusion

Just as each organisation maintains procedures in relation to the dispatch and receipt of mail and instant messaging, each organisation must also determine its policies on email; this is preferable to defending legal proceedings because of a failure to do so.

Email and other forms of electronic communication are replacing the traditional formal letter. Commercial expediency will win out. With this comes several challenges. Many commercial parties have jumped into electronic commerce with little consideration of the legal consequences. This too is not new. Commercial parties forged ahead in centuries past without law that dealt with their actions, and the result was the *lex mercatoria*, a reactive body of law. Electronic communicators must be aware of the current laws that affect their actions, and they must set up systems to validate their documents in terms of the place of dispatch and receipt, the timing of dispatch and receipt, the admissibility (in evidentiary terms) of the email and

---

24 For a common public example, see PGP: <www.pgpi.com>.

attachments sent. Disclaimers can be effective, but should be drafted with care; they may need to be specific to particular uses.

FURTHER READING

Alan Davidson, 'Email disclaimers', 2002 *Proctor* 39.

Alan Davidson, 'Email and documents', (2004) 26 *South Australian Law Bulletin* 19.

Matthew Nied, 'Clicking away privacy: Email and the tort of intrusion upon seclusion', (2014) 17(9) *Journal of Internet Law* 3.

10

CENSORSHIP ONLINE

The Australian Communications and Media Authority (ACMA) is responsible for administering legislation regarding the content and regulation of most forms of electronic communications. This chapter deals with the role of ACMA and the regulation of internet, television and radio communications.

The Australian Communications and Media Authority

ACMA is responsible for the regulation of broadcasting, radio communications, telecommunications and online content. Its responsibilities include:

- promoting self-regulation and competition in the telecommunications industry, while protecting consumers and other users;
- fostering an environment in which electronic media respect community standards and responds to audience and user needs;
- managing access to the radiofrequency spectrum, including the broadcasting services bands; and
- representing Australia's communications and broadcasting interests internationally.[1]

The internet

ACMA administers the scheme for dealing with content on the internet, enforces Australia's anti-spam law and can make rules about accessing the internet via premium mobile phone services.

Online content regulation is established under Schedules 5 and 7 of the *Broadcasting Services Act 1992* (Cth), which deal with offensive and illegal material on the internet and the protection of children from exposure to material that is unsuitable. The Act gives ACMA the following functions:

- investigation of complaints about Internet content and Internet gambling services;
- encouraging development of codes of practice for the Internet industry, registering, and monitoring compliance with such codes;
- providing advice and information to the community about Internet safety issues, especially those relating to children's use of the Internet;
- undertaking research into Internet usage issues and informing itself and the Minister of relevant trends;
- liaising with relevant overseas bodies.[2]

---

1 See the ACMA website: <www.acma.gov.au>.
2 Ibid.

The *Spam Act 2003* (Cth) bans the sending of unsolicited electronic messages, including email and SMS, and the harvesting of email addresses.

Consumers

Consumer codes are registered by ACMA, making them enforceable. ACMA monitors compliance and the strategies used to raise consumer awareness of the codes.

ACMA monitors and reports on the performance of telecommunications service providers against the timeframes for the provision and repair of the standard telephone service specified in the Customer Service Guarantee. It also administers the Universal Service Obligation (USO), which ensures that all people in Australia, no matter where they live or carry on business, have reasonable access to a standard telephone service, payphones, prescribed carriage services and digital data services.

ACMA raises community awareness about communications and consumer safeguards. There is a range of ACMA information products and campaigns, including widely used toolkits about mobile phone, fixed phone and internet services.

ACMA administers complaint schemes for radio, television and internet content and is responsible for ensuring that carriers and eligible carriage service providers, including internet service providers (ISPs), join the Telecommunications Industry Ombudsman (TIO) scheme. One of the TIO's main roles is to investigate complaints made against its members.

Industry

ACMA works with industry, through the regulatory framework, to foster self-regulation, provide benefits to users, readily accommodate technological change and contribute to an efficient and internationally competitive communications sector.

Internet content

Various degrees of censorship and restriction apply to television, radio, books, newspapers and films. However, any user of the internet knows that material that breaches those standards is available online.

The internet contains the most splendid educational and cultural material. It also contains offensive and disgraceful material. Internationally there is divergence of opinion regarding appropriate standards in cultural areas such as dress, literature and films. There is, however, consensus regarding the repugnance of the portrayal of actual extreme violence and child pornography. But there remains disagreement in relation to the age of a 'child', the upper limit of which varies from 12 to 21. According to Article 1 of the UN Convention on the Rights of the Child, 'child' refers to a person under 18 years of age. There are also disagreements as to the meaning of 'violence', 'offensive' and 'indecent'.[3]

No matter what one's definition is, though, there is consensus on the fact that offensive material is available on the internet. But keeping track of what is available is almost impossible for any government or organisation – Google, for example, has indexed more than one trillion web pages.

Some countries have made attempts to control specific kinds of offensive internet sites. German courts and legislators have sought to extend anti-Nazi law to other jurisdictions to restrict web-based Holocaust deniers. Similarly, France has pressured eBay and Yahoo to limit the sale of Nazi memorabilia. In Turkey the office of an ISP was demolished when it was found to have allowed images of women with uncovered arms and faces.

ABC (US) journalist Michael Malone wrote about child pornography:

> This is the very heart of darkness. These are images that are more than shocking and repulsive. They kill your soul, in part because you know that every poor child you see on these sites is dead, if not now at the hands of a sadist, then decades from now from drugs, alcoholism or suicide. The pictures first make you sick, then angry, and finally homicidal … There were already certain unspeakable images so burned into my brain that, even now, I wish I could take a scalpel and cut them out.[4]

Studies suggest that a majority of internet users have at some stage visited websites that may be regarded as pornographic: some suggest that 5–24 per cent of overall internet usage is spent accessing pornographic sites.[5] The figures vary according to the nature and type of survey, but with more than a trillion web pages, even the conservative figure yields several billion pages.

US cases

Reno v American Civil Liberties Union

The Clinton Administration recognised the potential danger of the booming internet pornography business and enacted the *Communications Decency Act 1996*

---

3 For example, see <www.ageofconsent.com/ageofconsent.htm>.
4 Michael Malone, 'Silicon insider. Dark world of child porn,' (2002) ABCNews.com.
5 See <www.eff.org>.

(US).[6] However, in *Reno v American Civil Liberties Union*,[7] the US Supreme Court regarded the definitions of 'indecent' and 'patently offensive' as vague and broad, and struck down most of the Act as unconstitutional. This case is the most significant in terms of pornography on the internet because it removed incentives for policing or enforcement of laws against pornography online. However, it is also true that such material could, both before and after the case, be hosted offshore.

US v American Library Association

In June 2003 the US Supreme Court, in *US v American Library Association*, held that anti-pornography filtering does not violate free speech rights. Congress can require public libraries that receive federal funds to provide public internet access to install filters. Chief Justice Rehnquist stated:

> Internet terminals are not acquired by a library in order to create a public forum for Web publishers to express themselves. Rather, a library provides such access for the same reasons it offers other library resources: to facilitate research, learning and recreational pursuits by furnishing materials of requisite and appropriate quality ... The decisions by most libraries to exclude pornography from their print collections are not subject to heightened scrutiny; it would make little sense to treat libraries' judgments to block online pornography differently.[8]

The decision gives US legislators the power to control the billion-dollar industry which internet pornography has become since the decision in *Reno v American Civil Liberties Union*. The negative result may be the limits on the extent to which members of the public may be able to access legitimate internet content. Justice Breyer stated that web surfers can ask librarians to disable filters to access a particular site, but counsel argued that even people undertaking legitimate research will not ask a librarian to turn off the anti-pornography filter. One witness, Dr Bertman, who maintained a medical site, expressed concern that young persons with sexually transmitted diseases may have their access to legitimate sites curtailed. The Bush Administration argued that federally funded libraries do not include X-rated movies and magazines, so they should be permitted to filter out such online material: this sets them up as an exception to the Reno case, with some control over such material returned to them.

---

6 *Communications Decency Act 1996* (US) (CDA).
7 521 US 844 (1997). Janet Reno was the Attorney General for the Clinton Administration.
8 539 US 194 (2003), 195.

Australia

Internet content has been the jurisdiction of ACMA[9] since January 2000. The *Communications Legislation Amendment (Content Services) Act 2007* (Cth) inserted Schedule 7 into the *Broadcasting Services Act 1992* (Cth) for the purpose of regulating all content delivered via carriage services, irrespective of the platform, and whether they consist of user-generated content or otherwise. Schedule 7 commenced on 20 January 2008. In developing the new content rules, ACMA stated that it was 'guided by its disposition to allow adults to continue to read, hear and see what they want, while protecting children from exposure to inappropriate content, regardless of the delivery mechanism'.[10]

The provisions are similar to the previous obligations relating to stored content. The rules provide that after receiving a complaint and investigating internet or mobile content, ACMA may require the content service provider to either remove the content or place the content behind specified access restrictions.

Under Schedule 7 the following categories of online content are prohibited content:

- any online content that is classified RC or X18+ by the Classification Board (formerly the Office of Film and Literature Classification). This includes real depictions of actual sexual activity, child pornography, depictions of bestiality, material containing excessive violence or sexual violence, detailed instruction in crime, violence or drug use, and/or material that advocates the doing of a terrorist act;
- content which is classified R18+ and not subject to a restricted access system that prevents access by children. This includes depictions of simulated sexual activity, material containing strong, realistic violence and other material dealing with intense adult themes; and
- content which is classified MA15+, that is provided by a mobile premium service or a service that provides audio or video content upon payment of a fee, and that is not subject to a restricted access system. This includes material containing strong depictions of nudity, implied sexual activity, drug use or violence, very frequent or very strong coarse language, and other material that is strong in impact.[11]

Where content has not been classified by the Classification Board, but if it were to be classified, there is a substantial likelihood that it would be prohibited content, it is defined as potential prohibited content, and the rules applying to prohibited content apply.

---

9 At the time it was known as the Australian Broadcasting Authority (ABA).

10 ACMA Chair Chris Chapman, <www.acma.org.au>.

11 Classifications are based on criteria outlined in the *Classification (Publications, Films and Computer Games) Act 1995* (Cth), National Classification Code and the Guidelines for the Classification of Films and Computer Games 2005.

In addition, Schedule 7 regulates for:

- providers of hosting services, live content services, link services and commercial content services to have in place access restrictions if providing R18+ and commercial MA15+ content;
- 'take-down', 'service cessation' and 'link deletion' notices to remove content or access to content that is the subject of a complaint; and
- a co-regulatory approach that provides for the development of industry codes to address issues including the classification of content, procedures for handling complaints about content and increasing awareness of potential safety issues associated with the use of content services.[12]

Mobile premium services including premium rate SMS and MMS[13] services and mobile content portals are regulated under the *Telecommunications Service Provider (Mobile Premium Services) Determination 2010 (No. 1)* (Cth), under subsection 99(1) of the *Telecommunications Act 1997* (Cth). A mobile carriage service provider must not supply content classified as MA15+ or R18+ to a customer unless the customer has requested access and has been verified as at least 18 years old. Content classified as MA15+ or R18+ must not be supplied by premium SMS or MMS services otherwise than on a number with a listed prefix.

Schedule 7 of the *Broadcasting Services Act 1992* (Cth) requires ACMA to develop a new restricted access systems declaration to regulate access to MA15+ content and R18+ content with an Australian connection, amend the mobile premium services determination to remove the access restrictions and designated prefix requirements that are made redundant by Schedule 7 and vary the Telecommunications Numbering Plan 1997 to allow the transfer of the designated prefix requirements from the mobile premium services determination.

'Content service' is defined as '(a) a service that delivers content to persons having equipment appropriate for receiving that content, where the delivery of the service is by means of a carriage service; or (b) a service that allows end-users to access content using a carriage service'.[14]

Referral to law enforcement agencies

If, in the course of an investigation, ACMA is satisfied that content is prohibited content or potential prohibited content and is of a sufficiently serious nature to warrant referral to a law enforcement agency, ACMA must notify a member of an

---

12 Internet content was previously regulated under the Restricted Access Systems Declaration 1999 under clause 4(1) of Schedule 5 to the *Broadcasting Services Act 1992* (Cth).
13 SMS is short for Short Message Service and MMS is short for Multimedia Message Service.
14 *Broadcasting Services Act 1992* (Cth) Schedule 7, cl2.

Australian police force. 'Sufficiently serious nature' is not defined, but would include evidence of child pornography or the commission of a crime such as sexual assault or common assault.

Take-down notices

If ACMA is satisfied that content hosted by a 'hosting service provider' is prohibited content and an Australian connection exists, and if the content has been classified RC or X18+, or R18+ or MA15+ (without a restricted access system in place) by the Classification Board, ACMA must give the hosting service provider a written final take-down notice.[15] ACMA can declare that a specified access control system is a restricted access system in relation to content for the purposes of Schedule 7.[16] Eligible electronic publications are exempt. Where:

(a) content consists of:
  (i) an electronic edition of a book, magazine or newspaper; or
  (ii) an audio recording of the text, or abridged text, of a book, magazine or newspaper; and
(b) a print edition of the book, magazine or newspaper is or was available to the public ... in Australia; then:
(c) the content is an *eligible electronic publication*.[17]

If the content is not classified and ACMA is satisfied that, if the content were to be classified by the Classification Board, there is a substantial likelihood that the content would be classified RC or X18+, or R18+ or MA15+ (without a restricted access system in place), ACMA must issue an interim take-down notice. ACMA must then apply to the Classification Board to have the content classified, and depending upon the classification, withdraw the notice or issue a final take-down notice.[18]

Service-cessation notices

If ACMA is satisfied that content hosted by a live content service provider is prohibited content and the service provider has an Australian connection, and if the content has been classified RC or X18+, or R18+ or MA15+ (without a restricted access system in place) by the Classification Board, ACMA must give the live content service a written service cessation notice.[19] Again, eligible electronic publications are exempt.

---

15 *Broadcasting Services Act 1992* (Cth) Schedule 7, cl47(1).
16 *Broadcasting Services Act 1992* (Cth) Schedule 7, cl14.
17 *Broadcasting Services Act 1992* (Cth) Schedule 7, cl11.
18 *Broadcasting Services Act 1992* (Cth) Schedule 7, cl47(2).
19 *Broadcasting Services Act 1992* (Cth) Schedule 7, cl56(1) .

If the content is not classified and ACMA is satisfied that if the content were to be classified by the Classification Board there is a substantial likelihood that the content would be classified RC or X18+, or R18+ or MA15+ (without a restricted access system in place), ACMA must issue an interim service-cessation notice. ACMA must then apply to the Classification Board to have the content classified, and depending upon the classification, withdraw the notice or issue a final service-cessation notice.[20]

Link deletion notices

If ACMA is satisfied that 'users in Australia can access content using a link provided by a links service', that 'the content is prohibited content and the links service has an Australian connection', and if the content has been classified RC or X18+, or R18+ or MA15+ (without a restricted access system in place), by the Classification Board, ACMA must give the hosting service provider a written final link deletion notice.[21] Eligible electronic publications are exempt.

If the content is not classified and ACMA is satisfied that if the content were to be classified by the Classification Board there is a substantial likelihood that the content would be classified RC or X 18+, or R18+ or MA15+ (without a restricted access system in place), ACMA must issue an interim link-deletion notice. ACMA must then apply to the Classification Board to have the content classified, and depending upon the classification, withdraw the notice or issue a final link deletion notice.[22]

Industry codes

Schedule 7 encourages bodies and associations that represent sections of the internet industry to develop industry codes. A Code of Practice drafted by the Australian Internet Industry Association (IIA)[23] has been accepted as the legislative guideline for ISPs, content providers and internet users. While the Code is not mandatory, Schedule 7 makes provision for ACMA to direct an ISP or content host to comply with a registered code.

Complaints and investigations

Complaints regarding prohibited and potential prohibited content may be lodged with ACMA.[24] ACMA is required to act on all complaints unless satisfied that the

---

20 *Broadcasting Services Act 1992* (Cth) Schedule 7, cl56(2).
21 *Broadcasting Services Act 1992* (Cth) Schedule 7, cl62(1).
22 *Broadcasting Services Act 1992* (Cth) Schedule 7, cl62(2).
23 See <www.commsalliance.com.au/__data/assets/pdf_file/0020/44606/content_services_code_registration_version_1_0.pdf>.
24 See generally *Broadcasting Services Act 1992* (Cth) Schedule 7, Part 3.

complaint is frivolous, vexatious or not made in good faith.[25] ACMA may also initiate investigations.

RC or X classifications include:

- material containing detailed instruction in crime, violence or drug use;
- child pornography;
- bestiality;
- excessively violent or sexually violent material; and
- real depictions of actual sexual activity.[26]

R classification includes:

- material containing excessive and/or strong violence or sexual violence;
- material containing implied or simulated sexual activity;
- material which deals with issues or contains depictions which require an adult perspective.[27]

Conclusion

Many content providers and hosts have little understanding of censorship law or of classification. The distinctions between classifications are intricate and difficult to ascertain, even for trained censors. This is one reason why the fee for classification is substantial and generally prohibitive. Content providers and hosts are not likely to be able to afford multiple applications. ACMA can request classification in response to a complaint, but not upon the request of a concerned content provider.

Some content providers and businesses use offshore service providers rather than risk dealing with Australian law and ACMA. The provisions in respect of offshore content regulation are unworkable.[28]

Given the global nature of the internet and online services, the scheme set up pursuant to Schedules 5 and 7 of the *Broadcasting Services Act 1992* (Cth) is largely a toothless tiger. Take-down notices, cessation service notices and link deletion notices will have an impact on Australian content, but most complaints made to ACMA are in relation to overseas content.[29] The result of decisions such as *Reno v ACLU* is that the law makers of nations such as the United States are powerless to enact controlling legislation. The international response is stalemated.

25 *Broadcasting Services Act 1992* (Cth) Schedule 7, cl43.
26 See the Classification Board's website: <www.classification.gov.au>.
27 Ibid.
28 See *Broadcasting Services Act 1992* (Cth) Schedule 5.
29 See <www.acma.gov.au>.

ACMA plays a significant role in administering, investigating and reporting on many forms of electronic communications. In relation to mass forms of communications – television and radio – in Australia, its responsibility is substantial, but in many respects the tools provided by the legislature are inadequate.

Perhaps more crucially, while the online content provisions of Australian legislation may reduce prohibited content that originates within Australia, they have no real impact on the amount of unclassified material reaching Australian users. This means that in the global context ACMA's effectiveness is limited. Cyberspace libertarians support this freedom of information flow, but the opposing view asks: at what cost?

FURTHER READING

Electronic Frontiers Australia, *Internet censorship laws in Australia*: <www.efa.org.au/Issues/ Censor/cens1.html>.

PART

3

ELECTRONIC COMMERCE

11

ELECTRONIC COMMERCE AND THE LAW OF CONTRACT

Commerce is typically about profit. It also always involves risk. Risk assessment in commerce involves consideration of such factors as the law of contracts, the parties, the goods or services and the legal forum. Many commercial parties have braved the new electronic commerce world without knowing or understanding the legal implications of their actions. In many instances commercial parties have embraced electronic commerce because of its efficiencies, and thus profits. A new order is emerging in this world in a manner not dissimilar to the onset of *lex mercatoria*.[1]

In an attempt to ensure confidence, many international organisations have proposed treaties, model laws and protocols to encourage certainty and stability for international electronic commercial practices and in relation to laws of contract.[2] The *UNCITRAL Model Law on Electronic Commerce* (Model Law) has proved the most popular, with significant international acceptance by national legislatures, including those of Australia and New Zealand. More recently the UN passed the *Convention on the Use of Electronic Communications in International Contracts*.[3]

This chapter addresses the regulation of, and legislative responses to, electronic contracting. It challenges the wisdom of and necessity for legislation based on the Model Law, and the introduction of the concept of consent as a precondition for the application of selected legislative provisions. This chapter does not deal with the basic principles of contract law; they are dealt with most satisfactorily in many texts.

UNCITRAL Model Law on Electronic Commerce and the Communications Convention

In 1996 the UN Commission on International Law Trade (UNCITRAL) released what is now the most popular model for consumer and commercial protection in

---

1 See Chapters 1 and 2.
2 These organisations have included the Organisation for Economic Cooperation and Development (OECD) <www.oecd.org/development/electroniccommerce.htm>; the United Nations; the Asia-Pacific Economic Cooperation forum (APEC) <www.apec.org>; the International Chamber of Commerce (ICC) <www.iccwbo.org>; the World Trade Organization (WTO) <www.wto.org/english/tratop_e/ecom_e/ecom_e.htm>; and the UN Commission on International Trade Law (UNCITRAL) <www.uncitral.org>.
3 The Convention entered into force on 1 March 2013.

an electronic environment. The *UNCITRAL Model Law on Electronic Commerce*[4] (Model Law) was intended to provide national legislatures with a template of internationally acceptable rules that would remove legal obstacles and create a more secure legal environment for electronic commerce. The Model Law was intended to facilitate the use of electronic communication and the digital storage of information. It provided standard ways to assess the legal value of electronic messages and legal rules for electronic commerce in specific areas such as carriage of goods.

The Model Law has gained significant international acceptance.[5] The drafting process was attended by representatives of over 50 nations and 10 international organisations.

The Model Law does not specifically refer to contract law. Instead it deals with the principle of functional equivalence of electronic media in commercial transactions.[6] That is, where the electronic form is functionally equivalent to the traditional form, it should be treated equally by the law. This principle permeates all legislation based on the Model Law. A second principle underlying the Model Law is that of technology neutrality (the term was chosen in response to the recognition that technology is constantly developing). For example, as 'electronic mail' connotes a certain medium, the Model Law uses the general expression 'data message'.

The Model Law addresses:

- legal recognition of data messages;
- writing;
- signatures;
- originals;
- admissibility and evidentiary weight of data messages;

---

4 *UNCITRAL Model Law on Electronic Commerce*, GA Res 51/162 (16 December 1996). Available at <www.uncitral.org/uncitral/en/uncitral_texts/electronic_commerce/1996Model.html>.

5 Legislation implementing provisions of, or influenced by, the Model Law has been adopted in Australia 1999, Bahrain 2002, Bangladesh 2006, Barbados 2001, Belize 2003, Brunei Darussalam 2000, Cabo Verde 2003, Canada 2000, China 2004, Hong Kong 2000, Macao 2005, Colombia 1999, Dominican Republic 2002, Ecuador 2002, Fiji 2008, France 2000, Gambia 2009, Ghana 2008, Grenada 2008, Guatemala 2008, India 2000, Iran 2004, Ireland 2000, Jamaica 2006, Jordan 2001, Lao People's Democratic Republic 2012, Liberia 2002, Malaysia 2006, Mauritius 2000, Mexico 2000, New Zealand 2002, Oman 2008, Pakistan 2002, Panama 2001, Paraguay 2010, Philippines 2000, Qatar 2010, Republic of Korea 1999, Rwanda 2010, Saint Kitts and Nevis 2011, Saint Lucia 2011, Saint Vincent and the Grenadines 2007, Samoa 2008, San Marino 2013, Saudi Arabia 2007, Seychelles 2001, Singapore 2010, Slovenia 2000, South Africa 2002, Sri Lanka 2006, Syrian Arab Republic 2014, Thailand 2002, Trinidad and Tobago 2011, United Arab Emirates 2006, United Kingdom of Great Britain and Northern Ireland 1999, United States of America 1998, Vanuatu 2000, Venezuela 2001, Vietnam 2005 and Zambia 2009. See <www.uncitral.org>.

6 See (2007) *Official Guide to Enactment of the UNCITRAL Model Law on Electronic Commerce*, (2007), paragraph 15 : <www.uncitral.org/pdf/english/texts/electcom/05-89450_Ebook.pdf>.

- retention of data messages;
- formation and validity of contracts;
- recognition by parties of data messages;
- attribution of data messages;
- acknowledgment of receipt; and
- time and place of dispatch and receipt of data messages.[7]

The Model Law represented a giant step forward in relation to the regulation of electronic commerce and largely achieved its objectives of removing legal obstacles, promoting certainty, providing a more secure legal electronic commerce environment and being 'of use to individual users of electronic commerce in the drafting of some of the contractual solutions that might be needed to overcome the legal obstacles'.[8] Nevertheless, the Model Law represents 1990s thinking and reflects the limited understanding of the issues at that time. It has become dated with the advent of newer technology and the even greater uptake of that technology. More significantly, case law has closely scrutinised the provisions and revealed flaws.

In 2005 UNCITRAL released the *Convention on the Use of Electronic Communications in International Contracts (Communications Convention)*.[9] The Communications Convention is intended to assure companies and traders internationally that contracts negotiated electronically are as valid and enforceable as traditional paper-based transactions. The provisions build on the Model Law and the UNCITRAL Model Law on Electronic Signatures (2001).[10] The Communications Convention made the following improvements:

- extended definitions;
- improved the test for an electronic signature;
- reformulated the test for time of dispatch and time of receipt; and
- introduced provisions applying to contracts involving electronic communications, invitation to make offers, use of automated message systems for contract formation and errors in electronic communications.

To date the *Communications Convention* has been signed by many nations and ratified by seven.[11] Australia has stated that it will ratify the *Convention*.

7 See Model Law, arts 5 to 15.
8 See UNCITRAL, above n 6, para 2.
9 Available at <www.uncitral.org/pdf/english/texts/electcom/06-57452_Ebook.pdf>.
10 Available at <www.uncitral.org/pdf/english/texts/electcom/ml-elecsig-e.pdf>. The *Model Law on Electronic Signatures* has not achieved the same level of acceptance as the *Model Law on Electronic Commerce*. Nevertheless, its principles and deliberations have influenced the *Communications Convention*.
11 Montenegro, Sri Lanka, Congo, Dominican Republic, Honduras, Russian Federation and Singapore. For an up-to-date list, see <www.uncitral.org/uncitral/en/uncitral_texts/electronic_commerce/2005Convention_status.html>.

Australia

All Australian states and territories and the Commonwealth have passed amending legislation to conform to the *Communications Convention*. In 2010 the Attorneys-General of the Commonwealth, states and territories agreed to amend their respective Electronic Transactions Acts, following which the Commonwealth government stated that it will accede to the *Convention*. However, to date this has not taken place.

The *Electronic Transactions Act 1999* (Cth) is based on the Model Law and was amended in 2011 to adopt the terms of the *Communications Convention*. All Australian states and territories have enacted parallel legislation.[12] The Federal Attorney General stated that the 'enactment of the uniform Bill will achieve the Commonwealth's goal of national uniform legislation to remove the legal impediments facing electronic transactions'.[13] The stated objects within the Act are to provide a regulatory framework that:

- recognises the importance of the information economy to the future economic and social prosperity of Australia; and
- facilitates the use of electronic transactions; and
- promotes business and community confidence in the use of electronic transactions; and
- enables business and the community to use electronic communications in their dealings with government.[14]

Background to the Australian legislation

In 1997 the Wallis Report on the financial industry in Australia recognised the need 'to adopt appropriate internationally recognised standards for electronic commerce, including for electronic transactions over the Internet and the recognition of electronic signatures'.[15] Specifically, the Report recommended:

- amendments to legislation and industry codes to permit the appropriate use of digital signatures, electronic notices and documents to improve the efficiency of financial transactions and reduce costs;

---

12 *Electronic Transactions Act 2000* (NSW), *Electronic Transactions (Queensland) Act 2001* (Qld), *Electronic Transactions Act 2000* (SA), *Electronic Transactions Act 2000* (Tas), *Electronic Transactions (Victoria) Act 2000* (Vic), *Electronic Transaction Act 2011* (WA), *Electronic Transactions Act 2001* (ACT), *Electronic Transactions (Northern Territory) Act 2000* (NT). References to Acts in this chapter will be to the corresponding Acts listed here.
13 News release by Federal Attorney General Daryl Williams, April 2000.
14 Section 3.
15 Australian Government, *Financial System Inquiry Final Report*, (1997), Chapter 2, para 2.67.

- endorsement by industry and government of the Public Key Authentication Framework; and
- amendments to the *Evidence Acts* to take account of electronic transactions and record keeping.

In May 1999, at a meeting of the Standing Committee of Attorneys General, the states agreed to enact parallel legislation based on the Commonwealth Bill. All states and territories have prepared legislation in accordance with the agreement. The nine pieces of legislation are:

Cth	*Electronic Transactions Act 1999*
NSW	*Electronic Transactions Act 2000*
Qld	*Electronic Transactions (Queensland) Act 2001*
SA	*Electronic Transactions Act 2000*
Tas	*Electronic Transactions Act 2000*
Vic	*Electronic Transactions (Victoria) Act 2000*
WA	*Electronic Transactions Act 2011*
ACT	*Electronic Transactions Act 2001*
NT	*Electronic Transactions (Northern Territory) Act 2000*

The *Electronic Transactions Act 1999* (Cth) came into full operation on 1 July 2001 and applies to all laws of the Commonwealth except those specifically exempted by its regulations.[16] For constitutional reasons the Commonwealth Act applies only 'for the purposes of a law of the Commonwealth'.[17] 'Laws of the Commonwealth' are specified in the regulations.[18] The Federal legislature relies primarily upon the corporations power, the trade and commerce power and the territories power to give it the ability to deal with electronic commerce issues.[19] The corresponding state and territory legislation has no need of such a restriction.

Because there are minor changes in the legislation across the states, territories and the Commonwealth, choice of law provisions will play an important part in the application of the rules in this area. All these Acts bind the Crown.[20]

---

16 More than 150 exemptions have been proclaimed by regulations, see *Electronic Transactions Regulations 2000* (Cth).

17 Section 8.

18 *Electronic Transactions Act 1999* (Cth) s5.

19 *Australian Constitution* ss51(xx), 51(i) and 122 respectively.

20 Cth – s6; NSW – s6; Qld – s7; SA – s6; Tas – s4; Vic – s6; WA – s6; NT – s6. The ACT Act omits the provision.

Provisions of the Australian Electronic Transactions Acts

Provisions	Cth	ACT	NSW	NT	Qld	SA	Tas	Vic	WA	NZ[21]
Short Title	1	1	1	1	1	1	1		1	1
Commencement	2		2	2	2	2	2	2	2	2
Object	3	3	3	3	3	3		1,4	3	3
Simplified Outline	4	4	4	4	4,5	4		5	4	4
Definitions	5	5	5	5	6	5	3	3	5	5–6
Crown to be Bound	6		6	6	7	6	4	6	6	7
External Territories	7									
Validity of electronic transactions	8	7	7	7	8	7	5	7	8	8
Writing	9	8	8	8	9–13	8	6	8	9	18–21
Signature	10	9	9	9	14–15	9	7	9	10	22–24
Production of document	11	10	10	10	16–18	10	8	10	11	28–29
Retention	12	11	11	11	19–21	11	9	11	12	25–26
Exemptions	7A–7B	6A	6A	6A	Sch	6A	4A	6A	7	14
Time of dispatch	14	13	13	13	23	13	11	13	13	10
Time of receipt	14A	13A	13A	13A	24	13A	11A	13A	14	11
Place of dispatch and receipt	14B	13B	13B	13B	25	13B	11B	13B	15	12–13
Attribution of electronic communications	15	14	14	14	26	14	12	14	16	
Additional provisions applying to contracts involving electronic communications	15A–15F	14A–14E	14A–14E	14A–14E	26A–26E	14A–14E	12A–12E	14A–14E	17–21	
Regulations	16	15	15	15	27	15	13	15	22	36
Transitional Provisions	17		16	16	28		13A	16	23	

---

21 The New Zealand Act also includes provisions dealing with access, originals, copyright and consent.

New Zealand

The New Zealand *Electronic Transactions Act 2002* and the *Electronic Transactions Regulations 2003* came into force on 21 November 2003. Their stated purpose is to facilitate the use of electronic technology by reducing uncertainty regarding the legal effect of information that is in electronic form or that is communicated by electronic means, and the time and place of dispatch and receipt of electronic communications by functional equivalence. The Act provides that in its interpretation, reference may be made to the Model Law and any document that relates to the Model Law that originates from UNCITRAL.[22] New Zealand has taken no steps to date to conform to the *Communications Convention*.

United States

The United States *Uniform Electronic Transactions Act 1999* is the product of the National Conference of Commissioners on Uniform State Laws and uses the UNCITRAL Model Law as its template. The Act applies only to transactions between parties who have agreed to conduct transactions by electronic means.[23] The Act defines an 'electronic record' as 'a record created, generated, sent, communicated, received, or stored by electronic means'.[24] Forty-seven states, the District of Columbia, Puerto Rico, and the Virgin Islands have adopted the *Uniform Electronic Transactions Act*. The remaining three US states have not adopted the Act, but have enacted their own legislation relating to electronic transactions.

United Kingdom

In the United Kingdom the two relevant pieces of legislation are the *Land Registration Act 2002* (UK) and the *Electronic Communications Act 2000* (UK).

The *Land Registration Act 2002* replaced 1925 legislation relating to registered land and dealings with unregistered land in England and Wales. Part 8 implements electronic conveyancing processes. An electronic document to which section 91 applies is to be regarded for the purposes of any enactment as a deed. Section 91 applies to certain dispositions (including documents used in conveyancing) in an electronic form which make provision for the time and date when they take effect and include certified electronic signatures of each person by whom they purport to be authenticated. In these circumstances the dispositions are to be regarded as in writing and signed by each individual, and sealed by each corporation whose electronic signature they have. Where notice of assignment made by means of a document pursuant to section 91

---

22 Section 6.
23 See Consent, below.
24 The US Act is available at <euro.ecom.cmu.edu/program/law/08-732/Transactions/ueta.pdf>.

is given in electronic form, it is to be regarded for the purposes of any enactment as having been given in writing.[25] Where conveyancing parties utilise an electronic document that states the time and date that it takes effect, and contains the certified electronic signature of relevant parties, it is deemed to be a document in writing.

Subsequent provisions of the *Land Registration Act 2002* allow the registrar to arrange an electronic communications network for a range of purposes such as electronic registration and electronic settlement. Separate rules deal with the communication of documents in electronic form to the registrar and the electronic storage of documents communicated to the registrar in electronic form.

The *Land Registration Act 2002* refers to the *Electronic Communications Act 2000* (UK) to identify what would qualify as an electronic signature and what constitutes a certification.[26] The Explanatory Memorandum to the Act states that the provisions do 'not disapply the formal statutory or common law requirements relating to deeds and documents but deems compliance with them'. The *Electronic Commerce (EC Directive) Regulations 2002* (UK) implemented the EU's Electronic Commerce Directive 2000. The Directive was introduced to clarify and harmonise the rules of online business throughout Europe with the aim of boosting consumer confidence. The United Kingdom did not make specific separate provisions on electronic transactions because the government viewed the statutory requirements for writing and a signature as already capable of being satisfied by email and by online trading. This view is based on the report on electronic commerce by the Law Commission for England and Wales in 2001.[27]

India

India has developed as a world leader in information technology. In 2000 it enacted the *Information Technology Act 2000*, based on the UNCITRAL Model Law on Electronic Commerce 1996. As with the many nations adopting the Model Law, the Act deals with provisions validating electronic signatures and electronic writing, attribution, acknowledgement and dispatch of electronic records. The Indian legislation was substantially amended by the *Information Technology (Amendment) Act 2008* and now provides comprehensive laws dealing with electronic security, certification authorities for digital signatures and electronic evidence. It includes extensive provisions dealing with cyberterrorism and data protection. Most notably, the Act makes provision for a range of cyber offences and sets up the Cyber Appellate Tribunal.[28]

---

25 Section 91(10) is to be read in accordance with section 7(2) and (3) of the *Electronic Communications Act 2000* (Cth).
26 See Signatures, below.
27 Law Commission for England and Wales, *Electronic Commerce: Formal Requirements in Commercial Transactions*, 2001.
28 See <catindia.gov.in>.

Electronic contracts

Contract formality does not alter merely because an electronic medium was used. Simple contracts requiring no formality are entered into daily. A contract which can be entered into orally can of course be entered into by use of email and other forms of electronic communication. This is not new. The first electronic contract was entered into in the mid-1800s, when the telegraph was first in commercial use.[29] The courts have had little difficulty recognising contract formation by electronic means.[30] However, the perception in the 1990s was that commercial parties were uncertain of the use of electronic media where formal requirements such as writing, signature, production and retention were concerned.

The term 'transaction' is defined as including:

(a) any transaction in the nature of a contract, agreement or other arrangement; and

(b) any statement, declaration, demand, notice or request, including an offer and the acceptance of an offer, that the parties are required to make or choose to make in connection with the formation or performance of a contract, agreement or other arrangement; and

(c) any transaction of a non commercial nature.[31]

The Electronic Transactions Acts do affect key elements of contracts, such as the timing and place of communications, records and documents, and the basic constructs of offer and acceptance. These Acts are predicated on the use of 'electronic communication', defined as:

(a) a communication of information in the form of data, text or images by means of guided and/or unguided electromagnetic energy; or

(b) a communication of information in the form of speech by means of guided and/or unguided electromagnetic energy, where the speech is processed at its destination by an automated voice recognition system.[32]

---

29 The first Australian case to mention electronic commerce, by referring to the 'telegraph', was *R v Rowlands* [1837] TASSupC 10 in the Supreme Court of Van Diemen's Land, 22 August 1837. The first English case to refer to a contract by 'electric telegraph' was *Walsh v Ionides* [1853] EngR 64; 118 E.R. 479.

30 For example, see *Brinkibon Ltd v Stahag Stahl und Stahlwarenhandelsgesellschaft mbH* [1983] 2 AC 34, *Reese Bros Plastics Ltd v Hamon-Sobelco Aust. Pty Ltd* (1988) 5 BPR 11, 106, *Databank Systems Ltd v Commissioner of Inland Revenue* [1990] 3 NZLR 385 and *Walsh v Ionides* [1853] EngR 64; 118 E.R. 479.

31 Cth – s5, NSW – s5, Qld – Sch 2, SA – s5, Tas – s3, Vic – s3, WA – s5, ACT – s5, NT – s5. The New Zealand Act defines 'transaction' as including a transaction of a non-commercial nature, a single communication and the outcome of multiple related communications.

32 Cth – s5, NSW – s5, Qld – Sch 2, SA – s5, Tas – s3, Vic – s3, WA – s5, ACT – s5, NT – s5. The New Zealand Act defines 'electronic communication' as 'a communication by electronic means', and defines 'electronic' as including 'electrical, digital, magnetic, optical, electromagnetic, biometric, and photonic'.

Common law

In their zeal, legislators seem to have assumed that the common law would not recognise functional equivalence nor the validity of electronic communications and electronic documents. Historically, the courts have proved most flexible in such circumstances. However, the case evidence is mixed. Australian courts have appropriately recognised the validity of electronic writing and electronic signatures even in the absence of the guiding legislation. Unfortunately, there are recent cases where the courts have failed to apply the legislation and arrived at examples and tests which do not meet the criteria of functional equivalence.

Application of the common law

Despite the fact that for more than a century the common law has recognised electronic communications – by telegraph, radio and telephone, and more recently by telex and facsimile – the emergence of the internet, EDI (Electronic Data Interchange) and email has led governments to legislate new rules.

In *McGuren v Simpson*,[33] McGuren claimed Simpson was barred by the *Limitation Act 1969* (NSW) from commencing legal proceedings for debt. Section 54 of that Act provides that the limitation period recommences where a confirmation or acknowledgement is made before expiry of the period, provided such acknowledgment is in writing and signed by the maker. The plaintiff's cause of action arose on 26 November 1993, the disputed email acknowledgement was sent and received on 29 September 1999 and proceedings commenced on 26 August 2002. The limitation period was 6 years. Initially, in holding that the limitation period had been extended, Lulham LCM incorrectly applied the *Electronic Transactions Act 2000* (NSW). On appeal to the NSW Supreme Court all parties agreed that as the Act commenced in 2001 it did not apply to the 1999 email. However, Lulham LCM stated that his decision was also based on the common law:

> If the name of the party to be charged is printed or written on a document intended to be a memorandum of the contract, either by himself of [sic] his authorised agent, it is his signature whether it is at the beginning or middle or foot of the document.[34]

The issue before the NSW Supreme Court was whether at common law the email amounted to writing and signature for the purposes of section 54 of the *Limitations*

---

33 [2004] NSWSC 35.
34 Lulham LCM cited a passage from Cheshire and Fifoot's *Law of Contract* (7th edn) and *Darryl v Evans* (1962) H&C 174 at 191. See also the conflicting US decisions of *Ballas v Tedesco* 41 F Supp 2d 531, at 541, *Graham Technology Solutions Inc. v Thinking Pictures Inc.* 949 F Supp. 1427 (ND Cal 1997) and *Lockheed-Arabia v Owen* [1993] 3 WLR 468.

Act 1969 (NSW). The court concluded: 'It is [this court's] view that …s54 of the Act ought to be read to accommodate technological change and that, accordingly, the email sent by the plaintiff constitutes a written document.' The court regarded the words of the email 'yes I spent the money and I shouldn't have', together with the name appearing in the email, as a written and signed confirmation of McGuren's obligation to Simpson.[35]

In 2007, in *Hume Computers Pty Ltd v Exact International BV*, Jacobson J applied 'domestic law' because, for international jurisdictional reasons, *lex fori* applied. His Honour rejected the submission that an email is an electronic representation of writing and therefore does not constitute writing itself as required by [the Distributorship agreement between the parties]'.[36] He stated:

> The requirement of written notice is to be construed in light of the fact that this is a commercial agreement made between two companies engaged in the computer software business. I would be blinding myself to commercial and technological realities to find that an email communication in the present circumstances was not written notice.[37]

In *Wilkens v Iowa Insurance Commissioner*,[38] the Iowa Court of Appeals held that a requirement to keep a written record of an insurance contract was satisfied by an insurer keeping written records on its computer system. The Court of Appeals applied the common law as the case preceded the US legislation.

The Law Commission for England and Wales, in its paper 'Electronic commerce: Formal requirements in commercial transactions – advice from the Law Commission', reached a view consistent with that expressed in *Wilkens*: a document which can be printed and stored is 'in writing'.[39]

A brief obiter comment by de Jersey CJ in *Exceptional Sunrise Pty Ltd v Jones*[40] indicates that parties may impliedly exclude email as a method of writing. The parties used the existing Real Estate Institute of Queensland and Queensland Law Society's contract for houses and land. The buyer purportedly gave written notice by email. Clause 10.4 provided that notices are effectively given if 'delivered or posted' or 'sent to the facsimile number of the other party'. There was no mention of notice by email. De Jersey CJ stated that a submission by counsel that email was not written notice 'did, I feel, gain strength from … the absence, in cl 10.4, of any reference to email communication'. His Honour made no reference to the applicable *Electronic Transactions (Queensland) Act 2001* (Qld). Clause 10.4 does not

35 See also *Stuart v Hisbon* [2013] NSWSC 766.
36 [2007] FCA 478, para 48.
37 Ibid., para 49.
38 (1990) 457 NW 2d ('*Wilkens* case').
39 Law Commission for England and Wales, *Electronic Commerce: Formal Requirements in Commercial Transactions*, 19 December 2001. Available at <www.lawcom.gov.uk/docs/e-commerce.pdf>.
40 [2008] QSC 190, para 30.

in fact exclude notice by email, and in conveyancing practice notice by email has become a common practice. The *Electronic Transactions (Queensland) Act 2001* would have required his Honour to apply the functional equivalence test and hold that an email notice would be complying 'written notice'.[41]

Exemptions

Each of the nine Australian jurisdictions permits exemptions from the application of their respective Electronic Transactions Acts.[42] All except Queensland permit exemptions by regulations. Queensland's exemptions appear in the Schedule to its Act.[43] There are considerable inconsistencies in the approaches taken among the jurisdictions. Uniform legislation would remedy this defect. The Commonwealth's jurisdiction is inherently different from that of the states and territories and its Act's regulations list more than 150 specific exemptions.[44]

Only one state exempts interests in land.[45] Some exempt testamentary dispositions specifically.[46] Others use a variation of the words 'a requirement or permission for a document to be attested, authenticated, verified or witnessed by a person other than the author of the document'.[47] This expression is a minefield, applying to many transactions, contracts, affidavits, statutory declarations, notices, deeds and much more. Curiously, the order of words varies. In New South Wales and Western Australia it is 'verified, authenticated, attested or witnessed'; in Queensland 'attested, authenticated, verified or witnessed'; and in South Australia it is 'witnessed, attested, verified or authenticated'. One might wonder why the drafters chose different phrases and whether the courts might interpret the phrases differently. The 'attested, authenticated, verified or witnessed' exemption may also arise from a perceived impracticality of witnessing electronic documents and a lack of understanding as to

---

41 See also *Islamic Council of South Australia Inc v Australian Federation of Islamic Councils Inc* [2009] NSWSC 211, discussed below.
42 The ACT is the only jurisdiction not to enact exemptions.
43 This is in accordance with the Queensland parliament's principle that legislation should not contain Henry VIII clauses. See *Legislative Standards Act 1992* (Qld) s4(5).
44 *Electronic Transactions Regulations 2000* (Cth) Schedule 1. For example, bills of exchange and cheques.
45 *Electronic Transactions Regulations 2007* (SA) regulations 4 and 5. See *Lucke v Cleary* [2011] SASCFC 118.
46 *Electronic Transactions (Northern Territory) Regulations* (NT) regulation 2; *Electronic Transactions Regulations 2011* (Tas) regulation 4(a); *Electronic Transactions (Victoria) Regulations 2010* regulation 6; *Electronic Transactions Regulations 2012* (WA) regulations 3 and 4.
47 *Electronic Transactions Act 2001* (Qld) clause 6, Schedule 1; *Electronic Transactions Regulations 2012* (NSW) regulation 5(f) and 6(f); *Electronic Transactions Regulations 2002* (SA) regulation 5; *Electronic Transactions Regulations 2012* (WA) regulations 3 and 4.

how such witnessing can be achieved.[48] Other exemptions include filing and producing documents for judicial proceedings, personal service and powers of attorney.

The rationale for these exemptions is unstated. However, it seems clear that there is a perception by the drafters that electronic communications and documents ought not be regarded as functionally equivalent in certain circumstances. The Guide to the UNCITRAL Model Law explains that the matter of specifying exclusions should be left to enacting states, to take better account of differences in national circumstances. However, it warned that the objectives of the Model Law 'would not be achieved' if legislators used 'blanket exceptions'.[49] The Commonwealth, with its numerous exemptions, and the four states which use the 'attested, authenticated, verified or witnessed' document exemption, risk falling into this blanket exemption category. More serious is the effect on the principle of functional equivalence. Underlying these exemptions is an apparent mistrust of electronic communications and documents.

Exemption does not equate to a paper requirement

Many of the Commonwealth exceptions and the state exemptions may be based on the assumption that traditional paper or hardcopy will be required in exempted situations. Such an assumption is fundamentally flawed. An exemption does not equate to a paper or hardcopy requirement. It merely means that the Act does not apply in that situation. The situation then falls to the common law: the courts will in these circumstances independently determine that a given electronic communication or document will or will not suffice for a particular requirement. Indeed there are a handful of cases which have already so held (discussed above).[50]

New Zealand

The *Electronic Transactions Act 2002* (NZ) provides for exemptions to be listed in the Schedule to the Act (section 14). The Schedule lists more than 40 specific and general exemptions, including: notices that are required to be given to the public; information that is required to be given in writing either in person or by registered post; affidavits, statutory declarations, or other documents given on oath or affirmation; powers of attorney; testamentary instruments; negotiable instruments; and documents to files or produced in connection with judicial proceedings. The list is so broad as to risk falling into the UNCITRAL Guide's 'blanket exemption' and

---

48 See A McCullagh, W Caelli and P Little, 'Signature stripping: A digital dilemma', (2001) 1 *Journal of Information, Law and Technology*.

49 See UNCITRAL, above n 6, paras 52, 69.

50 See Common law, above; *McGuren v Simpson* [2004] NSWSC 35; *Hume Computers Pty Ltd v Exact International BV* [2007] FCA 478; *Wilkens v Iowa Insurance Commissioner* (1990) 457 NW 2d 1.

to thwart functional equivalence. Parties entering into contracts using electronic means under New Zealand law must be cognisant of the length and breadth of these exemptions, which substantially reverse the Act's effect.

National Electronic Conveyancing System

The National Electronic Conveyancing System (NECS) aims to provide a single point of entry in each jurisdiction. The project has been agreed to by the Council of Australian Governments (COAG). Implementation in stages by the various states and territories has commenced. New South Wales and Victoria both undertook the first stage of the system in 2013. The Appendix to the NSW legislation contains the model Electronic Conveyancing National Law, to be adopted in due course by all other Australian juris-dictions.[51] The first stage of electronic conveyancing includes single party transactions such as standalone discharges of mortgage, standalone mortgages and most refinances.

Validity of electronic transactions

The Australian Electronic Transactions Acts provide that:

> a transaction is not invalid because it took place wholly or partly by means of one or more electronic communications.[52]

The New Zealand *Electronic Transactions Act 2002* states:

> To avoid doubt, information is not denied legal effect solely because it is
> (a) in electronic form or is in an electronic communication;
> (b) referred to in an electronic communication that is intended to give rise to that legal effect.[53]

The immediate distinction is that the Australian provision is predicated on a trans-action, whilst the New Zealand provision is predicated on information. Both are variations on the Model Law, which provides that:

> Information shall not be denied legal effect, validity or enforceability solely on the grounds that it is in the form of a data message.[54]

---

51 See *Electronic Conveyancing (Adoption of National Law) Act 2012* (NSW), *Electronic Conveyancing National Law (Queensland) Act 2013* (Qld), *Electronic Conveyancing National Law (South Australia) Act 2013* (SA), *Electronic Conveyancing (Adoption of National Law) Act 2013* (Tas), *Electronic Conveyancing (Adoption of National Law) Act 2013* (Vic).

52 Cth – s8, NSW – s7, Qld – s8, SA – s7, Tas – s5, Vic – s7, WA – s7, ACT – s7, NT – s7. Queensland added the word 'merely' before the word 'because', perhaps giving rise to an argument that it may be a factor.

53 NZ – s8.

54 UNCITRAL Model Law, Art. 5. See also Art. 5bis (added in 1998) and Art. 11, specifically dealing with the formation and validity of contracts.

This general rule is subject to other provisions that deal with the validity of transactions, specific requirements of such elements as writing and signature, and the specific exemptions. Common law courts have never questioned the validity of electronic contracts.[55] Should an electronic communication of a document be challenged, it is more likely that one of the specific provisions of the Act would be utilised rather than this general provision. Nevertheless, this provision establishes the general rule and context for validity, and the form of functional equivalence underlying the legislation.

Writing

The writing provisions of the Electronic Transactions Acts are designed to provide functional equivalence of electronic writing, on conditions, where writing is otherwise required or permitted by law.

Many pieces of legislation require contracts to be in writing or evidenced in writing. Such legislation is typically based on the *Statute of Frauds 1677* (Imp.), the aim of which was to help protect people and their property against fraud and sharp practices by legislating that certain types of contract could not be enforced unless there was written evidence of its existence and of its terms.[56]

The decision by UNCITRAL to formulate the template legislation was taken because in 'a number of countries the existing legislation governing communication and storage of information is inadequate or outdated because it does not contemplate the use of electronic commerce'.[57] In most common law jurisdictions, the *Statute of Frauds* has been re-enacted in several pieces of legislation. Section 4 of the original statute[58] applies to charges on, among other things, agreements upon consideration of marriage or upon sale of lands, tenements or hereditaments. It also states that a person is not able to sue upon such contracts unless 'some memorandum or note thereof shall be in writing, and signed by the party to be charged therewith, or some other person thereunto by him lawfully authorised'. Section 17 has similar provisions on the purchase of goods for £10 or over:

> *no action shall be brought* whereby to charge any executor or administrator upon any special promise, to answer damages out of his own estate; or *whereby to charge the defendant upon any special promise to answer for the debt, default or miscarriages of*

---

55 See above n 29.
56 See Sharon Christensen and Rouhshi Low, 'Moving the Statute of Frauds to the digital age', (2003) 77 *Australian Law Journal* 416 and Alan Davidson, 'Electronic transactions and contracts', (2001) 21(6) *Proctor* 38.
57 Guide to the UNCITRAL Model Law, para 3.
58 *Statute of Frauds 29 Car 2. c. 5.3.4.*

another person; … or upon any contract or sale of lands, tenements or hereditaments, or any interest in or concerning them; or upon any agreement that is not to be performed within the space of one year from the making thereof, unless the agreement upon which such action shall be brought, or some memorandum or note thereof shall be in writing, and signed by the party to be charged therewith, or some other person thereunto by him lawfully authorized.[59]

Legislation based on the Model Law does not change the impact of *Statute of Frauds* legislation. Instead it dictates circumstances in which electronic writing is to be regarded as equivalent. Australian legislation derived from the *Statute of Frauds* typically permits transactions of certain interests subject to stated formalities (such as the requirement for writing).[60]

Australian provisions

If, under a law of this jurisdiction, a person is required to give information in writing, that requirement is taken to have been met if the person gives the information by means of an electronic communication, where:

(a) at the time the information was given, it was reasonable to expect that the information would be readily accessible so as to be useable for subsequent reference, and

(b) the person to whom the information is required to be given consents to the information being given by means of an electronic communication.[61]

In all Australian Electronic Transactions Acts this provision is repeated with the word 'permitted' replacing 'required'.[62] Hence the provisions apply to any requirement or permission to give information in writing. Information is defined as 'information in the form of data, text, images or sound'.[63] Let us examine these provisions in more detail.

---

59 Emphasis added.
60 See, for example in relation to dispositions of land: *Conveyancing Act 1919* (NSW) s54A; *Property Law Act 1958* (Vic) s53 and *Property Law Act 1974* (Qld) ss 10, 59. Also bills of exchange, *Bills of Exchange Act 1909* (Cth) s8; promissory notes, *Bills of Exchange Act 1909* (Cth), s89; cheques, *Cheques Act 1986* (Cth) s10; assignments of copyright, *Copyright Act 1968* (Cth) s196(3); marine insurance contracts, *Marine Insurance Act 1909* (Cth) ss27, 28. Some sale of goods legislation has similar restrictions: for example, see *Sale of Goods Act 1895* (WA) s4.
61 *Electronic Transactions Acts*: NSW – s8(1), Qld – s11, SA – s8(1), Tas – s6(1), Vic – s8(1), WA – s9(1), ACT – s8(1), NT – s8(1). The Commonwealth has substantially similar provisions in s9(1), but also makes special provision for Commonwealth entities.
62 Cth – s9(2), NSW – s8(2), Qld – s12, SA – s8(2), Tas – s6(2), Vic – s8(2), WA – s9(2), ACT – s8(2), NT – s8(2).
63 Except in the Commonwealth Act, where 'speech' was used instead of 'sound'. The state and territory legislators chose the wider term with hindsight.

'required to give information in writing'

The expression 'required to give information in writing' is a clear reference to the *Statute of Frauds* requirements. The provision has no application to simple contracts, which can be formed orally.

'requirement is taken to have been met'

The expression deems electronic writing to be equivalent.

'electronic communication'

The expression 'electronic communication' is defined as:

(a) a communication of information in the form of data, text or images by means of guided or unguided electromagnetic energy, or both, or

(b) a communication of information in the form of sound by means of guided or unguided electromagnetic energy, or both, where the sound is processed at its destination by an automated voice recognition system.[64]

This media-neutral and technology-neutral approach allows the provision to apply to as broad a range of circumstances as possible.

'at the time the information was given, it was reasonable to expect'

In this phrase the use of the expression 'reasonable' is both a strength and a weakness. The term gives those who write legislation (the drafters) and those who interpret the law (in the end, the courts) great flexibility. There are myriad factual circumstances in which the provision could apply, including in the future with technology not yet developed. This gives the provision strength to be applied where sound judgement and reason so dictate. But the provision is also a weakness. One of the fundamental objects of the legislation is to provide certainty, but here a party to a transaction may be unable to predict with precision what a court would regard as reasonable. The lawyer in court will argue various meanings and permutations; first, what is reasonable and second, whether it was reasonable 'at the time the information was given'. The uncertainty cancels out the benefit of the provision. The provision is no better than leaving the issue to the courts, which in any event would have found functional equivalence where it was reasonable to do so.

---

64 The Commonwealth Act again limits application to 'speech' instead of 'sound'.

'the information would be readily accessible so as to be usable for subsequent reference' 'reasonable to expect'

The expression 'the information would be readily accessible so as to be useable for subsequent reference' is predicated on the principle of functional equivalence. A feature of ink and paper writing is that it is typically accessible for subsequent reference. Again, interpreters of the provision may question the distinction between 'accessible' and the use in this provision of 'readily accessible'. Is this broader or narrower than for paper, or the same? Paper has different durability. The drafters of wills and other important documents typically use a high grade paper, aware that the document may be required many years in the future. Ink can and does fade. Some government departments require documents to be in black ink. This has been based on the traditional concern that ink fades and the modern concern that light-coloured ink does not photocopy faithfully. Paper oxidises and can disintegrate. In these circumstances it is appropriate to read the expression in conjunction with the qualifying expression 'reasonable to expect'. For example, it would be reasonable to expect that electronic mail which is stored when created and by the recipient on receipt, would be readily accessible for subsequent reference.[65] However, the typical chat room uses electronic exchanges without the expectation that the communications will be stored; such a use would fall foul of the provision.

In *Islamic Council of South Australia Inc. v Australian Federation of Islamic Councils Inc.*[66] Brereton J gave a broad description of writing whilst ignoring the applicable NSW *Electronic Transactions Act*. His Honour stated: 'the concept of "writing" is concerned with the form in which words are used, and not the surface on which they are written'. However, he took the point further, stating:

> While 'writing' often contemplates writing on paper, it is nonetheless writing and not speech, if written in invisible ink. It is nonetheless writing, if written in the sky by an aircraft engaging in skywriting. To my mind, it is nonetheless writing, if it appears on a computer screen, as a result of the entry of data into a computer.[67]

The conclusion, on the facts, that the email was writing, and that the single name at the end of the email was a signature may be regarded as correct, but the analysis is flawed. The key attribute of paper writing is that it is usable later for other purposes. There are many forms of writing which do not meet this basic test; skywriting is one such example, and should not, therefore, be regarded as meeting a

---

65 For a discussion on whether it is reasonable to send an email with an attachment in an unusual compressed format see *Re David Scott Ellis; Ex Parte Triple M Mechanical Services Pty Ltd [No 2]* [2013] WASC 161.

66 [2009] NSWSC 211.

67 Ibid., para 20.

legal writing requirement. His Honour's second example, where 'it appears on a computer screen', is similarly flawed. Emails and saved computer documents can be recalled – that is, used later for other purposes – and so serve a similar function as paper writing. However, the mere typing of data on a screen of writing without more would be insufficient. Without taking some action to save the data or file, the data disappears when the computer is turned off, and so becomes unavailable for subsequent use. His Honour, in this instance, should have made reference to the standard and test contained in the applicable Electronic Transactions Act.

With instant messaging, the exchange appears on each party's computer screens and disappears after a short period of time or when the session is ended. Hence it is unavailable for subsequent reference. However, it is possible to save the exchange, by copying and pasting it to a regular computer file, or logging the conversations, or using a screenshot or screen capture. Should the parties agree to record the exchange in one of these ways, then it may be reasonable to expect that the information would be 'readily accessible so as to be useable for subsequent reference'.

'giving information'

For the purposes of the section, 'giving information'[68] is defined in each of the Australian Acts and applies to a requirement or permission to give information, whether the word 'give', 'send' or 'serve', or another expression, is used. 'Giving information' is defined as including:

> making an application, making or lodging a claim, giving, sending or serving a notification, lodging a return, making a request, making a declaration, lodging or issuing a certificate, making, varying or cancelling an election, lodging an objection and giving a statement of reasons.[69]

It has been argued that these examples do not include the creation of a contract.[70] However, subsequent case law has accepted the application of the writing provision to both offers and acceptances leading to the formation of a contract.[71] In any

---

68 The expression 'give information' is used in the Queensland Electronic Transactions Act.

69 Cth – s9(5), NSW – s8(5), Qld – s10, SA – s8(5), Tas – s6(5), Vic – s8(5), WA – s9(5), ACT – s8(5), NT – s8(5), NZ – s20(4) . For an application, see *Johanson and Civil Aviation Safety Authority* [2012] AATA 239.

70 S Christensen, W Duncan and R Low, 'The requirements of writing for electronic land contracts: The Queensland experience compared with other jurisdictions', (2003) 10(3) *eLaw Journal: Murdoch University Electronic Journal of Law*, para 26.

71 See, for example, *Luxottica Retail Australia Pty Ltd v 136 Queen Street Pty Ltd* [2011] QSC 162, where the court stated 'Luxottica communicated acceptance of all the terms the respondent asked for ... (except price) on 15 November 2010' by email. The price was later determined by an exchange of emails. See also *Golden Ocean v Salgaocar* [2012] EWCA Civ 265, *Rosenfeld v Zarneck* (Supreme Court, King's County, New York, 2004) and *Shattuck v Klotzbach* (Superior Court, Massachusetts, 2001).

event 'information' is broadly defined as 'information in the form of data, text, images or speech' and is otherwise uncontroversial. The provision applies to service where 'written notice is required'. For example, in *Kavia Holdings Pty Limited v Suntrack Holdings Pty Limited* the NSW Supreme Court considered a requirement that the notice be in writing, stating:

> The email satisfies this requirement. The clause then provides that the written notice 'may be given or served upon a party hereto by being left at that address specified as that party's address in the relevant item of the reference schedule.' I do not read this language as imposing a mandatory requirement for physical delivery. By its express terms it is permissive.[72]

In the subsequent decision of *C&P Syndicate Pty Ltd v Reddy* the NSW Supreme Court approved this statement, affirming that the approach was 'consistent with the policy objectives of the *Electronic Transactions Act 2000* (NSW) section 8 as well as modern business practice and the routine course of communications between the respective solicitors for the plaintiff and the first defendant'.[73]

Paragraph (b) Consent

The consent precondition – that the person the information is required to be given to must consent to the information being given by means of an electronic communication – has had incongruous and unintentional consequences. The consent provision is considered separately below.[74]

New Zealand

The New Zealand provision avoids the use of the terms 'requirement' and 'permission', removes the condition 'reasonable to expect' and uses the expression 'electronic form'. The provision is uncomplicated yet positive:

> A legal requirement that information be in writing is met by information that is in electronic form if the information is readily accessible so as to be usable for subsequent reference.[75]

---

72 [2011] NSWSC 716, para 33.
73 [2013] NSWSC 643, para 111. Cf *Exceptional Sunrise Pty Ltd v Jones* [2008] QSC 190. See also *Curtis v Singtel Optus Pty Ltd* [2014] FCAFC 144, where a Bankruptcy Notice with a judgement 'attached' was duly served electronically.
74 See Consent, below.
75 *Electronic Transactions Act 2002* (NZ) s18.

Signatures

Legislation which requires writing typically also requires a signature by the maker.[76] A person who under a law is required to give a signature may, pursuant to and subject to conditions under the Electronic Transactions Acts, use an alternative method of authenticating their identity in relation to an electronic communication.[77]

Legislation should not be based on the various functions that a signature may have in a paper-based environment. Such an approach places undue emphasis upon concepts peculiar to paper, and also risks tying the legislation to a particular state of technical development. The UNCITRAL Model Law and the UN Communications Convention concentrate upon two basic functions of a signature: first, to identify the author of a document and second, to indicate the person's intention in respect of the information being communicated. It does not deal specifically with the integrity of the document itself.[78]

Australian provisions

Each of the nine Australian Electronic Transactions Acts includes a provision deeming electronic signatures, on meeting certain conditions, to fulfill the requirements under the law of signatures:

> If, under a law of this jurisdiction, the signature of a person is required, that requirement is taken to have been met in relation to an electronic communication if:
>
> (a) a method is used to identify the person and to indicate the person's intention in respect of the information communicated, and
> (b) the method used was either:
>   (i) as reliable as appropriate for the purpose for which the electronic communication was generated or communicated, in the light of all the circumstances, including any relevant agreement, or
>   (ii) proven in fact to have fulfilled the functions described in paragraph (a), by itself or together with further evidence, and
> (c) the person to whom the signature is required to be given consents to that requirement being met by way of the use of the method mentioned in paragraph (a).[79]

---

76 For example, legislation based on the *Statute of Frauds*: see *Conveyancing Act 1919* (NSW) s54A, *Law of Property Act 1936* (SA) s26, *Property Law Act 1974* (Qld) s59, *Conveyancing Law of Property Act 1884* (Tas) s36, *Instruments Act 1958* (Vic) s126, *Statute of Frauds 1677* (Imp.)(WA) s2, *Civil Law (Property) Act 2006* (ACT) s201, *Law of Property Act 2000* (NT) s62.
77 Cth – s10; NSW – s9; Qld – ss14–15; SA – s9; Tas – s7; Vic – s9; WA – s10; ACT – s9; NT – s9.
78 See UNCITRAL, above n 6; and *United Nations Convention on the Use of Electronic Communications in International Contracts* (entered into force 1 March 2013), Explanatory Note by the UNCITRAL secretariat, 13.
79 NSW – s9(1), Qld – s14, SA – s9(1), Tas – s7(1), Vic – s9(1), WA – s10(1), ACT – s9(1), NT – s9(1). The Commonwealth has substantially similar provisions in s10(1), but also makes special provision for Commonwealth entities.

The Australian signature provision is substantially similar to the 'writing' provision.[80] Curiously, however, whereas the provision regarding writing applies where there is a requirement for writing or where writing is permitted, the provision for signatures only applies where the signature is required. This provision does not deem functional equivalence to signatures where they are not required, but are simply permitted. For example, where a signature is used as corroborating evidence proving the existence of a contract or transaction where the signature was not required, the Electronic Transactions Acts have no application. The acceptability and equivalence of an electronic signature in such circumstances should be a matter for the common law. This issue was raised in *Stuart v Hisbon*,[81] where it was argued that the NSW signature provision should not apply because the signature was not 'required'.[82] However, Harrison J applied the provision to a single name typed at the end of an email, stating that it was capable of meeting the requirements of the section and noting: 'Electronic signatures are a fact of modern commercial life.'[83]

'signature of a person'

'Signature of a person' is a surprisingly thorny concept.[84] The meanings, and the use and custom, of a signature have been many and varied. 'Person' can mean an individual or a corporation. The signature of a corporation can be its corporate seal accompanied by one or more officers' personal signatures. The seal may be a rubber stamp, an impressed indentation into paper or even a wax seal.

Traditional signatures most typically are physically written, printed or impressed. They can be readily reproduced by the maker and recognised and identified by other parties and experts. To varying degrees they are difficult to forge. Traditional signatures have acquired fungibility such that they have been the standard for identification and for the execution of legal instruments, and used in financial institutions, for credit cards, accounts, cheques and so forth. Additionally, alteration and removal are difficult. When faced with a new form of signature, the common law courts looked to the accepted functions and purposes of signatures and to the signatory's intention to determine if the electronic signature offered the same.

---

80 See above.
81 [2013] NSWSC 766.
82 Ibid., para 16.
83 Ibid., para 34. See also *Attorney-General (SA) v Corporation of the City of Adelaide* [2013] HCA 3.
84 See Chapter 13 for a discussion of the nature and form of traditional signatures.

'signature of the person ... in relation to an electronic communication'

The type of signature envisaged by the provision is an 'electronic signature', although that expression is not used. Instead the provision applies to the broader expression, 'signature of the person ... in relation to an electronic communication'. There is no definition of 'electronic signature' in Australian legislation. The common law courts would most likely look to the pertinent attributes of a traditional signature to determine whether a given electronic signature meets legal requirements.

The term 'electronic signature' should not be confused with 'digital signature'. The latter refers to a specific attachment which uses an asymmetric cryptosystem, a hash function and public and private 'keys' for authentication and verification. An 'electronic signature' is any means of electronic authentication of the identity of a person and of the intent of that person associated with an electronic record. The term has no universally accepted meaning and internationally is variously defined.

Paragraph (a) – Method used

Paragraph (a) establishes the principle that, in an electronic environment, the basic legal functions of a signature are performed by way of a method that identifies the originator of a data message and confirms the originator's intention in respect of the content of that message.

In 2006, in *Mehta v J Pereira Fernandes SA*,[85] the English courts had cause to consider the nature of an electronic signature. Mehta emailed Fernandes' solicitors offering to provide a personal guarantee in favour of Fernandes and to make a payment of £5000 on certain terms. The email did not show Mehta's name at the foot of the message, but was described in the header as having come from 'Nelmehta@ aol.com'. On receiving the email, a clerk employed by the solicitors telephoned Mehta and agreed to the proposal. The solicitor then sent a written guarantee to Mehta. However, Mehta did not sign or return it.

Judge Pelling QC held that the email would be a note or memorandum to which section 4 of the Statute of Frauds applied. However, his Honour also considered whether or not it was sufficiently signed:

> a party can sign a document for the purposes of Section 4 by using his full name or his last name prefixed by some or all of his initials or using his initials, and possibly by using a pseudonym or a combination of letters and numbers (as can happen for example with a Lloyds slip scratch), providing always that whatever was used was inserted into the document in order to give, and with the intention of giving, authenticity to it.[86]

85 [2006] EWHC 813.
86 Ibid., para 26.

In determining what would amount to a signature, Judge Pelling QC examined the underlying purpose. His Honour stated that the purpose of the *Statute of Frauds*:

> is to protect people from being held liable on informal communications be-
> cause they may be made without sufficient consideration or expressed am-
> biguously or because such a communication might be fraudulently alleged
> against the party to be charged.[87]

In relation to an electronic document his Honour commented that:

> if a party creates and sends an electronically created document then he will
> be treated as having signed it to the same extent that he would in law be
> treated as having signed a hard copy of the same document. The fact that the
> document is created electronically as opposed to as a hard copy can make
> no difference.[88]

The issue before the court was whether the automatic insertion of a person's email address after the document has been transmitted constitutes a signature for the purposes of the *Statute of Frauds*. His Honour's conclusion was that an email address insertion was 'incidental'. The header is 'divorced from the main body of the text of the message'. If there is no further evidence in relation to the maker's intention, 'it is not possible to hold that the automatic insertion of an email address is ... intended for a signature'. To conclude otherwise would, in his Honour's view, undermine, or potentially undermine, the purpose of the *Statute of Frauds*. Although decided before amendments were made pursuant to the *Communications Convention*, the decision today would be the same.

'electronic communication'

The expression 'electronic communication' is defined as:

(a) a communication of information in the form of data, text or images by means of guided or unguided electromagnetic energy, or both, or

(b) a communication of information in the form of sound by means of guided or unguided electromagnetic energy, or both, where the sound is processed at its destination by an automated voice recognition system.[89]

This is a media-neutral and technology-neutral approach, allowing the provision to apply to as broad a range of circumstances as possible.

---

87 Ibid., para 16.
88 Ibid., para 28.
89 The Commonwealth Act again limits application to 'speech' instead of 'sound'.

The placing of files in a cloud facility will not of itself be an electronic communication, where, for example, an email includes a direct link to the files in the cloud. In *Conveyor & General Engineering Pty Ltd v Basetec Services Pty Ltd*,[90] one party attempted to serve another party with documents by placing digital files in Dropbox[91] and sending an email with a link to the files via the Dropbox facility. The Queensland Supreme Court held that digital files were not 'electronically communicated' because the files were not communicated 'by guided or unguided electromagnetic energy'. Instead there was 'an electronic communication of the means by which other information in electronic form could be found, read and downloaded at and from the Dropbox website'.[92] If the files were attached to the email, the court stated that it would have regarded the documents as served. However, 'the use of the Dropbox meant that the whole of the application was not within an "electronic communication", thereby precluding the operation of [the Electronic Transactions Act]'.[93]

'a method used to identify the person and to indicate the person's intention'

This expression is used in place of the simpler concept of 'electronic signature'. It ensures technology neutrality. The 'method used' could be as simple as a sender typing a name at the end of an email,[94] or it could be an unseen digital signature logically associated and integrated with an electronic file authenticating the identity of the sender to a mathematical certainty and ensuring the integrity of the message.[95] The former is insecure. Anyone can type such a signature. Some email senders may place a digitised image of their signature at the end of their emails. This is equally insecure, as anyone can cut and paste the image. The 'method used' could be a simple code. Two parties may by agreement determine that, for example, the number '37' should be placed at the end with the intention that it will signify both the identity and intention of the sender. Others may improve on this rudimentary approach and require the code to be dynamic, yet simple, such as today's date multiplied by five plus the number of the month multiplied by eight. The resulting number appearing at the end of each email appears random, and yet it would allow the parties to accept, with some deal of certainty and security, the authenticity and integrity

---

90 [2014] QSC 30.

91 Dropbox is a cloud service that allows users to store digital files securely. Users can share their files, if they choose, by providing others with the login details or sending a direct link.

92 [2014] QSC 30, para 28.

93 Ibid., para 29.

94 As approved by Judge Pelling QC in *Mehta v J Pereira Fernandes SA* [2006] EWHC 813, para 8.

95 For more on digital signatures, see Chapter 13.

of the message.[96] Digital signatures that use an asymmetric cryptosystem, or public and private 'keys' and a hash function, to ensure authentication and verification of the message and authorship are very secure.

Paragraph (b)(i) – Reliability of the method used

Paragraph (b)(i) provides a flexible approach to the level of security to be achieved by the method of identification used under paragraph (a). In determining whether or not the method used is appropriate, legal, technical and commercial factors should be taken into account. These might include, for example:

- the sophistication of the equipment used by each of the parties;
- the nature of their trade activity;
- the frequency with which commercial transactions take place between the parties;
- the kind and size of the transaction;
- the function of signature requirements in the given statutory and regulatory environment;
- the capability of communication systems;
- compliance with authentication procedures set forth by intermediaries;
- the range of authentication procedures made available by the intermediary;
- compliance with trade customs and practice;
- existence of insurance coverage against unauthorised messages;
- the importance and value of the information contained in the data message;
- the availability of alternative methods of authentication and the cost of their use; and
- the degree of acceptance or non-acceptance of the method of identification in the relevant industry or field both at the time the method was agreed upon and at the time the data message was communicated.[97]

Although this is unstated, the provision envisages the 'method used' including electronic signatures. An electronic signature may be defined here as:

> any letters, characters, numbers or other symbols in digital form attached to or logically associated with an electronic record or document, and executed or adopted with the intention of authenticating or approving the electronic record or document.[98]

---

96 The example for 5 November would be 113.
97 See UNCITRAL, above n 6, para 58; and UN *Convention on the Use of Electronic Communication in International Contracts*, above n 78, para 162.
98 Modified from the definition of electronic signature in the Singapore *Electronic Transactions Act 1998*, s2.

This would cover the simple email signature, a code attached or appended to an email or an electronic document, and the use of a digital signature.[99]

In *Faulks v Cameron*,[100] the NT Supreme Court considered emails that ended with the type-written words 'Regards Angus' and 'Regards Angus Cameron'. The court had to determine whether the emails were 'signed' as a consequence of the *Electronic Transactions (Northern Territory) Act 2000* (NT). With surprisingly little analysis, it was held that the emails had been signed. Young AM was satisfied that:

> the printed signature on the defendant's emails identifies him and indicates his approval of the information communicated, that the method was reliable as was appropriate and that the plaintiff consented to the method. I am satisfied that the agreement is 'signed'.[101]

'the purpose for which the electronic communication was generated or communicated'

These words require a connection between the electronic communication and the signature. Hence the method used must indicate the signatory's intention that the signature be attached to or logically associated with the electronic communication.

In *McGuren v Simpson*,[102] the NSW Supreme Court regarded the words of an email 'yes I spent the money and I shouldn't have', together with the name appearing in the email, as a written and signed confirmation of McGuren's obligation to Simpson for the purposes of the *Limitation Act 1969* (NSW). The court approved the passage in *Halsbury's Laws of Australia*:

> Where the name of the party to be charged appears on the alleged note or memorandum, for example, because it has been typed in by the other party, the so-called 'authenticated signature fiction' will apply where the party to be charged expressly or impliedly acknowledges the writing as an authenticated expression of the contract so that the typed words will be deemed to be his or her signature.[103]

The court held that the email was recognisable as a signed note of a concluded agreement.

Paragraph (b)(i) envisages that technological advances may result in signature technology becoming unsuitable even though it may have been suitable for a

---

99 See Chapter 13 for a discussion of the nature and form of electronic and digital signatures.
100 [2004] NTSC 61; (2004) 32 Fam LR 417.
101 [2004] NTSC 61, para 64.
102 [2004] NSWSC 35. See Writing, above.
103 110 *Contract* at [110–1030].

particular transaction at an earlier time. The legislature's intention was to link this requirement to the time that the signature method was used, to ensure that a signature method that was appropriate at the time it was used is not later rendered invalid. This technology-neutral standard enables signature methods to meet appropriate subjective standards at the time they are used.[104]

Paragraph (b)(i) establishes a 'reliability test' to ensure functional equivalence for electronic signatures. Without paragraph (b)(i) there was concern that only signature methods that employed high-level security methods would be considered adequate.[105]

Paragraph (b)(ii) – Proven to have fulfilled the functions in paragraph (a)

The former paragraph (b)[106] was based on 1990s reasoning and was flawed. Paragraph (b)(ii) was inserted to address this defect. A strict application of the former provision could lead a court to invalidate a contract on the ground that the electronic signature was not appropriately reliable even if there was no dispute about the identity of the person signing or of the fact of signing. UNCITRAL recognised this flaw, describing it as 'unfortunate', because it potentially allows one party to try to escape its obligations by denying the validity of one of the signatures, not on the ground that it was not signed, but on the spurious ground that the method was not 'as reliable as appropriate' in the circumstances.[107]

Paragraph (b)(ii) now validates a signature method, regardless of its reliability under paragraph (b)(i), where the method used is proven in fact to have identified the signatory and indicated the signatory's intention in respect of the electronic communication.[108] Care needs to be taken that the correct version of the signature provision is applied to the facts. Two cases to date have incorrectly applied the amendments to facts predating the amendments.[109]

---

104 *Electronic Transactions Bill 1999* (Cth) Explanatory Memorandum.
105 Explanatory note by the UNCITRAL secretariat on the Communications Convention, para 163.
106 Amendments were made between 2010 and 2013 to the Electronic Transactions Acts, to conform to the UNCITRAL Communications Convention.
107 Explanatory note by the UNCITRAL secretariat on the Communications Convention, para 164.
108 Ibid.
109 See *Conveyor & General Engineering Pty Ltd v Basetec Services Pty Ltd* [2014] QSC 30 and *Austral-Asia Freight Pty Ltd v Turner* [2013] FCCA 298. The commencement dates of the respective amendments are: Cth – 22 June 2011, NSW – 15 October 2010, Qld – 29 August 2013, SA – 1 March 2012, Tas – 1 January 2011, Vic – 1 December 2011, WA – 1 August 2012, ACT – 1 June 2012, NT – 23 May 2011.

Paragraph (c) Consent

Paragraph (c) duplicates the consent provision for 'writing', and raises the same issues, comments and concerns. The consent provision is considered separately.[110]

New Zealand provisions

22 Legal requirement for signature

(1) Subject to subsection (2), a legal requirement for a signature other than a witness' signature is met by means of an electronic signature if the electronic signature–

    (a) adequately identifies the signatory and adequately indicates the signatory's approval of the information to which the signature relates; and

    (b) is as reliable as is appropriate given the purpose for which, and the circumstances in which, the signature is required.

(2) A legal requirement for a signature that relates to information legally required to be given to a person is met by means of an electronic signature only if that person consents to receiving the electronic signature.[111]

The New Zealand provisions for signatures are based on the UNCITRAL Model Law. Unlike Australia, however, the New Zealand provision above refers specifically to the use of 'electronic signatures' and to their equivalence in set circumstances. 'Electronic signature' in relation to information in electronic form is defined as 'a method used to identify a person and to indicate that person's approval of that information'.[112] The provision parallels the Australian provision in relation to being 'as reliable as is appropriate given the purpose for which, and the circumstances in which, the signature is required'.

Section 22 duplicates the consent provision for 'writing', and raises the same issues, comments and concerns. The precondition that the person receiving the signature is required to have given consent to that requirement being met by way of the use of the method mentioned is considered separately.[113]

The New Zealand *Electronic Transactions Act* includes a specific provision for witnessing a document by way of an electronic signature. The requirements parallel the provision in section 22. An electronic signature used to witness a document must comply with section 22 and:

---

110 See Consent, below.
111 *Electronic Transactions Act 2002* (NZ) s22.
112 *Electronic Transactions Act 2002* (NZ) s5.
113 See Consent, below.

23(1)(b) in the case of the witnessing of a signature or a seal, the electronic signature of the witness–

(i) adequately identifies the witness and adequately indicates that the signature or seal has been witnessed; and

(ii) is as reliable as is appropriate given the purpose for which, and the circumstances in which, the witness' signature is required.[114]

Section 24 contains a presumption that certain electronic signatures are reliable for the purposes of the Act;

24(1) For the purposes of sections 22 and 23, it is presumed that an electronic signature is as reliable as is appropriate if–

(a) the means of creating the electronic signature is linked to the signatory and to no other person; and

(b) the means of creating the electronic signature was under the control of the signatory and of no other person; and

(c) any alteration to the electronic signature made after the time of signing is detectable; and

(d) where the purpose of the legal requirement for a signature is to provide assurance as to the integrity of the information to which it relates, any alteration made to that information after the time of signing is detectable.

This section describes the operation of a digital signature but does not preclude other secure forms of electronic signatures.[115]

Production of documents

If, under a law of this jurisdiction, a person is required to produce a document that is in the form of paper, an article or other material, that requirement is taken to have been met if the person produces, by means of an electronic communication, an electronic form of the document, where:

(a) having regard to all the relevant circumstances at the time the communication was sent, the method of generating the electronic form of the document provided a reliable means of assuring the maintenance of the integrity of the information contained in the document, and

(b) at the time the communication was sent, it was reasonable to expect that the information contained in the electronic form of the document would be readily accessible so as to be useable for subsequent reference, and

---

114 *Electronic Transactions Act 2002* (NZ) s23(1)(b).
115 For a description on the operation of digital signatures, see Chapter 13.

(c) the person to whom the document is required to be produced consents to the production, by means of an electronic communication, of an electronic form of the document.[116]

The underlying assumption of both the Model Law and the Australian legislation has been that original documents are 'paper-based ones'; the provisions deal with an electronic equivalent. The New Zealand *Electronic Transactions Act* includes a provision not foreshadowed in either of these: section 29 deals with situations where the electronic form is the original. The section aims to give a paper copy functional equivalence if certain criteria are met:

29 Legal requirement to provide or produce information that is in electronic form

A legal requirement to provide or produce information that is in electronic form is met by providing or producing the information–

(a) in paper or other non-electronic form; but, if the maintenance of the integrity of the information cannot be assured, the person who must provide or produce the information must–

    (i) notify every person to whom the information is required to be provided or produced of that fact; and

    (ii) if requested to do so, provide or produce the information in electronic form in accordance with paragraph (b); or

(b) in electronic form, whether by means of an electronic communication or otherwise, if–

    (i) the form and means of the provision or production of the information reliably assures the maintenance of the integrity of the information, given the purpose for which, and the circumstances in which, the information is required to be provided or produced; and

    (ii) the information is readily accessible so as to be usable for subsequent reference; and

    (iii) the person to whom the information is required to be provided or produced consents to the provision or production of the information in an electronic form and, if applicable, by means of an electronic communication.

Consent

The Commonwealth Parliament introduced consent as an additional precondition for functional equivalence of electronic writing, electronic signatures and electronic production.[117] The person to whom the electronic writing or signature is

---

116 NSW – s10, Qld – ss16–18, SA – s10, Tas – s8, Vic – s10, WA – s11, ACT – s10, NT – s10; New Zealand – s28. The Commonwealth has substantially similar provisions in s11, but also makes special provision for Commonwealth entities. For an example of the application of para (b) see *Curtis v Singtel Optus Pty Ltd* [2014] FCAFC 144.

117 See *Electronic Transactions Act 1999* (Cth) ss9(1)(d), 9(2)(d), 10(1)(d), 11(1)(e) and 11(2)(e) and the state and territory equivalents.

required to be given, or to whom documents are required to be produced, must consent to that requirement being met electronically. This change was followed by the states, territories and New Zealand. In New Zealand, however, consent is required for retention and access as well as for writing, signatures and the production of documents.

Although the underlying principle of the legislation is functional equivalence,[118] the notion of consent was considered significant enough to override that precept. It has been suggested that the consent provision thwarts functional equivalence.[119] In my view, the reasoning for its inclusion is ill-conceived and it creates an unwarranted impediment.

The consent provision is absent from the UNCITRAL Model Law. The Model Law is based on 'the recognition that legal requirements prescribing the use of traditional paper-based documentation constitute the main obstacle to the development of modern means of communication'.[120] The UNCITRAL drafters based its template on the 'functional equivalent approach', stating that it is 'based on an analysis of the purposes and functions of the traditional paper-based requirement with a view to determining how those purposes or functions could be fulfilled through electronic-commerce techniques'.[121]

They noted that:

> Among the functions served by a paper document are the following: to provide that a document would be legible by all; to provide that a document would remain unaltered over time; to allow for the reproduction of a document so that each party would hold a copy of the same data; to allow for the authentication of data by means of a signature; and to provide that a document would be in a form acceptable to public authorities and courts.[122]

The UNCITRAL drafters also considered that:

> electronic records can provide the same level of security as paper and, in most cases, a much higher degree of reliability and speed, especially with respect to the identification of the source and content of the data, provided that a number of technical and legal requirements are met.[123]

---

118 See Writing, above.
119 Alan Davidson, 'The Electronic Transaction Acts – in action or inaction?', (2007) 27 *Proctor* 7, 47; Alan Davidson, 'A matter of consent', (2004) 24 *Proctor* 11, 23. See also CC Nicoll, 'Consent – Luddite's lifeline', (2000) 9(3) *Information & Communications Technology Law* 195.
120 UNCITRAL, above n 6.
121 Ibid., para 16.
122 Ibid.
123 Ibid.

Their only stated reservation was that the adoption of the functional equivalence approach 'should not result in imposing on users of electronic commerce more stringent standards of security (and the related costs) than in a paper-based environment'.[124]

When adopting the functional equivalence approach, the UNCITRAL drafters gave due attention to the existing hierarchy of form requirements, which provides distinct levels of reliability, traceability and inalterability with respect to paper-based documents. The Model Law does not attempt to define a computer-based equivalent to any kind of paper document. Instead, it sets out basic functions of paper-based form requirements. Once these requirements have been met, all transactions should 'enjoy the same level of legal recognition'.[125]

The Explanatory Memorandum to the Commonwealth's *Electronic Transactions Act* states that the inclusion of the consent provision was based on the government's:

> general policy that a person should not be compelled to use an electronic communication to conduct a transaction in order to satisfy requirements or permissions to give information in writing under Commonwealth law.[126]

The definition of 'consent' in the Australian Acts includes consent that can reasonably be inferred from the conduct of the person concerned,[127] but does not include consent given subject to conditions unless the conditions are complied with. The definition is intended to ensure that express consent is not required prior to every electronic communication.[128]

The Explanatory Memorandum states that the power only applies where a person is receiving an electronic communication and that it is not necessary to state whether or not that person consents beforehand because 'the provisions are clearly drafted to provide a person with the ability to *choose* whether or not to satisfy their legal obligations by using an electronic communication' (emphasis added). However, this statement is questionable. For example, for a contract to be formed utilising the deeming features of the Electronic Transactions Acts, consent must be given by the recipient, and be known to be given, in advance. It is insufficient for the recipient to consent after receipt.

Example

If the law requires writing or a signature, and a person emails an acceptance, what is the effect of the consent provision on the timing of the formation of the contract?

---

124 Ibid.
125 Ibid., para 18. For example, see Art. 11 – Formation and validity of contracts.
126 *Electronic Transactions Act 1999* (Cth), Explanatory Memorandum, 49.
127 See, for example, *Luxottica Retail Australia Pty Ltd v 136 Queen Street Pty Ltd* [2011] QSC 162.
     See also *Rockhampton Regional Council v GKI Resort Pty Limited* [2013] QPEC 40, para 29.
128 See *Ilich and Baystar Corp Pty Ltd* [2004] WASTR 25.

To simplify the problem, let us ignore the postal acceptance rule and assume that the contract is formed on communication. Assume an offer is made by letter and contains the requisite material terms and the signature of the offeror. The offeree sends an email acceptance including an otherwise acceptable electronic signature. If it is known that the offeror will consent to an electronic communication of acceptance in advance, whether expressly, impliedly or by prior conduct, the Act applies and the requirement of writing and signature 'is taken to have been met'.

If the offeror has not consented in advance, two possibilities arise. First, on receipt of the acceptance the offeror considers his or her position, weighing up whether or not to consent to the 'electronic' writing and signature, and after some deliberation – minutes or days – the offeror decides to consent and all appears to be well. This seems to be the position taken by the Explanatory Memorandum. What is not addressed by the legislation is the timing of the formation of the contract. Is the contract formed at the point of communication by the offeree or when the offeror actually consents to the use of electronic writing? What if the offeror obtains legal advice regarding the electronic writing and so takes one or two weeks to consider whether or not to consent? What would be the effect should a 'time is of the essence' provision operate during the deliberation period? To suggest that a contract is entered into not on communication but at a later time would be to create a new concept: deferred formation of contract.

These issues were encountered in *Ilich and Baystar Corp Pty Ltd*.[129] The WA Strata Titles Referee determined that the language of the WA writing provision[130] requires consent to be known in advance. Kronberger R stated:

> both the 'giving' of the information and the 'consent' are expressed in the present tense, which may well indicate a legislative intention that, at the time the information was given, consent must exist. In other words, subsequent words or conduct are, strictly, irrelevant.[131]

The only result can be that where consent is not known in advance, the requirements of writing and signature are not 'taken to have been met' for the application of the Electronic Transactions Acts. This is contrary to express statements in the Explanatory Memorandum, although the Explanatory Memorandum was not specifically referring to contract formation. This leads to two unusual and perhaps surprising consequences. First, where consent cannot be determined in advance, the offeror cannot enforce a contract on receiving an email acceptance. Second, the offeree sending the email knows that the acceptance cannot be enforced against him or her, to the same extent that the offeree knows that on oral acceptance

---

129 [2004] WASTR 25.
130 *Electronic Transactions Act 2003* (WA) s8.
131 [2004] WASTR 25, para 11. See also *Thorn Airfield Lighting Pty Ltd v W* [2012] TASWRCT 11.

cannot be enforced. Of course, additional conduct may give the offeror a remedy using doctrines of estoppel or part performance, but, in the absence of any other factor, a contract has not been formed.[132] So the Australian consent provisions remove functional equivalence, one of the stated aims of the Model Law, and lead to incongruous unintentional results. A recipient of paper-based communications has no choice but to accept them (in terms of contract formation). Treating electronic communications differently erodes the functional equivalence principle and downgrades electronic commerce.

In *Legal Services Board v Forster* the Supreme Court of Victoria concluded that the Board must have consented 'because it instituted the proceedings on the basis that the resolution had been agreed to by the four members required'.[133] This improperly disregards the submission that '[c]onsent would have to have been given at the time of the resolution, and not subsequently'. The correct answer would be that there was consent in advance because of prior practice or by the Board's use of an email to send out the relevant form.

In *Bellaire Pty Ltd v Roselink Enterprises Pty Ltd*, a notice required in writing was given by email. The recipient argued lack of consent to the electronic communication. The Master of the Court stated that the 'ultimate question' was whether consent could be reasonably inferred from the inaction of the recipient to inform the sender that this objection would be made. The Master expressed concern that when the email was received 'no one contacted the (sender) to point out the deficiencies in the notice'. The Master noted that the first objection was made in the submissions to the court, concluding, '(i)n this case, the fact of silence speaks volumes'.[134] The Master appears to be an enthusiastic advocate for electronic commerce, stating that:

> [t]he pedantic insistence on a notice being in writing is entirely inconsistent with commerce being conducted as it is today ... To accept the (recipient's) argument would be to ignore the realities of the world of commerce in this day and age.[135]

However, the Master goes too far. In stating that consent emerges at some time after an unknown period of silence is to read into the provision an interpretation which is absent from the legislation.[136]

---

132 United Nations *Convention on the Use of Electronic Communications in International Contracts*, above n 78, para 173.
133 [2010] VSC 102.
134 [2014] WASC 142, para 26.
135 Ibid., para 27.
136 The Master would be better off stating that there was no consent, which results in no application of the *Electronic Transactions Act* to validate the notice as writing; and in the absence of a legislative provision, the common law would apply, which, the Master may rule, would recognise the email as writing.

In three separate cases the Resource Management and Planning Appeal Tribunal of Tasmania considered the issue of consent under the Tasmanian *Electronic Transactions Act*. On each occasion the Tribunal held that the respective local Council had not consented to the receipt of writing electronically from residents. The Tribunal reiterated that 'the validity of any purported transmission or sending of a representation in these circumstances is dependant [sic] upon the recipient's consent' and noted that the absence of providing for an electronic mode of receipt was a 'manifest clear intention not to consent to receipt of a representation electronically'.[137] In a later case the Tribunal stated that consent should be 'express and unequivocal' and ruled that consent could be reasonably inferred where an email address is provided in a formal notice in a newspaper or on its website.[138] Such an inference does not arise where the recipient does not provide an email address in any form, and 'more to the point the *only* address given is a postal one'.[139] In a third case the Tribunal accepted the position that consent may be given by reference to an email address on the Council's website or advertisement.[140] In each of these cases, there was nothing to indicate the acceptance of consent in advance, so the ruling was that there was no consent.

There remains one significant caveat. These comments are made for the purposes of the application of the Electronic Transactions Acts only. The relevant provisions merely state that equivalence requirements are not met if certain preconditions apply. The Act does not state that if the preconditions are not met the electronic writing shall not be equivalent. The next step is to determine whether the common law would regard the electronic writing and signature as equivalent.[141]

Consent – Other countries' provisions

Several others countries have consent provisions. The US *Uniform Electronic Transactions Act 1999* contains a general provision for the entire Act:

> This [Act] applies only to transactions between parties each of which has agreed to conduct transactions by electronic means. Whether the parties agree to conduct a transaction by electronic means is determined from the context and surrounding circumstances, including the parties' conduct.[142]

137 *KM Ravich v King Island Council and BH Hassing* [2007] TASRMPAT 226, para 6.
138 *Heritage Protection Society (Tasmania) Inc. v Tasmanian Heritage Council and Ireneinc Planning* [2011] TASRMPAT 165, para 17.
139 Ibid., emphasis added.
140 *Tarkine National Coalition Inc v Circular Head Council and Shree Minerals* [2012] TASRMPAT 146, para 8.
141 See Common law, above.
142 Section 5(b).

The Official Comments to this Act state, incongruously, that 'the paradigm of this Act is two willing parties doing transactions electronically'. The drafters considered this consent provision to demonstrate that the application of the Act is to be voluntary and to allow 'the greatest possible party autonomy to refuse electronic transactions'.[143]

The US *Electronic Signatures in Global and National Commerce Act* includes a similar consent provision to protect consumers. The Federal Trade Commission argues that the provision discourages deception and fraud by those who might fail to provide consumers with information the law requires that they receive.[144]

The *Electronic Commerce Act* of Ireland contains a consent provision substantially similar to that in the Australian Acts. In a section headed 'Use not mandatory', the Canadian *Electronic Transactions Act 2001* states: 'Nothing in this Act requires a person to provide, receive or retain information or a record in electronic form without the person's consent.'[145] The Official Comment explains that the section ensures that the Act will not be used to compel people to use electronic documents against their will as some people are still 'uncomfortable' with such documents and do not have the 'capacity' to use them. The Act, it explains, is intended to provide 'certainty, not compulsion'.

The Canadian *Uniform Electronic Commerce Act 1999* provides that 'Nothing in this Act requires a person to use or accept information in electronic form, but a person's consent to do so may be inferred from the person's conduct.'[146] The Official Comment to the Act explains that the section ensures that the Act will not be used to compel people to use electronic documents 'against their will'. It too states that many people 'are still uncomfortable with such documents', and do not yet have the capacity to use them.

Consent – Final comment

Two final comments to this section are warranted. The first – that the Australian consent provision thwarts functional equivalence – has been made. Under normal circumstances parties cannot refuse traditional paper communications and documents. Instead of providing certainty by recognising equality where the electronic writing, signature or production is functionally equivalent, the consent provision adds an unnecessary precondition creating less certainty, with consequences that are yet to be tested and analysed in court, in the end leaving such matters to the common law.

---

143 Official Comment to s5 US *Uniform Electronic Transactions Act 1999*, cl2.
144 Federal Trade Commission, 'Report to Congress on the Electronic Signatures in Global and National Commerce Act: The Consumer Consent Provision in Section 101(c)(1)(C)(ii)', (2001) <www.ftc.gov/reports/report-congress-electronic-signatures-global-national-commerce-act-consumer-consent>.
145 *Electronic Transactions Act 2001* (Canada) s4.
146 *Uniform Electronic Commerce Act 1999* (Canada) s6(1).

Second, the consent provision is futile. Where there is no applicable consent, the relevant provision does not state that the electronic writing, signature or production shall not be legally and functionally equivalent. The consequence is that this provision of the Act does not apply in any circumstances. Where the Act does not apply the courts must turn to the common law. The common law has, in the few cases to date, held equivalence in any event.[147]

Retention of information and documents

The requirement to record information in writing may be met by recording the information in electronic form.[148] To be acceptable it must be reasonable to expect that the information will continue to be accessible for future reference and the method of storing the information must comply with any requirements of the regulations under the Act as to the kind of data storage device on which the information is to be stored.

Retention in paper form

The requirement to retain a document in the form of paper, an article or other material for a particular period[149] may be met by recording or retaining the information in electronic form:

> If under a law of this jurisdiction, a person is required to record information in writing, that requirement is taken to have been met if the person records the information in electronic form, where:
>
> **(a)** having regard to all the relevant circumstances at the time of the generation of the electronic form of the document, the method of generating the electronic form of the document provided a reliable means of assuring the maintenance of the integrity of the information contained in the document, and
>
> **(b)** at the time of the generation of the electronic form of the document, it was reasonable to expect that the information contained in the electronic form of the document would be readily accessible so as to be useable for subsequent reference, and

---

147 See Common law, above; *McGuren v Simpson* [2004] NSWSC 35; *Hume Computers Pty Ltd v Exact International BV* [2007] FCA 478; *Wilkens v Iowa Insurance Commissioner* (1990) 457 NW 2d 1; *SM Integrated Transware v Schenker Singapore* Ltd [2005] 2 SLR 651.

148 Cth – s12(1), NSW – s11(1), Qld – s19, SA – s11(1), Tas – s9(1), Vic – s11(1), WA – s12(1), ACT – s11(1), NT – s11(1); New Zealand – s25.

149 The New Zealand provisions refer to 'paper or other non-electronic form', and do not refer to any particular period.

(c) if the regulations require that the electronic form of the document be retained on a particular kind of data storage device, that requirement has been met throughout that period.[150]

The integrity of information contained in a document is maintained 'if, and only if'[151] the information has remained complete and unaltered, apart from (a) the addition of any endorsement, or (b) any immaterial change, which arises in the normal course of communication, storage or display.[152] Applying this provision, it has been held that an audio recording of a meeting such as via a digital voice recorder or tape recorder, is a 'record' in the same way as a written transcript or minutes of the meeting.[153]

Retention in electronic form

The requirement to retain information the subject of an electronic communication for a particular time may be met by recording or retaining the information in electronic form. To be acceptable, that requirement is taken to have been met:

if ... the person is required to retain ... or causes another person to retain, in electronic form, the information throughout that period, where:

(a) ... at the time of commencement of the retention of the information, it was reasonable to expect that the information would be readily accessible so as to be useable for subsequent reference; and

(b) ... having regard to all the relevant circumstances at the time of commencement of the retention of the information, the method of retaining the information in electronic form provided a reliable means of assuring the maintenance of the integrity of the information contained in the electronic communication; and

(c) ... throughout that period, the first person also retains, or causes the other person to retain, in electronic form, such additional information obtained by the first person as is sufficient to enable the identification of the following:

   (i) the origin of the electronic communication;

   (ii) the destination of the electronic communication;

   (iii) the time when the electronic communication was sent;

   (iv) the time when the electronic communication was received; and

---

150 Cth – s12(2), NSW – s11(2), Qld – s20, SA – s11(2), Tas – s9(2), Vic – s11(2), WA – s12(2), ACT – s11(2), NT – s11(2), New Zealand – s25.
151 The Northern Territory altered this to 'only if'.
152 This additional provision is absent from the New Zealand provision.
153 *The Astor Centre* [2013] QBCCMCmr 249, para 18.

(d) ... at the time of commencement of the retention of the additional information covered by paragraph (c), it was reasonable to expect that the additional information
would be readily accessible so as to be useable for subsequent reference; and

(e) if the regulations require that the information be retained, in electronic form, on a
particular kind of data storage device–that requirement has been met throughout
that period.[154]

The requirements for origin, destination and time are aimed at electronic mail. The
application to other technologies such as SMS messaging, instant messaging and
chat rooms, where communication is often effectively instantaneous, may prove
problematic.

As with the previous requirement to retain in a paper form, the integrity of information contained in a document is maintained 'if, and only if'[155] the information
has 'remained complete and unaltered, apart from the addition of any endorsement, or any immaterial change, which arises in the normal course of communication, storage or display'.[156]

Time and place of dispatch and receipt of electronic communications

The time and place of the dispatch and receipt of electronic communications can
have significant impact in commerce, particularly in the law of contract. Strict
rules have developed in relation to the time and place of offer and acceptance in
contract law. This may have a bearing on the applicable jurisdiction or contract
formation. The *Electronic Transactions Acts* of Australia and New Zealand include
provisions based initially on the UNCITRAL Model Law and modified in Australia
by amendments in conformity with the UN *Communications Convention* that attempt to resolve uncertainties in this area. The time of dispatch and time of receipt
must be considered in conjunction with common law rules of offer and acceptance
and the timing of contract formation. One must also ask whether the postal acceptance rule can or should apply to electronic mail and other forms of electronic
communications and, if it does, how it interacts with the legislation.

154 Cth – s12(4), NSW – s11(4), Qld – ss19–21, SA – s11(4), Tas – s9(4), Vic – s11(4), WA –
s12(4), ACT – s11(4), NT – s11(4); NZ – ss26–27. The Commonwealth provision includes the
words 'in all cases' at the beginning of paragraphs (a)–(d).
155 The Northern Territory altered this to 'only if'.
156 Cth – s12(3), NSW – s11(3), Qld – s 20(3), SA – s11(3), Tas – s9(3), Vic – s11(3), WA – s12(3),
ACT – s11(3), NT – s11(3); this additional provision is absent from the New Zealand provision.

Time of dispatch

For the purposes of a law of this jurisdiction, unless otherwise agreed between the originator and the addressee of an electronic communication, the time of dispatch of the electronic communication is:

(a) the time when the electronic communication leaves an information system under the control of the originator or of the party who sent it on behalf of the originator, or

(b) if the electronic communication has not left an information system under the control of the originator or of the party who sent it on behalf of the originator – the time when the electronic communication is received by the addressee.[157]

The dispatch of the electronic communication occurs when it leaves the control of the originator. In the most typical case this would be when the originator clicks the 'Send' button of an email. The broad term 'electronic communication' applies to emails and SMS messages, and to present and future technologies. The provision for time of dispatch is a default rule. The parties may have 'otherwise agreed' to alternative arrangements. All nine Australian Electronic Transactions Acts were amended to conform to the UN *Communications Convention*. In doing so the former flawed test, which was that receipt occurs when 'entering an information system outside the control of the originator', was removed.

Problems not envisaged when the former provision was drafted by UNCITRAL in 1996 arose with regard to email and communication systems. Today, some systems permit the originator to recall an email before it has been flagged as read. However, it is also possible for a recipient to read the name of the sender and the subject line without opening an email. Changing the test to 'leaving the information system under the control of the originator' resolves this dilemma.[158] Where the electronic communication has not left the information system under the control of the originator, it is deemed dispatched when received. This rule also addresses the recall concern.[159] Even where an email has been successfully recalled, it has been dispatched, although knowledge of that fact, and subsequent proof, may be problematic. In the short term, practitioners must be careful not to apply the amended provisions to facts predating the amendments.[160]

---

157 NSW – s13. Other Australian jurisdictions have identical or substantially identical provisions: Cth – s14, Qld – s23, SA – s13, Tas – s11, Vic – s13, WA – s13, ACT – s13, NT – s13.

158 Alan Davidson, *The Law of Electronic Commerce*, Cambridge University Press, 2009, p. 33.

159 'This provision anticipates the exchange of electronic communications within the same information system', Electronic Transactions Amendment Bill 2011 (Cth), Explanatory Memorandum para 54.

160 This has occurred on at least two occasions: see *Conveyor & General Engineering Pty Ltd v Basetec Services Pty Ltd* [2014] QSC 30 and *Austral-Asia Freight Pty Ltd v Turner* [2013] FCCA 298. For the commencement date of the amendments see above n 109.

The New Zealand provision in relation to the time of dispatch is much less verbose than the Australian equivalents, but contains the same notions and principles:

> An electronic communication is taken to be dispatched at the time the electronic communication first enters an information system outside the control of the originator.[161]

Time of receipt

The Electronic Transactions Acts provide:

(1) For the purposes of a law of this jurisdiction, unless otherwise agreed between the originator and the addressee of an electronic communication:

   (a) the time of receipt of the electronic communication is the time when the electronic communication becomes capable of being retrieved by the addressee at an electronic address designated by the addressee, or

   (b) the time of receipt of the electronic communication at another electronic address of the addressee is the time when both:

     (i) the electronic communication has become capable of being retrieved by the addressee at that address, and

    (ii) the addressee has become aware that the electronic communication has been sent to that address.

(2) For the purposes of subsection (1), unless otherwise agreed between the originator and the addressee of the electronic communication, it is to be assumed that the electronic communication is capable of being retrieved by the addressee when it reaches the addressee's electronic address.[162]

The section distinguishes between a communication sent to a designated electronic address and where no electronic address is designated. Where the electronic address is designated, receipt of an electronic communication occurs when it is 'capable of being retrieved'. This is 'assumed' to be when it reaches the addressee's electronic address.[163] Where the electronic address is not designated, not only must the electronic communication be capable of being retrieved, but the addressee

---

161 *Electronic Transactions Act 2002* (NZ) s10(1).

162 NSW – s13A. Other Australian jurisdictions have identical or substantially identical provisions: Cth – s14A, Qld – s24, SA – s13A, Tas – s11A, Vic – s13A, WA – s14, ACT – s13A, NT – s13A. For cases dealing with receipt at common law see *Jalun Pool Supplies Pty Ltd v Onga Pty Ltd* [1999] SASC 20, [18] and *Premium Grain Handlers Pty Ltd v Elite Grains Pty Ltd* [2005] WASC 103, [65]–[71].

163 UN *Convention on the Use of Electronic Communications in International Contracts*, above n 78, para 16: 'capable of being retrieved' 'is presumed to happen when the electronic communication reaches the addressee's electronic address'. See para 16.

must also become aware that it has been sent to that address.[164] In *Bauen Constructions Pty Ltd v Sky General Services Pty Ltd*,[165] the Supreme Court of NSW examined the meaning of the expression 'capable of being retrieved' in circumstances where an email was caught by the recipient's spam filter. The court described the expression as 'ample in their [sic] reach', quoting the Oxford dictionary definition of 'retrieve' in its primary sense as 'to get or bring back from somewhere' and in its secondary sense as 'to find or extract (information stored in a computer)'.[166] The court concluded that even where the email is caught by the recipient's 'spam filter, it is nonetheless archived and accessible by (the addressee) via its external IT consultant'.[167] That is, where an 'an email is sent, but not opened or read, but it is capable of being retrieved, it has been received'.[168] An email filter may be external and may be for a range of 'sanitation' purposes, such as quarantining emails with viruses or text which includes profanity, quarantining spam, rejecting oversized emails or stripping attachments with undesirable components. The operation of the filter is typically unknown to and beyond the control of the sender. Innocent emails may fall foul of such filters; for example, by the use of otherwise innocuous expressions such as 'pharmaceutical'.[169] Cases have held that emails may be regarded as received even where caught in such a filter system and deleted or placed into a dead-letter box.[170] Files attached to an email in an unusual compressed format unknown to the recipient were nevertheless capable of being retrieved.[171]

Again, the broad term 'electronic communication' applies to emails and, SMS messages, and to present and future technologies. Depositing electronic documents in a dropbox facility[172] and then sending the links to the recipient by email will not be regarded as an electronic communication.[173] The provision for time of

---

164 In *Spiral Tube Makers Pty Ltd v PIHA Pty Ltd* [2010] APO 16, an email communication consented to a draft deed being sent by facsimile within 14 days. The opponent erroneously believed the draft deed could be sent by email and did so after close of business on the 14th day. However, in the absence of a designation of the email address, the court appropriately applied what is now subsection (2) of the time of receipt provision, namely that the communication is received when it comes to the attention of the addressee, which in this case was the next morning, the 15th day, and so was out of time.

165 [2012] NSWSC 1123.

166 Ibid., para 77, brackets added.

167 Ibid.

168 Ibid., para 78.

169 As discussed at para 87 in *William Close Pty Ltd v City of Salisbury (No 2)* [2012] SAERDC 26.

170 For example *William Close Pty Ltd v City of Salisbury (No 2)* [2012] SAERDC 26.

171 See *Re David Scott Ellis; Ex Parte Triple M Mechanical Services Pty Ltd [No 2]* [2013] WASC 161; however, the court questioned and discussed whether the '.rar' files were readily accessible so as to be useable for subsequent reference, as required by the writing test to be functionally equivalent.

172 A dropbox facility is a service by which electronic files may be stored by a third party remotely so that another person with the appropriate access code can access the files. See above n 91.

173 See *Conveyor & General Engineering Pty Ltd v Basetec Services Pty Ltd* [2014] QSC 30, para 29.

receipt is also again a default rule as the parties may have agreed to alternative arrangements. All nine Australian Electronic Transactions Acts were amended to conform to the UN *Communications Convention*. In doing so, the concept that receipt occurs when 'entering a designated information system of the recipient' was removed. Many cases struggled with the meaning of 'designated information system'.[174] In the short term, practitioners must be careful not to apply the amended provisions to facts predating the amendments.

The time of receipt of electronic communications has significant practical consequences and has been the subject of several cases. Many bodies, both governmental and non-governmental, make provision for the receipt of documents, and set up consequences for non-receipt. However, various expressions, which do not necessarily equate to 'receipt', are used: such bodies may require documents to be lodged, served, provided, left, given, delivered or made, or information to be notified. In contract law, a contract is typically formed when the acceptance is communicated to the offeror. The courts must grapple with the application of a test of functional equivalence for 'receipt' in circumstances where other expressions are used.

In *Westpac Banking Corporation v Dixon*[175] the court equated 'receipt' under the Commonwealth *Electronic Transactions Act* with the requirement to 'give' a notice pursuant to section 64D of the *Bankruptcy Act 1966* (Cth).

Most Australian states, and New Zealand, have legislation to ensure payment under a construction contract, by a procedure that involves a payment claim by the claimant followed by a payment schedule by the respondent detailing reasons, if any, for withholding payment. If the respondent fails to respond within a strict statutory time limit, the right to object is lost. However, a mixture of terminology has been used in the various jurisdictions. In four states and New Zealand the relevant section states that the claimant may 'serve' the payment claim and the respondent may 'provide' a payment schedule in response.[176] Western Australia and the ACT use the expression, 'giving' a payment claim and 'giving' a payment schedule (or notice of dispute) in response.[177] Only Queensland uses the expression to 'serve' for both the claim and response.[178]

---

174 For example *Austar Finance v Campbell* [2007] NSWSC 1493 and *Reed v Eire* [2009] NSWSC 678.

175 [2011] FMCA 211.

176 *Building and Construction Industry Security of Payment Act 1999* (NSW), ss13 and 14, *Building and Construction Industry Security of Payment Act 2009* (SA), ss13 and 14, *Building and Construction Industry Security of Payment Act 2009* (Tas), ss17 and 18, *Building and Construction Industry Security of Payment Act 2002* (Vic), ss14 and 15, *Construction Contracts Act 2002* (NZ), ss20 and 21.

177 *Construction Contracts Act 2004* (WA), Schedule 1, *Building and Construction Industry (Security of Payment) Act 2009* (ACT), ss14 and 15.

178 *Building and Construction Industry Payments Act 2004* (Qld), ss17 and 18.

In *Falgat Constructions Pty Ltd v Equity Australia Corporation Pty Ltd*,[179] Hodgson JA discussed the expressions 'serve', 'provide', 'notice', 'receipt' and 'made' under the NSW Act. His Honour stated that where a 'document has actually been received and come to the attention of a person to be served or provided with the document ... there has been service, provision and receipt'.[180] He noted that a payment claim is a notice and that section 31, dealing with the service of notices, thus applied. However, he questioned whether section 31 'also applies to provision of payment schedules'. He considered it 'highly unlikely' that it was the intention of the legislature that 'provision' of the payment schedule only occurs when it 'actually comes into the hands of some person on behalf of the claimant',[181] because the legislative scheme would be thwarted by a claimant ensuring that no one was at the claimant's address or registered office within the time period. His Honour considered whether the 'use of the word "provide" rather than the word "serve" carries a suggestion that a different meaning is intended'. However, he concluded that for the purposes of the Act, they have the same meaning.[182] The legislation requires an adjudication application to be 'made' to a relevant authority; his Honour equated 'made' with 'received'. Finally, his Honour stated that:

> mail delivered to a registered office or place of business is received at that place when it is put into the mail box of that registered office or place of business, without the necessity of anyone actually seeing it ... [and] would be satisfied once the document has arrived at the claimant's registered office or place of business and is there during normal office hours.[183]

In *Bauen Constructions Pty Ltd v Sky General Services Pty Ltd*,[184] the court equated receipt with 'lodged' under section 20 of the *Building and Construction Industry Security of Payment Act 1999* (NSW).

In *Hickory Developments Pty Ltd v Schiavello (Vic) Pty Ltd*,[185] both the counsel and the judge, Vickery J, appear to have ignored the Victorian *Electronic Transactions Act*. In deciding the date and time of an electronic application for adjudication made under the *Building and Construction Industry Security of Payment Act 2002* (Vic), the judge initially stated that:

> from general experience I accept that shortly after each email was received by the server computer, it sent an electronic notification to a

179 [2006] NSWCA 259.
180 Ibid., para 58.
181 Ibid., para 60.
182 Ibid., para 61.
183 Ibid., paras 62 and 63.
184 [2012] NSWSC 1123.
185 [2009] VSC 156.

computer operated by (the adjudicator), indicating that the emails had been received.[186]

His Honour reasoned that the adjudicator was then in a position to discover the notification from the server and open the email and attachments. 'Until at least these steps had been taken ... it could not be said that the email in each case and its attachments had been "received" at the place of business of (the adjudicator).' His Honour regarded the documents at this stage as merely being 'accessible to the intended recipient'.[187] However, his Honour then reasoned by analogy to the electronic filing of origination process in the Supreme Court of Victoria and the County Court of Victoria, that the date and time of filing of an originating process that is filed electronically is 'governed by the date and time when the email transmission arrives at the court server where it may be accessed by the court'.[188] His Honour concluded that the date and time of filing of the application before him 'may be determined by the date and time when the email transmission *arrives at the authority's server* where it may be accessed'.[189] In arriving at this conclusion his Honour considered the previous conduct of the adjudicator in accepting such applications, statements contained in the Victorian Adjudication Application Checklist and the text of the email in question which 'unequivocally demonstrated an intention that [the] email and attachments' were to constitute a formal application.

In *Austar Finance v Campbell*, Austin J, whilst making no reference to the NSW *Electronic Transactions Act*, raised the question whether service occurs where an email is sent to an email address where the recipient routinely accesses his or her computer (which is located at the address of the place of business) even though the email is not read. To add to the profusion of terminology Austin J uses the expression 'left', stating that:

> where the electronic message is received and held by a remote third-party server rather than in the receiver's computer, and there is no hard copy document unless the receiver accesses the email and transmits it to a printer, nothing can be said to have been 'left' at the receiver's premises, at least until the e-mail is accessed.[190]

In *Reed v Eire*, MacReady AJ stated: 'The first question is whether "receipt" as defined in the Electronic Transactions Act equates to service.'[191] His view was that

---

186 Ibid., para 126. Note that His Honour is using the word 'received' without any reference to the Victorian *Electronic Transactions Act*.
187 Ibid.
188 Ibid., para 131.
189 Ibid., para 132, emphasis added; see also para 133.
190 [2007] NSWSC 1493, para 60.
191 [2009] NSWSC 678, para 29.

the time of receipt provision (as it was at that time) 'does away with the requirement of notice of the documents in a readable form being given to the person to be served'.[192] MacReady AJ's view was that this had the benefit of preventing the recipient from deliberately not downloading and opening an email to avoid service. In these circumstances, once the addressee has designated an electronic address, the onus is on the addressee to become aware of communications received at that address.

Evidence of receipt

Information recorded by ink on paper has the feature of singularity in two senses. In the first sense a unique record is created.[193] In the second, the information contained within the paper is expressed and represented by the writing alone. This is not necessarily the case with electronic records. By their very nature, electronic records can be, and often are, designed to contain both information with the appearance of writing, and additional information (metadata) – often copious amounts of it. It typically includes the date of the transmission, the date of receipt by various servers, a detailed list of recipients and linkages between messages sent and replies received. Any knowledgeable person may be able to find and read this additional information.[194] Unfortunately, in a number of Australian cases where evidence of such metadata would have greatly assisted the court in reaching its decision, no such person has been invited to assist the court.

In *Reed v Eire* MacReady AJ expressed frustration about the lack of metadata, stating: 'What is important ... is the point at which the communication reaches a mail server from which the recipient can access it.'[195] His Honour complained of the lack of 'technical evidence', which he described as 'some kind of email exchange log generated by that server' to assist in determining the precise time an email entered the recipient's Internet Service Provider or personal computer. In the absence of the email's metadata the court could not satisfactorily apply the receipt provision of the NSW *Electronic Transactions Act*, and could make no determination that an email was 'received' before it had been opened by the recipient. His Honour was aware that such evidence ought to exist: 'The evidence does not indicate whether this is data that is regularly logged by mail servers and if so, whether there may be a question as to the length of time this information is stored.'[196] Similarly, in *Austar*

---

192 Ibid., para 32.
193 Miriam Golby, *Electronic Documents in Maritime Trade*, Oxford University Press, Oxford, 2013, p. 35.
194 For an example dealing with metadata in Microsoft Word documents and the law of evidence, see Chapter 19.
195 [2009] NSWSC 678, para 34.
196 Ibid., para 31.

Finance v Campbell, Austin J complained that there was 'no evidence' on when the email was received and that 'the evidence that has been provided at this technical level is less than satisfactory'.[197] His Honour was attempting to determine what was held at the computer located at the business address. The evidence was indeed available in the metadata for both cases, and one can only surmise that it was not presented because a sufficiently knowledgeable computer person was not called on.

In both *Austar Finance v Campbell* and *Reed v Eire* the sender was unable to prove that the notice was received in time; had the relevant metadata been made available to the court, the result may well have been different in both cases. MacReady AJ addressed this issue stating that in the absence of evidence to assist he would be 'reluctant to infer that the recipient server received the email on the same day' because it may have been the case that the sending mail server could not 'for some reason dispatch the communication' or the destination mail server may have been 'off-line for some reason'.[198]

This places the sender of an email at a disadvantage. Only the recipient has direct access to the received email with the pertinent metadata. The sender must use discovery to gain access, not to a printout of the email, but to an electronic copy.[199] This unsatisfactory position was addressed and rectified by the Queensland Court of Appeal in *Queensland Building Services Authority v JM Kelly (Project Builders) Pty Ltd*[200] by imposing an onus on the recipient to adduce evidence in respect to the receipt of the email. The sender dispatched an email with a notice pursuant to the *Queensland Building Services Authority Act 1991* (Qld). The evidence did not satisfactorily establish if or when it was received, although the general manager of the recipient company indicated that if it had been received, it would have been dealt with by an administrator, who would have decided whether or not it should be passed on to the general manager. The general manager stated that he had no recollection of such an email being brought to his notice on the date in question. The Court of Appeal considered that the recipient 'did not fulfil the *onus* which lay upon it to prove that it had not opened the email'.[201] The court pointed out that the recipient did not adduce direct evidence that the attachment to the email was '*not* received and opened by an employee of the (recipient)'; and did '*not* adduce evidence explaining why the staff member did not give evidence, so that the (recipient's) failure to adduce evidence from the staff member at least made it less likely that the court would draw the inferences for which the (recipient) contended'.[202] The Court of Appeal concluded: 'There is no reason to doubt that the (sender)

197 [2007] NSWSC 1493, para 18. See also para 22.
198 [2009] NSWSC 678, para 35.
199 See Chapter 19.
200 [2013] QCA 320.
201 Ibid., para 11, emphasis added.
202 Ibid., para 16, emphasis added.

effectively directed the (recipient) to rectify the building work.'[203] It must be noted that had the metadata been adduced as evidence, there would have been no need for the Court of Appeal to make these presumptions and shift the onus of proof.

For the purposes of contract formation, the provision can form a quasi postal acceptance rule, as the email is deemed received before communication. The problem is complicated by rules relating to acceptances and, in common law countries, by the possible application of the postal acceptance rule.

Migration Act – bankruptcy rules – time of receipt

The former test for time of receipt was considered to be so flawed and so uncertain that the Federal Parliament made amendments to the *Migration Act 1958* (Cth) in 2001 to include a provision to 'disapply' the time of receipt provision. Section 494C(5) of the *Migration Act 1958* (Cth) provides that where the Minister gives a document to a person by fax, email or other electronic means, it is deemed received at the end of the day on which the document was transmitted. Section 494C(6) states that subsection (5) applies 'despite section 14 of the *Electronic Transactions Act 1999*'.[204] The Explanatory Memorandum states that the effect is to 'disapply the deemed receipt provisions of the ET Act in favour of the deemed receipt provision in subsection 494C(5), as this is more certain'. The Explanatory Memorandum expressed concern about the test under the Commonwealth *Electronic Transactions Act*, stating that the time of receipt:

> might never be known ... There is a need in the migration context for receipt to be easily determinable ... it was preferable to expressly provide for deemed receipt ... and not rely on the default provisions in section 14 of the ET Act.[205]

In *American Express Australia Limited v Michaels*,[206] the court regarded the *Bankruptcy Regulations 1996* (Cth) dealing with the time of receipt of electronic documents as implicitly excluding the application of the time of receipt provision of the Commonwealth *Electronic Transactions Act*. The court considered the time of receipt provision in the Bankruptcy Rules as 'simple to establish', whereas it described at length the difficulties and 'uncertainties in applying the *Electronic Transactions Act 1999*'.[207] Much of the difficulty has been removed with the 2011 amendments.

---

203 Ibid., para 14, emphasis added.
204 See, for example, *Tay v Minister for Immigration & Citizenship* [2010] FCAFC 23
205 It should be noted that the *Migration Act* stills refers to s14 of the *Electronic Transactions Act 1999*, even though the time of receipt provision was renumbered to s 14A in June 2011. See also *Chidbundid v Minister for Immigration* [2012] FMCA 59.
206 [2010] FMCA 103.
207 Ibid., see paras 23–30.

New Zealand

As with the time of dispatch, the New Zealand provision, in relation to the time of receipt, is much less verbose than the Australian equivalents. However, it contains the former test of entering a designated information system. For New Zealanders, the time of receipt is:

(a) in the case of an addressee who has designated an information system for the purpose of receiving electronic communications, at the time the electronic communication enters that information system; or

(b) in any other case, at the time the electronic communication comes to the attention of the addressee.[208]

Acceptance by electronic communication and the postal acceptance rule

Contracts are formed only when there is a meeting of minds. There is an offer and a corresponding acceptance. The general common law principle is that acceptance must be communicated to the offeror, at which point a legally enforceable contract comes into existence. However, from the 19th century cases of *Henthorn v Fraser*,[209] based on *Adams v Lindsell*,[210] an exception known as the postal acceptance rule arose. As propounded by Lord Herschell in the former case:

> Where the circumstances are such that it must have been within the contemplation of the parties that ... the post might be used as a means of communicating the acceptance of an offer, the acceptance is complete as soon as it is posted.[211]

This exception applies whether the letter is delivered, delayed or even lost. It has been regarded by the House of Lords as a rule of 'commercial expediency' and as a 'foundation of convenience'.[212] Without the rule the acceptor may be placed in an uncertain position, not knowing when or whether the acceptance has been received and communicated. The rule avoids the necessity of a confirmation and of a confirmation of the confirmation *ad infinitum*.

While the rule has been held to apply to telegrams, the courts have consistently held that it does not apply to instantaneous forms of communication such as the telephone and (in some cases) telexes.

---

208 *Electronic Transactions Act 2002* (NZ) s11. See also *Petterson v Gothard No.3* [2012] NZHC 666.
209 [1892] 2 Ch 27.
210 (1818) B & Ald 681.
211 [1892] 2 Ch 27, 33.
212 Lord Wilberforce, in *Brinkibon Ltd v Stahag Stahl* [1983] 2 AC 34.

In *Entores Ltd v Miles Far East Corp.*[213] Lord Denning discussed various scenarios, such as acceptance shouted across a river which was not heard due to a passing plane, the telephone going dead, and where a recipient informs a sender of the failure of the teleprinter during the transmission of a telex. Initially Lord Denning commented: 'In all the instances I have taken so far, the man who sends the message of acceptance knows that it has not been received or he has reason to know it. So he must repeat it.' However, he then considered the position where the sender does not know the acceptance had not been communicated. Perhaps 'the listener on the telephone does not catch the words of acceptance' and does not ask that the words be repeated, or 'the ink on the teleprinter fails at the receiving end' and the clerk does not ask for the message to be repeated. As a result, 'the man who sends an acceptance reasonably believes that his message has been received ... The offeror in such circumstances is clearly bound because he will be estopped from saying that he did not receive the message of acceptance. It is his own fault ...'.[214] However, his Lordship continued, if the offeror 'without any fault on his part does not receive the message of acceptance – yet the sender of it reasonably believes it has got home when it has not – then I think there is no contract'.[215] Parker LJ in the same case notes that although the operation of a telex 'is not completely instantaneous, the parties are to all intents and purposes in each other's presence, just as if they were in telephonic communication'.[216]

The same cannot be said of all electronic communications. The parties often regard the communications as akin to mail. There may be no expectation of being in each other's presence.[217]

In *Brinkibon Ltd v Stahag Stahl und Stahlwarenhandelsgesellschaft mbH*[218] the House of Lords confirmed on the facts before them that the telex should be treated as instantaneous communication. However, Lord Wilberforce qualified the principle. Although it was still too early to consider electronic mail, his Lordship set out a number of guidelines, reminiscent of electronic mail use, which could be used to assess whether a form of communication might have the postal acceptance rule applied to it:

> The message may not reach, or be intended to reach, the designated recipient immediately. Messages may be sent out of office hours, or at night, with the intention, or upon the assumption, that they will be read at a later time. There may be some error or default at the recipient's end which prevents

213 [1955] 2 QB 327 ('*Entores*' case').
214 Ibid., 333.
215 Ibid.
216 Ibid., 337.
217 See Eliza Mik, 'The effectiveness of acceptances communicated by electronic means, or – does the postal acceptance rule apply to email', (2009) 26(1) *Journal of Contract Law*, 68.
218 [1983] 2 AC 34 ('*Brinkibon's* case'.

> receipt at the time contemplated and believed in by the sender. The message may have been sent and/or received through machines operated by third persons. And many other variations may occur. No universal rule can cover all such cases: they must be resolved by reference to the intention of the parties, by sound business practice and in some cases by a judgment where the risks should lie.[219]

There is no blanket rule. That is, 'no universal rule can cover all such cases'. His Lordship envisaged that a threefold test should be applied, taking into account the intention of the parties, sound business practice and, in some cases, a judgement of where the risks should lie.[220] The mistake made by many commentators has been to examine only the technology and to categorise it as instantaneous or not. This has led to misdirection. The correct approach should be to examine the use of the technology, as described by Lord Denning in *Entores'* case, and Lord Wilberforce (above). There have been misgivings about the blanket categorisation of the telex and facsimile as instantaneous. When employed via third parties (indeed on occasions through the post office) similar delays, if not identical delays, occur as occur with standard post. If the use anticipates such delay, there is no reason in principle that the postal acceptance rule should be regarded as inapplicable.

Messenger systems and chat rooms provide users with real-time communications that should be categorised as instantaneous. Acceptance of offers made using such technology should follow the rule of acceptance on communication. Acceptances may be by numerous means – voicemail, VOIP, SMS, bulletin boards, email, to name a few. To classify the application of the 19th century rule based purely on whether or not it can be instantaneous is fraught with danger.[221]

Some technologies may be used in more than one way: like the post and in an instantaneous manner. Email is sometimes used as a chat room or instant messaging. Two users may send and receive numerous emails within a matter of minutes. It may be conversational, with questions and answers clarifying each other's position before a formal offer and acceptance occurs. This use of communications should be regarded as instantaneous, in which case the general 'communication acceptance rule' ought to apply. Similar use of other technology should be treated likewise.

However, some users utilise electronic mail like standard mail. A given office's protocol may be to access email once per day and then carefully draft a reply for sending later in the day. Such an office may require a supervisor to check

---

219 Ibid., 42.
220 See Mik, above n 217, 17.
221 See Marwan Al Ibrahim, Ala'eldin Ababneh and HishamTahat, 'The Postal Acceptance Rule in the digital age', (2007) 2(1) *Journal of International Commercial Law and Technology.*

the contents of all mail before it is sent, whether it is standard or electronic mail. Once approved, the electronic mail may be sent in one batch; for example, at a time similar to the dispatch of regular mail. Clearly this use would be more akin to standard mail.

The focus of the application of the rule should be on the use, bearing in mind Wilberforce's threefold test of intention, sound business practice and risk.

Four scenarios may be considered in determining whether and how the postal acceptance rule should apply to electronic communications:

1   The postal acceptance rule does not apply because the Electronic Transactions Acts override the common law and specifically provide that 'receipt' occurs when the email enters the recipient's 'designated information system'. Hence it is the intention of the legislature that a quasi postal acceptance rule applies to electronic communications.

2   The postal acceptance rule does not apply to electronic communications because such communications are to be regarded as instantaneous communications.

3   The postal acceptance rule applies to electronic communications independently of the Electronic Transaction Acts.

4   The postal acceptance rule applies in circumstances involving commercial expediency, depending upon the intention of the parties and use.

The first approach is unsustainable because the stated rationales of the Electronic Transactions Acts do not deal directly with contracts or the postal acceptance rule.[222] The Acts are designed to deal with a broad range of electronic transactions. The second and third approaches presume that the postal acceptance rule is technology-based. This is a misconception perpetuated by scant reading of the cases. The cases refer to use, intention, sound businesses practice and risk. For example, Lord Wilberforce in *Brinkibon's* case[223] envisaged circumstances where facsimiles may nevertheless be subject to the postal acceptance rule. The fourth approach looks to the ramifications of usage, such as the inconvenience of delay in the context of intention, business practice and commerce. If the intention of the parties cannot be determined, the 'rule of commercial expediency' should apply according to the nature and use made of the technology involved.

The Singapore High Court expressed an obiter view on the postal acceptance rule applying to emails, describing it as an 'important issue' and stating that 'email does not really differ from mail that has to be opened'.[224] Rajah JC considered that 'unlike a fax or a telephone call, [email] is not instantaneous. E-mails are processed through servers, routers and Internet service providers.'[225]

222 See Electronic Transactions Bill 1999 (Cth), Explanatory Memorandum.
223 [1983] 2 AC 34.
224 *Chwee Kin Keong v Digilandmall.com Pte Ltd* [2004] 2 SLR 594, para 97.
225 Ibid.

His Honour added that once an offer sent by email 'the sender loses control over the route and delivery time of the message. In that sense, it is *akin to ordinary posting.*'[226] Ultimately Rajah JC stated:

> Notwithstanding some real differences with posting, it could be argued cogently that the postal rule should apply to e-mail acceptances; in other words, that the acceptance is made the instant the offer is sent.[227]

Logan J in the Federal Court of Australia stated:

> Experience suggests that email is often, but not invariably, a form of near instantaneous communication ... there are analogies to be drawn with the way the law developed in relation to telex communications in an earlier era where what I have termed 'the instantaneous communication rule' came to be adopted ... by analogy with cases concerning the position with what were, or were treated as, other forms of instantaneous communication, I consider that the contract was made where the acceptance was received.[228]

However, while leaving the door open for the future, his Honour decided that the rule did not apply to the case before him on the facts and because the issue was not 'explored' by the parties.

Today, commercial parties have at their disposal numerous methods of communication virtually beyond comprehension at the time of Lord Denning in *Entores'* case and Lord Wilberforce in *Brinkibon's* case. Prophetically, Lord Brandon, in *Brinkibon's* case, stated:

> The reason for the exception is commercial expediency ... That reason of commercial expediency applies to cases where there is bound to be a substantial interval between the time when the acceptance is sent and the time when it is received. In such cases the exception to the general rule is more convenient, and makes on the whole for greater fairness, than the general rule itself would do.[229]

Where the parties' intention is that communications shall be electronic and there is expected to be, and is, a substantial interval between the time when the acceptance is sent and the time when it is received, the postal acceptance rule ought to apply.[230]

---

226 Ibid., para 98, emphasis added.
227 Ibid.
228 *Olivaylle Pty Ltd v Flottweg GMBH & Co KGAA (No. 4)* [2009] FCA 522, para 25.
229 Ibid., 48.
230 See comments made in para 174 Explanatory Note by the UNCITRAL secretariat on the *UN Convention on the Use of Electronic Communications in International Contracts,* above n 78, para 174.

The rationale remains commercial expediency, sound business practice and an appropriate assessment of risk. The Explanatory Memorandum to the amending Bill of the Commonwealth stated that the postal acceptance rule 'may be confined to situations where it can be inferred an offeror intended acceptance to be communicated upon dispatch of an electronic communication'.[231]

The application of the postal acceptance rule is typically limited to applicable common law jurisdictions. However, the rule does not apply where the contract is an international sale of goods, as the applicable law defers to the *United Nations Convention on Contracts for the International Sale of Goods* (CISG). The CISG does not apply to contracts for personal, family or household use,[232] and so would not apply in personal internet purchases. The CISG is law in all Australian states and territories and New Zealand.[233]

Place of dispatch and place of receipt

(1) For the purposes of a law of this jurisdiction, unless otherwise agreed between the originator and the addressee of an electronic communication:

   (a) the electronic communication is taken to have been dispatched from the originator's place of business, and

   (b) the electronic communication is taken to have been received at the addressee's place of business.

(2) For the purposes of the application of subsection (1) to an electronic communication:

   (a) a party's place of business is assumed to be the location indicated by that party, unless another party demonstrates that the party making the indication does not have a place of business at that location, and

   (b) if a party has not indicated a place of business and has only one place of business, it is to be assumed that that place is the party's place of business, and

   (c) if a party has not indicated a place of business and has more than one place of business, the place of business is that which has the closest relationship to the underlying transaction, having regard to the circumstances known to or contemplated by the parties at any time before or at the conclusion of the transaction, and

---

231 Electronic Transactions Amendment Bill 2011 (Cth), Explanatory Memorandum, para 56.
232 Article 2, *United Nations Convention on Contracts for the International Sale of Goods*.
233 *Sale of Goods (Vienna Convention) Act 1986* (NSW), *Sale of Goods (Vienna Convention) Act 1986* (Qld), *Sale of Goods (Vienna Convention) Act 1986* (SA), *Sale of Goods (Vienna Convention) Act 1987* (Tas), Part VI *Goods Act 1958* (Vic), *Sale of Goods (Vienna Convention) Act 1986* (WA), *Sale of Goods (Vienna Convention) Act 1987* (ACT), *Sale of Goods (Vienna Convention) Act* (NT), and *Sale of Goods (United Nations Convention) Act 1994* (NZ).

(d) if a party has not indicated a place of business and has more than one place of business, but paragraph (c) does not apply-it is to be assumed that the party's principal place of business is the party's only place of business, and

(e) if a party is a natural person and does not have a place of business-it is to be assumed that the party's place of business is the place of the party's habitual residence.[234]

These rules may be important in determining the law to be applied, or the forum, in the event of a dispute. It is not proposed to deal with the various rules of private international law and domestic conflict of laws rules here. However, circumstances may arise where the place of contract formation determines which laws or which forum may be applicable.[235]

Again, the term 'electronic communication' applies to emails, instant messages and SMS, present and future technologies. The provision is a default rule. The parties may have 'otherwise agreed' to alternative arrangements.

Attribution of electronic communication

Traditional forms of paper-based communication can be typically attributed to the author by such factors as handwriting, signature and letterhead. Electronic communications can be generic. The electronic text can be indistinguishable regardless of the source. However, to whom do we attribute the message? For example, using one of the popular public email services, such as Gmail or Yahoo, an impersonator could register a person's name.[236] A second example is where the impersonator accesses another's computer and, using the actual email system on the computer, sends a message. The recipient of such a message has every indication that the message is genuine.

The Australian Electronic Transactions Acts resolve this conundrum in a manner that is functionally equivalent to that of the paper world. A person is not bound by an electronic communication unless the communication was sent by, or with the authority of, that person:

234 NSW – s13B. Other Australian jurisdictions have identical or substantially identical provisions: Cth – s14B, Qld – s25, SA – s13B, Tas – s11B, Vic – s13B, WA – s15, ACT – s13B, NT – s13B, New Zealand – ss12–13. The New Zealand provisions contain the same principle, but are much less verbose.

235 See *Rock Solid Surfaces Pty Ltd v Biesse Group (Australia) Pty Ltd* [2011] FCA 42.

236 Gmail and other such email services are so popular that a given name may not be available, but registrants typically use a variation with a number or other characters. Nevertheless the impersonation remains.

unless otherwise agreed between the purported originator and the addressee of an electronic communication, the purported originator of the electronic communication is bound by that communication only if the communication was sent by the purported originator or with the authority of the purported originator.[237]

In the paper world a person is not bound by forgeries or communications sent without authority, unless there is some culpability. Such authority may be given ostensibly or impliedly in accordance with agency principles. Importantly, the parties may agree to exclude this provision in advance. Authority includes delegation, agency and the employer–employee relationship. Culpability may arise though estoppel or negligence.

This Australian provision differs from the UNCITRAL Model Law. The advantage of the Australian approach is its functional equivalence. The disadvantage is that a person receiving an apparently genuine message may be faced with a subsequent argument or defence that it was sent without authority. In addition, the Model Law provides for a presumption that the purported originator is in fact the originator.

The recipient may act on the electronic communication where, in order to ascertain whether the communication is of the originator, the recipient properly applied a procedure previously agreed to for that purpose, or the communication, as received, resulted from the actions of a person whose relationship with the originator, or with any agent of the originator, enabled that person to gain access to a method used by the originator to identify the electronic communication as his or her own.[238]

The Australian Acts preserve the law of agency.[239] The decision to reject the UNCITRAL model follows a recommendation made by the Electronic Commerce Expert Group (ECEG). The ECEG argued that the UNCITRAL proposal favoured electronic commerce over paper-based communication. It noted that the use of signatures on paper for commerce at a distance (by mail or facsimile) involves the risk of forged or unauthorised signatures but there is no general legislative rule that entitles the addressee to presume that the signature is genuine. If the UNCITRAL proposal were accepted, addressees of electronically signed data messages would be better placed than those who received manually signed paper-based messages.

The New Zealand *Electronic Transactions Act* does not include an attribution provision. The result should be that the courts apply the same standards for non-electronic communications.

---

237 Cth – s15(1); NSW – s14;(1) Qld – s26(1); SA – s14(1); Tas – s12(1); Vic – s14(1);
     WA – s16(1); ACT – s14(1); NT – s14(1).
238 UNCITRAL *Model Law on Electronic Commerce*, Art. 13.
239 Cth – s15(2), NSW – s14(2), Qld – s26(2), SA – s14(2), Tas – s12(2), Vic – s14(2),
     WA – s16(2), ACT – s14(2), NT – s14(2).

Originals

The New Zealand *Electronic Transactions Act* includes a provision dealing with originals:[240]

> A legal requirement to compare a document with an original document may be met by comparing that document with an electronic form of the original document if the electronic form reliably assures the maintenance of the integrity of the document.[241]

The section is predicated on the assumption that the original document is a hard-copy. No provision exists where the original is the electronic document. The UNCITRAL Model Law makes the same narrow assumption.[242]

Electronic Case Management System

Schedule 1 of the NSW *Electronic Transactions Act* includes specific provisions for electronic documents to be used in a court which has adopted the Electronic Case Management System. These provisions override the general provisions of the Act. Schedule 1 permits the NSW Attorney General to establish an electronic case management system to enable documents with respect to legal proceedings to be created, issued, used, served and communicated in electronic form.

Critique

The impact of the legislation has been broad, extending beyond internet transactions. Those jurisdictions with broad blanket exemptions should reconsider them. The impact has not been fully appreciated, and such exclusions impact functional equivalence and are outdated in the modern digital age. Within Australia the differences between the states and territories' legislation must be noted. There are several stylistic changes, particularly in the Queensland legislation, which a court may regard as deliberate and significant in a given factual situation. Though the states and territories generally resisted divergences in an attempt to maintain national uniformity, stability and certainty, uniform legislation would be preferable.

---

240 The Australian legislators choose not to include a provision dealing with originals.
241 *Electronic Transactions Act 2002* (NZ) s30.
242 Article 8.

The major advantage of legislation based on the UNCITRAL Model Law and the UN *Communications Convention* is that it provides an even platform for national legislatures. An international approach provides a level of uniformity that is desirable, if not necessary, for international commerce.

Although the Electronic Transactions Acts create a regulatory regime for the use of electronic communications in transactions, they do not remove any legal obligations that may be imposed upon a person by other laws. The major purpose of the Acts is to enable people to use electronic communications in the course of business operations and to satisfy their legal obligations.

However, the legislation is largely unnecessary and often redundant. It was introduced before the courts had had the opportunity to adequately apply common law precepts to the new technologies and circumstances. The limited cases to date support this view.[243] The analysis of the provisions of the legislation, the misconceived consent requirement and the advent of new and changing technologies not considered by the legislators all lead to the conclusion that the legislation should be reviewed. The Law Commission for England and Wales, in its paper 'Electronic Commerce: Formal requirements in Commercial Transactions – Advice from the Law Commission', recommended that there was 'no need' for legislation based on the *UNCITRAL Model Law* for most purposes:

> We conclude that in most contexts e-mails (and attachments) and website trading (but not EDI) are already capable of satisfying the statutory form requirements existing in English law in the areas considered in this Advice. To that extent we suggest that there is no need to consider adoption in this country of the UNCITRAL Model Laws.[244]

The consent provisions are ill-considered and unsound. The writing, signature, production and retention requirements are superfluous. The exemptions are inconsistent across jurisdictions, giving rise to confusion and inconsistencies. The exemptions under the Commonwealth legislation are so broad as to frustrate the Act's operation. A major joint state and territory review is recommended, with a view to curtailing unwarranted and undesirable provisions and enacting streamlined uniform legislation.

FURTHER READING

Sharon Christensen, William Duncan and Rouhshi Low, 'The requirements of writing for electronic land contracts: the Queensland experience compared with other

---

243 See Common law, above; *McGuren v Simpson* [2004] NSWSC 35, *Hume Computers Pty Ltd v Exact International BV* [2007] FCA 478 and *SM Integrated Transware v Schenker Singapore Ltd* [2005] 2 SLR 651.

244 Paragraph 2.15, available at <www.lawcom.gov.uk/docs/e-commerce.pdf>.

jurisdictions', (2003) 10(3) *eLaw Journal: Murdoch University Electronic Journal of Law*, <www.murdoch.edu.au/elaw/issues/v10n3/christensen103.html>.

Henry Gabriel, 'The new United States Uniform Electronic Transactions Act: Substantive provisions, drafting history and comparison to the UNCITRAL Model Law on Electronic Commerce', (2000) <www.unidroit.org/english/publications/review/articles/2000–4-gabriel-e.pdf>. The author was a Commissioner on the National Conference of Commissioners on Uniform State Laws at the time of the drafting.

Minyan Wang, 'The impact of information technology development on the legal concept – a particular examination on the legal concept of 'signatures'', (2006) 15(3) *International Journal of Law and Information Technology*.

D Witte, 'Comment: Avoiding the un-real estate deal: Has the Uniform Electronic Transactions Act gone too far?', (2002) 35 *John Marshall Law Review* 311 at 321. Also see *Uniform Electronic Transactions Act 1999* (US), comment 4 to s5(b).

12

CONTRACTING ONLINE

Principles of contracting have evolved over the eons, from simple tribal bartering to formal contracting, which has been in place, and enforced, since ancient Egypt times. Plato recognised basic rules for the cancellation of agreements and Roman law placed contracts into various classes. However, mass communications and connections between potential contracting parties have expanded contracting in a manner not envisaged. Although the fundamental principles of contract law will continue to apply in the digital world, new and unusual circumstances arise which must be addressed and managed by commercial parties and legal systems. Online commerce, local and global, has become commonplace in the past two decades. Numerous traders have embraced the new opportunities by creating global meeting places and auction houses such as eBay and Amazon. The sale of software, cars, travel, books, music and videos are just some of the many commercial transactions carried out in cyberspace. Trillions of dollars' worth of goods and services transactions occur online annually. Online contracts are typically entered into without paper, without the use of a pen and without the use of the spoken word. This chapter explores how such contracts may be entered into and how conditions may be incorporated into them. This chapter also addresses the changes to the Electronic Transactions Acts as a result of the adoption of the UN's *Convention on the Use of Electronic Communications in International Contracts* (New York, 2005).

Offers online

Undertaking business in person has certain unspoken advantages. The shopkeeper can make assumptions, from the person's appearance, about their capacity to enter into a contract: the person may appear to be an adult, and to not be afflicted with some legal incapacity (mental or otherwise). Similarly, goods on display are typically regarded as being an invitation to treat and not a formal offer until presented for payment. This gives the shopkeeper the opportunity to withdraw the goods from sale.[1] Questions arise as to the nature of the 'display' of goods on a website by an online merchant. Should the 'display' be regarded as a formal offer or merely an invitation to treat? The Commonwealth, all Australian states, and both territories have amended their respective Electronic Transactions Acts to conform to the UN's *Convention on the Use of Electronic Communications in International Contracts* to make it clear that to be an offer, the online seller must clearly indicate the intention to be bound in case of acceptance:

---

1 *Pharmaceutical Society of Great Britain v Boots Cash Chemists (Southern) Ltd* [1952] 2 QB 795.

15B Invitation to treat regarding contracts

(1) A proposal to form a contract made through one or more electronic communications that:

    (a) is not addressed to one or more specific parties; and

    (b) is generally accessible to parties making use of information systems; is to be considered as an invitation to make offers, unless it clearly indicates the intention of the party making the proposal to be bound in case of acceptance.

(2) Subsection (1) extends to proposals that make use of interactive applications for the placement of orders through information systems.[2]

Terms and conditions online

Accepting terms and conditions by conduct, notice, click of the mouse or touch on a tablet computer has raised questions reminiscent of the contract cases known as the 'ticket cases'.[3] The typical ticket case scenario arises where a person is handed a ticket – for example, for train travel, parking or dry cleaning. The ticket may state that the holder is subject to terms which the holder may have had little or no chance to read, negotiate or agree to. The courts have been required to determine the point of time at which these contracts are entered into and their terms and conditions. The starting point has been determining which terms are to be incorporated into the contract. In *Thornton v Shoe Lane Parking Station*, Lord Denning, referring to an extremely onerous exclusion of liability clause on a parking ticket, stated:

> It [the exclusion clause] is so wide and so destructive of rights that the court should not hold any man bound by it unless it is drawn to his attention in the most explicit way ... In order to give sufficient notice, it would need to be printed in red ink with a red hand pointing to it – or something equally startling.[4]

Similarly, in *Interfoto Picture Library Ltd v Stiletto Visual Programmes Ltd*,[5] the English Court of Appeal held that to incorporate onerous terms into a contract, reasonable notice must be given.

---

2 *Electronic Transactions Act 1999* (Cth) s15B, *Electronic Transactions Act 2000* (NSW) s14B, *Electronic Transactions (Queensland) Act 2001* (Qld) s26B, *Electronic Transactions Act 2000* (SA) s14B, *Electronic Transactions Act 2000* (Tas) s12B, *Electronic Transactions (Victoria) Act 2000* (Vic) s14B, *Electronic Transaction Act 2011* (WA) s18, *Electronic Transactions Act 2001* (ACT) s26B, *Electronic Transactions (Northern Territory) Act 2000* (NT) s14B.

3 For example, *Parker v The South Eastern Railway Co.* (1877) 2 CPD 416; *Olley v Marlborough Court* [1949] 1 KB 532; *Sydney City Council v West* (1965) 114 CLR 481; *Thornton v Shoe Lane Parking Station* [1971] 2 QB 163.

4 [1971] 2 QB 163, 170. See also *Oceanic Sun Line Special Shipping Company Inc v Fay* [1988] HCA 32, para 15.

5 [1989] 1 QB 433.

Such an approach is prophetic for contracts in cyberspace. The principles of the ticket cases – such as the opportunity to access terms and conditions and the extent to which such clauses will be binding – have been explored and paralleled progressively in the shrinkwrap and online contract cases.

Shrinkwrap

Shrinkwrap contracts derive their name from the clear plastic wrapping that encloses the goods (such as software packages). The software packages typically include a notice saying that by opening the shrinkwrap, the purchaser agrees to the terms and conditions enclosed. Such contracts typically include provisions such as an arbitration clause, a choice of law and forum clause, disclaimers, limitations of warranties and limitations of remedies. The major criticism of such contracts is that the consumer will be bound by terms and conditions unknown at the time the contract is entered into. In a Dilbert cartoon, Scott Adams parodied shrinkwrap contracts thus:

> Dilbert: I didn't read all of the shrinkwrap license on my new software until after I opened it. Apparently I agreed to spend the rest of my life as a towel boy in Bill Gates' new mansion.
>
> Dogbert: Call your lawyer.
>
> Dilbert: Too late. He opened software yesterday. Now he's Bill's laundry boy.[6]

The initial response was to limit the application of such clauses. In *Step-Saver Data Sys Inc. v Wyse Tech*[7] the court held that the terms of the shrinkwrap licence were not enforceable because Step-Saver had not assented to them. However, later, in *ProCDInc v Zeidenberg,*[8] the appeal court noted that it would be impossible to print the entire contract on the exterior of the box. The court found that:

> notice on the outside, terms on the inside, and a right to return the software for refund if the terms are unacceptable ... may be a means of doing business valuable to buyers and sellers alike.[9]

The implications have extended to mass marketing, the distribution of software online, which is most significant, and to the purchase of tickets for concerts, air

---

6 Scott Adams, *Dilbert*, United Feature Syndicate Inc., 14 January 1997. It is interesting that as early as 1997 the problem was perceived to be broad enough to warrant public parody.

7 939 F. 2d 91 (3d Cir 1991).

8 86 F. 3d 1447 (7th Cir 1996) ('*ProCD* case').

9 See G Evans and B Fitzgerald, 'Information transactions under UCC Article 2B: The ascendancy of freedom of contract in the digital millennium?', (1998) 21(2) *UNSW Law Journal* 416.

travel and sporting events where the purchaser pays in advance and receives the tickets with the terms included. In *Hill v Gatway 2000 Inc.*,[10] Easterbrook J commented that cashiers and sales personnel cannot be expected to read the terms of each contract to the customer before ringing up the sale. In that case his Honour explicated the cost benefits to the customer where 'telephonic recitation' was avoided and use was made of a 'simple approve-or-return device'. His Honour concluded, 'Competent adults are bound by such documents, read or unread.'[11]

Electronic affirmation

Electronic affirmation is a method of including terms and conditions in an online contract, where the user, for example, assents to a list of terms and conditions by clicking or touching an onscreen button marked, for example, 'Agree' or 'I accept'. The electronic affirmation approach has the advantage of allowing the user to read the terms and conditions before assenting. The vendor can dictate the number of steps for the user to pass through before reaching the assent stage. Many commentators have used the expression 'clickwrap agreement', but no Australian cases have used the expression to date.[12] Electronic affirmation is widely used, and to a large extent it is not even controversial. In Chapter 1 it was noted that there was no test case arguing the validity of electronic communications – in the use of the electronic telegraph, from the 1830s, or in the case of the telephone, since the 1880s.

In the typical situation the vendor uses an interactive web page which may ultimately require personal and payment details. The contract needs no paper or signature, although there is authority for the proposition that a simple mouse click is an electronic signature. Affirmation may be given by numerous methods. The simplest uses a mouse click or finger tap alone to indicate assent. The trader must take reasonable steps to bring the terms and conditions to the attention of the buyer at or before the time the contract is formed.[13] On some websites the user may

---

10   105 F. 3d 1147 (7th Cir 1997).

11   Ibid., 1149.

12   The expression 'clickwrap' colloquially derived from the incorporation of terms into 'shrinkwrap' agreements. For examples of the use of the expression 'clickwrap' see Dale M Clapperton and Stephen G Corones, 'Unfair terms in "clickwrap" and other electronic contracts', (2007) 35 *Australian Business Law Review* 152, Kayleen Manwaring, 'Enforceability of clickwrap and browsewrap terms in Australia: Lessons from the US and the UK', 2011 5(1) *Studies in Ethics, Law, and Technology* and Alan Davidson, *Electronic Commerce Law* Cambridge University Press, 2009. The expression 'click through' has also been utilised.

13   *Parker v The South Eastern Railway Company* (1877) 2 CPD 416.

be required to check a box and then click or tap the 'I agree' or equivalent button. A more circumspect site may require the user to type a word such as 'yes', or to sign the page by typing his or her name and then clicking or tapping the button. In each of these examples, provided a clear and unambiuguous choice is made, the user should be bound by the terms and conditions.

The first decision on the enforceability of electronic affirmation contracts was the US case of *Hotmail Corp. v Van$ Money Pie Inc.*, in 1998.[14] At the time, Hotmail provided free email services to more than 10 million customers.[15] An email account would be allocated to the user only after the user clicked an 'I agree' button which listed hotmail's specific terms and conditions. These included the prohibition on transmitting unsolicited commercial email – that is, spam. Assent occurred by clicking the appropriate button. The defendant sent spam mail with pornographic material, and altered the return address to make it appear that it came from a different source. Hotmail applied for an injunction to restrain both the spamming and the false source. The defendant claimed, among other things, that the terms could not form part of any agreement as he had not agreed to the terms. The court had little difficulty in holding that there was an enforceable agreement. The key is to determine whether or not the user had given consent to the terms and conditions by a positive and unambiguous act.

In *eBay International AG v Creative Festival Entertainment Pty Limited*,[16] Gold Coast concert tickets were purchased online by clicking on a box next to the words 'I have read and agreed to the following terms and conditions' and then clicking the word 'OK'. Creative Festival Entertainment Pty Ltd (Creative Festival) unsuccessfully attempted to argue that the contract was finalised only when the payment and nominated purchaser details were accepted by Creative Festival. This argument was based on the decision in *Toll (FGCT) Pty Limited v Alphapharm Pty Limited*.[17] Creative Festival was attempting to include additional terms restricting the resale of the tickets (known as scalping). The court held that an online contract was completed when the relevant computer icons were clicked, stating, a 'reasonable person in the position of the parties would have regarded the transaction completed'.[18] In general terms the court stated:

> Where a ticket or other document is intended by the issuer to contain terms
> of the contract such as an exemption clause or a foreign jurisdiction clause or
> other special condition, the issuer cannot rely on those terms unless, at the

---

14 47 USPQ 2d 1020 (1998).
15 By 2014 the number had grown to more than 400 million and Hotmail has changed to Outlook.
16 [2006] FCA 1768.
17 [2004] HCA 52.
18 [2006] FCA 1768, para 25.

time of contract, it did all that was reasonably necessary to bring the terms to the other party's attention.[19]

The court concluded that the:

> online purchase was a contract in writing signed by the parties. By clicking on the relevant buttons and, by the computer bringing up all terms needed to purchase a ticket, ... the whole transaction was in writing, signed and agreed by the parties.[20]

Similarly, in *Steven J Caspi v Microsoft Network*[21] the terms of the agreement appeared in a scrollable window next to two blocks containing the words 'I agree' and 'I disagree'. The user could not use Microsoft's network without selecting the affirmative choice. The US appellate court held that this created an enforceable contract:[22]

> To conclude that plaintiffs are not bound by [the forum] clause would be equivalent to holding that they were bound by no other clause either, since all provisions were identically presented. Plaintiffs must be taken to have known that they were entering into a contract; and no good purpose, consonant with the dictates of reasonable reliability in commerce, would be served by permitting them to disavow particular provisions or the contracts as a whole.[23]

In *Register.com Inc. v Verio Inc.*, the court described the key to electronic affirmation being that the decision to accept or reject must occur before access is given. The electronic affirmation must 'expressly and unambiguously manifest assent prior to the user being given access to the product'.[24]

In *AV et al. v Paradigms LLC*,[25] a US court applied the principle to minor high school students:[26]

---

19 Ibid., para 19 citing *Oceanic Sun Line Special Shipping Company Inc v Fay* [1988] HCA 32 per Brennan J; *MacRobertson Miller Airline Services v Commissioner of State Taxation (WA)* [1975] HCA 55 per Stephen J and Jacobs J; *Sydney Corporation v West* [1965] HCA 68 per Barwick CJ, Taylor and Windeyer JJ.

20 Ibid., para 49. See also L Sayer-Jones and M Averill, 'Intellectual property: The importance of minimising risk in online agreements', (2014), 1(6) *Law Society Journal of NSW*.

21 323 NJ Super 118 (1999).

22 See also *I Lan Systems Inc. v Netscout Service Level Corp.* (D Mass 2002).

23 323 NJ Super 118 (1999), para 6.

24 356 F. 3d 393 (2nd Cir 2004), 53–4.

25 Company Civ Act. No. 07–0293 (ED Va 2008).

26 In relation to the applicability to minors, the court quoted from *Williston on Contracts*, Section 9: 14, 4th edn, 2007: 'if an infant enters into any contract subject to conditions or stipulations, he cannot take the benefit of the contract without the burden of the conditions or stipulations'. The court concluded: 'Plaintiffs received benefits from entering into the agreement with iParadigms. They received a grade from their teachers, allowing them the opportunity to maintain good standing in the classes in which they were enrolled ... Plaintiffs cannot use the infancy defense to void their contractual obligations while retaining the benefits of the contract. Thus, plaintiffs' infancy defense fails' (p. 10).

The Court finds that the parties entered into a valid contractual agreement when Plaintiffs clicked 'I Agree' to acknowledge their acceptance of the terms of the Click-wrap Agreement. The first line of the Clickwrap Agreement, which appears directly above the 'I Agree' link, states: 'Turnitin and its services ... are offered to you, the user, conditioned on your acceptance without modification of the terms, conditions and notices contained herein.' Also the Clickwrap Agreement provides that iParadigms will not be liable for any damages 'arising out of the use of this web site'. By clicking 'I Agree' to create a Turnitin profile and enter the Turnitin website, Plaintiffs accepted iParadigm's offer and a contract was formed based on the terms of the Clickwrap Agreement.[27]

Electronic affirmation for contracts requiring writing and a signature

When a person browses the internet, electronic writing typically appears. If the writing simply disappears when the web page is exited, it cannot be said to be functionally equivalent to writing on paper, which is typically usable for subsequent reference.[28] If, however, there is a reasonable expectation that the writing will be available for subsequent reference, then the writing equivalency test is fulfilled.

However, there is an important distinction to be made where a signature is required and where a signature is not required. Contracts are most often entered into without writing or a signature. In such cases, a contract entered into by email, in chat rooms, by texting, or by the use of a computer mouse or finger tap should be uncontroversial. As with oral contracts, evidence may be required to prove the elements of the contract, such as the offer and acceptance, but given the facts of such an offer and corresponding acceptance (and the other usual elements required by contract law), a contract is formed.

On the other hand, where a signature is required, further analysis is required. A contract without the signature would be unenforceable, as would an oral acceptance in person or by telephone. This is the case for assurances (dispositions) of land, certain guarantees, insurance contracts, certain intellectual property assignments, for example. The expression 'electronic signature' is not defined in the Australian Electronic Transactions Acts. From the case law to

---

27 Company Civ Act. No. 07–0293 (ED Va 2008) at 8.
28 See Chapter 11.

date there is no doubt that it includes digital signatures, and a name typed on emails at the end of the email. Notwithstanding the sparsity of cases to date, a disposition of land in an email transaction with a signature at the end would conform to the writing and signature requirements of the respective property law Acts within Australia.

An internet chat room is quite different. The test pursuant to the writing provision of the Electronic Transactions Acts is that the electronic writing must be available for subsequent reference.[29] The Electronic Transactions Acts signature provisions instead require a method to identify the person and to indicate the person's intention in respect of the information communicated. Simply put, can a mouse click or finger tap in itself both identify the person and indicate the person's intention? Perhaps surprisingly, it does so with relative ease. First, for 'traditional' signatures courts have accepted an 'X' as a signature for the most formal of documents and deeds. The identity of the signor cannot be ascertained by the signature, but by other circumstances, such as witnesses. In addition, many traditional signatures are unreadable to the point of illegibility, although appropriate experts may testify to their authenticity. Indeed parties may use a code known to select persons for security purposes to identify and verify the parties involved.

A digital signature is indeed invisible to the user, but it readily identifies the signor to a high degree of certainty. The mouse click or finger tap can identify the person by reference to the online IP address connecting the person to the online agreement in question. A commercial web host typically retains information about visitors to web pages: which pages are visited, time spent, and identifying information. It is true that another person may be using the device at that time, but the same could be said of email accounts, where a person accesses the account and sends an email in the name of another whilst typing in the name of the account holder. The Electronic Transactions Acts address this issue in two ways. First, the method used for identification must be 'as reliable as appropriate for the purpose for which the electronic communication was generated or communicated, in the light of all the circumstances, including any relevant agreement' or 'proven in fact to have fulfilled the (method) functions ... by itself or together with further evidence'.[30] Under this test, a person who admits that he or she was the person who initiated the mouse click (for example) would be identifiable by the IP address, and so satisfy the Electronic Transactions Acts identification and signature requirement.

---

29 *Electronic Transactions Acts*: Cth – s9(1), NSW – s8(1), Qld – s11, SA – s8(1), Tas – s6(1), Vic – s8(1), WA – s9(1), ACT – s8(1), NT – s8(1).

30 *Electronic Transactions Acts*: Cth – s10(1), NSW – s9(1), Qld – s14, SA – s9(1), Tas – s7(1), Vic – s9(1), WA – s10(1), ACT – s9(1), NT – s9(1).

Aashish Srivastava states: 'with the electronic signature approach when one clicks the mouse on the I-Agree button, that act probably amounts to signing an agreement'.[31]

Browsewrap

Where there is no positive and unambiguous act to indicate assent the position is less certain. The term 'browsewrap' refers to the situation where a user enters into an agreement without giving unambiguous consent to the terms and conditions. For example, a vendor of software to be downloaded may have given the user the opportunity to browse the terms but has not made access to the product conditional on reading the terms and conditions. The vendor may merely place a link to the 'terms of download' on the download page, leaving it optional to view those terms.

In *Specht v Netscape Communications Corp.*,[32] Specht downloaded Netscape's SmartDownload software. Specht claimed that as a result, private information was wrongfully and surreptitiously transmitted to Netscape. Netscape sought to compel arbitration, arguing the applicability of the online agreement, which included an arbitration clause. To download the software, users clicked the button marked 'Download'. The only reference to the terms and conditions appeared only if the user scrolled down the page. The user would then see the words 'please review and agree to the terms of the Netscape SmartDownload license agreement before downloading and using the software'. Next to this was a link which, if clicked, opened a web page containing the terms, including the arbitration clause. The court held that Specht was not bound by the terms. The fact that users were not required to give a positive assent before proceeding was critical to the court's reasoning. The court doubted whether such browsewrap agreements were enforceable:

> Promises become binding when there is a meeting of the minds and consideration is exchanged. So it was at King's Bench in common law England; so it was under the common law in the American colonies; so it was through more than two centuries of jurisprudence in this country; and so it is today. Assent may be registered by a signature, a handshake, or a click of a computer mouse transmitted across the invisible ether of the Internet. Formality is not a requisite; any sign, symbol or action, or even wilful inaction, as long as it is unequivocally referable to the promise, may create a contract.[33]

---

31 Aashish Srivastava, *Electronic Signatures for B2B Contracts*, Springer, India, 2013.
32 150 F. Supp. 2d 585 (SD NY 2001) ('*Specht's* case').
33 Ibid., 587.

Where clickwrap licence agreements and the shrinkwrap agreement at issue in *ProCD* require users to perform an affirmative action unambiguously expressing assent before they may use the software, that affirmative action is equivalent to an express declaration stating, 'I assent to the terms and conditions of the licence agreement'. For example, Netscape's Navigator will not function without the clicking of a box constituting assent. Netscape's SmartDownload, in contrast, allows a user to download and use the software without taking any action that plainly manifests assent to the terms of the associated licence or indicates an understanding that a contract is being formed.[34]

Actual or presumptive knowledge of the browsewrap terms and conditions, for example by prior access, will suffice. The reasoning in *Ticketmaster Corp. v Tickets. com Inc.*[35] was consistent with *Specht's* case, but without deciding the point the court left open the possibility that prior use of a website, together with knowledge of the terms and conditions, could create a subsequent binding contract. The plaintiff offered tickets to entertainment events for sale online. The website included terms and conditions purporting to govern use of the site. These were located at the bottom of the website's front page. Users were not required to confirm assent to the terms and conditions or to indicate whether or not the terms and conditions had been read. The defendant sold similar tickets online but also provided information for other sites which included deep links to the plaintiff's site. These deep links bypassed the plaintiff's front page, but included the statement: 'These tickets are sold by another ticketing company. Although we can't sell them to you, the link above will take you directly to the other company's web site where you can purchase them.' The plaintiffs sued for breach of contract, infringement of copyright, unfair competition, unjust enrichment and interference with business advantage. The court left open the possibility that use of a website together with knowledge of the terms and conditions could create a binding contract, but stated:

> [The terms and conditions provide] that anyone going beyond the home page agrees to the terms and conditions set forth, which include that the information is for personal use only, may not be used for commercial purposes, and no deep linking to the site is permitted. In defending this claim, Ticketmaster makes reference to the 'shrink-wrap license' cases, where the packing on the outside of the CD stated that opening the package constitutes adherence to the license agreement (restricting republication) contained therein. This has been held to be enforceable. That is not the same as this case because the 'shrink-wrap license agreement' is open and obvious and in fact hard to miss. Many web sites make you click on 'agree' to the terms and conditions before

---

34 150 F. Supp. 2d 585 (SD NY 2001), 587. See also *In re Zappos.com, Inc., Customer Data Security Breach Litigation* (2012) WL 4466660 (D. Nev).
35 54 USPQ 2d 1344 (CD Cal 2000).

going on, but Ticketmaster does not. Further, the terms and conditions are set forth so that the customer needs to scroll down the home page to find and read them. Many customers instead are likely to proceed to the event page of interest rather than reading the 'small print'. It cannot be said that merely putting the terms and conditions in this fashion necessarily creates a contract with anyone using the web site.[36]

In relation to deep linking, the court added that:

[H]yperlinking does not itself involve a violation of the Copyright Act ... since no copying is involved ... the customer is automatically transferred to the particular genuine web page of the original author. There is no deception in what is happening. This is analogous to using a library's card index to get reference to particular items, albeit faster and more efficiently ... deep linking by itself (i.e. without confusion of source) does not necessarily involve unfair competition.[37]

In *Net2Phone Inc. v Los Angeles Superior Court* the court stated that knowledge or even presumptive knowledge of the existence of the terms may be sufficient to form a contract. The court preferred a firm assent by a 'clickthrough' process, but noted that cases involving cruise tickets and parking tickets have established that such assent is not necessary for formation.[38]

In *Register.com Inc. v Verio Inc.* the court recognised that contract offers on the internet often required the offeree to click on an 'I agree' icon. However, the court stated that this was not necessary 'in all circumstances':

While new commerce on the Internet has exposed courts to many new situations, it has not fundamentally changed the principles of contract. It is standard contract doctrine that when a benefit is offered subject to stated conditions, and the offeree makes a decision to take the benefit with knowledge of the terms of the offer, the taking constitutes an acceptance of the terms, which accordingly become binding on the offeree.[39]

The approach in Australia and New Zealand is yet to be firmly determined, though the US cases are a good guide. The approach will most likely be to use or modify dicta such as Lord Denning's 'red hand' passage in *Thornton v Shoe Lane Parking Station Ltd*, where the clause did not exempt the defendants from liability as they had not taken reasonable steps to bring it to the attention of Thornton.

---

36 Ibid.
37 Ibid.
38 109 Cal App 4th 583 (Cal Ct App 2003). See also *Comb v PayPal Inc*. 218 F. Supp. 2d 1165 (ND Cal 2002).
39 356 F. 3d 393 (2d Cir NY 2004), 403.

In the absence of cases in Australia and New Zealand, some attempts have been made to consider the application of the unconscionability provisions of the Australian Consumer Law, the *Contracts Review Act 1980* (NSW), selected parts of the Fair Trading Acts, or to enact specific legislation to protect electronic contracts.[40] However, internationally the courts have provided an adequate response in the past decade and there is no reason to assume that Antipodean courts will not respond in the same way. At the very least, legislation which protects consumers generally applies equally to electronic contracts.

Electronic agents

It is possible for computer users to instruct the computer to carry out transactions automatically. For example, in today's supermarket the computer updates its inventory as items are scanned for sale. When the stock of an item falls to a predetermined level the computer is programmed, without human intervention, to contact the computer of the supplier and place an order for replacement stock. The supplier's computer, without human intervention, accepts the order and the next morning automatically prints out worksheets and delivery sheets for the supply and transport staff.

These electronic agents are programmed by and with the authority of the buyer and supplier. The computer is a tool programmed by or with a person's authority to implement their intention to make or accept contractual offers.[41] The legal status of electronic agents has now been clarified by amendments to the Commonwealth, state and territory Electronic Transactions Acts:[42]

> Use of automated message systems for contract formation–non-intervention of natural person
>
> A contract formed by:
>
> **(a)** the interaction of an automated message system and a natural person; or
> **(b)** the interaction of automated message systems;

---

40 See D Clapperton and S Corones, above n 12.
41 For an example of a legislative provision see *Uniform Electronic Transactions Act* (US) s14.
42 See, for an example, *Curtis v Singtel Optus Pty Ltd* [2014] FCCA 1286, where it was noted at para 47 that 'approximately 95 per cent of bankruptcy notices issued thereafter have been applied for and issued electronically'. Lloyd-Jones J stated at para 50: 'In my view, since the introduction of the online system for the electronic application for and issuing of bankruptcy notices on 11 February 2013, the operation of the *Electronic Transactions Act* has been relevant.'

is not invalid, void or unenforceable on the sole ground that no natural person reviewed or intervened in each of the individual actions carried out by the automated message systems or the resulting contract.[43]

FURTHER READING

Dale M Clapperton and Stephen G Corones, 'Unfair terms in "clickwrap" and other electronic contracts', (2007) 35 *Australian Business Law Review* 152.

Alan Davidson, 'Shrinkwrap, clickwrap and browsewrap contracts', (2003) 23 *Proctor* 9, 41.

Debora Halbert, 'The open source alternative: Shrink-wrap, open source and copyright', (2003) 10 *eLaw Journal* 4.

---

43 *Electronic Transactions Act 1999* (Cth) s15C;NSW – s14C; Qld – s26C; SA – s14C; Tas – s12C; Vic – s14C; WA – s19; ACT – s26C; NT – s14C.

13

ELECTRONIC SIGNATURES

The first electronic contracts were entered into with the use of the telegraph in the 1830s; in the 1880s they could be entered into by the use of the telephone. The earliest reported case validating electronic signatures comes from the New Hampshire Supreme Court in *Howley v Whipple* in 1869, where the court stated:

> It makes no difference whether [the telegraph] operator writes the offer or the acceptance in the presence of his principal and by his express direction, with a steel pen an inch long attached to an ordinary penholder, or whether his pen be a copper wire a thousand miles long. In either case the thought is communicated to the paper by the use of the finger resting upon the pen; nor does it make any difference that in one case common record ink is used, while in the other case a more subtle fluid, known as electricity, performs the same office.[1]

The traditional signature has been the prime method a person uses as a proof of identity, and as a material expression of intent and execution of documents. A signature on a document indicates the provenance of the document and the intention of the signatory with regard to that document. With the advent of the electronic era, a form of signature is adopted for electronic documents. This chapter examines the regulation, use and security of electronic signatures and the types of electronic signatures, such as digital signatures, biometric signatures and Transport Layer Security (TLS) technology, being used in social media and electronic commerce.

Traditional signatures

Understanding an electronic signature involves understanding the purpose and use of the traditional signature. The status of traditional signatures has been taken for granted or assumed. The law has developed for centuries with notions of deeds and documents being signed, sealed and delivered, witnessed, notarised and so forth. In some situations a signatory is bound on signing, and in others the signatory is not bound until there is an affirming act. The underlying intention of the signatory may be to be bound only by the subsequent act of delivery. There may be many signatures on a contract: one person may sign intending to be bound by the terms of the contract, while another is merely a witness, with no legal interest in the terms. Their intention is paramount. Even if a signature appears on a document, the signor may not be not bound because he or she lacked the requisite intention – there could be duress, undue influence, *non est factum*, unconscionability or some other vitiating factor. The signature of an illiterate may be an 'X'. An

---

1 48 NH 487 (1869).

incapacitated person such as a quadriplegic may use another person to place the signature on the document. In all circumstances it is the underlying intention of the signatory that is determinative.

The cases assist in determining the characteristics of a signature. The inclusion of a mark in some form intended as the signatory's authorisation, approval or execution of the contents of the document is paramount.

In 1682 in *Lemayne v Stanley*,[2] the full court regarded a will, handwritten by the testator, with his name appearing in the will, as 'sufficient signing'.[3] The majority also held that the testator's seal was a sufficient signing, stating, 'for *signum* is no more than a *mark*, and sealing is a sufficient *mark* that this is his will'.[4] In 1745 in *Ellis v Smith*,[5] the court held that 'signing' for legal purposes means the affixing of a personal signature. In 1794, in *Knight v Crockford*,[6] a letter beginning 'I James Crockford, agree to sell' was held to be sufficiently signed under s 4 of the *Statute of Frauds*.[7] The case of *Lobb v Stanley*[8] in 1844 considered the effect of a signature in the body of writing. Lord Denman CJ stated:

> it is a signature of a party when he authenticates the instrument by writing his own name in the body. Here it is true, the whole name is not written, but only 'Mr Stanley'. I think more is not necessary.[9]

Wightman J stated, 'if a party insert his name, either at the beginning or in the body of the document, for the purpose of authenticating it, that is enough, and no other signature is wanted'.[10] In 1892, in *Evans v Hoare*,[11] the defendant prepared a document which showed the plaintiff's address at the top, and the defendant's name and address in the body. Cave J stressed the importance of the 'intention for a signature' whether the purported signature is at the beginning, in the body or at the end.

These cases regarded the writing of one's name within the document as equivalent to a signature. However, the case of *Tourret v Cripps*[12] in 1879 dealt with the

---

2 (1682) 3 Lev 1; 83 ER 545.

3 (1682) 3 Lev 1, 1 per North, Wyndham, Charlton and Levinz JJ; 83 ER 545, 546.

4 83 ER 545, 546.

5 (1754) 1 Ves Jun 11 at 12; 30 ER 205. As late as 1954, Denning LJ, in a dissenting judgement, stated that 'the virtue of a signature lies in the fact that no two persons write exactly alike, and so it carries on the face of it a guarantee that the person who signs has given his personal attention to the document': *Goodman v J Eban Ltd* [1954] 1 QB 550 at 561.

6 (1794) 1 Esp NPC 190; 170 ER 324.

7 For the text of *Statute of Frauds* s4 and its implications see Chapter 11.

8 (1844) 5 QB 574; 114 ER 1366.

9 114 ER 1366, 1369.

10 Ibid.

11 [1892] 1 QB 593, see Cave J at 597. See also *Schneider v Norris* (1814) 2 M & S 286.

12 (1879) 48 LJ Ch 567; 27 WR 706.

proposed terms of a lease in the defendant's own handwriting on a sheet of paper on which was printed at the head of the page 'From Richd L. Cripps', with the defendant's address. The court held that the document had been signed. The essential element of intention was rising to the fore. In *Caton v Caton*, in 1867, Lord Westbury said that what is alleged to constitute the signature must:

> be so placed as to show that it was intended to relate and refer to, and that in fact it does relate and refer to, every part of the instrument … It must govern every part of the instrument. It must shew that every part of the instrument emanates from the individual so signing, and that the signature was intended to have that effect. It follows that if a signature be found in an instrument incidentally only, or having relation and reference only to a portion of the instrument, the signature cannot have legal effect and force which it must have in order to comply with the statute, and to give authenticity to the whole of the memorandum.[13]

The case of *R v Moore; Ex Parte Myers*[14] in 1884 dealt with a pawnbroker's pledge ticket that was not signed in accordance with the relevant legislation but was signed by an authorised agent. The name of the pawnbroker was printed on the ticket. Higginbotham J stated:

> A signature is only a mark, and where the Statute merely requires a document shall be signed, the Statue is satisfied by proof of the making of the mark upon the document by or by the authority of the signatory … where the Statute does not require that the signature shall be an autograph, the printed name of the party who is required to sign the document is enough … or the signature may be impressed upon the document by a stamp engraved with a facsimile of the ordinary signature of the person signing … proof in these cases must be given that the name printed on the stamp was affixed by the person signing, or that such signature has been recognised and brought home to him as having been done by his authority so as to appropriate it to the particular instrument.[15]

Binding oneself to the contents of the document therefore does not require the physical act of putting pen to paper, but can be achieved by an agent or through the use of some mechanical means. *R v Moore* determines that the object of a signature

---

13 (1867) LR 2 HL 127.
14 (1884) 10 VLR 322.
15 (1884) 10 VLR 322, 324. See also *Smith v Greenville County* 188 SC 349; 199 SE 416, 419 (1938), where it was held: 'A signature may be written by hand, printed, stamped, typewritten, engraved, photographed or cut from one instrument and attached to another, and a signature lithographed on an instrument by a party is sufficient for the purpose of signing it: it being immaterial by what kind of instrument a signature is made.'

affixed to a document is to authenticate the genuineness of the document.[16] Further, the case holds that a person, in order to be bound, must put his or her mind to the act of signing the document, as opposed to simply providing an autograph.

In *Lazarus Estates Ltd v Beasley*, Denning LJ (as he then was) made the following comment in relation to a company stamp:

> The statutory forms require the documents to be 'signed' by the landlord, but the only signature on these documents (if such it can be called) was a rubber stamp 'Lazarus Estates Ltd', without anything to verify it. There was no signature of a secretary or of any person at all on behalf of the company. There was nothing to indicate who affixed the rubber stamp. It has been held in this court that a private person can sign a document by impressing a rubber stamp with his own facsimile signature on it ... but it has not been held that a company can sign by its printed name affixed with a rubber stamp.[17]

In *Jenkyns v Gaisford & Thring*, Sir C Cresswell stated:

> a testator sufficiently signs by making his mark ... whether the signature is made by the testator himself or by some other person in his presence and by his direction. ... whether the mark was made by a pen or by some other instrument cannot make any difference; neither can it in reason make a difference that a fac-simile of the whole name was impressed on the will, instead of a mere mark or X. The mark ... was intended to stand for and represent the signature of the testator.[18]

Modern signatures

In the United States in 1948, in *Joseph Denunzio Fruit Company v Crane*, the Californian District Court commented that it 'must take a realistic view of modern business practices',[19] suggesting that the court should take judicial notice of the extensive use of the teletype machine. In holding that the point was *res nova*, the court held that teletype messages satisfy the *Statute of Frauds* in California.

In relation to facsimiles and telexes it could be argued that each message contains identifying information which could be regarded as a signature in law.[20] However,

---

16 Higginbotham J added, 'It was observed by Patterson J in *Lobb v Stanley*, that the object of all Statutes which require a particular document to be signed by a particular person is to authenticate the genuineness of the document.'

17 [1956] 1 All ER 341.

18 (1863) 3 SW & TR 93, 95.

19 79 F. Supp. 117 (DC Cal 1948).

20 See C Reed, 'Authenticating electronic mail messages – some evidential problems, (1989) 52(5) *Modern Law Review* 649 and Queensland Law Reform Commission Issues Paper, *The receipt of evidence by Queensland courts: Electronic records*, Issues Paper WP No 52 (1998). Available at <www.qlrc.qld.gov.au/wp52.html>.

the identifiers indicate the machine used, not necessarily the particular user or author of the message. Office facsimiles may be used by many parties. It is possible to alter the telex machine or facsimile machine so that it sends a false identification message. These possibilities may weigh heavily against any suggestion that a telex or facsimile should be treated as signed.[21]

Electronic signing

Electronic documents may be signed electronically with the same underlying intent and purpose as traditional documents. Cases requiring a mark with a corresponding intent of authorising or executing the document have equal application to electronic documents with electronic signatures. Thus signing an electronic communication such as an email by simply typing the sender's name at the end would be an acceptable electronic signature if inserted with the requisite intention. Similarly, including the sender's name in the body of the email, as envisaged in *Lobb v Stanley*[22] and *Evans v Hoare*,[23] will suffice.

In the Queensland Court of Appeal, in *R v Frolchenko*,[24] Williams J recognised that modern communication, such as email, may not bear a personal signature. His Honour stated that such an electronic document could be authenticated by looking at other factors, such as whether the name appears in typescript at the end of the document.

In the US case *Doherty v Registry of Motor Vehicles*,[25] Agnes J held that a police report made 'by means of email or some other electronic method' is regarded as signed, subjecting the reporting officer to possible perjury charges.

Email header as a signature

Where the sender of an email does not sign the email in the usual way, including by intentionally inserting a pre-programmed signature,[26] an email header cannot be regarded as a signature even if it includes the sender's name. The inclusion of the email address in the header is an automatic function of the email process.

---

21 In the United States, some commentators have adopted a pragmatic attitude to the potential difficulties raised by authentication; see B Wright, 'The verdict on plaintext signatures: They're legal', (1994) 10 *The Computer Law and Security Report* 311–12.
22 (1844) 5 QB 574; 114 ER 1366.
23 [1892] 1 QB 593, see Cave J at 597.
24 [1998] QCA 43.
25 No. 97CV0050 (Mass 1997).
26 See, for example, *Dursol-Fabrik Otto Durst GmbH & Co v Dursol North America Inc.* (2006) FC 1115, para 57 where Phelan J noted that it was 'confirmed' that the sender would see the default signature.

In *Mehta v J Pereira Fernandes SA*,[27] the court considered an email which was not signed at the foot of the message, but was described in the header of the email as having come from Nelmehta@aol.com. The court cited *Evans v Hoare* with approval and determined that whether or not an email address in the header amounts to a signature depends upon the intention of the sender. The defendant, by the email, offered to provide a personal guarantee in favour of the plaintiff in relation to a payment of £5000, on certain terms. The *Statute of Frauds* requires such guarantees to be in writing. Judge Pelling QC held that the email would be a note or memorandum to which section 4 of the *Statute of Frauds* applied. However, his Honour considered whether it was sufficiently signed, stating:

> a party can sign a document for the purposes of Section 4 by using his full name or his last name prefixed by some or all of his initials or using his initials, and possibly by using a pseudonym or a combination of letters and numbers (as can happen, for example, with a Lloyds slip scratch), providing always that whatever was used was inserted into the document in order to give, and with the intention of giving, authenticity to it. Its inclusion must have been intended as a signature for these purposes.[28]

In determining what would amount to a signature Judge Pelling QC examined the underlying purpose. The purpose of the *Statute of Frauds:*

> is to protect people from being held liable on informal communications because they may be made without sufficient consideration or expressed ambiguously or because such a communication might be fraudulently alleged against the party to be charged.[29]

In relation to an electronic document his Honour commented that:

> if a party creates and sends an electronically created document then he will be treated as having signed it to the same extent that he would in law be treated as having signed a hard copy of the same document. The fact that the document is created electronically as opposed to as a hard copy can make no difference.[30]

However, the issue before the court was whether the automatic insertion of a person's email address after the document has been transmitted constitutes a signature for the purposes of the *Statute of Frauds*. His Honour's conclusion was that an

---

27 [2006] EWHC 813.
28 Ibid., para 26.
29 Ibid., para 16.
30 Ibid., para 28.

email address insertion was 'incidental', and that the header was 'divorced from the main body of the text of the message'. If there is no further evidence in relation to the maker's intention, 'it is not possible to hold that the automatic insertion of an email address is ... intended for a signature'.[31] To conclude otherwise would, in his Honour's view, undermine or potentially undermine the purpose of the *Statute of Frauds*. His Honour questioned: 'Can it sensibly be suggested that the automatically generated name and fax number of the sender of a fax on a faxed document that is otherwise a Section 4 note or memorandum would constitute a signature for these purposes?'[32] Judge Pelling QC relied on the passage from Lord Westbury in *Caton v Caton*[33] (quoted earlier), and stressed the importance of the signatory's intention in placing or inserting the purported signature, stating: 'it is not possible to hold that the automatic insertion of an email address is, to use Cave J's language, "intended for a signature"'.[34]

The result is a victory for functional equivalence. To deem all emails as signed by the automatic header would deprive the sender of the ability to send unsigned notes. Many senders would and should be aware of the significance of placing their name at the end of an email or, as in *Evans v Hoare*,[35] the intentional placing of the name. In that case, Hoare's clerk, 'acting with the defendant's authority' had physically 'drawn up' a document with the defendant's name.[36] The modern parallel would be that where the email sender types the sender's name within the email body, it should be regarded as signing. The contrary view is put forward by Mason,[37] who concludes that the header and other automatic parts of the email, such as the source code and metadata, are parts of the email with 'considerable evidential value'.[38]

Acceptance at face value and risk

Parties to traditional hardcopy documents had accepted signatures at face value, accepting the associated practical and legal risks. An email can be made to appear

---

31 Ibid., para 29.
32 Ibid., para 23.
33 (1867) LR 2 HL 127.
34 [2006] EWHC 813, para 29.
35 [1892] 1 QB 593.
36 Ibid., 593.
37 Stephen Mason, *Electronic Signatures in Law*, Cambridge University Press, 3rd edn, 2012, 227–45.
38 Ibid., 238.

to be from a third party, and false addresses and pseudonyms can be employed. However, this is not new. Letters, facsimiles, telexes and so forth have also been faked. Fraudsters utilise all means at their disposal.

The genuineness of a document does not rely solely on the signature. Typically, a range of proofs are used for verification purposes. It is quite rare that standard hardcopy documents are adduced into evidence and proven as genuine only by the signature. More often the origin and genuineness are determined from the facts, conduct and acts of the parties and the surrounding circumstances of the case. Parties to contracts generally accept signatures at face value. They have no technical process to prove the genuineness of a signature, handwritten or otherwise, and there is typically no practice of requiring additional verification until a dispute arises. Similarly, there is no technical proof of origin of a telegram or telex. Commercial parties have accepted this risk in the past.

The courts and legislators should resist establishing any rule, principle or law that claims that an electronic signature is not valid merely because of the possibility of fraud or tampering, or that such signatures are fallible. Law makers should recognise commercial parties' acceptance of risk for commercial expediency, particularly in like circumstances.

Functions of signatures

Historically, the signature of a person does much more than merely authenticate the genuineness of a document. For example, three signatures typically appear on a testamentary disposition such as a will. The intention and function depend on whether the signature is that of the testator or witness. Functions include:

- to identify the signatory;
- to clarify and identify the personal involvement of the signatory in the act of signing;
- to associate a particular person with the contents of the document;
- to witness another person's signature;
- to approve the contents of the document;
- to indicate authorship of the document by the signatory.[39]

In the absence of vitiating factors such as fraud, *non est factum*, undue influence and unconscionable conduct, the law regards a signature as binding on the

---

39 See A McCullagh, P Little and W Caelli, 'Electronic signatures: Understand the past to develop the future, [1998] *UNSWLJ* 56 and A McCullagh, W Caelli and P Little, 'Signature stripping: A digital dilemma', (2001) 1 *Journal of Information, Technology and Law*.

signatory in relation to the contents of the document even if the signatory has not read the document. Scrutton LJ, in *L'Estrange v Graucob Ltd*, stated that when 'a document containing contractual terms is signed, then, in the absence of fraud, or, I will add, misrepresentation, the party signing it is bound, and it is wholly immaterial whether he has read the document or not'.[40] In *Foreman v Great Western Railway Company*,[41] an illiterate drover, in charge of cattle, signed a contract of carriage by rail which contained an exclusion clause. The court held that the drover's employer was bound by the clause, stating 'the plaintiff who sends the (illiterate) servant to sign the document is in no better or worse position than if he had signed it himself without reading it'.[42] More recently, the Full High Court stated:

> to sign a document known and intended to affect legal relations is an act which itself ordinarily conveys a representation to a reasonable reader of the document. The representation is that the person who signs either has read and approved the contents of the document or is willing to take the chance of being bound by those contents.[43]

There appear to be five main functions of signature requirements:

1. evidentiary – to ensure the availability of admissible and reliable evidence when applying legislation such as the *Statute of Frauds*;
2. cautionary – to act as a warning that this is a serious document with legal consequences;
3. reliance – the signature requirement may indicate that the veracity of the document or record may be relied on by others later;
4. channelling – to act as a demarcation between 'intent to act in a legally significant way and intent to act otherwise'; and
5. record-keeping – for compliance with laws such as taxation, money-laundering and statutes of limitation.[44]

---

40 [1934] 2 KB 394, 403.

41 (1878) 38 LT 851.

42 Ibid., 853, brackets added.

43 *Toll (FGCT) Pty Ltd v Alphapharm Pty Ltd* [2004] HCA 52, para 38 per Gleeson CJ, Gummow, Hayne, Callinan and Heydon JJ. See also *Oceanic Sun Line Special Shipping Company Inc. v Fay* [1988] HCA 32 para 15, per Brennan J (as he then was): 'If a passenger signs and thereby binds himself to the terms of a contract of carriage containing a clause exempting the carrier from liability for loss arising out of the carriage, it is immaterial that the passenger did not trouble to discover the contents of the contract.'

44 See Electronic Commerce Expert Group, 'Electronic commerce: Building the legal framework, Report of the Electronic Commerce Expert Group to the Attorney-General', (1998), para 2.7.28.

Electronic Transactions Acts

The requirement for signature in documents, particularly those that document, evidence or create contracts, was discussed in Chapter 11.

Where the law requires a signature, the Electronic Transactions Acts deem that the requirement is taken to have been met in relation to an electronic communication where certain conditions are met. The underlying rationale is functional equivalence. Where the electronic signature is functionally equivalent to the traditional signature, it ought to be treated equally in law. Each of the nine Australian Electronic Transactions Acts includes a provision deeming electronic signatures, on certain conditions, to meet the requirements under the law of signatures. The signature provision states:[45]

> If, under a law of this jurisdiction, the signature of a person is required, that requirement is taken to have been met in relation to an electronic communication if:
>
> **(a)** a method is used to identify the person and to indicate the person's intention in respect of the information communicated, and
> **(b)** the method used was either:
>> **(i)** as reliable as appropriate for the purpose for which the electronic communication was generated or communicated, in the light of all the circumstances, including any relevant agreement, or
>> **(ii)** proven in fact to have fulfilled the functions described in paragraph (a), by itself or together with further evidence, and
> **(c)** the person to whom the signature is required to be given consents to that requirement being met by way of the use of the method mentioned in paragraph (a).[46]

The former requirement that the court must have 'regard to all the relevant circumstances at the time the method was used, [and that] the method was as reliable as was appropriate for the purposes for which the information was communicated' was a serious weakness of the signature provision. However, the current provision

---

45 NSW – s9(1), Qld – s14, SA – s8(1), Tas – s7(1), Vic – s9(1), WA – s9(1), ACT – s9(1), NT – s9(1). The Commonwealth has substantially similar provisions in s10(1), but also makes special provision for Commonwealth entities. Note that these provisions were amended to conform to the *UN Convention on the Use of Electronic Communications in International Contracts (2005)*.

46 The following expressions and phrases from the legislation were considered in detail in Chapter 11: 'signature of person'; 'signature of the person … in relation to an electronic communication'; 'method used'; 'electronic communication'; 'a method used to identify the person and to indicate the person's intention'; 'reliability of the method used'; 'the purposes for which the information was generated or communicated'; 'proven to have fulfilled the functions in paragraph (a)'; and 'consent'.

will require the court, through counsel, to cover a significant number of factors –
legal, technical and commercial – before making the equivalence determination.
These might include, for example:

- the sophistication of the equipment used by each of the parties;
- the nature of their trade activity;
- the frequency with which commercial transactions take place between the parties;
- the kind and size of the transaction;
- the function of signature requirements in a given statutory and regulatory environment;
- the capability of communication systems;
- compliance with authentication procedures set forth by intermediaries;
- the range of authentication procedures made available by the intermediary;
- compliance with trade customs and practice;
- the existence of insurance coverage mechanisms against unauthorised messages;
- the importance and value of the information contained in the data message;
- the availability of alternative methods of authentication and the cost of implementing them;
- the degree of acceptance or non-acceptance of the method of identification in the relevant industry or field both at the time the method was agreed upon and the time when the data message was communicated; and
- any other relevant factor.[47]

'Electronic signature' defined

An 'electronic signature' is any means of electronic authentication of the identity
of a person and of the intent of that person to indicate approval or to be associated with an electronic record. The term has no universally accepted meaning and
internationally is variously defined. An 'electronic signature' may be defined as any
electronic data, including any letters, characters, numbers or other symbols, attached to or logically associated with an electronic record, used with the intention
of authenticating or approving the electronic record.

The Electronic Transactions Acts in Australia do not define 'electronic signature'. They do not need to. Instead, they logically connect the use of a 'signature'

---

47 *UNCITRAL Model Law on Electronic Commerce with Guide to Enactment* (1996) paras 52–61,
<www.uncitral.org/pdf/english/texts/electcom/05-89450-Ebook.pdf>.

with an 'electronic communication'. By necessity, such a signature must be electronic. The expression 'electronic communication' is defined as:

(a) a communication of information in the form of data, text or images by means of guided or unguided electromagnetic energy, or both, or

(b) a communication of information in the form of sound by means of guided or unguided electromagnetic energy, or both, where the sound is processed at its destination by an automated voice recognition system.[48]

The expression 'electronic communication' may be regarded as narrower than 'electronic record' or 'electronic document', but this point remains untested. In all likelihood a court would apply the expression to all forms.

The *UNCITRAL Model Law on Electronic Commerce* does not use the expression 'electronic signature'. However, the *UNCITRAL Model Law on Electronic Signatures* defines an 'electronic signature':

'Electronic signature' means data in electronic form in, affixed to or logically associated with, a data message, which may be used to identify the signatory in relation to the data message and to indicate the signatory's approval of the information contained in the data message.[49]

The New Zealand *Electronic Transactions Act 2002* provides: '"electronic signature", in relation to information in electronic form, means a method used to identify a person and to indicate that person's approval of that information'.

The expression only appears once in each of the Australian Acts, and then only to provide that 'Certain other laws [are] not affected.' This savings provision is designed to ensure that the general deeming provision of the Electronic Transactions Acts does not affect the operation of a specific law which may call for an electronic signature 'howsoever described'.

The Singapore *Electronic Transactions Act 1998* included extensive provisions dealing with electronic and digital signatures. The Singapore Act defined 'electronic signature' as:

any letters, characters, numbers or other symbols in digital form attached to or logically associated with an electronic record, and executed or adopted with the intention of authenticating or approving the electronic record.[50]

---

48 NSW – s5, Qld – s6, SA – s5, Tas – s3, Vic – s3, WA – s5, ACT – s5, NT – s5. The Commonwealth *Electronic Transactions Act 1999* uses the narrower word 'speech' in place of 'sound'. New Zealand defines 'electronic communications' in s5: '"electronic communication" means a communication by electronic means'.

49 Art. 2.

50 *Electronic Transactions Act 1998* (Singapore) s2.

An electronic signature may be as simple as typing a name at the end of an email. It may be a complex mathematical transformation designed to provide a level of security to ensure that the electronic message is from the purported sender and is unaltered. Both forms of signatures have data in digital form attached to or logically associated with an electronic document. The level of security to be used is a matter for the parties, depending upon factors such as the commercial and legal risk involved. Parties entering into transactions over the internet frequently need to authenticate the message and verify the identity of the sender.

Uses

An electronic signature may be used to sign any electronic document or record, with the same intention and for the same purpose as a traditional signature on a paper record or document. However, certain types of electronic signature have a much higher level of security than the traditional signature, and may be used for authentication and verification purposes with a greater degree of certainty.

Security of electronic signature

Traditional signatures can be easily forged. Nevertheless the traditional signature is used extensively in commerce, on contracts, cheques and other negotiable instruments. Electronic signatures have different risks. While the simple electronic signature merely typed at the end of an electronic record may be less secure than the traditional signature, there are many choices available to parties, commercial and otherwise, to raise the level of authentication and verification to well in excess of that of a handwritten signature.

Anyone could type a person's name at the end of a typed electronic communication. Such a signature, while valid in the right circumstances, is most insecure. Two parties could agree upon a simple code. Parties could agree upon a simple number or a string of characters. For example, parties agree on the number '333'. This number may be placed at the end of the message with the agreed meaning that this verifies that the communication came from the other party. Such a simple signature identifies the signor by agreement, and indicates authentication or approval. The number may be dynamic; for example, the agreed number could be the sum of five times the date plus six times the month: 5 November would thus be '91'. It would be difficult for a third party to work out the authenticating signature even by intercepting a handful of communications. There are more sophisticated methods available commercially.

Digitised signatures

A digitised signature is a handwritten signature, scanned into a computer and then placed electronically into an electronic document, such as an email, to give the appearance of a traditional signature. Such a signature is an electronic signature, and if placed with the requisite intention operates in the same manner as any other electronic signature. A digitised signature has a low level of security, as anyone intercepting such an email can extract it and use it.

Digital signatures

The digital signature is a subset of the electronic signature. Digital signatures are attached to specific data, such as an email, computer file or web page. Although often used as a signature in the usual sense, the expression 'digital signature' is a misnomer. It may be better described as a 'digital certificate', as it functions as certification of the document and sender (or creator) rather than as a formal signature. A digital signature is:

> an electronic signature consisting of a transformation of an electronic record using an asymmetric cryptosystem and a hash function such that a person having the initial untransformed electronic record and the signer's public key can accurately determine –
>
> **(a)** whether the transformation was created using the private key that corresponds to the signer's public key; and
>
> **(b)** whether the initial electronic record has been altered since the transformation was made.[51]

A digital signature permits both verification and authentication of data.

The recipient verifies the digital signature by a simple automatic computation involving the data, the purported digital signature and the sender's public key. The computation determines whether or not the correct mathematical relationship exists. If it does, it reports that the digital signature is verified. An unverified digital signature may be an indication that there is a hoax sender or that the message has been altered. The recipient should then take appropriate steps, such as determining the bona fides of the message, and seek a retransmission.

Standard encryption requires that the sender and the recipient of a message know and use the same secret code. This method is symmetrical: the process to decrypt is the reverse of the process to encrypt. The method is called private encryption. The major difficulty with it is agreeing on the secret code with confidence that no one else finds out. Anyone who overhears or intercepts the key can potentially read all encrypted messages. Accordingly, private encryption has its own inherent security risks. Also, in modern communications one may have little notice of who one's correspondent may be, and thus of when one may need this level of encryption.

---

51 *Electronic Transactions Act 2010* (Singapore) Third Schedule. The Act also defines 'asymmetric cryptosystem' and 'hash function'. See also the *UNCITRAL Model Law on Electronic Signatures*.

Public encryption was developed in 1976 to resolve private encryption dilemmas. The sender and recipient each possess a pair of keys: the public key and the private key. Each person's public key is freely available to anyone. The private key is kept secret. There is no need for both parties to share information about the private key. All communications involve only the public key; no private key is ever transmitted or shared. There is a mathematical relationship between the public key and the private key, but the private key cannot be determined from the public key. One or more public keys may be created from the private key. The program makes complex mathematical calculations to do this.

The holder of a private key uses that key to place a digital signature on the relevant electronic document. Any person holding the corresponding public key is able to verify that the message has not been altered and to authenticate that it could only come from the holder of the private key. The 'hash function' means applying an algorithm that maps or translates one sequence of the electronic record into another, generally smaller, set (the 'hash result') such that: a record yields the same hash result every time the algorithm is executed using the same record as input; it is computationally infeasible that a record can be derived or reconstituted from the hash result produced by the algorithm; and it is computationally infeasible that two records can be found that produce the same hash result using the algorithm. The level of security available is such that it is regarded as impossible to duplicate.

A verified result of a digital signature is regarded as certain in the industry as far as the computing aspects are concerned. However, there remains the issue of public key substitution. The holder of a public key must ensure that it comes from a reliable source. A rogue may pretend to be another person, or to represent an institution, and provide a substitute public key, with the result that the recipient will receive a verification and authentication message because the substituted public key will correspond with the rogue's private key. For this reason Certification Authorities have been established. They issue certificates which certify the ownership of a public key. Financial institutions, corporate and government entities and others provide the Certification Authority with the public key. The Certification Authority then undertakes identification due diligence. Certification Authorities have become a critical component of commercial data security and electronic commerce by confirming and guaranteeing public key identity. There are many commercial and government approved Certification Authorities in the marketplace. The courts should accept an authentication from any of these authorities.

Authentication of electronic data messages will become increasingly important for lawyers and commercial parties for evidentiary purposes. The Australian Evidence Acts do not address all aspects of email communications. Some state Acts make presumptions regarding the sending and receipt of postal articles, telexes, lettergrams and telegrams. However, there is no similar presumption regarding email. Nonetheless, the Commonwealth and NSW Evidence Acts state:

> The hearsay rule does not apply to a representation contained in a document recording a message that has been transmitted by electronic mail or by a fax, telegram, lettergram or telex so far as the representation is a representation as to:
>
> **(a)** the identity of the person from whom or on whose behalf the message was sent, or
>
> **(b)** the date on which or the time at which the message was sent, or
>
> **(c)** the message's destination or the identity of the person to whom the message was addressed.[52]

Nevertheless, courts will need to be satisfied regarding the authenticity of such transmissions.

The enactment of legislation dealing with digital and electronic signatures needs to be considered with caution. Only recently have international models been available for national legislatures. In July 2001 UNCITRAL released the Model Law on Electronic Signatures.[53] This Model Law is intended to bring greater legal certainty to the use of electronic signatures. It establishes the presumption that electronic signatures are to be treated as equivalent to handwritten signatures where certain criteria of technical reliability are met. The Model Law uses technology-neutral language and establishes rules of conduct for assessing responsibilities and liabilities of the signatory, the relying party and trusted third parties that might intervene in the signature process. In a similar vein, the European Union passed a Directive on a Community Framework for Electronic Signatures.[54] It establishes a legal framework for electronic signatures and certain certification services.

Given the pace of technological development, it is more appropriate for the market to determine practice issues, such as the levels of security and reliability required for electronic signatures. Legislation should deal simply with the legal effect of electronic signatures.

While the Commonwealth *Electronic Transactions Act 1999* is based on the *UNCITRAL Model Law on Electronic Commerce*, the federal Attorney-General's view is that a legislative regime concerning digital and electronic signatures is not required. The debate in relation to the legal issues raised by electronic commerce is often clouded by the discussion of digital and electronic signatures. 'Electronic signature' is a term used to refer to a range of technologies intended to ensure the security and certainty of electronic commerce.

---

52 *Evidence Act 1995* (Cth) s71 and *Evidence Act 1995* (NSW) s71.

53 The text of the *UNCITRAL Model Law on Electronic Signatures* was adopted on 5 July 2001. It is available at <www.uncitral.org/english/texts/electcom/ml-elecsig-e.pdf>. Australia has not enacted any legislation based on this Model Law.

54 *Directive 1999/93/EC of the European Parliament and of the Council of 13 December 1999 on a Community Framework for Electronic Signatures* [1999], available at <www.europa. eu.int/comm/internal_market/en/media/sign/Dir99–93-ecEN.pdf>.

Australian Business Number Digital Signature Certificates

To aid electronic commerce, the federal government developed the Australian Business Number Digital Signature Certificate (ABN-DSC), which is a digital certificate linked to an entity's ABN. It facilitates online service delivery and is intended to foster the use of digital certificates and electronic commerce in Australia. Since March 2001 Commonwealth agencies have accepted the use of these certificates to identify businesses for online transactions. Only Certification Authorities accredited under the Commonwealth's Gatekeeper Public Key Infrastructure framework are able to issue ABN-DSCs.

In 1997, the federal government established the Online Council following agreement by states, territories and local government to cooperate on online issues. In March 2002, all states and territories agreed to urgently consider accredited and cross-recognised certificates which are ABN-DSC compliant. This will help meet the e-commerce objectives of governments by making digital certificates widely available to businesses. This development has direct implications for B2G (business to government) electronic commerce and facilitates B2B (business to business) electronic commerce by providing authentication, confidentiality, integrity and non-repudiation.[55]

Secure Socket Layer – Transport Layer Security

Secure Socket Layer (SSL) technology refers to a sequence of processes that ensure that information stored in electronic form or transmitted over networks, such as the internet, is not accessible to any person not authorised to view that information.[56]

Transport Layer Security (TLS) is a security protocol that ensures privacy between communicating applications and their users on the internet. When a server and client communicate, TLS ensures that no third party may interfere with or read any message. TLS is the successor to SSL.

---

55 See generally the Australian Government Information Management Office: <www.finance. gov.au/agict/>.
56 ALRC, *Review of Australian Privacy Law*, Discussion Paper No. 72 (2007), para 6.5. For an example of an SSL application, see SSL-Explorer Enterprise Edition at <www.optimati.com/ index.php?option=com_content&task=view&id=47&Itemid=63>.

Both SSL and TLS use a form of digital signature technology. For evidentiary purposes, communications using this technology would be regarded as secure, authenticated and verified. SSL and TLS provide endpoint authentication and communications privacy over the internet using cryptography. In typical use, the server is authenticated and the client remains unauthenticated; mutual authentication requires deploying public key infrastructure to clients. The protocols allow server applications to communicate in a way designed to prevent eavesdropping, tampering and message forgery. This allows users to securely provide personal details – such as name, address and credit card numbers – to sites employing the protocol.

The SSL and TLS protocols exchange records. Each record can be compressed, encrypted and packed with a message authentication code. Each record has a content type field that specifies the type of protocol being used. When the connection is initiated, the record level encapsulates another protocol: the handshake protocol. Client and server negotiate a common secret called 'master secret'. Other key data is calculated from the 'master secret', which is passed through a 'Pseudo Random Function'.

Applications

The SSL and TLS protocols are commonly found with hypertext transfer protocol (HTTP), which is the most common protocol used on the World Wide Web. When used, the protocol becomes HTTPS. HTTPS is used to secure World Wide Web pages for applications such as electronic commerce. It uses public key certificates to verify the identity of endpoints.

FURTHER READING

Sharon Christensen, William Duncan and Rouhshi Low, 'The Statute of Frauds in the digital age – maintaining the integrity of signatures', (2003) 10(4) eLaw : Murdoch University Electronic Journal of Law 44.

Alan Davidson, 'Electronic signatures', (2002) 22 Proctor 8, 31.

Alan Davidson, 'Signatures on electronic documents', (2004) 24 Proctor 7, 29.

Yee Fen Lim, 'Digital signature, certification authorities and the law', (2002) 9(3) eLaw Journal 29.

A McCullagh, W Caelli and P Little, 'Signature stripping: A digital dilemma', (2001) (1) Journal of Information, Law and Technology.

Stephen Mason, Electronic Signatures in Law, Cambridge University Press, 3rd edn, 2012.

14

COPYRIGHT ISSUES IN ELECTRONIC COMMERCE

Prior to digital storage and the internet, the nature and architecture of the storage of information made access difficult and copying relatively arduous and time consuming. In the 21st century, information of all types is created, shared and, significantly, reproduced digitally. Material placed online is subject to unrestricted reproduction. The demand for all forms of information is a vast opportunity for order and structure – and for exploitation. The sheer number of users, and their voracious appetites, leads to increased supply. This is demonstrated by the vast number of websites which have emerged to reproduce material subject to copyright, and the almost complete disregard for the law by individual users.[1]

The internet facilitates the swift reproducing and exchange of digital material. Hyperlinking and framing can offer new possibilities for infringement of copyright. Works protected by copyright, such as music and videos, can be easily transferred in peer-to-peer dealings. Such transfers have become the target of copyright owners. This chapter explores these issues and developments and the relationship between copyright and electronic commerce. It is not intended to state the law relating to copyright, other than via a brief overview. The advent of electronic commerce and the internet have necessitated a rethink of intellectual property issues by the World Intellectual Property Organization (WIPO), the courts and the legislature. The proliferation of material on the internet – written, aural and graphic – has posed new questions and resulted in the creation of new rights internationally.

The nature of copyright

Intellectual property comprises state-sanctioned rights entitling the holder of such rights to a monopoly on exploiting and controlling a number of uses of the property for a predetermined period of time. The state gains the benefit of, for example, literary and musical works, new inventions, medicines, research, designs and innovation. Inventors, writers, composers and designers have the incentive of reward for their efforts. Their works, patents and designs will form part of the public domain when the predetermined period expires.

Copyright arose only after the invention of the printing press. Before that, copies were made by hand and were relatively expensive and time consuming. Charles II of England encouraged the passing of the *Licensing Act of 1662*. However, the *Statute of Anne* in 1702[2] is regarded as the first copyright legislation. It gave publishers rights for fixed periods. Copyright's initial application to books

---

1 For peer-to-peer filing sharing, see Chapter 4.

2 *8 Anne c 19*. Long title: 'An Act for the Encouragement of Learning, by vesting the Copies of Printed Books in the Authors or purchasers of such Copies, during the Times therein mentioned'.

and maps has now extended to such things as sound, films, choreography and software. The Berne Convention of 1886 established international recognition of copyright among member nations. The Berne Convention pioneered the concept that copyright automatically arose at the time of creation. That is, registration of copyright is not necessary. Copyright arises once a work is written down, painted or drawn, filmed or taped. It protects the expression of an idea, but not the idea itself; it protects only against the copying of a work, not against independent creation. An idea is not protected until it is documented in writing or recorded in some way. Copyright is intended to reward authors economically by giving them control of various uses of their work.

To qualify for copyright protection, works must be original.[3] Originality is assessed according to whether or not the creator produced the work using his or her own skill and effort and did not copy another's work. If two authors express the same idea and their respective works are created independently, they both have copyright protection.

The regulations of the Berne Convention are incorporated into the World Trade Organization's TRIPS agreement (1995), giving the Berne Convention near global application. The 2002 World Intellectual Property Organization (WIPO) Copyright Treaty enacted greater restrictions on the use of technology to copy works in the nations that ratified it.

Copyright, at its basic level, is the right to copy. Copyright arises only by the operation of statute: in Australia, the *Copyright Act 1968* (Cth).[4] The right usually vests in the creator or author of a work at the time when the work is first produced in material form. For example, if one is said to own the copyright in a musical work, no other person has the right to make a copy of that work without permission.[5]

Copyright covers two categories of material: 'works', which, as defined by the *Copyright Act*, may be literary, dramatic, musical or artistic, and 'subject matter other than works', such as sound recordings, cinematograph films (including computer-generated or interactive computer games), television and sound broadcasts and published editions of works.[6] 'Works' are dealt with by Part III of the Copyright Act, 'subject matter other than works' by Part IV. The copyright in 'subject matter other than works' exists independently of the copyright in the original work. From

---

3 See *Macmillan v Cooper* (1923) 93 LJPC 113; *Cramp & Sons Ltd v Frank Smythson Ltd* [1944] AC 328; *Feist Publications Inc. v Rural Telephone Service Co. Inc.* 737 F. Supp. 610, 622 (Kan 1990). See also *Lott v JBW & Friends PL* [2000] SASC 3.
4 Copyright is specifically a federal power pursuant to the *Constitution*, s51(xviii): Copyrights, patents of inventions and designs, and trade marks. The New Zealand legislation is the *Copyright Act 1994*.
5 See *APRA v Canterbury-Bankstown League Club Ltd* [1964] NSWR 138.
6 See *APRA v Commonwealth Bank of Australia* (1993) 25 IPR 157; *Telstra Corp. Ltd v APRA* (1997) 38 IPR 294.

a copyright perspective, the internet is a mixture of original works and secondary works. Web pages may include graphics and images, text, compilations, and music and video clips, each of which is likely to be protected by copyright.

Generally, copyright in a literary, dramatic, musical or artistic work lasts for 70 years after the end of the calendar year in which the author of the work died.[7] If, before the death of the author of a literary work (other than a computer program) or a dramatic or musical work, the work had not been published, performed in public or broadcast, and records of the work had not been offered or exposed for sale to the public, copyright lasts for 70 years after the end of the calendar year in which the work is first published, performed in public, or broadcast, or records of the work are first offered or exposed for sale to the public, whichever is the earliest of those events.[8] A reference to the doing of an act in relation to a work includes a reference to the doing of that act in relation to an adaptation of the work.[9] If the first publication of a literary, dramatic, musical or artistic work is anonymous or pseudonymous, copyright lasts for 70 years after the end of the calendar year in which the work was first published. However, if at any time before the end of the period the identity of the author of the work is generally known or can be ascertained by reasonable inquiry, the period is calculated from the death of the author.[10] Where the work is the product of joint authorship, the period of protection runs from the death of the last surviving joint author.

Exclusive rights

The *Copyright Act* grants certain exclusive rights to the holder of the copyright, depending upon the type of work:

> 31(1) For the purposes of this Act, unless the contrary intention appears, copyright, in relation to a work, is the exclusive right:
>
> > **(a)** in the case of a literary, dramatic or musical work, to do all or any of the following acts:
> >
> > > **(i)** to reproduce the work in a material form;
> > > **(ii)** to publish the work;
> > > **(iii)** to perform the work in public;
> > > **(iv)** to communicate the work to the public;

---

7 *Copyright Act* (Cth) s33(2); 50 years in New Zealand, *Copyright Act 1994* (NZ) s22.
8 *Copyright Act* (Cth) s33(3).
9 *Copyright Act* (Cth) s33(4).
10 *Copyright Act* (Cth) s24.

      (v) to make an adaptation of the work;

     (vi) to do, in relation to a work that is an adaptation of the first-mentioned work, any of the acts specified in relation to the first mentioned work in subparagraphs (i) to (iv), inclusive; and

  (b) in the case of an artistic work, to do all or any of the following acts:

      (i) to reproduce the work in a material form;

      (ii) to publish the work;

      (iii) to communicate the work to the public; and

  (c) in the case of a literary work (other than a computer program) or a musical or dramatic work, to enter into a commercial rental arrangement in respect of the work reproduced in a sound recording; and

  (d) in the case of a computer program, to enter into a commercial rental arrangement in respect of the program.[11]

The relief that a court may grant in an action for an infringement of copyright includes 'an injunction (subject to such terms, if any, as the court thinks fit) and either damages or an account of profits'.[12] There may be additional damages for flagrant breaches or as punishment, to deter the infringer (and, presumably, others). The aggrieved party may also claim damages for conversion and delivery up of infringing copies or plates used for making such copies.[13]

Where a proved infringement on a commercial scale involves a communication of a work to the public, and it is likely that there were other infringements of the copyright by the defendant that the plaintiff did not prove in the action, the court is directed by the *Copyright Act* to have regard to the likelihood of other infringements, as well as the proved infringement. In determining whether the proved infringement and the likely infringements were on a commercial scale, the court must take into account the volume and value of any articles that are infringing copies and any other relevant matter. For the purposes of this consideration, 'article' includes a reproduction or copy of a work in electronic form.[14]

Infringement

Infringement may be direct or indirect. Direct infringement is where a person exercises an exclusive right of the copyright owner without permission.[15] The downloading of music from the internet, for example, involves direct copying. Indirect

---

11 For New Zealand, see *Copyright Act 1994* (NZ) s16.

12 *Copyright Act 1968* (Cth) s115(2).

13 *Copyright Act 1968* (Cth) s116, and ss119–125.

14 *Copyright Act 1968* (Cth) s115(5), (6), (7) and (8).

15 *Coogi Australia Pty Ltd v Hysport International Pty Ltd* [1998] FCA 1059.

infringement includes the importing of infringing articles, selling or conducting other trade dealings with infringing articles and permitting a place of public entertainment to be used for a public performance of a work.[16]

Generally the infringement occurs where a 'substantial part' of the work is copied.[17] In addition, generally there needs to be proof of a sufficient degree of objective similarity between the work and the copy, and a causal connection between the two works.

Substantial part

Copyright is infringed where the work or a substantial part of the work has been copied.[18] What constitutes a substantial part is a question of fact, and is determined on a case-by-case basis. In 1853 Harriet Beecher Stowe sued to stop an unauthorised German translation of her novel *Uncle Tom's Cabin* – and lost.[19] Notwithstanding that the entire work was involved, Judge Robert Grier held that copyright applies only to the 'precise words'. Calling a translation 'a copy of the original', his Honour described as ridiculous the proposition that the translation was a breach of the copyright. In 1870 the US Congress remedied this position, as have all modern jurisdictions. The copyright holder now has the right to make an adaptation (this includes translations) of the work and to do all the things with that adaptation that are allowed to be done with the work itself.[20]

Prior to the internet and computer programs, the cases established that the most important factor in determining whether or not the part of the work copied was a substantial part was the quality of what was copied, not the quantity.[21] Copying a few notes of music of a popular song could constitute a substantial part if those notes constitute the main theme of the song.[22] In the High Court of Australia in *IceTV Pty Limited v Nine Network Australia Pty Limited*, French CJ, Crennan and Kiefel JJ stated: 'whether a part reproduced is a "substantial part", a matter often referred to is whether there has been an "appropriation" of the author's skill and labour'.[23]

---

16 See *Copyright Act 1968* (Cth) s39(1). See Peer-to-peer file sharing, below.
17 *Copyright Act 1968* (Cth) s14.
18 See *Copyright Act 1968* (Cth) ss14, 31(1)(a)(i) and (b)(i).
19 *Stowe v Thomas* 23 F. Cas. 201 (CCED Pa 1853).
20 *Copyright Act 1968* (Cth) s31(1)(a)(vi) and (vii).
21 *Ladbroke (Football) Ltd v William Hill (Football) Ltd* [1964] 1 WLR 273, House of Lords. See also *EMI Songs Australia Pty Limited v Larrikin Music Publishing Pty Limited* [2011] FCAFC 47.
22 *Hawkes & Son (London) Ltd v Paramount Film Service Ltd* [1934] 1 Ch 593. See also *Blackie & Sons Ltd v Lothian Book Publishing Co. Pty Ltd* (1921) 29 CLR 396; *Warner Bros Pictures v Majestic Pictures Corp.* (1934) 70 F. 2d 310, titles of works; *Exxon Corp. v Exxon Ins. Consultations* [1982] Ch 119; *Arica Institute Inc. v Palmer* (1992) 970 F. 2d 1067, short phrases and slogans.
23 [2009] HCA 14, para 49.

The question of whether or not something is a substantial part of a computer program created difficulty in *Autodesk Inc. v Dyason No. 1*[24] and *Autodesk Inc. v Dyason No. 2*.[25] The question centred on a 127-bit series. The 127 bits were tiny, typically representing a mere 16 characters in a typed document. But as used in the program they were an important construct. Dawson J said that the 127-bit series was 'a substantial, indeed *essential*,part of that program ... [it] processes the information which it receives'.[26] Brennan J said that the series was 'but a minute fraction of the bytes in the whole ... program. Nevertheless, the series ... is both *original and critical*'.[27] Gaudron J said that the series was 'the *linchpin* of the program ... It was *critical* ... there is, in my view, simply no basis for an argument that the [series] was not a substantial part'.[28]

In *Data Access Corporation v Powerflex Services Pty Ltd*[29] the High Court considered the approaches in the *Autodesk* cases to come close to a 'but for' analysis: 'but for' the 127-bit series, the program would not work. The reasoning in the *Autodesk* cases did not find favour with the High Court, although Gaudron J published a separate judgement explaining her Honour's position. The High Court noted that in general, a computer program may not work, or may not work as planned, if even one character is altered, and so it could be argued that each character is 'essential'. In *Cantor Fitzgerald International v Tradition (UK) Ltd*,[30] in the English Patents Court, Pumfrey J observed of *Autodesk (No. 1)* that it 'would result in any part of any computer program being substantial since without any part the program would not work, or at best [would] not work as desired'.[31] In *Autodesk (No. 2)* Mason CJ had dissented, stating that 'substantial part':

> refers to the *quality* of what is taken rather than the *quantity* ... it is important to inquire into the importance which the taken portion bears in relation to the work as a whole: is it an 'essential' or 'material' part of the work?[32]

The High Court in *Data Access* was unable to agree with the approach taken by the majority in the *Autodesk* cases. The High Court felt that there was 'great force' in the criticism that the 'but for' essentiality test was not practicable. Mason CJ's dissenting

24 (1992) 173 CLR 330.
25 (1993) 176 CLR 300. ('*Autodesk* cases').
26 (1992) 173 CLR 330 at 346, emphasis added.
27 (1992) 176 CLR 300 at 311, emphasis added.
28 Ibid. at 330, emphasis added.
29 [1999] HCA 49 ('*Data Access* case'). Gleeson CJ, McHugh, Gummow and Hayne delivered a joint judgment with which Gaudron J agreed effectively in full, only making a separate comment regarding her Honour's earlier judgment in *Autodesk v Dyason No. 2* (1993) 176 CLR 300.
30 [2000] RPC 95.
31 Ibid., 131.
32 (1993) 176 CLR 300, 305, emphasis added.

opinion was preferred. Accordingly, a person who does no more than reproduce those parts of a program which are data or related information and which are irrelevant to its structure, will be 'unlikely' to have reproduced a substantial part of the computer program. The High Court used the term 'unlikely' in preference to 'impossible' because it conceived that data, considered alone, could be sufficiently original to be a substantial part of the computer program in the right circumstances.

In *Data Access* the High Court also considered whether a 'Huffman Compression' table was a literary work. The Huffman compression is a method of reducing the amount of memory space consumed by data files. In evidence, Dr Bennett, the third respondent, explained the method, stating, for example, that the letter 'e' was normally encoded as the bit string '01100101', but as a common character it might be encoded instead as the bit string '101', with a space (and thus also efficiency) saving of 62.5 per cent.[33] This process could be used for many letters, strings and phrases. There was no allegation that Dr Bennett copied the source code of the Huffman algorithm from the original program. Dr Bennett wanted the plaintiff's original program to be able to compress and decompress his files, and for his program to compress and decompress other files in an identical way so that the programs could work together.[34] Consequently, he needed to be able to replicate precisely the default Huffman Compression table. Dr Bennett did not have access to the original file. His evidence was that he refrained from 'decompiling or looking inside the Dataflex runtime', and instead carried out a process to recreate and deduce the original table. This 'reverse engineering method' was highly ingenious. Nevertheless, the High Court held that the original Huffman table fell 'squarely within the statutory definition of a literary work'. Both the High Court and the Full Federal Court considered that the process undertaken by Dr Bennett constituted a 'reproduction' of the original Huffman table:

> The fact that Dr Bennett used an ingenious method of determining the bit string assigned to each character does not make the output of such a process any less a 'reproduction' than if Dr Bennett had sat down with a print-out of the table and copy-typed it.[35]

Objective similarity and causal connection

The requisite degree of similarity depends on the type of work. An exact duplicate will be objectively similar. Objective similarity may arise after transformation into another media, such as a book into a film. Two pieces of computer software may be objectively similar if one has been translated into another computer language;

---

33 [2000] RPC 95, 114.
34 See Software, below.
35 [2000] RPC 95, 124.

the deliberate copying of computer data may also produce something that is objectively similar.

Gibbs CJ, in *SW Hart & Co. Pty Ltd v Edwards Hot Water Systems*, described the test in the following terms:

> The notion of reproduction, for the purposes of copyright law, involves two elements – resemblance to, and actual use of, the copyright work, or, to adopt the words which appear in the judgment of Willmer LJ in *Francis Day & Hunter Ltd v Bron* (1963) Ch 587, at p 614, 'a sufficient degree of objective similarity between the two works' and 'some causal connection between the plaintiffs' and the defendants' work'.[36]

Lord Reid said, in *Ladbroke (Football) Ltd v William Hill (Football) Ltd:*

> Broadly, reproduction means copying, and does not include cases where an author or compiler produces a substantially similar result by independent work without copying. And, if he does copy, the question whether he has copied a substantial part depends much more on the quality than on the quantity of what he has taken.[37]

Causal connection may be proved directly or indirectly. The copying may be unconscious, such as the reproduction of music heard years before.

Software

In the past three decades the courts and the legislature have grappled with copyright issues of software and computer programs. In 1986, in *Computer Edge v Apple*,[38] the High Court of Australia held that the *Copyright Act* did not apply to software. The High Court was unable to classify computer code as a literary work, or any other type of work. Computer code may be as basic as a series of unintelligible (to the human reader) ones and zeros, in machine language, or one of dozens of other computer languages with varying degrees of readability. It was not denied that great care and skill were involved in creating the code, but it did not fit in with the then definition of literary work. This resulted in an amendment to the *Copyright Act* expanding 'literary works' to include a computer program, defined as:

> a set of statements or instructions to be used directly or indirectly in a computer in order to bring about a certain result.[39]

---

36 (1985) 159 CLR 466, 472. See also *EMI Songs Australia Pty Limited v Larrikin Music Publishing Pty Limited* [2011] FCAFC 47.
37 (1964) 1 WLR 273, 276. See also *Francis Day & Hunter Ltd v Bron* [1963] Ch 587.
38 (1986) 161 CLR 171.
39 *Copyright Act 1968* (Cth) s10.

The new definition was tested by the High Court in *Data Access*.[40] The court's finding that the respondents infringed the appellant's copyright in the computer compression table was described as having 'considerable practical consequences'.[41] There are significant ramifications for anyone who seeks to produce a computer program that is compatible with a program produced by others. The court, concerned about the impact of its decision, stated, 'matters … can be resolved only by the legislature reconsidering and, if it thinks it necessary or desirable, rewriting the whole of the provisions that deal with copyright in computer programs'.[42]

Dr Bennett, as noted above, became familiar with the applicant's 'Dataflex' system and decided to create and market an application development system which would be compatible with the Dataflex database file structure so that persons who were familiar with the Dataflex system would be able to use his new product. By a process of reverse engineering and study of both the documentation and operation of the Dataflex system, Dr Bennett created computer programs compatible with the Dataflex system. He 'duplicated' and used certain commands and 'Reserved Words' (the precise words used by Dataflex to operate the program). The underlying source code, however, was quite different from the original. He was aware that copying the original source code would be a copyright breach, so he avoided doing so directly. The Full Court of the Federal Court of Australia held that commands in a computer program were not original literary works within the meaning of the definition in section 10 of the *Copyright Act*, and so copyright did not subsist in them.

The High Court asked whether each of the Reserved Words constituted a 'computer program' within the meaning of section 10(1) of the Act, and held that although each Reserved Word was 'undoubtedly' in 'code or notation', each one was merely a single word. None of the Reserved Words met the criteria set out in section 10. The majority went to some lengths to explain the nature and characteristics of computer code and even set out three short examples of such code.[43] The High Court held that it is not appropriate to relate the Reserved Word back to the underlying computer code to which it refers. It is the particular selection, ordering, combination and arrangement of instructions within a computer program which provide its expression. Similarly, a set of Reserved Words is not a 'computer program'. The simple listing does not cause a computer to perform any identifiable function. The definition of a 'computer program' requires that the set of instructions be intended to cause the computer to perform a particular function.

---

40 [1999] HCA 49. Gleeson CJ, McHugh, Gummow and Hayne JJ delivered a joint judgment with which Gaudron J agreed effectively in full, only making a separate comment regarding her Honour's earlier judgment in *Autodesk v Dyason No. 2* (1993) 176 CLR 300.
41 [1999] HCA 49, para 125.
42 Ibid.
43 Computer programmers will observe curious use of computer code in their Honours' judgement.

Right of communication

In 2000 the centrepiece of amendments to the *Copyright Act* was a new broadly based, technology-neutral right of communication to the public. The right is an exclusive right (for the copyright holder) in literary, musical, artistic and dramatic works, sound recordings, films and broadcasts.[44]

'Communicate' is defined as: 'make available online or electronically transmit (whether over a path, or a combination of paths …)'.[45] The right replaced and extended the pre-existing technology-specific broadcasting right. 'Broadcast' is defined as: 'a communication *to the public* delivered by a broadcasting service within the meaning of the *Broadcasting Services Act 1992* (Cth)'.[46] However, a broadcasting service does not include 'a service, such as a teletext service, that provides no more than data or no more than text (with or without associated images); or a service that makes programs available on demand on a point-to-point basis, including a dial-up service'.[47] The communication right includes cable transmissions and encompasses the uploading of material onto an internet server. The technology-neutral approach can apply to an electronic transmission by copper wires, optic fibre cables and microwaves. The right does not apply to the physical distribution of copyright material in a tangible form (such as the distribution of hard copies of books). The expression 'to the public' includes the public within or outside Australia, so it permits Australian copyright holders to control communication directed to overseas audiences.

Exemptions

The *Copyright Act* exempts dealing with copyright material without the permission of or payment to copyright owners where such use is for the purposes of 'research and study, criticism and review, parody or satire, reporting the news, and professional legal advice'. These are referred to as the 'fair dealing' exemptions.[48] Specific provisions which deal with electronic works are now included as well: there is a fair dealing for research and study related to a published literary work in electronic form (except a computer program or an electronic compilation, such as a database), a published dramatic work in electronic form or an adaptation published in

---

44 *Copyright Act 1968* (Cth) s31(1)(a)(iv) and (b)(iii). The new right does not apply to published editions.
45 *Copyright Act 1968* (Cth) s10.
46 *Copyright Act 1968* (Cth) s10, emphasis added.
47 *Broadcasting Services Act 1992* (Cth) s6.
48 See *Copyright Act 1968* (Cth) ss40–42 and *Copyright Act 1994* (NZ) ss42, 43, 176.

electronic form of such a literary or dramatic work. The fair dealing under these circumstances is either 10 per cent of the number of words in the work or adaptation, or if the work or adaptation is divided into chapters, a single chapter.[49] There are several other exemptions.

Libraries and archives

Libraries and archives are permitted to make reproductions of copyright material for library users for the purposes of research and study, and for other libraries for certain purposes. This access must be provided in a way which will not unreasonably prejudice the interests of copyright owners. The *Copyright Act* includes such permission for electronic reproduction and communication of copyright material. However, certain restrictions apply: for example, a library may only request an article or a portion of a work in electronic form from another library if that portion or article is not available 'within a reasonable time at an ordinary commercial price'. This is designed to minimise unreasonable conflict with the emerging markets of copyright owners.[50]

Infringing copies made on machines installed in libraries and archives

Following concern over the possibility of legal action against libraries when photocopiers were first introduced, the *Copyright Act* was amended to remove liability from the library where conspicuous warning notices are in place.[51] More recently this was extended to copies by computers:

> Where:
>
> **(a)** a person makes an infringing copy of, or of part of, a work on a machine (including a computer), being a machine installed by or with the approval of the body administering a library or archives on the premises of the library or archives, or outside those premises for the convenience of persons using the library or archives; and
>
> **(b)** there is affixed to, or in close proximity to, the machine, in a place readily visible to persons using the machine, a notice of the prescribed dimensions and in accordance with the prescribed form;
>
> neither the body administering the library or archives nor the officer in charge of the library or archives shall be taken to have authorized the making of the infringing copy by reason only that the copy was made on that machine.[52]

---

49 *Copyright Act 1968* (Cth) s40.
50 *Copyright Act 1968* (Cth) Div 5.
51 See *University of New South Wales v Moorhouse* (1975) 133 CLR 1.
52 *Copyright Act 1968* (Cth) s39A. The provision also applies to archives.

Educational statutory licences

Part VB of the *Copyright Act* permits educational institutions with a statutory licence to make copies of works subject to the payment of equitable remuneration. The Part applies to the reproduction and communication of works in hardcopy form or in electronic form.

Temporary reproductions

When a web page is accessed, the user's web browser makes a copy of the text and graphics on the website and places both in a temporary directory or cache. Depending on the extent of use of the web browser and the size reserved for such files, the text and graphics may remain in place indefinitely. Early questions arose about unauthorised copies of material subject to copyright. One early opinion was that there was an implied licence.[53] That is, if the holder of the copyright placed material on the internet, normal use of the internet, including the making of such temporary files, must be implied. However, should the user make any other copy, such as cutting and pasting or some other use of the temporary files, such an implication could not be drawn.

The *Copyright Act* provides that temporary or incidental reproductions made in the course of the technical processes of exercising the communication right are exempt, giving statutory effect to the implied licence concept. The Act covers both temporary reproductions made in the course of communication and temporary reproductions of works as part of a technical process of use.[54]

Enforcement measures

The *Copyright Act* helps copyright owners enforce their rights in the digital environment by providing enforcement regimes for circumvention devices and services, rights management information and broadcast decoding devices. The enforcement measures are designed to combat piracy.

The Act includes civil remedies and criminal sanctions against the manufacture, commercial dealing, importation, making available online, advertising, marketing and supply of a circumvention device or service used to circumvent technological protection measures such as program locks.[55] A 'circumvention device' is defined as:

---

53 Alan Davidson, 'Digital agenda amendments to the Copyright Act', (2001) 21–3 *Proctor* 30.
54 *Copyright Act 1968* (Cth) ss43A, 43B respectively.
55 *Copyright Act 1968* (Cth) ss116AK–116AQ.

> ...a device, component or product (including a computer program) that:
>
> **(a)** is promoted, advertised or marketed as having the purpose or use of circumventing the technological protection measure; or
>
> **(b)** has only a limited commercially significant purpose or use, or no such purpose or use, other than the circumvention of the technological protection measure; or
>
> **(c)** is primarily or solely designed or produced to enable or facilitate the circumvention of the technological protection measure.[56]

This definition includes software tools and is intended to exclude general purpose electrical equipment, such as DVD recorders and computers. A 'circumvention service' has a corresponding meaning:[57]

> A 'technological protection measure' means:
>
> **(a)** an access control technological protection measure; or
>
> **(b)** a device, product, technology or component (including a computer program) that:
>
> > **(i)** is used in Australia or a qualifying country by, with the permission of, or on behalf of, the owner or exclusive licensee of the copyright in a work or other subject-matter; and
> >
> > **(ii)** in the normal course of its operation, prevents, inhibits or restricts the doing of an act comprised in the copyright; but does not include such a device, product, technology or component to the extent that it:
> >
> > **(iii)** if the work or other subject-matter is a cinematograph film or computer program (including a computer game) – controls geographic market segmentation by preventing the playback in Australia of a non-infringing copy of the work or other subject-matter acquired outside Australia; or
> >
> > **(iv)** if the work is a computer program that is embodied in a machine or device– restricts the use of goods (other than the work) or services in relation to the machine or device.[58]

Many products now incorporate Rights Management Information (RMI). The *Copyright Act* includes criminal offences and civil remedies regarding the intentional removal and alteration of RMI, or the commercial dealing with copyright material where the RMI has been removed.[59] 'Electronic rights management information' is defined as:

> ... information that is or was attached to, or is or was embodied in, a copy of the work or subject-matter, or [which] appears in connection with a communication, or the making

---

56 *Copyright Act 1968* (Cth) s10.
57 *Copyright Act 1968* (Cth) s10.
58 *Copyright Act 1968* (Cth) s10.
59 *Copyright Act 1968* (Cth) ss116B–116D.

available, of the work or subject-matter, [which] identifies the work or subject-matter, and its author or copyright owner ... identifies or indicates some or all of the terms and conditions on which the work or subject-matter may be used.[60]

This includes digital watermarks.

A person will only be directly liable for copyright infringements involved in a communication where they have determined the content of that communication. This provides an exemption for the carrier or the Internet Service Provider (ISP), unless it can be proven that either had authorised the infringement by a user.[61]

Time-shifting, format-shifting and space-shifting

Time-shifting of television and radio programs for later private use is permitted. The recording of television or radio programs solely for private and domestic use by watching or listening to the material broadcast at a time more convenient does not infringe copyright.[62] The exception does not generally apply to podcasts or webcasts, and does not apply if the recording is later sold, rented or distributed (other than to a member of the person's family or household), or played or shown in public or broadcast. There is no express obligation to destroy the recording at any time, although it may be implied that the exception is not meant to permit permanent copies or repeated use.

The issue came before the Full Federal Court in the case of *National Rugby League Investments Pty Limited v Singtel Optus Pty Ltd*.[63] In 2011 Optus offered a new service called 'TV Now', which gave users the ability to record TV programs and play these back on certain mobile devices. The programs were stored on Optus's cloud storage facility. The National Rugby League (NRL) and Australian Football League (AFL) objected and threatened Optus with certain actions. Both football leagues had sold online rebroadcasting rights to Telstra. Optus initially commenced proceedings under section 202 of the *Copyright Act 1968* (Cth), claiming that the NRL and AFL had made unjustified threats. Optus claimed that the recordings were made and initiated by users who were permitted to time-shift their private recordings. Rares J at first instance agreed with Optus, and the NRL and AFL appealed. The Full Federal Court reversed the decision. The court decided that the recordings were made by Optus or by Optus and the user together, and hence Optus infringed

---

60 *Copyright Act 1968* (Cth) s10.
61 See *Copyright Act 1968* (Cth) ss39B, 116AA–116AJ, 195AW, 195AXI.
62 *Copyright Act 1968* (Cth) s111.
63 [2012] FCAFC 59.

copyright. This will impact many aspects of cloud computing. A user may view programs on a portable television device, but under this decision may not use a service to make a recording and watch the same program later.

Space-shifting means that a person who owns a copy of a sound recording, such as a CD, is allowed to make a copy of that recording, for private and domestic use, to play on another device owned by that person. The device could be a CD player, a computer, a car CD player, or a portable device such as an MP3 player or iPod.[64] The provision does not apply if the initial copy is an infringing copy (such as a pirated CD or an unauthorised digital download). The provision also does not apply if the second copy is later sold, rented or distributed (other than to a member of the person's family or household), or played or shown in public or broadcast. The provision may apply to recorded music from a digital download, but does not apply to podcasts.

Format-shifting involves copying from one format to another for private use. An individual may copy books (including novels, children's books, reference books), newspapers and other periodical publications (such as magazines and journals), photographs, and films on videotape but not DVDs, provided the copy is made from a non-infringing copy owned by the individual. For example, print material maybe scanned for viewing on a computer screen. A photograph may be converted from a print to an electronic image, or conversely an electronic image may be printed. A video may be copied into a digital format. The provision does not apply to sales, rent or distribution other than to a member of the person's family or household.

Piracy and enforcement

Conduct regarded as 'substantial infringement on a commercial scale' attracts special attention; it includes likely infringements as well as proved infringements when infringement takes place online on a commercial scale. Colloquially this is referred to as 'piracy'. There are also offences relating to unauthorised access to encoded broadcasts, such as pay television.[65]

Hyperlinking

Hyperlinks permit a copy of data, images and other material to be downloaded onto the user's computer. Trade mark and copyright issues arise.

---

64 *Copyright Act 1968* (Cth) s109A.
65 See *Copyright Act 1968* (Cth) ss115(5)–(8), 132AC, Part VAA.

Hyperlinks are fundamental to internet use and navigation. With a simple click of a computer mouse a massive amount of information and data is available. Some links are internal: that is, the link will take the user to another web page created by the same designer and author as the initial page. Most links will cause the web browser to retrieve the web page of another host, anywhere in the world, and display the contents. The target site will have a unique URL (Universal Resource Locator).

The contents of a retrieved website may be protected by trade mark or copyright regulation.[66] The question of the status and extent of protection available in relation to the 'sign' (for trade marks) or 'copy' (for copyright) displayed on the user's computer has been the subject of speculation. When viewing a website, the content is not a continuous stream, such as with television. Instead a connection is made with the host, typically for a fraction of a second, during which time the contents are copied to a cache or temporary area. The text, graphics files and any other data are copied to the user's computer. The web browser assembles the copied material in a predetermined meaningful way. Whether or not this amounts to a breach of trade mark right or copyright has been untested. However, it would be reasonable to assume that the host of the data has granted, at the very least, an implied licence for the user to view the content. The host knows, or ought to know, that temporary copies are made as part of the operation of the World Wide Web. The host almost always wants or expects the data to be displayed by web users. It is the host that has placed the material into a public area for access on the World Wide Web.

In *Ticketmaster Corporation v Tickets.com Inc.* the court held that:

> hyperlinking does not itself involve a violation of the Copyright Act ... since no copying is involved ... the customer is automatically transferred to the particular genuine web page of the original author. There is no deception in what is happening. This is analogous to using a library's card index to get reference to particular items, albeit faster and more efficiently.[67]

In Australia the issue was resolved with the inclusion of section 43A(1) of the *Copyright Act*, which provides:

> The copyright in a work, or an adaptation of a work, is not infringed by making a temporary reproduction of the work or adaptation as part of the technical process of making or receiving a communication.

Temporary reproductions made in the course of the technical process of making or receiving electronic communications are excluded from the scope of copyright. However, if any further step is taken to make a copy, such as 'cutting and pasting'

---

66 In relation to trade marks, see Chapter 15.
67 54 USPQ 2d 1344 (CD Cal 2000).

text from the screen, or copying the temporary files to another part of the user's storage, the protection is inapplicable.

Placing a link on a website which directs users to a website which contains infringing material ought not to be considered a breach in itself. Such an action is clearly not a primary breach, and to establish a secondary breach, the fact that the targeted site contained an infringing copy would need to be proved. In the US case of *Intellectual Reserve Inc. v Utah Lighthouse Ministry Inc.*,[68] a critic of the Mormon Church placed some 17 pages of an 160-page 'Church Handbook of Instruction' on his website. The court ordered the material to be removed. In a cunning move, the critic posted on his website an email from a reader stating that the 'Church Handbook of Instructions is back online!' and listing three other websites where the handbook could be located. In a subsequent action the Utah District Court granted an injunction prohibiting the critic from directly posting either the contents of the Handbook or the 'addresses to Web sites that defendants know, or have reason to know, contain the material alleged to infringe plaintiff's copyright'. This judgement is unlikely to be followed by a court. A visitor who accesses the third party web-sites via such links would not be committing a breach in any event.

FURTHER READING

Australian Copyright Council: <www.copyright.org.au>.

Intellectual Property Society of Australia and New Zealand: <www.ipsanz.com.au>.

IP Australia: <www.ipaustralia.gov.au>.

World Intellectual Property Organization (WIPO): <www.wipo.org>.

WIPO (Copyright): <www.wipo.int/copyright/en/>.

---

68 75 F Supp 2d 1290 Utah DC (1999).

15

TRADE MARKS, PATENTS AND CIRCUIT LAYOUTS

The digital revolution has necessitated a re-examination of intellectual property issues by intellectual property holders, users and law makers. The nature of the digital age enables data to be easily copied, published and disseminated. Placing data, images, logos and text on websites, for example, is child's play. This means that trade mark holders have a new frontier to battle. Misuse of their trade mark rights, deliberate or incidental, commercial or personal, arises in relation to cyber-squatting and domain names, hyperlinking (particularly deep linking), framing in web pages and the use of meta-tags.

This chapter addresses issues relating to the impact of electronic commerce on the specific intellectual property rights of trade marks, patents and circuit layouts. It is intended to be only a brief overview of the law in these areas.

The nature of trade marks

A trade mark is 'a sign used, or intended to be used, to distinguish goods or services dealt with or provided in the course of trade by a person from goods or services so dealt with or provided by any other person'.[1] A trade mark is used in the course of trade to show a connection between a particular business and the goods or services it supplies. Trade marks indicate a standard of quality associated with a product or service and protect consumers from confusion and deception. Trade marks are protected under common law and under the *Trade Marks Act 1995* (Cth).[2]

Registrants only have the right to use their registered trade mark for the goods and services for which it is specifically registered. In Australia there are 45 classes in which a trade mark can be registered and there is no limit on the number of classes in which an application can be made, as long as the trade mark is actually used or intended to be used with respect to the goods or services nominated. A 'sign' is defined as 'including the following or any combination: any letter, word, name, signature, numeral, device, brand, heading, label, ticket, aspect of packaging, shape, colour, sound or scent'.[3] The inclusion of any 'aspect of packaging, shape, colour, sound and scent' in 1995 significantly broadened the range of features or signs which can be registered.

The system for registering trade marks effectively entitles a person to 'own' a word, logo, phrase or other distinctive sign and to stop others from using that mark or a deceptively similar mark in relation to the same or similar sorts of goods or services. Provided the trade mark is used continually and renewed, typically every 10 years, it may be retained indefinitely.

---

1 *Trade Marks Act 1995* (Cth) s17.
2 For the New Zealand equivalent, see *Trade Marks Act 2002* (NZ).
3 *Trade Marks Act 1995* (Cth) s6.

Trade mark registration is territorial and each country has its own system of registration. An Australian trade mark registration is effective throughout Australia. Those wishing to protect trade marks (for trade purposes, say) in other countries need to register them in those other countries.

A registered owner of a trade mark has the exclusive rights:

(a) to use the trade mark; and
(b) to authorise other persons to use the trade mark;
in relation to the goods and/or services in respect of which the trade mark is registered.[4]

A registered owner also has 'the right to obtain relief under the Act if the trade mark has been infringed'.[5]

A person may apply for the registration if 'the person claims to be the owner of the trade mark' and 'the person is using or intends to use the trade mark', 'the person has authorised or intends to authorise another person to use the trade mark' or 'the person intends to assign the trade mark to a body corporate that is about to be constituted'.[6]

Business names are not trade marks. The purpose of registering a business name or company name is to identify the owners operating under that name. Registration of a business name or a company name is not, in itself, a defence to an action of infringement of a registered trade mark. Nevertheless, business and company names become valuable identifiers, and they may be protected by provisions of the Australian Consumer Law, the states' and the ACT's Fair Trading Acts and the tort of passing off.

Infringement

Section 120 of the Act details circumstances where a registered trade mark is infringed:

120

(1) A person infringes a registered trade mark if the person uses as a trade mark a sign that is substantially identical with, or deceptively similar to, the trade mark in relation to goods or services in respect of which the trade mark is registered.

(2) A person infringes a registered trade mark if the person uses as a trade mark a sign that is substantially identical with, or deceptively similar to, the trade mark in relation to:

---

4 *Trade Marks Act 1995* (Cth) s20(1).
5 *Trade Marks Act 1995* (Cth) s20(2).
6 *Trade Marks Act 1995* (Cth) s27.

(a) goods of the same description as that of goods (*registered goods*) in respect of which the trade mark is registered; or

(b) services that are closely related to registered goods; or

(c) services of the same description as that of services (*registered services*) in respect of which the trade mark is registered; or

(d) goods that are closely related to registered services.

However, the person is not taken to have infringed the trade mark if the person establishes that using the sign as the person did is not likely to deceive or cause confusion.

(3) A person infringes a registered trade mark if:

(a) the trade mark is well known in Australia; and

(b) the person uses as a trade mark a sign that is substantially identical with, or deceptively similar to, the trade mark in relation to:

(i) goods (*unrelated goods*) that are not of the same description as that of the goods in respect of which the trade mark is registered (*registered goods*) or are not closely related to services in respect of which the trade mark is registered (*registered services*); or

(ii) services (*unrelated services*) that are not of the same description as that of the registered services or are not closely related to registered goods; and

(c) because the trade mark is well known, the sign would be likely to be taken as indicating a connection between the unrelated goods or services and the registered owner of the trade mark; and

(d) for that reason, the interests of the registered owner are likely to be adversely affected.

For the purposes of the Act, goods or services are similar to other goods or services if they are the same, or if they are of the same description as the other goods or services.[7] A trade mark is taken to be deceptively similar to another trade mark if it so nearly resembles that other trade mark that it is likely to deceive or cause confusion.[8]

Sections 120(3) and (4) have extended the infringement action to restrain activities which are likely to adversely affect the interests of the owner of a famous or well-known trade mark by the 'dilution' of its distinctive qualities or of its value to the owner.

---

7 *Trade Marks Act 1995* (Cth) s14.

8 *Trade Marks Act 1995* (Cth) s10. See *Koninklijke Philips Electronics NV v Remington Products Australia Pty Ltd* (2000) 100 FCR 90; *Shell Co. of Australia Ltd v Esso Standard Oil (Aust.) Ltd* (1963) 109 CLR 407; *Berlei Hestia Industries Ltd v Bali Co. Inc.* (1973) 129 CLR 353; *Polaroid Corp. v Sole N Pty Ltd* [1981] 1 NSWLR 491; *Transport Tyre Sales Pty Ltd v Montana Tyres Rims and Tubes Pty Ltd* (1999) 93 FCR 421.

The courts have held that this:

> dilution theory of liability 'does not require proof of a likelihood of confusion'; rather, what is protected is 'the commercial value or "selling power" of a mark by prohibiting uses that dilute the distinctiveness of the mark or tarnish the associations evoked by the mark'.[9]

Hyperlinking

Hyperlinks are fundamental to internet use and navigation.[10] The value of the World Wide Web lies in the process of hyperlinking, which allows users to connect to vast quantities of information, text, graphics and data with a simple mouse click. However, websites can also be designed in a way that may be prejudicial to the trade mark rights and copyright of others.[11]

Trade mark infringement can arise where one website links to another with registered trade marks.[12] The linking process can be regarded as a 'use' of such a mark in contravention of section 120(1) and (2). For example, users who link directly to targeted pages within a particular website bypass the home page. This form of hyperlinking is referred to as deep linking. Whatever the intention, the effect may be to reduce the site's advertising revenue, if that is dependent on 'hits' on the home page. Revenue is typically tied to the number of hits, or depends upon actual use of the advertising links. Also, the use of a deep link may give the impression that there is a connection, affiliation or some relationship between the owners of the two sites. This impression may deceive or cause confusion to a user.

The first such case before the courts was the Scottish case *Shetland Times Ltd v Wills and Zetnews Ltd*,[13] before Lord Justice Hamilton in 1996. The defendant ran the newspaper the *Shetland News* and a corresponding website; the applicant[14] ran the *Shetland Times* and a website. The defendant created hyperlinks using the headlines from the applicant's newspaper. The hyperlinks pointed directly to articles on the applicant's website. Because the links bypassed the applicant's home page, his Lordship considered that: 'there is a clear prospect of loss of potential advertising revenue in the foreseeable future'. The appearance gave some users the impression that the articles were part of the defendant's website.

---

9 *Campomar Sociedad Limitada v Nike International Limited* [2000] HCA 12, paras 42–43, citing *Restatement Third, Unfair Competition*, §25, Comment (a).
10 On hyperlinking generally, see Chapter 14.
11 See Katia Bodard, Bruno de Vuyst and Gunther Meyer, 'Deep linking, framing, inlining and extension of copyrights: Recent cases in common law jurisdictions' (2004) 11(1) *eLaw Journal* 2.
12 Ibid.
13 [1997] 37 IPR 71; [1997] FSR 604.
14 Described in the judgement as 'the pursuers'.

Additionally, his Lordship stated that:

> [t]here was, in the circumstances, no substance, in my view, in the suggestion that the pursuers were gaining an advantage by their newspaper items being made available more readily through the defenders' website.[15]

The court issued an 'interim interdict' requiring the defendants to remove the links. Unfortunately, the judgement was given at a preliminary stage, and the case did not proceed to a full hearing where argument could be made in full. The matter was subsequently settled.

In *Ticketmaster Corporation v Microsoft Corporation*,[16] Microsoft provided a link, on its Seattle Sidewalk entertainment site, to the Ticketmaster home page. Ticketmaster argued that a formal licence agreement would be required before anyone could link to its site. Ticketmaster had been negotiating such a licence with Microsoft, but negotiations had broken down. Instead, Ticketmaster entered into an agreement with CitySearch, a competitor of Microsoft's Sidewalk site. Ticketmaster claimed that Microsoft misused Ticketmaster's name and trade mark, diluting the value of the trade mark and damaging its relationship with sponsors. Microsoft claimed that the use of links is fundamental to the operation of the web and relied on the *US Constitution's* protection of free speech and the fair use doctrine. It further asserted that by placing a website online web hosts impliedly consented to links, including deep links. Ticketmaster claimed that Microsoft was 'feathering its own nest at Ticketmaster's expense ... committing electronic piracy'. This case was settled out of court, but it demonstrates the commercial concerns involved. The concept of property in a link was unknown to the legal and internet community. Many would argue that freedom of access and use was an inherent feature of the World Wide Web, particularly for websites placed in the public domain and intended to be readily accessed by the public.[17]

Implementing a hyperlink in itself should not be regarded as a trade mark infringement. To succeed in an action, an aggrieved party must show deception or confusion. Since these early cases, such problems have been resolved by technology. Web designers can restrict access to 'deep linked' pages so that a user can only access such pages from the home page. The structure and design of the home page can be such as to reveal the correct authorship, minimise confusion, and of course make available the advertising previously bypassed.[18]

In *Zoekallehuizen.nl v NVM*[19] the respondent operated a specialist search engine that searched for houses for sale and placed links to such information on the

---

15 [1997] 37 IPR 71; [1997] FSR 604, para 22.

16 No. 97–3055 DDP (CD Cal 1997).

17 See also *Washington Post Company v Total News Inc.* 97 Civ. 1190 (PKL) (SD NY).

18 See *Bernstein v JC Penny Inc.* 50 USPQ 2d 1063 (CD Cal 1998).

19 District Court (Arrondissementsrechtbank) Arnhem, 2006 (1). Available at <www.ivir.nl/files/database/sources/HofZAH.pdf>.

websites of local real estate agents. The applicants were the Dutch Association of Real Estate Agents and two local real estate agents. The President of the District Court of Arnhem rejected the claim for a restraining order stating that the websites of the real estate agents did not show substantial investment and were therefore not protected.

In *Bixee v Naukri*,[20] the Delhi High Court in India prohibited Bixee.com from deep linking to Naukri.com. The preliminary injunction was issued on a prima facie finding that Naukri suffered significant financial loss due to the diversion of readers away from the advertisements.

In Europe, in response to concerns that information is inadequately protected by the law, Directive 96/9/EC of the European Parliament and of the Council of 11 March 1996 on the legal protection of databases was passed. The preamble provides that the rationale for the directive is that databases 'are not at present sufficiently protected by Member States' and 'such differences in the legal protection of databases offered by the legislation of the Member States have direct negative effects on the functioning of the internal market as regards databases'. This directive concerns the legal protection of databases in any form.

In Australia, if links are used in a manner which causes deception or confusion, and a trade mark is involved, the aggrieved party may seek redress through section 120 of the *Trade Marks Act* (Cth). In addition, section 121(2) provides that it is a prohibited act to apply or use a trade mark in an altered manner or in relation to registered goods in a manner that is likely to injure the reputation of the trade mark.

If no trade mark is involved, remedies may be available under the copyright legislation,[21] the Australian Consumer Law,[22] the corresponding provisions of the state and territory Fair Trading Acts and the tort of passing off.

Framing

Web pages may be displayed in sections called frames. The web designer may create a heading or menu along the top of the page or on the left or right margin. This heading or menu remains static while the body of the web page changes when links, internal or external, are selected. This permits navigation within a website.

However, hypertext mark-up language (HTML) permits any web page to be displayed within any frame, including within the body of the original site. Problems arise where the static heading or menu continues, but the body of the web page displayed is in fact from another source. Users may well think that the outside

---

20 (2005) IA no. 9733/2005, reported as India's first deep linking case.
21 See Chapter 6.
22 In particular, ss18 and 29.

contents are part of the framer's web page. Indeed the displayed URL in the web browser may indicate the framed website, not the site that is actually being displayed in the body of the page. Such unauthorised framing can be misleading and deceptive and can amount to infringement of trade mark.

In *Washington Post Co. v Total News*,[23] the defendant used framing to present the content of external news sites such as CNN, Times Mirror, Dow Jones and Reuters. The advertisements from the external sites were reduced in size or obscured. The plaintiffs claimed:

> Simply put, Defendants are engaged in the Internet equivalent of pirating copyright material from a variety of famous newspapers, magazines or television news programs; packaging those stories to advertisers as part of a competitive publication or program produced by the Defendants and pocketing the advertising revenue generated by the unauthorized use of that material ... just as that conduct would not be tolerated in the world of print and broadcasting it is equally unlawful in the world of cyberspace.[24]

In their written preliminary statement to the court, *The Washington Post* had this to say about linking without permission:

> This action arises out of blatant acts of misappropriation, *trademark dilution and infringement*,wilful copyright violations, and other related tortious acts all committed by Defendants in connection with their operation of a parasitic site known as 'total-news.com' on that portion of the Internet known as the World Wide Web.[25]

The dispute was settled on terms that included permitting Total News to continue linking to the plaintiff's website. However, Total News could not use the framing technique.

In *Futuredontics Inc. v Applied Anagramatics Inc.*,[26] another US case, framing was used with respect to referrals to dental websites. The frame was one of several on the defendant's website. Other frames contained information on its business operations. The plaintiff's cause of action was based on copyright infringement and unfair competition. The court refused to grant an interim injunction. However, the reason for this refusal was that the plaintiff failed to prove that any harm had resulted from the conduct of the defendant. This decision was affirmed on appeal. Nevertheless, the case accepted that framing in appropriate circumstances could be the basis for an infringement claim.

---

23 97 Civ 1190 (SD NY 1997).
24 Ibid.
25 Ibid., Preliminary Statement (emphasis added).
26 CV 97–6991 ABC (Manx), 1998 US Dist. Lexis 2265 (9th Cir 1998).

Meta-tags

Meta-tags are pieces of information in the source code of a website. Meta-tags are not displayed on the website, but can be viewed by selecting the 'source' view.[27] There are many types of meta-tags. The 'keyword meta-tag' was designed to assist search engines. Search engines are based on algorithms designed to produce valuable and meaningful results for the user. One important criterion involves the words and phrases used, their frequency and location. A score is given and search results list the results with the highest scores first. One significant factor in allocating a score is the use of words in the keyword meta-tag. The website designer inserts keywords into the meta-tag to indicate the purpose of the website and to assist search engines. In *Playboy Enterprises Inc. v Hie Holdings Pty Ltd*,[28] the Registrar of the Australian Trade Marks Office described a meta-tag in these terms:

> [M]eta-tags are words embedded in the code for homepages on the Internet ... It is common for traders to embed meta-tags in their homepages so that those who are searching on the Internet find those pages via the meta-tags which are located by the search engine that the searcher is using. Thus a cheese-vendor on the Internet might include the various trade marks or generic names of cheeses as meta-tags on his homepage: these words are found by the search engines used by the public. Thus, these tags are invisible to the person trying to locate the cheese but will bring the merchant's homepage up on the search.[29]

Some website authors have misused the meta-tags. The information may be misleading and deceptive. For example, the designer may insert 'best' or 'top ten' before other keywords describing the product or service. Such a tactic increases that website's search engine score for searches that include the word 'best'. Such a manipulation may be a breach of the Australian Consumer Law.[30]

Trade mark infringement becomes a factor where the website designer uses another's trade mark in the meta-tag. The purpose may be to deflect patronage

---

27 For example, the following code may be inserted in the 'head' section of the website's code for a law firm: <meta name='keywords' content='law legal resource solicitor lawyer securities litigation intellectual property patent trade marks trade secret copyright software computer technology mediation confidential information australia'>.

28 [1999] ATMO 68.

29 In this case the ATMO refused to the application to register 'Playbabe' on the basis of its similarity to the Playboy trade marks.

30 For example, ss18 and 29, dealing with deceptive and misleading conduct.

from a competitor, or merely to interfere with the search engine research for another site. Even though the code is hidden from view, such a misuse can amount to an infringement. The 9th Circuit court in the United States described the use in this manner:

> The meta tags are not visible to the websurfer although some search engines rely on these tags to help websurfers find certain websites. Much like the subject index of a card catalog, the meta tags give the websurfer using a search engine a clearer indication of the content of a website.[31]

In the US case of *Playboy Enterprises Inc. v Calvin Designer Label*,[32] the court granted an injunction to restrain the use of Playboy's trade mark in the defendant's domain names (playboyxxx.com and playmatelive.com) in any 'machine-readable code', and in meta-tags:

> The Court finds that Plaintiff PEI is likely to succeed on the merits in proving inter alia trademark infringement, unfair competition, including a false designation of origin and false representation, in Defendants' use of the domain names ... and the repeated use of the PLAYBOY trademark in machine readable code in Defendants' Internet Web pages, so that the PLAYBOY trademark is accessible to individuals or Internet search engines which attempt to access Plaintiff under Plaintiff's PLAYBOY registered trademark.[33]

In *Playboy Enterprises Inc. v Welles*,[34] the defendant had been a Playboy playmate of the year, and used the playboy trade marks on her website, including in her site's meta-tags. The 9th Circuit court stated that the defendant 'used the terms "Playboy" and "Playmate" as meta tags for her site so that those using search engines on the Web can find her website if they were looking for a Playboy Playmate'. The court held that misuse of the trade mark in a meta-tag can be an infringement.

However, the defendant's use of the words 'playboy' and 'playmate'in this instance were regarded as fair use because the use was 'nominative'. The court applied a 'three-factor test for nominative use' in the following terms:

> First, the product or service in question must be one not readily identifiable without use of the trademark; second, only so much of the mark or marks may be used as is reasonably necessary to identify the product or

31 *Playboy Enterprises Inc. v Welles* 162 F. 3d 1169 (9th Cir 1998).
32 985 F. Supp. 2d 1220 (ND Cal 1997).
33 Ibid., para 6.
34 279 F.3d 796 (9th Cir 2002).

service; and third, the user must do nothing that would, in conjunction with the mark, suggest sponsorship or endorsement by the trademark holder.[35]

The court concluded that the trademarked terms in Welles' metatags were used in an editorial fashion and were 'nominative'.

In *Kailash Center for Personal Development Inc. v Yoga Magik Pty Limited,*[36] Jonn Mumford, also known as Swami AnandakapilaSaraswati, had developed a reputation with regard to yoga and Eastern spirituality. He entered into an agreement to permit his names and reputation to be associated with the promotion of several websites. After a falling out between the parties Mumford demanded the removal of meta-tags which included his names and the cancellation of the registration of certain domain names. Mumford's name was in the source code, as a meta-tag and on 44 web pages of the defendant. Notwithstanding the prior authorisation and agreement, the Federal Court held that such conduct was misleading and deceptive, contravening of section 52 of the *Trade Practices Act 1974* (Cth). Allsop J regarded the use of Mumford's name and pseudonyms as a misappropriation and ordered the discontinuance of such use.

Although not applied in Australian case law to date, section 146 of the *Trade Marks Act 1995* (Cth) is also well suited for a imposing a sanction against the misuse of a trade mark in a meta-tag:

146 Falsely applying a registered trade mark

(1) A person commits an offence if:

(a) the person applies a mark or sign to goods, or in relation to goods or services; and

(b) the goods or services are being, or are to be, dealt with or provided in the course of trade; and

(c) the mark or sign is, or is substantially identical to, the registered trade mark; and

(d) the person applies the mark or sign without:

(i) the permission of the registered owner, or an authorised user, of the trade mark; or

(ii) being required or authorised to do so by this Act, a direction of the Registrar or an order of a court.

---

35 Ibid., at 801. See also *Natural Floor Covering Centre Pty Ltd v Monamy (No. 1)* [2006] FCA 518, *Athens v Randwick City Council* [2005] NSWCA 317, *Insituform Technologies Inc. v National Envirotech Group* (1997) Civil Action No. 97–2064 (ED La 1997) and the German Federal Supreme Court judgement May 2006 I ZR 183/03.

36 [2003] FCA 536.

Patents for software and internet processes

A patent provides protection for inventions. The invention may be a device, a substance, a composition, a living organism, a method or a process.[37] A patent will be granted to protect any novel and non-obvious technological development. Patents evolved from mere legal instruments protecting intellectual property into valuable corporate assets and competitive commercial weapons. Businesses have relied upon the application of copyright law to protect computer programs and other software-related intellectual property. However, businesses are now more likely to choose patent protection as their most powerful offensive and defensive weapon in protecting intellectual capital on the internet. Recent amendments to the *Patents Act 1990* (Cth) have included patent protection for business processes and other technology, changes to thresholds for the grant of a patent, and exempting patent infringement of research and experimental activities.[38]

Developments in the United States

For many years, methods of doing business were not patentable. In the United States, there has been a deluge of applications for cyberpatents as a result of the 1998 decision in *State Street Bank and Trust Co. v Signature Financial Group Inc.*[39] The court held that 'methods of doing business' are patentable, provided the other statutory criteria are met. The decision applies to electronic commerce, internet technology, banking, insurance and finance.

The US *Patent Act* requires that patentable inventions must be new, non-obvious and useful. Potentially patentable internet inventions since the *State Street* decision include communications protocols, data compression schemes, encryption and security procedures, hardware, computer software (including servers, browsers and search engines), user interfaces and methods of conducting business online.

In response to the dramatic increase in applications for cyberpatents, the US *Business Method Patent Improvement Act*[40] was passed by Congress in 2001. The Act was intended to regulate business method patents and the conditions of issue and to make sure that the Patent Office issued these patents only where the method was new and innovative. Business method patent applications are to be

---

37 See, generally, <www.ipaustralia.gov.au/patents/>.
38 Amendments from the *Intellectual Property Laws Amendment (Raising the Bar) 2012* (Cth).
    For the New Zealand equivalent see *Patents Act 1953* (NZ).
39 149 F. 3d 1368; 47 USPQ 2d (Fed Cir 1998) ('*State Street* case').
40 HR 5364.

published for 18 months, allowing the public the opportunity to present information about prior inventions or request a hearing to determine whether an invention was known, used by others, or was in public use. The Act aims to provide a speedy and less costly alternative to litigation. Where the business method invention is merely a computer implementation of an existing practice, a presumption of obviousness applies and the invention is not patentable. The Act also reduces the burden of proof for challenges to the validity of a patent.

Developments in Europe

Article 52(1) of the *European Patent Convention* (EPC) provides that European patents may only be granted for inventions susceptible of industrial application which are new and which involve an inventive step.[41] The term 'invention' is not defined in the EPC, but Article 52(2) expressly excludes methods of doing business, mathematical methods, presentation of information and programs for computers. However, decisions of the Board of Appeal of the European Patent Office have allowed patents for computer programs. This was contingent upon the program being able to produce a 'technical effect' (that is, something beyond normal physical interactions between software and hardware) when the hardware executes the program's instructions.

These decisions bring the European Union's position on the patentability of internet and other software-related inventions closer to that of the United States, Japan and Australia. The UK *Patents Act* has identical provisions to the EPC. However, in *Merrill Lynch's Application*,[42] the UK Court of Appeal held that a computerised trading system for stocks and shares was capable of being patented. This confirmed that inventions whose novelty and non-obviousness reside in unpatentable subject matter such as computer programs are still capable of being patented.

Developments in Australia

In Australia, section 18 of the *Patents Act 1990* (Cth) provides that a patentable invention must be a manner of manufacture, novel, involve an inventive step, be useful and not secretly used before the priority date of a patent claim. The Australian Patent Office (APO) followed the United States in rejecting patent applications for software-related inventions because they were not a 'manner of manufacture' within the meaning of the Act.[43] Software-associated inventions were unpatentable

---

41 The EPC originally came into force in 1973. A revised version has been in operation from December 2007.

42 [1989] RPC 561.

43 See *British Petroleum Co. Ltd's Application* (1968) 38 AOJP 1020.

because they were perceived as schemes for operating a known machine, or abstract ideas, or intellectual processes or algorithms.[44]

IBM Corporation v Commissioner of Patents[45] concerned a 'method and apparatus for generating curves on computer graphics displays'. One objection by the Commissioner of Patents was that it was a mathematical algorithm, not a 'manner of manufacture'. The court considered an algorithm to be 'a procedure for solving a given type of mathematical problem'.[46] In applying the High Court decision of *National Research Development Corp. v Commissioner of Patents*,[47] the Federal Court determined the 'manner of manufacture' test to be whether the invention 'belongs to a useful art as distinct from a fine art ... that its value to the country is in the field of economic endeavour'.[48] It was held that while the mathematics of the invention was not new, its application to computers was commercially useful in the field of computer graphics: IBM was successful.

CCOM Pty Ltd v Jiejing Pty Ltd[49] followed the *IBM* decision. At issue was the validity of a 'petty patent'[50] relating to the input of Chinese characters into a word processing system. The Full Federal Court distinguished 'manner of manufacture' from the novelty and inventive step requirement in section 18 of the *Patents Act*, and confirmed the *NRDC* 'manner of manufacture' test. Further, the court held that the invention was useful in the economic endeavour of using word processing to assemble text in Chinese language characters.[51]

In recognition that patents for business processes and other technology should be protected, the *Patents Act* was amended in 2000 to significantly lower the inventiveness threshold. Patentable inventions must demonstrate an 'innovative step' when compared to the prior base, rather than the current 'inventive step', and must be 'obvious to a skilled person in the relevant field'. An innovative step involves a variance from the prior state of knowledge in a way which is meaningful in terms of how the invention actually works. The amendment is intended

---

44 See Alan Davidson, 'Patents for software and computers processes', (2001) 21 *Proctor* 1, 33.

45 (1991) 22 IPR 417 ('*IBM* case').

46 Ibid. at 419.

47 (1959) 102 CLR 252 ('*NRDC* case').

48 (1991) 22 IPR 417 at 423.

49 (1994) 27 IPR 481.

50 'The innovation patent was introduced in 2001 following an Advisory Council on Intellectual Property (ACIP) review of the petty patent system. The petty patent system was designed to provide a form of protection that was quick and easy to obtain, was relatively inexpensive and provided short term protection especially for inventions that had a short commercial life. Although the majority of users of the petty patent system were small to medium sized enterprises (SMEs), the system had limited success in meeting its intended objectives': Australian Government/IP Australia, 'Review of the innovation patent issues paper', September 2005.

51 (1994) 27 IPR 481 at 514.

to allow cheese and wine making, brewing and certain industrial processes as patentable inventions.[52]

In *Grant v Commissioner of Patents*,[53] Justice Branson of the Federal Court considered the validity of a business method-type patent. The claim related to a method for protecting an asset, comprising the following steps:

(a) establishing a trust [and] having a trustee,

(b) the owner making a gift of a sum of money to the trust,

(c) the trustee making a loan of said sum of money from the trust to the owner, and

(d) the trustee securing the loan by taking a charge for said sum of money over the asset.[54]

Justice Branson stated that 'an invention should only enjoy the protection of a patent if the social cost of the resulting restrictions upon the use of the invention is counterbalanced by resulting social benefits'. Her Honour found that the trust structure proposal lacked the appropriate:

> value to the country ... in the field of economic endeavour ... The perform-
> ance of the invention will not add to the economic wealth of Australia or
> otherwise benefit Australian society as a whole. For this reason, in my view,
> the invention the subject of the Patent is not a proper subject of letters patent
> according to the principles which have been developed for the application
> of s6 of the Statute of Monopolies.[55]

In this case, the patent applicant was required to demonstrate that the performance of the invention 'adds to the economic wealth of Australia or otherwise benefits Australian society as a whole' and 'advances the public interest'. This may be of particular concern for foreign applicants. This approach is in line with the European approach, which requires a 'technically useful' effect.[56]

Australian developments in software-related patents have paralleled those of the United States. Both nations consider software inventions patentable, and have formulated similar tests for determining patentable subject matter. Australia regards software-related internet inventions in much the same way as other software-related inventions. Many Australian internet patents mirror US patents through the medium of the Patent Co-operation Treaty.

---

52 See the Patents Amendment (Innovation Patents) Bill 2000, Explanatory Memorandum.
53 [2005] FCA 1100.
54 Ibid., para 2.
55 Ibid., paras 20–21. The original law was the *Imperial Statute of Monopolies 1623* (UK); its s6 is the equivalent of *Patents Act 1990* (Cth) s18(1A).
56 See also *State Street v Signature* 149 F. 3d 1368 (1998), which raised a test of 'a useful, concrete and tangible result'.

Patents and hardware

Electronic hardware is most suitable for patent application. The criteria are typically novelty and inventiveness. Provided the invention works in an improved manner over previously known devices, the patent application will be granted. Examples include computer systems, computer components and accessories.

Circuit layout rights

A circuit layout is a two-dimensional representation of a three-dimensional integrated circuit (these are also referred to as computer chip designs or semiconductor chips).[57] Circuit layouts are highly complex and the intellectual input required to create them may be of significant value. Integrated circuits are an integral part of modern electronics, and so are used in items such as computers and pacemakers.

Integrated circuits and circuit layouts are both protected under the *Circuit Layouts Act 1989* (Cth).[58] The purpose of the Act is to protect the intellectual property component of circuit layouts and integrated circuits, to give the owner rights, especially the right to make an integrated circuit from the plans. The Act assists in preventing billions of dollars being lost from unauthorised replication and distribution. Like copyright, there is no requirement for registration for the granting of rights to owners.

The Act became operative in 1990. It is part of Australia's obligation under GATT (the General Agreement on Tariffs and Trade). Member nations of the World Trade Organization Agreement are required by the Agreement on Trade-Related Aspects of Intellectual Property Rights (TRIPS) to protect circuit layout designs in accordance with the *Treaty on Intellectual Property in Respect of Integrated Circuits* adopted at Washington DC in 1989.[59]

The Act protects original circuit layouts made by an Australian citizen or an Australian corporation, or first commercially exploited in Australia.[60] A layout originating in a country formally declared in the Circuit Layout Regulations will also be given protection by the Act. The Act excludes layouts where the making involved no creative contribution by the maker, or was commonplace at the time it was made.[61]

The Act grants the owner of an original circuit layout rights to copy the layout, directly or indirectly, in a material form, to make an integrated circuit in accordance with the layout (that is, a three-dimensional version of the layout), and to exploit the layout commercially in Australia.[62] The rights include commercial exploitation, such as import and export, sale, hire and distribution. Where another person

---

57 *Circuit Layouts Act 1989* (Cth) s5.
58 For the New Zealand equivalent see the *Layout Designs Act 1994* (NZ).
59 Available at <www.wipo.int/treaties/en/ip/washington/trtdocs_wo011.html>.
60 See definition of 'eligible layout', *Circuit Layouts Act 1989* (Cth) s5.
61 *Circuit Layouts Act 1989* (Cth) s11.
62 *Circuit Layouts Act 1989* (Cth) s17.

commercially exploits a layout, if the person knew or ought reasonably to have known that they did not have licence to do so, the rights of the owner will have been infringed.[63] The holder's rights are not infringed where a person copies the layout for his or her private use, where copying is for research or teaching purposes, where copying is done in the process of evaluation or analysis of a layout, or where the uses of the layout is for Commonwealth defence or security.[64]

If the layout is not commercially exploited, the protection period runs for 10 years after the end of the calendar year in which the layout was made. If the layout is first commercially exploited within 10 calendar years of its being made, the protection period runs until the end of the 10th year after the end of the calendar year in which the layout was first commercially exploited.[65] This can result in a maximum period of 20 years.

The holder of the rights may take civil action for infringement: possible remedies are an injunction, damages, an account of profits or 'additional damages'.[66] Where there is a flagrant infringement or the infringer has gained some benefit, a court has discretion to award additional damages.[67] Action must be commenced within 6 years of the alleged infringement.

Circuit layout designs made before 1 October 1990 are not protected by the *Circuit Layouts Act*. The owners of such must resort to the law of copyright and designs protection.

Countries that are signatories to the WTO Agreement must protect circuit layouts and give the same level of protection to foreigners who make or exploit circuit layouts in their country as they do to their own citizens.[68] Layouts made or originating outside Australia in listed countries are given the same level and kind of protection in Australia as is given to layouts made in Australia.[69]

---

63 *Circuit Layouts Act 1989* (Cth) s19(3).
64 *Circuit Layouts Act 1989* (Cth) ss21(1), 22, 23 and 25 respectively.
65 *Circuit Layouts Act 1989* (Cth) s5.
66 *Circuit Layouts Act 1989* (Cth) s27(1) and (2).
67 *Circuit Layouts Act 1989* (Cth) s27(4).
68 Required by the TRIPS Agreement, Art. 3.
69 The listed countries are: Antigua and Barbuda, Argentina, Austria, Bahrain, Bangladesh, Barbados, Belgium, Belize, Bolivia, Botswana, Brazil, Brunei Darussalam, Burkino Faso, Burundi, Canada, Central African Republic, Chile, Colombia, Costa Rica, Cote d'Ivoire, Cuba, Cyprus, Czech Republic, Denmark, Djibouti, Dominica, Dominican Republic, Egypt, El Salvador, Finland, France, Gabon, Germany, Ghana, Greece, Guatemala, Guinea, Guinea Bissau, Guyana, Honduras, Hong Kong, Hungary, Iceland, India, Indonesia, Ireland, Israel, Italy, Jamaica, Japan, Kenya, Korea (Republic of), Kuwait, Lesotho, Liechtenstein, Luxembourg, Macau, Malawi, Malaysia, Maldives, Mali, Malta, Mauritania, Mauritius, Mexico, Morocco, Mozambique, Myanmar, Namibia, Netherlands (for the Kingdom in Europe and the Netherlands Antilles), New Zealand, Nicaragua, Nigeria, Norway, Pakistan, Paraguay, Peru, Philippines, Poland, Portugal, Romania, Saint Lucia, Saint Vincent and the Grenadines, Senegal, Sierra Leone, Singapore, Slovak Republic, Slovenia, South Africa, Spain, Sri Lanka, Suriname, Swaziland, Sweden, Switzerland, Tanzania, Thailand, Togo, Trinidad and Tobago, Tunisia, Turkey, Uganda, United Kingdom, United States of America, Uruguay, Venezuela, Zambia and Zimbabwe.

FURTHER READING

Katia Bodard, Bruno de Vuyst and Gunther Meyer, 'Deep linking, framing, inlining and extension of copyrights: Recent cases in common law jurisdictions', (2004)11(1) *eLaw Journal* 2.

IP Australia (Patents): <www.ipaustralia.gov.au/get-the-right-ip/patents/>.

IP Australia (Trade marks): <www.ipaustralia.gov.au/get-the-right-ip/trade-marks/>.

WIPO Treaties: <www.wipo.int/treaties/en/>.

16

DOMAIN NAMES

The internet manages to deal with more than 100 trillion hits per month on websites using 300 million domain names. For most, this process runs smoothly, with ingenious search engines, catalogues, structures, notices, gateways and myriad other methods developed to fashion a semblance of order and structure. This endogenous order reflects and parallels the emergence of principles of custom, trade and usage. With limited government input, and a willingness by altruistic individuals and organisations, a global web, in a literal sense, has materialised, impacting commerce and our social lives, entertaining us and informing us. One such participant in the process, Tim Berners-Lee, comments: 'Happily, the Web is so huge that there's no was any one company can dominate.'[1] It is a product of its users in a time of global communications technology. The development and implementation of domain names is a living testament to the way in which order emerges from a chaos of disconnected and unchoreographed minds and data.

This chapter is in three parts. The first part examines the mapping of cyberspace and the nature of domain names. Parts two and three deal with domain name disputes, with the former dealing with remedies using the courts, and the latter dealing with the compulsory Uniform Dispute Resolution policies and procedures of the domain name administrators.

Part 1 – Mapping cyberspace

Cyberspace is chaos. Almost half the world's population of 7.3 billion trawl unreal space for the gold, tidbits and junk released by a multitude of undisciplined hosts. The domain name system forms a map in cyberspace, indexing and listing material. Domain names have unwittingly become valuable business identifiers and valuable assets.[2]

Information in cyberspace is so vast that it cannot be properly catalogued. It is metamorphic in nature, growing, twisting and changing continuously. A semblance of order emerges in part by using meaningful identifiers for human interaction. The internet recognises no boundaries, yet existing laws are territorially based. The use and misuse of domain names have raised conflicts previously unknown

---

1   Tim Berners-Lee, *Weaving the Web*, Orion Business Books, 1999, p 144. Tim Berners-Lee is regarded by many as the inventor of the internet. In 1989, as a scientist at CERN (Centre Européan pour la Recherche Nucléaire; European Laboratory for Particle Physics), his contribution was to merge the technologies of personal computers, computer networking and hypertext into an information system. This would be modest at first, but it had the potential to be worldwide, subject to network connections. The initial purpose was to communicate among colleagues and access large quantities of data. During 1990 and 1991 Berners-Lee developed the underpinnings of the system which was the foundation of the World Wide Web.
2   See, for example, Berners-Lee, above n1, 138.

in law. Existing legal remedies have proven inadequate, expensive and inconvenient, and often they have been unenforceable. Compulsory arbitration clauses
have been placed into domain name licence agreements in an attempt to address
these deficiencies. But new problems continue to arise, resulting in inconsistent
determinations.

Commercial entities place great importance on their trade name, spending considerable time and money on research and marketing to make a selection which
will reflect the nature of the business and yield the greatest profits. Individuals have
the right to use their own name. Most jurisdictions have enacted rules in relation to
registering business names and company names.

Trade mark legislation usually includes provisions from international conven-
tions and agreements to assist in standardising the global position. A trade mark is
a distinctive sign which identifies certain goods or services as those produced or
provided by a specific person or enterprise.[3]

In the absence of trade mark registration, the laws of passing off and misrepresentation usually protect the use of a name within a specific geographic area.

The nature of domain names

Each internet page has a unique address, referred to as a Uniform Resource Locator
(URL). Protocols exist for various parts of each URL. Each URL can have a number
of parts: for example, the protocol, login, host, port, path, query, file, anchor/frag-
ment. Here is a typical URL for an html file: <http://www.auda.org.au/policies/
index.html>.

Protocol:	http
Domain name:	www.auda.org.au
Directory(ies) (path):	policies
File:	index.html

There is a range of possible protocols, but internet users are most familiar with
Hypertext Transfer Protocol (HTTP). Domain names are centrally organised and
registered and must be unique. There may be a number of directories or none at
all (in the latter case, files are on the root directory). Files are typically in hypertext
markup language (HTML) but may be any type of file. Where there is no file specified, a default file will apply.

The domain name has prescribed protocols which expand and evolve according to demand and usage. That part of the domain name selected by the individual

---

3 For more, see the WIPO home page and <www.wipo.int/trademarks/en/>. See also
   Chapter 15.

may be referred to as the identifier. In the example above it is 'auda'. In addition, the protocols may involve a top level domain name and second, third and fourth level domain names.

Top Level Domain names (TLDs)

ICANN is the international private/public non-profit corporation responsible for managing and coordinating the domain name system (DNS), the Internet Protocol (IP) address space allocation, protocol identifier assignment, generic top level domain names (gTLDs), country code top level domain name (ccTLD) systems and root server system management. Its role is to ensure that each IP address and domain name is unique and that internet users are able to locate all addresses. ICANN maintains each domain name map.[4]

The most well known open gTLDs are .com .org and .net. However, more recently ICANN has permitted the release of new gTLDs to increase competition and facilitate greater choice. There now exists several hundred gTLDs: for example, .fish .holiday and .photography.[5]

The expansion of gTLDs is long overdue. The reasons for limiting domain names to those with the appendage .com, .org and the like are purely historical. There have been no technical or logistical reasons, other than size, not to expand domain names to almost any combination or language. A restrictive approach continues in countries such as Australia, where there are a limited number of choices, such as .com.au, .org.au. The United States, and more recently the United Kingdom, have no such limitation, requiring only .us or .uk respectively. India permits the gTLD.in as well as other categories (such as .com.in and .org.in).

There are some 240 ccTLDs, such as .au for Australia, .nz for New Zealand, .in for India and .uk for the United Kingdom. Initially the United States did not have an assigned ccTLD and users simply omitted the code. However, this disadvantaged US users as many domain names without a ccTLD were registered internationally. The code .us has now been added to the list.

.au

In Australia 2TLDs are restricted. The non-profit company .au Domain Administration Ltd (auDA) has operated the .au domain since gaining government

---

4 These services were originally performed under US government contract by the Internet Assigned Numbers Authority (IANA) and certain other bodies. See <www.icann.org> for more detail.

5 Foreshadowed by web pioneer, Berners-Lee, above n 1, 139.

endorsement. auDA has put in place a system of registrars who compete with each other to provide a variety of packages to registrants.

.com.au	commercial
.net.au	network services
.edu.au	education
.gov.au	government
.id.au	limited individual use
.csiro.au	CSIRO
.org.au	miscellaneous (for registered organisations)
.asn.au	associations and non-profit organisations

.nz

The New Zealand Domain Name Commissioner (DNC) is responsible for the day-to-day oversight of the .nz domain name registration and management system, for the authorisation of registrars, and the transfer of management of specific domain names. Under the .nz Shared Registry System, authorised registrars can register and manage .nz domain names directly with the registry. Registrars are authorised by the DNC. The DNC is an operational office of InternetNZ (the Internet Society of New Zealand Inc.).[6]

NZ domain names cannot be owned by any party and are regarded by the DNC as licensed. A registrant must be an identifiable individual over 18 or a properly constituted organisation.[7]

.us

In the United States there is one top-level domain: .us. There are no secondary categories such as .com.us. Other than reserved words, there is no restriction on the use of a 2TLD. The .us domain is administered by NeuStar and was launched in April 2002.[8]

The .us structure is a locality-based hierarchy modelled on the geography of the United States. Branches in the locality space are overseen by delegated managers known as delegees or locality delegees. This hierarchical design provides structure, name uniqueness and a geographic reference point for all registrants.

6 See <www.internetnz.net.nz>.
7 NZ Domain Name Commission, *Registering, Managing, and Cancelling Domain Names:* <dnc.org.nz/content/registering_managing_cancelling.pdf>.
8 See <www.neustar.us>.

.uk

The .uk TLD was first used during the 1980s. At that time a voluntary group called the Naming Committee managed the registrations. This was replaced in 1996 by Nominet UK, a private non-profit company limited by guarantee. The Policy Advisory Board develops proposals for policies and rules for consideration by the Council of Management. Day-to-day operations are carried out by three departments: operations, technical and legal.[9] Nominet manages more than 11 million domain names, making it the fourth-largest internet registry in the world.

The .co.uk domain is open. Nominet does 'not impose restrictions' on the 'status as applicant for the registration' of the domains .co.uk or .org.uk.[10]

.in

The National Internet Exchange of India[11] (NIXI) is the official .in registry. The INRegistry was created by NIXI.[12] It functions as an autonomous body maintaining the .in ccTLD and ensuring its operational stability, reliability and security. It implements the policies set out by the government of India through its Ministry of Communications and Information Technology and Department of Information Technology. NIXI and the INRegistry assumed responsibility in January 2005. The INRegistry does not carry out registrations itself: it accredits registrars.

ICANN

The Internet Corporation for Assigned Names and Numbers (ICANN) implemented the Uniform Domain Name Dispute Resolution Policy (UDRP) in 1999. This is an efficient and cost-effective method of resolving disputes over domain names.

ICANN maintains relationships with governments, international treaty organisations, businesses, associations and individuals, and is the leading example of an alliance by the many constituents of the internet society.

Whois

Whois is an internet protocol for users to find details of the owner of a domain name, an IP address, or an autonomous system number on the internet. It is the policy of ICANN and other domain name administrators to provide and maintain registers of domain name licensees and all registrars. This facility better informs the

---

9 See <www.nominet.uk>.
10 Nominet UK, *Registering a .uk domain: Rules*, rule 4.4.
11 See <www.nixi.in>.
12 See <www.registry.in>.

public, facilitates legitimate dispute resolution concerns, allows rapid resolution of technical problems and permits enforcement of consumer protection, trade marks and other laws. Where a potential conflict in use of a domain name arises, initial contact can be made using the Whois database. Failure to maintain accurate details is regarded as a breach of the licence agreement, which may result in forfeiture of the domain name.

For TLDs, InterNIC maintains a Whois site at <www.internic.net/whois.html>. The country code Whois database is at <www.iana.org/cctld/cctld-whois.htm>.

Whois databases are maintained by auDA in Australia,[13] NeuStar in the United States,[14] Nominet in the United Kingdom,[15] the Office of the Domain name Commissioner in New Zealand[16] and INRegistry in India.[17]

Nexus requirements

Before registering a domain name some national domain administrators require a nexus with the jurisdiction or affiliation with the type of domain used.

gTLD nexus requirements

The single 'nexus' requirement for the open domains such as .com, .org and .net is that the applicant must complete a declaration that there is no infringement of another's rights in respect of the domain name. However, there is no process to check the legitimacy of such declarations. The .com domain is a gTLD originally intended for commercial businesses around the world. The .net domain is a gTLD for many types of organisations and individuals globally. Historically it was intended for and is still commonly used by Internet Service Providers (ISPs). The .org domain is unrestricted, but was intended to serve the non-commercial community.

Persons who claim that they have been aggrieved have only two courses of action: they may use ICANN's UDRP[18] or take the issue to a court of law and rely on established legal principles.[19]

There have been multiple illegitimate registrations of domain names in the .com TLD. The main reason is the ability to register anyone with any combination of

---

13 See <www.ausregistry.com.au/whois>.
14 See <www.whois.us>.
15 See <www.nic.uk>.
16 See <dnc.org.nz>.
17 See <www.inregistry.in/whois_search>.
18 ICANN, above n 13.
19 There are serious concerns with the directions taken by the UDRP arbitrators. The remedies available by the legal system were not designed to meet the particular exigencies of domain names.

letters and numbers without there being any effective nexus requirement. This has led to considerable speculation in registering domain names. Bad faith registrations are referred to as 'cybersquatting'.[20]

The domain name administrators for each country code determine their own policies with regard to a nexus with the jurisdiction. Some, such as .in require no nexus. Others, such as .au and .us, require a connection with the jurisdiction, such as citizenship, residency, a locally registered company or trade mark.[21]

Part 2 – Domain name disputes

Domain names disputes arise for a number of reasons. The uniqueness of each domain name leads to the potential for conflicts with businesses and individuals with similar names. In addition to these relatively accidental conflicts, some parties deliberately register names to hijack businesses, extort money from or disrupt the operations of established organisations. Such an action is known as cyberpiracy, cybersquatting or typosquatting. The extent of the problem has been reduced in three ways. First, in the 1990s there was a scramble to be the first to register domain names.[22] Those entities which were slow or underestimated the corporate and commercial value of domain names found themselves gazumped. In recent times established entities have dealt with the issue and new entities check for the availability of domain names at the time of incorporation. Second, many domain name administrators dealing with country codes have put in place nexus requirements, such as having in place a registered, company, trade mark or business name. This reduces sharp practice and speculation. Third, ICANN has opened up gTLDs to permit a much greater variety and choice in specialist fields, thus increasing the number of possible combinations.

Cybersquatting

Speculating on the resale value of internet domains names has become a profitable pastime for internet devotees. For example, VacationRentals.com sold for US$35

---

20 See below.
21 For .au see <www.auda.org.au>; for .nz see dnc.org.nz/content/registering_managing_cancelling.pdf>; for .us see <www.neustar.us/the-ustld-nexus-requirements>; for .uk see <www.nominet.org.uk>; for .in see <www.registry.in>.
22 More recently, in 2014, the UK domain name administrator released the open TLD .uk, raising concern that similar hijacking will be duplicated. This is largely minimised by allowing current registrants the first option to take up the new option.

million, Insure.com for US$16 million and Fund.com for £9.9 million.[23] These trans-
actions are part of commerce and offend no legal precepts. ICANN and most
National Domain Administrators accept the principle of first come first served. Also,
many country code domain administrators restrict the selling of domain names;
those who breach such a rule risk forfeiting the domain name.[24] However, a person
who registers a domain name identical to a well-known or famous name for the
purpose of subsequently demanding an exorbitant fee for 'transfer' (that is, sale)
is referred to as a cybersquatter. The value to the cybersquatter lies in the fact that
every domain name is unique. The term 'cybersquatting' originates from 'squatting',
typically used to refer to physically taking over 'tenements' and refusing to move.
In many jurisdictions squatters attain real proprietary interests through continuous
possession and the passage of time.[25]

Some registrations offend particular sensitivities: for example, when the names
of eminent political, scientific and religious persons, and the names of countries,
cities or indigenous peoples are registered by people with no actual association
with those names. The possibility of registering these identifiers as domain names
is a consequence of the highly automated and efficient first-come, first-served system used for domain name registration, a system that does not involve any screen-
ing of domain name applications, but that has allowed tremendous growth in the
use of the internet, and helped preserve universal connectivity.

In 1994 Joshua Quittner, a journalist, contacted the McDonalds Corporation
to ask why they had not registered mcdonalds.com. Quittner then registered the
domain name, in part to generate a story. He created the email address ronald@
mcdonalds.com and asked readers for comments. Some suggested he use the mc-
donalds.com site to promote vegetarianism, others suggested requesting an exorbitant price for its sale. Quittner published an article offering the name back
to McDonalds in exchange for computer equipment for a local school. Under
pressure from the corporate giant, InterNIC first agreed to revoke the registration, then changed its mind, leaving the registration with Quittner. McDonalds
ultimately agreed to donate $3500 to purchase the equipment.[26] This is the
first known instance of a person obtaining an economic benefit from a willing
registrant.[27]

23 For example, see <www.greatdomains.com>, <www.dotcomagency.com> and <www.
   domainbarn.com>.
24 For an example, see the policy by auDA at <www.auda.org.au/policies>.
25 Squatting can lead to the establishment of possessory title or historical title and is well
   established in common law jurisdictions.
26 Joshua Quittner, 'You deserve a break today', *Newsday*, October 1994, A05.
27 See James W Marcovitz, 'ronald@mcdonalds.com – Owning a bitchin' corporate trademark as
   an internet address – infringement?', (1995) 17 *Cardozo L Rev* 85.

Remedies using the court process

Electronic commerce has been embraced by a broad range of bodies and individuals, for commercial and personal reasons. In the majority of situations standard legal principles can resolve the issues. However, new technologies may permit new relationships and interactions at a scale not previously anticipated. Domain name rights and issues are such areas, and inevitably disputes arise concerning interests in given domain names. The law did not have an obvious remedy for this, and courts have considered trade mark rights, misrepresentation, fraud, consumer protection and the tort of passing off. The latter particularly requires consideration, as the courts have moulded and shaped pre-existing elements to suit new factual situations.

Cause of action

Whether innocently registered, as in *Pitman Training Limited v Nominet*,[28] or deliberately registered with the aim of extortion, as in *Panavision International v Toeppen*,[29] claimants maintained some form of proprietary right.[30]

Domain name registration authorities have taken a simplistic first-come first-served approach to the allocation of the domain names. However, the internet encompasses one jurisdiction, and each domain name is a unique international address. There can be no identical domain names in different countries. This problem is exacerbated by the typically short domain names most registrants prefer, but has been relieved in part by the release of the new gTLDs. In 1997 the case of *Pitman Training Limited v Nominet*[31] was the first decision on internet domain names in the United Kingdom and described domain name competition:

> The Internet is a network of computer networks. A computer which is attached to an appropriate network can use appropriate software to communicate and exchange information quickly with any other computer on the network. In order to receive or to make available information on the Internet a domain name is needed. A domain name can be likened to an address. It identifies a particular Internet site. A particular domain name will only be allocated to one company or individual. It represents that company's computer

---

28 [1997] EWHC Ch 367.
29 District Court California Case No. CV-96–03284-DDP (1996) and on appeal (1998) 141 F. 3d 1316 (9th Cir).
30 For early examples see *The Princeton Review Management Corp. v Stanley H Kaplan Educational Centre Ltd* 84 Civ 1604 (MGC) (SD NY 1994); *The Comp Examiner Agency Inc. 25th Century Internet Publishers v Juris Inc.* No. 96–0213-WMB US Dist LEXIS 20259 (CD Cal 1996).
31 [1997] EWHC Ch 367.

site and is the means by which that company's customers can find it on the Internet.[32]

Two UK organisations held the right to use the trading name 'Pitman' and wanted to use the domain name pitman.co.uk. One had been established for 150 years and the other for 12 years. Due to an administrative error, the domain name was wrongly allocated to Pitman Training Ltd. After receiving a complaint from Nominet, the UK naming committee transferred the domain name back. The plaintiff then commenced proceedings on the grounds of passing off, tortious interference with contract and (later) abuse of process. The court also considered a number of additional causes of action which might justify granting relief and concluded that as no wrong had been committed, no relief could be justified. The court held that, given that both parties had a prima facie right to use 'Pitman' in their business name, the first to register had the better interest in the domain name. Other jurisdictions have taken the same approach.[33] The law did not recognise the plaintiff's 150-year-old use as giving it any greater right than the registration by the defendant.

On its own, *Pitman v Nominet* was an open invitation to domain name squatters. An avalanche of cybersquatting occurred. Knowledgeable internet users made a grab for well-known word-based corporate marks, symbols and logos, relying on the initial ignorance of the future power and significance of domain names.

Section 120 *Trade Marks Act 1995* (Cth)

The majority of domain names are ordinary words, personal names, acronyms and abbreviations, and a substantial number include a registered trade mark. In Australia, section 120(1), (3) and (4) of the *Trade Marks Act 1995* (Cth) provides that a person infringes a registered trade mark if a person uses a trade mark as a sign,[34] where 'the trade mark is well known in Australia', 'is substantially identical with, or deceptively similar to' particular goods or services and is 'likely to be taken as indicating a connection' to those goods or services. Also, 'one must take account of the extent to which the trade mark is known within the relevant sector of the public, whether as a result of the promotion of the trade mark or for any other reason'.[35]

---

32 Ibid.
33 See *Prince plc v Prince Sportswear Group* [1998] FSR 21 and *Fry's Electronics v Octave Systems Inc*. No. 95-CV-02525 (N.D. Cal. 1997).
34 The word 'sign' is defined in s6 as including 'the following or any combination of the following, namely, any letter, word, name, signature, numeral, device, brand, heading, label, ticket, aspect of packaging, shape, colour, sound or scent'.
35 See *Bing! Software Pty Ltd v Bing Technologies Pty Ltd (No. 1)* [2008] FCA 1760 for a discussion on the application of s120, particularly with regard to different registered classes. See also *CSR Ltd v Resource Capital Australia Pty Ltd* [2003] FCA 279 and *AMI Australia Holdings Pty Ltd v Bade Medical Institute (Aust) Pty Ltd (No. 2)* [2009] FCA 1437.

Mantra Group Pty Ltd v Tailly Pty Ltd (No. 2)[36] is the first Australian case to use the expression 'typosquatting', describing its purpose as: 'to either capture web traffic if someone mistypes a domain name into an internet browser like Internet Explorer, or to attract search engines that are programmed to pick up such mis-spellings'.[37] In that case the Applicant claimed the Respondent used its trade mark in nine domain names with a misspelling of the word 'Cavill' such as 'Cavile' or 'Cavil'. The court stated that it had previously 'doubted' whether the mere use of the words of the trade mark in a domain name would constitute an infringement under section 120.[38] What is required is conduct in combination with the domain name which would raise it to a level of infringement. Reeves J suggested that the linking of the domain name to a website with advertising material promoting goods or services in relation to which the trade mark is registered might so qualify. It would be more likely to be an infringement if the website used the words of the trade mark to promote the goods or services concerned.[39] The court ordered the transfer of the infringing domain names.[40]

In relation to the use of ordinary English words used as a trade mark and a potentially infringing domain name see *Organic Marketing Australia Pty Limited v Woolworths Limited.*[41]

In *Sydney Markets Limited v Sydney Flower Market Pty Limited,*[42] the Federal Court of Australia stated:

> where two domain names are sufficiently similar so as to make it difficult for a member of the public to know in advance exactly which site they will be taken to (as, for example, where the only difference between them is the presence or absence of '.au'), there is considerable scope for the public to be misled.[43]

In *Campomar Sociedad, Limitada v Nike International Limited*[44] the High Court of Australia (in obiter) stated that subsections 120(3) and (4) have:

> extended the infringement action to restrain activities which are likely ad-versely to affect the interests of the owner of a 'famous' or 'well-known' trade

---

36 [2010] FCA 291.
37 Ibid., para 38.
38 Referring to *CSR Ltd v Resource Capital Australia Pty Ltd* [2003] FCA 279 at para 42, per Hill J.
39 [2010] FCA 291, para 50(g).
40 For a European case on trade mark infringement see *InterfloraInc v Marks & Spencer plc* [2011] EUECJ C-323/09, [2012] ETMR 1, a decision of the Court of Justice of the European Communities.
41 [2011] FCA 279, using the expression 'honest to goodness'.
42 [2002] FCA 124.
43 Ibid., para 149.
44 [2000] HCA 12.

mark by the 'dilution' of its distinctive qualities or of its value to the owner. The 'dilution' theory of liability 'does not require proof of a likelihood of confusion'; rather, what is protected is the commercial value or 'selling power' of a mark by prohibiting uses that dilute the distinctiveness of the mark or tarnish the associations evoked by the mark.[45]

The *Trade Marks Act 2002* (NZ) provides:

89(1) A person infringes a registered trade mark if the person does not have the right to use the registered trade mark and uses in the course of trade a sign– …

(d)   identical with or similar to the registered mark in relation to any goods or services that are not similar to the goods or services in respect of which the trade mark is registered where the mark is well known in New Zealand and the use of the sign takes unfair advantage of, or is detrimental to, the distinctive character or the repute of the mark.

This may be contrasted with the UK, Singapore and Australian approaches.[46] New Zealand and Singapore use the expression 'well-known' trade marks; the UK Act refers to a trade mark which has a 'reputation' in the United Kingdom. The Australian provision deals with marks that are well known 'within the relevant sector of the public'. It may be reasoned that a mark may only be well known in New Zealand where a significant part of the general public know of the trade mark. The words 'take unfair advantage of, or is detrimental to the distinctive character or the repute of the mark' are from the UK Act. As a result, the UK case law may be most relevant. For example, the UK courts have held that detriment may be caused by the erosion of distinctiveness or the tarnishing of distinctiveness.[47] In Singapore the plaintiff must prove that the interests 'of the proprietor are likely to be damaged by such use'.[48] In Australia the plaintiff must prove that the interests 'of the registered owner are likely to be adversely affected'.[49] In New Zealand and the United Kingdom the emphasis is on the harm to the character or reputation of the mark. In Australia and Singapore it is the interests of the owner of the well-known mark that are primary.

The courts' decisions in trade mark domain name cases have been criticised for construing the principles of infringement, passing off and dilution too generously. It is argued that general common law principles have been either modified

---

45 Ibid., paras 42–43.
46 *Trade Marks Act 1994* (UK), *Trade Marks Act 1998* (Singapore) and *Trade Marks Act 1995* (Cth).
47 *Premier Brands v Typhoon* [2000] RPC 477.
48 *Trade Marks Act 1998* (Singapore) s27(3)(d).
49 *Trade Marks Act 1995* (Cth) s120(3)(d).

or negated to suit the requirement of trade mark owners.[50] For example, there is a general rule that a person has the right to use his or her own name for the purpose of honest trading.[51] This natural right has been consistently negated in favour of the reputation of the commercial enterprises.[52] Decided cases imply that the use of a domain name will override an individual's right if a prominent, well-known business has a similar name.[53]

In *Re Krupp*,[54] the defendant had registered the domain name krupp.com for his internet services in 1995, using his first name, 'krupp'. The word 'krupp' is also used as a trade mark by leading German steel company, which wished to obtain the domain name. The defendant's use of his first name was not allowed: the commercial reputation of the steel manufacturer was recognised as overruling his right to use his own name. The court found that the outstanding commercial reputation of the plaintiff meant it had a right not to tolerate other firms bearing the same name weakening the value of its mark. This decision, like many other cases, also highlighted the fact that in most of the cases, courts failed to consider even the basic principles of passing off – such as the effects or likelihood of confusion – and upheld the plaintiff's claim even though parties were in completely different industries (in this case a steel producer and an ISP).

The *Trade Marks Act 1995* (Cth) specifically preserves the rights of a claimant to maintain an action for the tort of passing off against a registered owner of a trade mark. Section 230(1) specifies 'this Act does not affect the law relating to passing off'.[55]

Domain name passing off

The expression 'domain name passing off' is coined here to refer to a new hybrid of the traditional tort of passing off. The tort of passing off is concerned with the protection of business reputation and with the protection of consumers from deceptive or misleading trading activities. The underlying elements are active conduct by a defendant which causes actual damage to the plaintiff's goodwill or business. However,

---

50 Adrian Wolff, 'Pursuing domain name into uncharted waters: Internet domain names that conflict with corporate trade marks', (1997) 34 *San Diego Law Review* 1463, 1468.
51 See *Marengo v Darly Sketch & Sunday Graphics* Ltd (1948) RPC 242.
52 Anri Engel, 'International domain name disputes: Rules and practice of the UDRP', (2003) 25 *European Intellectual Property Review* 351, 354.
53 See Andrea F Rush, 'Internet domain protection: A Canadian perspective', (1997) 11 *Internet Protocol Journal* 1, 11.
54 [1999] *EIPR* N24.
55 S 230(1). Note s230(2), which provides a defence in limited circumstances. For an application see *CI JI Family Pty Limited v National Australian Nappies (NAN) Pty Limited* [2014] FCA 79, where the Federal Court states, at para 40: 'Possession of a registered trade mark is, accordingly, no defence to an action for passing off where the elements of that tort are present.'

in an attempt to provide a remedy for domain name disputes, the courts have exercised great flexibility to reshape the passing off concept so as to yield a remedy.

Passing off involves appropriating a reputation that belongs to another and thus the misrepresentation of goods, services or goodwill, typically in a business situation. In 1896 Lord Halsbury, in *Reddaway v Banham*, stated, 'nobody has any right to represent his goods as the goods of somebody else'.[56] In *Reckitt & Colman Products Ltd v Borden Inc. (No. 3)*,[57] Lord Oliver of Aylmerton said, 'The law of passing off can be summarised in one short general proposition – no man may pass off his goods as those of another.'[58]

The leading case on passing off has been the House of Lords decision of *Erven-Warnink v Townsend & Sons*,[59] where Lord Diplock defined the necessary elements:

> A misrepresentation [is],
> – made by a trader in the course of trade,
> – to prospective customers of his or customers or ultimate consumers of goods or services supplied by him,
> – which is calculated to injure the business or goodwill of another trader (in the sense that this is a reasonably foreseeable consequence) and
> – which causes actual damage to a business or goodwill of the trader by whom the action is brought or (in a *quia timet* action) will probably do so.[60]

In the High Court of Australia, Isaacs J said, in *Orange Crush (Australia) Ltd v Gartrell*:

> the right protected by the tort of passing off is not a property in the mark, name or get-up, but in the business or goodwill likely to be injured by the misrepresentation conveyed by the defendant's use of the mark, name or get-up with which goods or services of another are associated in the minds of a particular class of the public. The plaintiff's property in the goodwill is in its nature transitory and exists only so long as the name is distinctive of the plaintiff's services in the eyes of the class of the public.[61]

This judgement was written in 1928, long before the internet and domain name rights were even contemplated.

---

56 [1896] AC 199, 204.
57 [1990] 1 WLR 491.
58 Ibid.
59 [1979] AC 731 ('Advocaat case'). See also *Reckitt & Colman Products Ltd v Borden Inc. (No. 3)* [1990] 1 WLR 491 and *Hodgkinson & Corby Ltd v Wards Mobility Services Ltd* [1994] 1 WLR 1564.
60 [1979] AC 731 at 742.
61 (1928) 41 CLR 282, 292.

Oggi Advertising Ltd v McKenzie

In 1998 the High Court of New Zealand, in *Oggi Advertising Ltd v McKenzie*,[62] used passing off as the underlying cause of action. McKenzie registered oggi.co.nz.

Baragwanath J stated that as a matter of law the plaintiff, in seeking the injunction to restrain the use of the domain name by the defendant, needed to establish the five elements of passing off listed by Lord Diplock. His Honour held that first, McKenzie had 'floated into Cyberspace' a misrepresentation that McKenzie was associated with Oggi Advertising Ltd. Second, the defendant projected a 'clear business implication'. Third, New Zealand users of the web were prospective customers. Fourth, the defendant's actions diverted business from Oggi Advertising Ltd, damaging its goodwill. Fifth, the defendant's conduct 'would probably cause actual damage' to Oggi Advertising Ltd. McKenzie was ordered to assign the domain name to Oggi and remove any link whereby users could access his site using the name Oggi.

This may have provided a remedy on the facts of this case, but upon any analysis it could prove to severely limit the possible remedies for other domain name disputes. His Honour made no attempt to extend passing off concepts any further. A significant proportion of cybersquatters may not intend to trade off the goodwill of the name of the target. They may not intend to trade, or to promote their activities on a website, or to set up a web page after registration. Should Baragwanath J's approach in *Oggi's* case be strictly applied, few plaintiffs would have a remedy.

Should a cybersquatter simply register a 'well-known' name and take no other steps, none of the five passing off elements would be met.

Marks & Spencer v One in a Million

In *Marks & Spencer v One in a Million*,[63] the English High Court was faced with a situation similar to that of the *Oggi* case, and pioneered the extension of the tort of passing off in a manner not previously contemplated. This is an example of the courts finding and moulding a remedy to suit new circumstances. The defendant had made no attempt to use the domain name. It had not placed any material online to be accessed via the domain name. The English High Court refused to allow the absence of a precedent to foil the plaintiff's 'right' to a remedy. The defendant registered several domain names in the hope of on-selling them to interested

---

62 (1999) 44 IPR 661; 6 NZBLA 102, 567, High Court of New Zealand, ('*Oggi's* case'). Baragwanath J.

63 *Marks & Spencer plc, Ladbrokes plc, J Sainsbury plc, Virgin Enterprises Ltd, British Telecommunications plc, Telecom Securicor Radio Ltd v One in a Million* [1997] EWHC Patents 357; and on appeal [1999] 1 WLR 903; [1998] EWCA Civ 1272 ('*Marks & Spencer* case'). See also *Hoath v Connect Internet Services* [2006] NSWSC 158, *Australian Stock Exchange Ltd v ASX Investor Services Pty Ltd* (Unreported, Supreme Court of Queensland, Burchett J, 1999) and *connect.com.au Pty Ltd v Go Connect Australia Pty Ltd* [2000] FCA 1148.

parties. One such domain name was marksandspencer.com, Marks & Spencer being a well-known chain of department stores. A cynical observer may remark that English judges would not permit such an established name as Marks & Spencer to be usurped. The defendant did not use the domain name in any form of trade; nor did it set up a website. It had merely registered the domain name. A strict application of the first-come first-served rule effectively blocked Marks & Spencer from acquiring registration of the name. Some of the other names registered by the defendant included: britishtelecom.co.uk, macdonalds.co.uk, burgerking.co.uk, marksandspencer.co.uk, motorola.co.uk, sundaytimes.co.uk and thetimes.co.uk.

Sumpton DJ,[64] at first instance, considered and discussed Lord Diplock's five passing off elements. To provide a remedy, his Honour expanded the meaning of passing off and its application to a level not previously contemplated. In particular, his Honour applied the principles of a *quia timet* injunction to restrain the '*threat* of passing off'. None of the five passing off elements was met. The judgement contained the broadest proposition for challenging a domain name under the tort of passing off.

His Honour described the 'essence of the tort of passing off' as a misrepresentation to the public, whether or not intentional, liable to lead them to believe that the goods and services offered are those of the plaintiff. He added that the tort is also committed 'by those who put or authorise someone to put an "instrument of deception" into the hands of others'.[65] However, His Honour added that the mere creation of this 'instrument of deception', without some further act, is not passing off: 'There is no such tort as going equipped for passing off.'[66] The mere registration of 'a deceptive Internet domain name is not passing off',[67] but a *quia timet* injunction may be ordered to restrain the threat of passing off rather than the actual tort: '[E]ven a final injunction does not require proof that damage will certainly occur. It is enough that what is going on is calculated to infringe the Plaintiff's rights in future.'[68]

Quia timet injunctions are distinguished from others in that they may be granted against apprehended wrongs. In *Fletcher v Bealey*,[69] Pearson J stated there are 'at least two necessary ingredients' for equity courts to grant a *quia timet* injunction:

> There must, if no actual damage is proved, be proof of imminent danger,
> and there must also be proof that the apprehended damage will, if it comes,

---

64 The court comprised Jonathan Sumpton QC sitting as a Deputy Judge of the High Court.
65 At para 16, his Honour, citing *Singer v Loog* (1880) 18 Ch D 395, 412, cited with approval by Lord Macnaughten in *Camel Hair Belting* [1896] AC 199, 215–16.
66 *Marks & Spencer plc v One in a Million* [1997] EWHC Patents 357, para 19.
67 Ibid.
68 Ibid.
69 (1885) 28 Ch D 688.

be very substantial. I should almost say it must be proved that it will be irreparable, because, if the danger is not proved to be so imminent that no one can doubt that, if the remedy is delayed, the damage will be suffered, I think it must be shown that, if the damage does occur at any time, it will come in such a way and under such circumstances that it will be impossible for the plaintiff to protect himself against it if relief is denied to him in a *quia timet* action.[70]

With respect, it is questionable whether the application of these principles should lead to the granting of a *quia timet* injunction. Actual damage was not imminent. The registrant may never have used the domain name registration at all and the evidence indicated that there was no intention to activate any website. His Honour reasoned that there was 'only one possible reason' to register the marksandspencer domain address: 'to pass himself off as part of that group or his products off as theirs'.[71] His Honour then contradicted this statement by acknowledging counsel's submission of two additional uses not involving passing off: the resale of the domain name to Marks & Spencer, and blocking the use of the name by Marks & Spencer in order to induce them to pay. Neither of these activities constitutes passing off. His Honour regarded the domain names as worthless to the defendant except as a negotiating tactic to extort payment from the plaintiff. He expressed concern that there is a danger of deception simply through registration, but determined that no relief is available for passing off which has not yet occurred:

> Someone seeking or coming upon a website called *marksandspencer.co.uk* would naturally assume that it was that of the Plaintiffs ... Any person who deliberately registers a domain name on account of its similarity to the name, brand name or trade mark of an unconnected commercial organisation must expect to find himself on the receiving end of an injunction to restrain the threat of passing off, and the injunction will be in terms which will make the name commercially useless to the dealer.[72]

His Honour ordered a *quia timet* injunction against the defendant. Note that the arguments of Sumpton DJ are directed at famous and well-known identifiers.

Not surprisingly, One in Million appealed this new interpretation of the threat of passing off. The Court of Appeal dismissed the appeal, stating that merely registering the domain name has the potential to amount to passing off:

> [Counsel] submitted that mere registration did not amount to passing-off. Further, Marks & Spencer Plc had not established any damage or likelihood

---

70 Ibid., 698.
71 *Marks & Spencer plc v One in a Million* [1997] EWHC Patents 357, para 20.
72 Ibid., paras 20 and 21.

of damage. I cannot accept those submissions. The placing on a register of a distinctive name such as marksandspencer makes a representation to persons who consult the register that the registrant is connected or associated with the name registered and thus the owner of the goodwill in the name.[73]

The Court of Appeal regarded the mere registration of the domain name as an erosion of the exclusive goodwill in the name which damaged or was likely to damage Marks & Spencer.

In an attempt to fashion a remedy the court drew a parallel with the cases to grant injunctive relief where a defendant is equipped with or is intending to equip another with an instrument of fraud. As Sumpton DJ had done, the Court of Appeal limited its reasoning to famous and well-known domain names (which would 'inherently lead to passing-off'). The factors to consider included the similarity of the identifier to the plaintiff's name, the intention of the defendant, and the type of trade. If the intention of the defendant was to appropriate the goodwill, a clear case of passing off would be made out 'even if there is a possibility that such an appropriation would not take place':[74]

> If, taking all the circumstances into account the court should conclude that the name was produced to enable passing-off, is adapted to be used for passing-off and, if used, is likely to be fraudulently used, an injunction will be appropriate. It follows that a court will intervene by way of injunction in passing-off cases in three types of case. First, where there is passing-off established or it is threatened. Second, where the defendant is a joint tortfeasor with another in passing-off either actual or threatened. Third, where the defendant has equipped himself with or intends to equip another with an instrument of fraud. This third type is probably mere *quia timet* action.[75]

The court proceeded on the basis that Marks & Spencer denotes Marks & Spencer plc and nobody else. A search on the 'whois' database reveals the defendant as the registrant. This, the court considered, would lead a substantial number of persons to conclude that the defendant must be connected or associated with Marks & Spencer plc, and that 'amounts to a false representation which constitutes passing-off'.[76] The court reasoned that the defendant's purpose was to threaten use and disposal, sometimes explicitly and on other occasions implicitly.

---

73 Lord Justice Stuart-Smith, Lord Justice Swinton Thomas and Lord Justice Aldous.
74 [1998] EWCA Civ 1272.
75 Ibid.
76 Ibid.

Developments

In *CI JI Family Pty Limited v National Australian Nappies (NAN) Pty Limited*,[77] the Australian Federal Court accepted the conduct of the respondent in *inter alia* registering a domain named amounted to passing off, stating:

> ... the Applicants had made out the elements of the tort of passing off. Using the list of elements identified by Diplock LJ in *Erven Warnink*, supra, it would have been concluded that:
>
> (1) the manner in which the Respondents targeted potential customers in their 'proactive marketing process' constituted a representation that the business was aligned with that of the Applicants and hence constituted a misrepresentation;
>
> (2) the misrepresentation was made in the course of trade;
>
> (3) the misrepresentation was made to prospective customers of the Applicants;
>
> (4) a reasonably foreseeable consequence of the misrepresentation was injury to the business of the Applicants; and
>
> (5) the misrepresentation would probably cause damage to the business of the Applicants.[78]

Architects (Australia) Pty Ltd (trading as Architects Australia) v Witty Consultants Pty Ltd[79] applied the *Marks & Spencer* case. The defendant registered architects-australia.com.au, but unlike the Marks & Spencer case, the defendants argued that the words 'Architects Australia' are general dictionary terms combining a profession and location without any necessary reference to the plaintiff. Chesterman J of the Supreme Court of Queensland considered the issue of domain name passing off. His Honour stated:

> The plaintiff must establish:
>
> – That it holds goodwill or reputation in a specific trade or business;
>
> – That the defendant has misrepresented, intentionally or unintentionally, that a connection exists between the defendant or the defendant's goods, services or business, and the plaintiff or the plaintiff's business; and
>
> – That the plaintiff has suffered, or is under threat of, damage either by diversion of custom, diminished reputation or some other like form of damage.[80]

---

77 [2014] FCA 79, para 68.
78 For the facts and a discussion of consumer protection provisions, see below.
79 [2002] QSC 139.
80 Ibid., para 13.

His Honour regarded the essence of an action for passing off to be the protection of goodwill 'as embodied in the warmth of public sentiment towards its product, service, name or other feature'.[81] The words 'Architects Australia' were held to be 'sufficiently fancy' to be distinctive of the plaintiff's business to amount to an instrument of fraud, and the court ordered deregistration. The placement of a disclaimer on the defendant's website was ineffective because in the view of the court it referred only to the plaintiff's company name, not to its trading name.

In *Yahoo! Inc. v Akash Arora*,[82] the defendants registered yahooindia.com. The plaintiff was the owner of the well-established internet site Yahoo, as well as the trade mark and the domain name yahoo.com. The Yahoo India site had also copied Yahoo's format, contents, layout, colour scheme and source code. Based on this usage, the Delhi High Court found that the defendant had 'appropriated' the identifier 'Yahoo', and granted an injunction based on the tort of passing off and trade mark infringement restraining the defendant from dealing in the identifier.[83]

A single judge of the Bombay High Court took the domain name passing off developments a step further. In *Rediff Communication Ltd v Cyberbooth*,[84] the court stated that a 'domain name is more than an Internet Address and is entitled to equal protection as trade mark'. This was an example of typosquatting. The plaintiff was the owner of the well-known portal rediff.com. The defendant had registered radiff.com. The court held that there was a clear 'intention to deceive' and that the only purpose of the registration was to trade on the goodwill and reputation of the plaintiff.

In *Sports Warehouse, Inc. v Fry Consulting Pty Ltd*,[85] the Federal Court refused to accept a trade mark application of a US-based company which had used the trade mark 'TENNIS WAREHOUSE' in its .com domain name for more than a decade.[86] The respondent, who had lodged an objection to the application, was an Australian company who had used the same words in its .com.au domain name for more than a decade. Most of the applicant's customers were in the US, but

---

81 Ibid., para 14.
82 (1999) PTC (19) 210 (Delhi).
83 See *Titan Industries Ltd v Prashanth Koorapati & Ors* (Application 787 of 1998 in action 179), Delhi High Court, finding a *prima facie* case of passing off where the trade mark application was pending.
84 AIR (2000) Bom 27.
85 [2010] FCA 664.
86 The Applicant was a Californian company which had made online retail sales from its website <www.tenniswarehouse.com> since 1995. The company also operated <www.runningwarehouse.com>, <www.racquetballwarehouse.com>, <www.skatewarehouse.com>, <www.inlinewarehouse.com> and <www.tacklewarehouse.com>.

sales in Australia had increased over several years. Kenny J of the Federal Court considered that, consistent with Australian authority, 'a domain name *may* constitute use of a trade mark'.[87] His Honour considered that the use of a trade mark within a domain name is evidence that a domain name might be used as a trade mark,[88] stating:

> not all domain names will be used as a sign to distinguish the goods or services of one trader in the course of trade from the goods or services of another trader ... whether or not a domain name is used as a trade mark will depend on the context in which the domain name is used. In this case, the domain name is more than an address for a website, the domain name is also a sign for the applicant's online retaining service available at the website. In the context of online services, the public is likely to understand a domain name consisting of the trade mark (or something very like it) as a sign for the online services identified by the trade mark as available at the webpage to which it carries the internet user.[89]

His Honour noted that the use of the domain name <www.tennis-warehouse.com> constituted use of the mark TENNIS WAREHOUSE as a trade mark. The use of 'www' or '.com' are 'merely indicia of a domain name' and the use of the hyphen between words is a 'well-known way in which domain name registrants overcome the need to exclude spaces from the name'.[90] Kenny J concluded that the applicant's trade mark had low distinctiveness and that the applicant's evidence as to its use of the trade mark was insufficient to distinguish the applicant's designated services from the services of other traders, such as the respondent.[91]

Australian Consumer Law

A statutory form of relief, similar to the tort of passing off, is contained in the Australian Consumer Law:[92]

---

87 [2010] FCA 664, paras 146–147, emphasis added.
88 His Honour referred to *CSR Limited v Resource Capital Australia Pty Limited* [2003] FCA 279, para 42 and *Ellerman Investments Ltd v C-Vanci* (2006) 69 IPR 215.
89 [2010] FCA 664, para 153.
90 Ibid., para 155.
91 The applicant had failed to make out its case as required by s 45(5)(c) *Trade Marks Act 1995* (Cth), so that in the circumstances 'TENNIS WAREHOUSE' is not capable of distinguishing the designated services of the applicant from the services of other persons and accordingly should not be registered.
92 Contained in *Competition and Consumer Act 2010* (Cth) Schedule 2.

> 18(1) A person must not, in trade or commerce, engage in conduct that is misleading or deceptive or is likely to mislead or deceive.
>
> 29 False or misleading representations about goods or services
>
> **(1)** A person must not, in trade or commerce, in connection with the supply or possible supply of goods or services or in connection with the promotion by any means of the supply or use of goods or services: …
>
> **(g)** make a false or misleading representation that goods or services have sponsorship, approval, performance characteristics, accessories, uses or benefits; or
>
> **(h)** make a false or misleading representation that the person making the representation has a sponsorship, approval or affiliation.[93]

Section 18 applies without intent and gives rise to civil action. Section 29 requires a form of intent. Civil action may be based on the section. In addition, a breach of section 29(g) and (h) conduct is an offence.[94]

The registration of a trade mark does not preclude an action pursuant to section 18. In *CI JI Family Pty Limited v National Australian Nappies (NAN) Pty Limited*,[95] two business partners, in 1996, had registered the business name 'Nappy Land'. After a disagreement the partnership was dissolved. For more than a decade both parties continued to use the name. One used it in New South Wales. The other used the name nationally, registered it as a trade mark, and registered the domain name <www.nappyland.com.au>. On the facts the court granted an injunction against the second party, concluding that the applicant had proved its case under section 18 of the Australian Consumer Law and the tort of passing off. Citing *CSR Ltd v Resource Capital Australia Pty Ltd*,[96] the court commented that the registration of a domain name may constitute misleading or deceptive conduct.

In *Kailash Center for Personal Development Inc. v Yoga Magik Pty Limited*,[97] the Federal Court of Australia followed the *Marks & Spencer* case. Jonn Mumford, also known as Swami Anandakapila Saraswati, had developed a reputation with regard to yoga and Eastern spirituality. He was approached to lend his name and reputation to the promotion of several websites. After a falling out between the parties Mumford demanded the removal of meta-tags for websites which included his names and the cancellation of the registration of the domain names omkarakriya.com and jonnmumford.com. Despite the prior authorisation and agreement, the Federal Court held that that there had been misleading and deceptive conduct within the meaning of section 52 of the *Trade Practices Act 1974* (Cth) (the predecessor of section 18 of

---

93 Formerly *Trade Practices Act 1974* (Cth) ss52 and 53, respectively.
94 See *Trade Practices Act 1974* (Cth) s75AZC.
95 [2014] FCA 79.
96 [2003] FCA 279, see below.
97 [2003] FCA 536.

the Australian Consumer Law) and ordered deregistration of the domain names. The court regarded the use of Mumford's name and pseudonyms as a misappropriation.

In *CSR Limited v Resource Capital Australia Pty Limited*,[98] Hill J, in the Federal Court of Australia, stated that anyone seeing the domain name would assume that CSR was the real owner of the domain name. CSR is a well-known Australia icon. It produces 4 per cent of the raw sugar traded on the world market and 40 per cent of Australia's total raw sugar. 'CSR' and 'CSR Sugar' are registered trade marks. The defendant registered the domain names csrsugar.com and csrsugar.com.au and wrote to CSR offering to sell the domain names. The defendant had previously written to another sugar company offering to sell domain names for $5000 to $10 000, for 'introductory purposes'.[99] Referring to the *Marks & Spencer* case, the court stated:

> a cyber squatter who registers a name intending to sell that name to the owner of a trade mark or threaten a sale to a competitor if the owner does not come up with the money may have registered the name as an instrument of fraud, and thereby be guilty of the tort of passing off as was held by the Court of Appeal in England.[100]

His Honour held that 'the act of obtaining registration' of both domain names amounted to misleading and deceptive conduct pursuant to section 52 of the *Trade Practices Act 1974* (Cth), and constituted a representation that CSR and the defendant were affiliated. Hill J ordered that the domain names be transferred to CSR and restrained both the defendant and the director from registering or using any other domain name where 'CSR' or 'CSR Sugar', or any other word or mark that is substantially identical or misleadingly, deceptively or confusingly similar, appears. His Honour ordered that a copy of the judgement be forwarded to the Australian domain name registration authority.[101]

Australian Competition and Consumer Commission v Chen[102] demonstrates international enforceability with domain name disputes. The defendant was a resident of the United States and had registered, among other domain names, sydneyopera. org. Chen falsely represented that the site was affiliated with the Sydney Opera House. Persons used their credit cards, believing they were purchasing tickets for events at the Sydney Opera House. The plaintiff did not raise passing off but relied on the consumer protection provisions of the *Trade Practices Act 1974* (Cth). Chen's

---

98 [2003] FCA 279.

99 A separate dispute against the defendant (RCA) dealing with www.tullochwines.com had been resolved before the Administrative Panel of WIPO Arbitration and Mediation Centre at the complaint of JY Tulloch Pty Ltd. The panel found that RCA acted in bad faith and that there was 'no clearer case of cybersquatting'.

100 [2003] FCA 279, para 42.

101 See also *Sheather v Staples Waste Removals Pty Limited (No. 2)* [2014] FCA 84.

102 [2003] FCA 897.

conduct was held to be misleading or deceptive or likely to mislead or deceive (in contravention of section 52) and to include misleading representations (in contravention of subsections 53(c) and (d), now section 29(g) and (h) of the *Australian Consumer Law*). His Honour expressed concern that 'cross-border fraud and misleading conduct, particularly through the Internet, is a growing problem for the international community'. Consumer protection and law enforcement agencies have established mechanisms for international cooperation to protect consumers. The Australian Competition and Consumer Commission (ACCC) informed the court that it would bring the orders to the attention of the US Federal Trade Commission and request its assistance. The extra-territorial enforcement of federal orders is ordinarily a matter for the domestic law of the country in which the orders are sought to be enforced. At common law, four conditions must be satisfied if a foreign judgement is to be recognised by an Australian court: first, the foreign court must have exercised a jurisdiction which Australian courts will recognise; second, the foreign judgement must be final and conclusive; third, there must be an identity of parties; and fourth, if based on a judgment *in personam,* the judgement must be for a fixed debt.

In *Hoath v Connect Internet Services*,[103] White J approved the contention that the right to sue for passing off was not dependent upon any title to a domain name, but on whether the plaintiff had developed goodwill or a reputation such that the defendant's use of the domain name, without the plaintiff's consent, misrepresented to the public that the defendant's business was the plaintiff's business, or that there was a trade connection between them.[104]

In *Satyam Infoway Ltd v Siffynet Solutions Pvt Ltd*,[105] the Supreme Court of India held that domain names are business identifiers and should be protected by the law of passing off as well as by trade mark legislation.

Fraud

Several domain name cases have raised fraud as grounds for relief. In *Marks & Spencer plc v One in a Million*,[106] the English Court of Appeal held that the domain names registered by the defendant were instruments of fraud. The value of the domain names, the court said, 'lay in the threat that they would be used in a fraudulent way':

> The registrations were made with the purpose of appropriating the [plaintiffs'] property, their goodwill, and with an intention of threatening dishonest use

---

103 [2006] NSWSC 158.
104 See *Fletcher Challenge Ltd v Fletcher Challenge Pty Ltd* [1981] 1 NSWLR 196 at 204, and *Nicholas v Borg* (1986) 7 IPR 1.
105 (2004) (28) PTC 566 (SC).
106 [1999] 1 WLR 903; [1998] EWCA Civ 1272.

by them or another. The registrations were instruments of fraud and injunctive relief was appropriate just as much as it was in those cases where persons registered company names for a similar purpose.

The classic statement of fraud, from the common law world, comes from *Derry v Peek*:[107] fraud exists 'when it is shown that a false representation has been made (1) knowingly, or (2) without belief in its truth, or (3) recklessly, careless whether it be true or not'.[108] Fraud includes equitable fraud. In equity, the term 'fraud' also embraces conduct which falls below the standard demanded in equity. There is no exhaustive definition of equitable fraud, but undue influence and unconscionability are applicable considerations.

In *Powell v Birmingham Vinegar Brewing Co. Ltd*,[109] Lord Halsbury LC said:

> A person who puts forward this 'Yorkshire Relish,' made as it is by the present defendants, is representing it as being a particular manufacture. It may be true that the customer does not know or care who the manufacturer is, but it is a particular manufacture that he desires. He wants Yorkshire Relish to which he has been accustomed, and which it is not denied has been made exclusively by the plaintiff for a great number of years. This thing which is put into the hands of the intended customer is not Yorkshire Relish in that sense. It is not the original manufacture. It is not made by the person who invented it. Under these circumstances it is a *fraud* upon the person who purchases to give him the one thing in place of the other.[110]

The primary relief sought by plaintiffs is the discontinuation of the use of the offending domain name; in cases of cybersquatting it is the transfer of the domain name. However, courts have made awards of damages – compensatory, aggravated and punitive – and have considered making an order of account of profits.[111] Punitive damages require a separate actionable wrong.

Typosquatting is a variation of cybersquatting but retains the bad faith and insidious features. Typosquatters typically register domain names which are spelling variations of existing sites that have substantial traffic. The offending site often directs browsers to sites offering adult entertainment, gambling or recursive advertising. Some count the accidental hits and then sell advertising in proportion to the

---

107 (1889) 14 App Cas 337, 374 per Lord Herschell.
108 In *Peek v Gurney* (1873) LR 6 HL 377, 403 Lord Cairns considered that fraud existed where there was a partial statement of fact in such a manner that the withholding of what is not stated 'makes that which is stated absolutely false'.
109 [1897] AC 710.
110 Ibid., 713–14, emphasis added; see also Lord Herschell at 715. See also *Sheather v Staples Waste Removals Pty Limited (No. 2)* [2014] FCA 84, para 5.
111 *Hoath v Connect Internet Services* [2006] NSWSC 158, para 209.

traffic generated. Reliance is placed on the fact that a percentage of accidental hits respond positively to the diversion.

In *Yahoo! Inc. and GeoCities v Data Art*,[112] the claimant, who owned geocities.com, had 1.7 billion hits in one month. The defendant had registered 36 domain name variations, including eocities.com and gocities.com. Even a small percentage of hits resulting from mistyping resulted in considerable traffic.[113] The arbitration panel ordered the transfer of these bad faith registrations. Similarly in *Eddie Bauer Inc. v Paul White*[114] the misspelt domain name was eddibower.com and the panel restrained its use.

Typosquatting includes taking advantage of the accidental omission of the dot after the initial www, such as <http://www.dowjones.com>.[115]

In 2001 Telstra Australia succeeded in forcing the transfer of the domain name telsra.com from a Melbourne-based typosquatter.[116] Upon accessing the site, the user was automatically redirected to an online gambling website. Telstra submitted that the practice caused embarrassment and tarnished Telstra's reputation and marks. Telstra had previously won other domain name disputes relating to telstrashop.com[117] and telstra.org.[118]

Part 3 – Uniform Dispute Resolution Policies

By the 1990s, ICANN was in need of a solution to the rising dispute resolution problem. The legal proceedings in court were slow, expensive and involved a minefield of jurisdictional issues.

In 1999 ICANN issued its Uniform Dispute Resolution Policy (UDRP)[119] as an alternative to legal proceedings before courts. The UDRP has become the international standard for resolving domain name disputes. It is intended to also discourage abusive registrations. The complainant is required to demonstrate that the disputed domain name is identical or confusingly similar to theirs, that the

---

112 WIPO Case No. D2000–0587.
113 Should one in a thousand visitors make the appropriate typo, the defendant would receive 1.7 million visits per month, an amount of traffic which would attract considerable advertising interest.
114 (2000) *eResolution* AF-204.
115 *Dow Jones v Powerclick Inc.*,WIPO Case No. D2000–1259.
116 *Telstra Corporation Ltd v David Whittle*, WIPO Case No. D2001–0434.
117 *Telstra Corporation Ltd v Barry Cheng Kwok Chu*, WIPO Case No. D2001–0423.
118 *Telstra Corporation Ltd v Nuclear Marshmallows*, WIPO Case No. D2000–0003.
119 ICANN, above n 13.

registrant does not have a right or legitimate interest in the domain name, and that the registrant has registered and used the domain name in bad faith.[120]

ICANN provides that domain name disputes must be resolved by agreement, court action or arbitration before a registrar will cancel, suspend or transfer a domain name. The process does not extend to any domain name ending with a country code unless that country's domain name authority has specifically adopted the UDRP. Many domain name administrators have issued their own Dispute Resolution Policies, which largely reproduce the ICANN policy.

The UDRP has been adopted by ICANN-accredited registrars in all gTLDs: it is included as a term in registration agreements between the applicant and the registrar. Dispute proceedings arising from alleged abusive registration of domain names may be initiated by parties claiming trade mark or service mark rights.

The purpose of the UDRP is to create global uniformity, reduce the costs for resolving domain name disputes and enable the laws of nation states to continue to operate.

In applying for an ICANN open domain name the registrant must represent and warrant that the statements made in the application are complete and accurate and that, to the registrant's knowledge, the registration does not infringe upon or violate the rights of any third party.[121] The numerous instances of cybersquatting are a testament to the fact that a considerable number of registrants ignore this contractual undertaking. ICANN makes no attempt to require its registrars to make any determination about whether or not the applicant may be in breach. Clearly there are examples of well-known and famous trade marks being registered without there having been any attempt to question or otherwise limit the applications. Registrars often rely, for their income, on turnover of domain names, so restricting registration would be an additional cost and thus against their own interests.

Registrants are required to submit to a mandatory administrative proceeding in the event that a third party makes a complaint:

> ... to the applicable Provider, in compliance with the Rules of Procedure, that
> (i) your domain name is identical or confusingly similar to a trademark or service mark in which the complainant has rights; and
> (ii) you have no rights or legitimate interests in respect of the domain name; and
> (iii) your domain name has been registered and is being used in bad faith.[122]

The complainant must prove that all three elements are present. The UDRP's administrative panel's decisions cannot be enforced in court.

---

120 In addition, ICANN has issued a number of specialist policies for particular TLDs.
121 It should be reiterated that the UDRP applies to the open gTLD and not directly to any of the approximately 240 country code domain names, such as .us, .au, .nz, .uk and .in.
122 ICANN, above n 13, para 4(a).

'Identical or confusingly similar'

Many cases simply involve the exact trade or service mark of the complainant, and there is little need for analysis. In *Blue Sky Software Corp. v Digital Sierra Inc*[123] the registrant had registered robohelp.com, which was identical to the complainant's trade mark 'ROBOHELP'. First, the WIPO panel made the somewhat obvious statement, 'The addition of .com is not a distinguishing difference.' Similarly, there is little scrutiny or examination required when, for example, 'i' is added to 'Toyota' to create itoyota.com[124] or 'girls' is added to 'nokia' to form nokiagirls.com.[125] In the latter case the WIPO panel stated, 'The ability of this word "girls" to distinguish the Domain Name from the trademark of the Complainant is limited. As a general noun, "girls" is indeed a rather neutral addition to this trademark.'[126]

'Identical or confusingly similar' are meant to be separate concepts. On occasion parties have attempted to argue that the use of an identical identifier should be identical *and* confusingly similar. The case of *BWT Brands Inc. and British American Tobacco (Brands) Inc. v NABR*[127] involved a well-known brand of cigarettes – Kool – and the registration of kool.com. The WIPO panel rejected the registrant's argument that an identical domain name must simultaneously be confusingly similar for the provision to become operative:

> The burden on the Complainant under this head is merely to demonstrate that the disputed domain name is similar or identical to the Complainants' trademark, without reference to the way in which the domain name is being used. Plainly enough, the disputed domain name *kool.com* is identical to the Complainant's registered trademark.[128]

The test of confusing similarity is limited to a comparison between the domain name identifier and the mark alone. The panel does not need to consider other trade mark or passing off issues. In a majority of cases the panels have concluded that the domain names were confusingly similar: for example, walmartcanadasucks.com,[129] salvationarmysucks.com,[130] guinness-reallysucks.com,[131] adtsucks.

---

123 WIPO Case No. D2000–0165.
124 *Toyota Jidosha Kabushiki Kaisha v S & S Enterprises Ltd*, WIPO Case No. D2000–0802.
125 *Nokia Corporation v Nokiagirls.com*, WIPO Case No. D2000–0102.
126 See also *The Stanley Works and Stanley Logistics Inc. v Camp Creek Co. Inc.*, WIPO Case No. D2000–0113.
127 WIPO Case No. D2001–1480.
128 Ibid., para 6.
129 *Wal-Mart Stores Inc. v Walsucks and Walmarket Puerto Rico*, WIPO Case No. D2000–0477.
130 *The Salvation Army v Info-Bahn Inc.*, WIPO Case No. D2001–0463.
131 *Diageo plc v John Zuccarini*, WIPO Case No. D2000–0996.

com,[132] accorsucks.com,[133] autotradersucks.com,[134] standardcharteredsucks.com[135] and wal-martsucks.com.[136] However, the opposite conclusion was reached with wallmartcanadasucks.com,[137] mclanenortheastsucks.com[138] and lockheedmartin-sucks.com.[139]

The panels have considered a 'mark for name comparison'. This involves the potential and the actual use of the domain name for the purpose of confusion.[140] While actual deceptive use is relevant to the second and third requirements, it is not for the first requirement. In *Koninklijke Philips Electronics NV v In Seo Kim*,[141] the panel considered that phillipssucks.com was confusingly similar to the trademark 'Philips'. The panel stated:

> Not all Internet users are English speaking or familiar with the use of 'sucks' to indicate a site used for denigration. Furthermore, it is not unknown for companies to establish complaint or comment sites or areas of sites to obtain feedback on their products; accordingly, some people might suppose that a website of this nature at the Domain Name was operated by the Complainant.[142]

However, the panel rightly stated that the addition of 'sucks.com' will not necessarily result in a successful challenge. Where a domain name is genuinely registered and used for the purposes of criticism, the second and third requirements of the rule will not necessarily be met.

Registrants often argue that the identifier is made up of generic or descriptive words which are not exclusively associated with complainant's mark or business. In *Energy Source Inc. v Your Energy Source*,[143] the domain name was youren-ergysource.com. The three-member panel focused on the domain name itself,

---

132 *ADT Services AG v ADT Sucks.com*, WIPO Case No. D2001–0213.
133 *Société Accor contre M Philippe Hartmann*, WIPO Case No. D2001–0007.
134 *TPI Holdings Inc. v AFX Communications*, WIPO Case No. D2000–1472.
135 *Standard Chartered PLC v Purge IT*, WIPO Case No. D2000–0681.
136 *Wal-Mart Stores Inc. v Richard MacLeod*, WIPO Case No. D2000–0662. See also *Direct Line Group Ltd v Purge IT*, WIPO Case No. D2000–0583 (directlinesucks.com); *Dixons Group PLC v Purge IT*, WIPO Case No. D2000–0584 (dixonssucks.com); *Freeserve PLC v Purge IT*, WIPO Case No. D2000–0585 (freeservesucks.com); *National Westminster Bank PLC v Purge IT*, WIPO Case No. D2000–0636 (natwestsucks.com); and *Vivendi Universal v Jay David Sallen*, WIPO Case No. D2001–1121 (vivendiuniversalsucks.com).
137 *Wal-Mart Stores Inc. v wallmartcanadasucks.com and Kenneth J Harvey*, WIPO Case No. D2000–1104.
138 *McLane Company Inc. v Fred Craig*, WIPO Case No. D2000–1455.
139 *Lockheed Martin Corporation v Dan Parisi*, WIPO Case No. D2000–1015.
140 See *Koninklijke Philips Electronics NV v Cun Siang Wang*, WIPO Case No. D2000–1778.
141 WIPO Case No. D2001–1195.
142 Ibid., para 6.
143 NAF No. FA0096364.

stating that it is 'undoubtedly similar, but not identical' to the complainant's mark, 'Energy Source'. The panel said that 'confusing similarity should be determined by comparing the mark and domain name alone, independent of the other marketing and use factors usually considered in a traditional infringement action'. The panel regarded the words 'energy source' as the salient feature and determined that the addition of 'your' would be likely to be regarded by internet users as something related to 'energy source'.[144] The application of these principles continues to prove problematic. Three panel decisions have included dissenting opinions on this issue.[145] However, the decisions of panels do not form precedents in the formal sense, so panels are not bound by them. Nevertheless, parties before panels do refer to earlier decisions, and panels refer to such decisions in their reasons for judgement.

Trade mark or service mark

The ICANN rules fit the US concept of common law trade mark and service marks much more neatly than they do the laws of other jurisdictions. Many jurisdictions define trade marks as the exclusive purview of trade mark legislation. The extended meaning of 'service mark' has been used to deal with unregistered marks which might otherwise fit within the US approach.

Common law trade mark rights are usually confined to the jurisdiction where the mark is used. In *ESAT Digifone Ltd v Colin Hayes*,[146] the complainant had failed to register its own name, though there was a trade mark application pending in respect of other marks. The panel resolved the dispute in favour of the complainant. This Ireland-based case referred to local trade mark law, which hitherto had not recognised common law trade marks.[147] In *Fiber-Shield Industries Inc. v Fiber Shield Ltd* (fibershield.net), the respondent had operated a legitimate, non-competing business under the name for more than 10 years but had nevertheless lost the domain registration.[148] In *State of the Netherlands v Goldnames Inc.*,[149] the complainant alleged that there was a common law mark Staten-Generaal (States General), representing the Dutch state, even though in the Netherlands no common law trade mark exists. The panel held that the complainant's mark,

---

144 See *Sony Kabushiki Kaisha v Sin Eonmok*, WIPO Case No. D2000–1007 and *MP3.com Inc. v Sander*, WIPO Case No. D2000–0579, dealing with the addition of 'my'.

145 For example, *Vivendi Universal v Jay David Sallen and GO247.com Inc.*,WIPO Case No. D2001–1121. See also *Bosley Medical Institute Inc. v Kremer* 403 F. 3d 672 (9th Cir 2005).

146 WIPO Case No. D2000–0600.

147 The Panel referred to *Coca-Cola v F Cade & Sons Limited* [1957] IR 196. See also *PA Consulting Services Pty Ltd v Joseph Barrington-Lew*, WIPO Case No. DAU2003–0002.

148 NAF (2000) No. FA0001000092054.

149 WIPO Case No. D2001–0520.

Staten-Generaal, was reasonably well known throughout the world, as well as within the Netherlands, and that the complainant might thus be viewed as having legally protectable rights.

The panels have ruled that registration as a registered trade mark or service mark was not necessary, and that even individual names have sufficient secondary association for complainants to maintain that 'common law trademark rights' exist. For example, well-known novelist Jeanette Winterson reclaimed her name, which had been registered as Jeanettewinterson.com (as well as .org and .net).[150] The registrant, Hogarth, was a research fellow at Cambridge University and claimed that he intended to develop websites with reviews, biographies and forthcoming works of authors. However, Hogarth had also stated that he wanted to make money, and had asked for a 3 per cent share of profits of books sold via the website. The panel stated that the 'Complainant does not rely upon any registered trade marks but on her common law rights in her real name'. She has achieved international recognition and critical acclaim for her works and 'use of that Mark has come to be recognised by the general public as indicating an association with words written and produced exclusively by the Complainant'. The panel was satisfied that Jeanette Winterson had established trade mark rights in the mark for the purpose of the UDRP and ordered that all three domain names be transferred.

The well-known singer and performer Madonna challenged Dan Parisi, who purchased madonna.com for US$20,000. Parisi argued that this complainant was named after the Virgin Mary, as was her mother and hundreds of thousands of other people throughout the world over the past 2000 years, and had no greater right than any other person so named. However, for the purposes of the panel decision, the identifier was identical, Parisi had no legitimate interest in the name, and he had acquired it and was using it in bad faith. This complainant had registered 'Madonna' as a trade mark, establishing her rights in the name.[151] In a not dissimilar case the registrant had registered the domain name mickjagger.com. The panel first noted that the domain name was identical except for the .com, the capitalisation and spacing. The singer had had 'continuous commercial use of that mark for more than thirty-five (35) years'.[152] The panel stated that the UDRP 'does not require that the Complainant have rights in a registered trademark or service mark' and decided that the complainant held a common law trademark in his famous name, Mick Jagger.[153]

---

150 See *Jeanette Winterson v Mark Hogarth*, WIPO Case No. D2000–0235.
151 *Madonna Ciccone v Dan Parisi*, WIPO Case No. D2000–0847 (madonna.com).
152 *Mick Jagger v Denny Hammerton*, NAF FA0095261.
153 Ibid.

Other celebrities who have succeeded in having their name transferred include Julia Roberts,[154] Isabelle Adjani,[155] the Wiggles,[156] Jethro Tull,[157] Gene Kelly,[158] Tiger Woods[159] and Jimi Hendrix.[160] In addition, Time Warner has been successful in seeking orders to have several domain names which include the fictitious name 'Harry Potter' transferred.

On the other hand, another well-known singer, Sting, failed in his attempt.[161] In the *Sting* case the panel agreed that unregistered or common law marks are sufficient, but the complainant did not provide any documentary evidence in support of his assertion that he was the owner of the unregistered trademark or service mark. The complainant did assert – and the panel took the equivalent of judicial notice – that the complainant is a world-famous entertainer known by the name Sting. However, after considering the fact that this identifier has common dictionary meanings, the panel stated:

> Although it is accepted that the Complainant is world famous under the name STING, it does not follow that he has rights in STING *as a trademark or service mark* ... the personal name in this case is also a common word in the English language, with a number of different meanings.[162]

In *Re Eilberg*,[163] a trade mark application was filed for <www.eilberg.com> in the class of intellectual property. The applicant used the mark on letterheads and business cards. The claim was made that by not including the prefix http://, the use operated as a trade mark rather than merely as an indicator of a way to contact the law firm. These contentions were rejected by the USPTO Trademark Trial and Appeal Board. It held that displaying the domain name on the letterhead did not function as a service mark.

'Registrant has no rights or legitimate interests'

The second limb of the UDRP[164] requires the complainant to show that the registrant has no rights or legitimate interests in the domain name. The mere assertion

154 *Julia Fiona Roberts v Russell Boyd*, WIPO Case No. D2000–0210.
155 *Isabelle Adjani v Second Orbit Communications Inc.*, WIPO Case No. D2000–0867.
156 *The Wiggles Touring Pty Ltd v Thompson Media Pty Ltd*, WIPO Case No. D2000–0124.
157 *The Ian Anderson Group of Companies Ltd v Denny Hammerton*, WIPO Case No. D2000–0475; referring to the musical group.
158 *Gene Kelly Image Trust v BWI Domain Manager*, WIPO Case No. D2008–0342
159 Tiger Woods (NAF Claim No: FA0902001245906).
160 By the estate of the late Jimi Hendrix, *Experience Hendrix LLC v Denny Hammerton and The Jimi Hendrix Fan Club*, WIPO Case No. D2000–0364.
161 *Gordon Sumner, Sting v Michael Urvan*, WIPO Case No. D2000–0596 .
162 Ibid., emphasis added.
163 49 USPQ 2d 1955 (1998).
164 UDRP para 4(a)(ii) provides the second of three assertions by the complainant: 'the registrant has no rights or legitimate interests in respect of the domain name'.

that the respondent has no such rights does not constitute proof. The panel is free to make reasonable inferences. Paragraph 4(c) of the UDRP sets out specific circumstances to assist the registrant in demonstrating legitimate rights or legitimate interests in the domain name. The circumstances are inclusive and useful in considering this issue. The title to the paragraph is 'How to Demonstrate Your Rights to and Legitimate Interests in the Domain Name in Responding to a Complaint':[165]

> Any of the following circumstances … shall demonstrate your rights or legitimate interests to the domain name for purposes of Paragraph 4(a)(ii):
> - before any notice to you of the dispute, your use of, or demonstrable preparations to use, the domain name or a name corresponding to the domain name in connection with a bona fide offering of goods or services; or
> - you (as an individual, business, or other organization) have been commonly known by the domain name, even if you have acquired no trademark or service mark rights; or
> - you are making a legitimate noncommercial or fair use of the domain name, without intent for commercial gain, to misleadingly divert consumers or to tarnish the trademark or service mark at issue.[166]

In relation to paragraph 4(c)(i), in *Libro Ag v NA Global Link*[167] (libro.com) the registrant argued that the complainant's trade mark 'libro' is common Spanish and Italian word for 'book'. However, although the registrant claimed it had registered the domain name to establish an online virtual book store, in fact users were redirected to restaurants.com. The panel held that the mere assertion of making preparations to use the domain name for the *bona fide* offering of goods is insufficient to demonstrate rights or legitimate interests.

In *Bruce Springsteen v Jeff Burgar and Bruce Springsteen Club*,[168] both the complainant and the registrant had rights in the name. The panel described Bruce Springsteen as 'the famous, almost legendary, recording artist and composer … his name is instantly recognisable in almost every part of the globe', and accepted the complainant's common law rights in the name. The registrant was the Bruce Springsteen Club, with Jeff Burger as the point of contact. When accessing the website users were immediately transferred to celebrity1000.com. In relation to paragraph 4(c)(i), the panel found there was no *bona fide* commercial use.

In relation to paragraph 4(c)(ii), the panel considered the meaning of 'commonly' and 'known by'. It found that the use of the name 'Bruce Springsteen Club' would not give rise to an impression in the minds of internet users that the proprietor was

---

165 The terms 'your' and 'you' refer to the registrant.
166 ICANN, above n 13, para 4(c).
167 WIPO Case No. D2000–0186.
168 WIPO Case No. D2000–1532.

effectively 'known as' Bruce Springsteen, let alone 'commonly' recognised in that fashion. Accordingly, the panel found that this requirement too was not met.

In applying paragraph 4(c)(iii), the panel considered the meaning of 'non-commercial' and 'fair use'. It observed that 'Bruce Springsteen', when inputted into a search engine, would yield thousands of hits, from which it would be apparent to users that some sites were official or authorised sites and others were not. Due to the number of sites, the panel noted that users would be 'unsurprised' to arrive at celebrity1000.com via the name 'Bruce Springsteen'. Accordingly, they stated that 'it is hard to infer from the conduct' of the registrant that the intent was for commercial gain or 'to misleadingly divert consumers'. In determining that such conduct does not 'tarnish' the common law rights of Bruce Springsteen by association with the celebrity1000.com website, the panel found there was 'fair use'. They considered that fair use would not exist if the domain name in question connected, for example, to 'sites containing pornographic or other regrettable material'.[169]

The panel found that the complainant, Bruce Springsteen, had not satisfied the second limb of the three-part test in paragraph 4(a) of the UDRP.

'Registration and use in bad faith'

The UDRP rules provide an explanation of 'Registration and Use in Bad Faith'. The circumstances include dealing with cybersquatting and the attempted extortion from trade mark and service mark owners:

> ... the following circumstances, in particular but without limitation, if found by the Panel to be present, shall be evidence of the registration and use of a domain name in bad faith:
>
> **(i)** circumstances indicating that you have registered or you have acquired the domain name primarily for the purpose of selling, renting, or otherwise transferring the domain name registration to the complainant who is the owner of the trademark or service mark or to a competitor of that complainant, for valuable consideration in excess of your documented out-of-pocket costs directly related to the domain name; or
>
> **(ii)** you have registered the domain name in order to prevent the owner of the trademark or service mark from reflecting the mark in a corresponding domain name, provided that you have engaged in a pattern of such conduct; or
>
> **(iii)** you have registered the domain name primarily for the purpose of disrupting the business of a competitor; or
>
> **(iv)** by using the domain name, you have intentionally attempted to attract, for commercial gain, Internet users to your web site or other on-line location, by creating a likelihood of confusion with the complainant's mark as to the source, sponsorship, affiliation, or endorsement of your web site or location or of a product or service on your web site or location.[170]

---

169 Ibid., para 6.
170 ICANN, above n 13, para 4(b).

These rules encompass and go beyond typical cybersquatting and typosquatting situations.[171]

The remedies available to the complainant pursuant to any proceeding before the panel are the cancellation of the domain name or the transfer of the domain name to the complainant. All panel decisions under the UDRP are published in full on the internet; the panel can determine to withhold portions in exceptional circumstances. The UDRP's mandatory administrative proceeding requirements do not prevent legal proceedings in any court of competent jurisdiction from being commenced before or after the UDRP proceedings.[172]

The UDRP allows a period of grace of 10 business days before taking action on any decision to cancel or transfer the domain name. This is to allow the registrant the opportunity to commence legal proceedings. All that is required to do this is notice of the legal proceedings by, for example, a plaint file-stamped by the clerk of the court.

The UDRP decision will not be implemented until ICANN receives satisfactory evidence of a resolution between the parties, or satisfactory evidence that the legal proceedings have been dismissed or withdrawn, or a copy of an order from the court dismissing the legal proceedings or ordering that the registrant has no right to continue to use the domain name.[173]

In *GlobalCenter Pty Ltd v Global Domain Hosting Pty Ltd*,[174] the panel members considered their right to make independent investigations. One took the view that the UDRP Rules[175] preclude panel members from conducting their own factual investigations and from visiting relevant websites unless invited to do so by a party to the dispute. A visit to the relevant websites might reveal the parties' compliance with the rules, their state of mind in relation to such issues as bad faith, and the validity of their respective submissions.[176] Another took the view that the panel is entitled to have regard to any freely available online public material 'germane to an issue in dispute'.[177]

The proceedings before panels are governed by the UDRP Rules.[178] These rules deal with the procedure and aspects such as fairness and evidentiary standards.

---

171 See *Miele Inc. v Absolute Air Cleaners and Purifiers*, WIPO Case No. D2000–0005 and *Telaxis Communications Corp. v William E. Minkle*, WIPO Case No. D2000–0756.

172 ICANN, above n 13, para 4(k).

173 ICANN, above n 13, para 4(d)–(k).

174 WIPO Case No. DAU2002–0001.

175 UDRP, Rules 10(a) and 15(a).

176 See also *Jazid Inc. Michelle McKinnon v Rennemo Steinar* eResolution, Case No. AF-0807, where the Panel stated that it is not 'the burden of the Panel to seek further evidence (other than judicial knowledge) to sustain the parties' allegations, as this may be disruptive of the arbitration process. Therefore, the burden rests on the parties to either support or sustain their allegations with the appropriate documentation whenever possible.'

177 WIPO Case No. DAU2002–0001, para 6.

178 UDRP, above n 175.

The panel must treat the parties equally, give each party a fair opportunity to present its case, and determine the admissibility, relevance, materiality and weight of the evidence.[179]

On occasion proceedings may be by teleconference, videoconference or web conference.[180]

In *Mary-Lynn Mondich and American Vintage Wine Biscuit Inc. v Big Daddy's Antiques*,[181] the panel held that merely offering to sell the domain name to the owner of the trade mark can be sufficient evidence for registration and use in bad faith where the registrant claimed more than any underlying costs. However, where the complainant initiated transfer discussions and the registrant had no prior plans to sell the domain name, the panel can find no bad faith.[182] Where the registrant concealed its identity by operating under a false name the panel can find bad faith.[183]

auDRP

In Australia the Australian Domain Name Administrator, auDA adopted a new .au Dispute Resolution Policy (auDRP) in 2010, replacing the original 2002 policy. This new policy is modelled on the UDRP and applies to all open 2TLDs, namely asn.au, com.au, id.au, net.au, .edu.au and org.au. The relevant provisions state:

> You are required to submit to a mandatory administrative proceeding in the event that a third party (a 'complainant') asserts to the applicable Provider, in compliance with the Rules of Procedure that:
>
> (i) your domain name is identical or confusingly similar to a name, trademark or service mark in which the complainant has rights; and
>
> (ii) you have no rights or legitimate interests in respect of the domain name; and
>
> (iii) your domain name has been registered or subsequently used in bad faith.[184]

There are three differences between the provisions of the UDRP and those of the auDRP. First, in paragraph (i), the auDRP added 'name'. The auDRP applies to domain names that are identical or confusingly similar, not only to a trademark or service mark, but also to any 'name' in which the complainant has rights. This

---

179 UDRP, above n 175, rule 10(a).
180 UDRP, above n 175, rule 13.
181 WIPO Case No. D2000–0004.
182 See *City Utilities v Ed Davidson*, WIPO Case No. D2000–0004 (cityutilities.com).See also *Blue Cross and Blue Shield Association and Trigon Insurance Company v Interactive Communications Inc.*, WIPO Case No. D2000–0788.
183 See *Telstra Corporation Ltd v Nuclear Marshmallows*, WIPO Case No. D2000–0003 (Telstra.org).
184 auDRP Schedule A, clause 4(a).

includes the complainant's company, business or other legal or trading name, as registered with the relevant Australian government authority, and the complainant's personal name.

Second, in paragraph (iii) the word 'and' has been replaced with 'or'. Under the auDRP, it is sufficient to prove that either registration 'or' subsequent use of the domain name by the registrant occurred in bad faith, whereas the UDRP requires the complainant to prove both elements.

Third, under the second circumstance of bad faith of the UDRP a pattern of conduct is required. Under the auDRP no such pattern is required.[185]

.nz DRSP

The registry responsible for the .nz (New Zealand) domain name extension instituted a new Dispute Resolution Service Policy (DRSP) in 2011 (applicable to .nz domains). It is similar to the .uk DRSP. However, it uses the expression 'Unfair Registration' in place of 'Abusive Registration':

> This Policy and Procedure applies to Respondents when a Complainant asserts to the DNC according to the Procedure, that:
> 4.1.1 The Complainant has Rights in respect of a name or mark which is identical or similar to the Domain Name; and
> 4.1.2 The Domain Name, in the hands of the Respondent, is an Unfair Registration.[186]

An 'Unfair Registration' is set out as non-exclusive circumstances in paragraph 5.1.

.usTLD Dispute Resolution Policy

The usTLD Dispute Resolution Policy is also based on the UDRP. The operative provisions state:

> You are required to submit to a mandatory administrative proceeding in the event that a third party (a 'Complainant') asserts to the applicable Provider, in compliance with the Rules, that:
> (i) Your domain name is identical or confusingly similar to a trademark or service mark in which the Complainant has rights;
> (ii) You have no rights or legitimate interests in respect of the domain name; and
> (iii) Your domain name has been registered in bad faith or is being used in bad faith.[187]

---

185 See *GE Capital Finance Australasia Pty v Dental Financial Services Pty Ltd*, WIPO Case No. DAU2004–0007; *University of Melbourne v union melb*, WIPO Case No. DAU2004–0004; and *The National Office for the Information Economy v Verisign Australia Limited* LEADR, Case No. 02/2003.
186 New Zealand DRSP clause 4.1.
187 See <www.neustar.us/ustld-dispute-resolution-policy>, clause 4(a).

.uk DRSP

The .uk Dispute Resolution Service Policy (DRSP) is part of the contract of registration for .uk domains. The .uk DRSP replaces the UDRP's concept of bad faith with the expression 'abusive registration' and provides a definition. Circumstances indicating abusive registration include that the registrant has registered or acquired the domain name primarily:

> (i) for the purposes of selling, renting or transferring the Domain Name to the Complainant or competitor for an amount valuable in excess of out-of-pocket costs; as a blocking registration against a name or mark in which the Complainant has rights; or
>
> (ii) for the purpose of unfairly disrupting the business of the Complainant.
>
> There shall be a presumption of Abusive Registration if the Complainant proves that [the] Registrant has been found to have made an Abusive Registration in three or more Dispute Resolution Service cases in the two years before the Complaint was filed.[188]

The operative provisions state:

> A Respondent must submit to proceedings under the Dispute Resolution Service if a Complainant asserts to us, according to the Procedure, that:
> - The Complainant has Rights in respect of a name or mark which is identical or similar to the Domain Name; and
> - The Domain Name, in the hands of the Respondent, is an Abusive Registration.[189]

INDRP

India the .in Domain Name Registry has published the .in Dispute Resolution Policy (INDRP). The operative provisions state:

> Any Person who considers that a registered domain name conflicts with his legitimate rights or interests may file a Complaint to the .IN Registry on the following premises:
> - (i) the Registrant's domain name is identical or confusingly similar to a name, trademark or service mark in which the Complainant has rights;
> - (ii) the Registrant has no rights or legitimate interests in respect of the domain name; and
> - (iii) the Registrant's domain name has been registered or is being used in bad faith.[190]

---

188 .uk DRSP clause 3.
189 Ibid., clause 2.
190 INDRP clause 4.

Practical ramifications

An aggrieved party who wishes to initiate proceedings may choose a dispute resolution process available from the domain name administrators, or legal proceedings before a court. These actions are not mutually exclusive, and a party may fail in one action and succeed in the other. The procedures, rules and approaches are for the most part unrelated.

The legal process is typically slow and the cost of lawyers is often prohibitive. The proceedings are in person and rely on a range of laws and malleable common law and general law principles. An aggrieved party may be able to establish the elements of passing off, but the same circumstances may not give rise to a remedy under the dispute resolution processes.

Conclusion

The domain name system was invented in 1983. The common law and statutes did not anticipate this new form of business identifier, and indeed debate continues about whether or not a domain name should be considered a new form of intellectual property.

The Australian Consumer Law provides a generalist remedy adopted in some domain name cases. In other cases an allegation of fraud can be made. However, disputants have seized upon the tort of passing off as the most favourable judicial cause of action to resolve their conflict. But even then, the traditional and strict approach required by the judiciary fails to provide a remedy in all situations. The courts have molded and fashioned the tort in a manner not previously anticipated or expected.[191] The result may be classified as a new tort, or at least a subset known as 'domain name passing off'. This kind of modification is not new; it is in the spirit of evolving law. To paraphrase Learned Hand, common law:

> stands as a monument slowly raised, like a coral reef, from the minute accretions of past individuals, of whom each built upon the relics which his predecessors left, and in his turn left a foundation upon which his successors might work.[192]

New and novel creations such as domain names call to the judiciary, as custodians of the common law, to do just this in order to serve law and society.

---

191 As in the *Marks & Spencer* case above.
192 Billings Learned Hand's review of Cardozo's 'The Nature of the Judicial Process', (1932) 35 *Harv LR* 479.

The policy of 'first come first served' was adopted and consistently followed by various domain name administrators, but in recent times it has frequently been negated by the various courts, UDRP panels and local DRP panels in favour of other rights (not exclusively those of trade mark owners). The rejection of the policy in cases of 'cybersquatting' is quite justified, in my view, but rejection of the policy in order to protect senior users of the trade mark is uncalled for.[193] Domain name registration policy rewards trade mark owners who have the foresight to register their trade marks as domain names.[194]

The initial run on established stakeholders who failed to record their interests on domain names registers has expired. The ignorance of the 1990s has passed. Nevertheless, new interests emerge. Cyberpiracy continues to take on various forms, not all of which are readily apparent. ICANN and its various constituents must maintain a constant vigil. The release of the new gTLDs will be a double-edged sword, providing both relief and choice for registrants on the one hand, but an opportunity for abuse by cybersquatters on the other.

FURTHER READING

Tim Berners-Lee, *Weaving the Web*, Orion Business Books, 1999.

Colm Brannigan, 'The UDRP: How do you spell success?', (2004) 5 *Digital Technology Law Journal*.

Neil Brown, 'Arbitration of Celebrity Domain Name Disputes', 13 *International Trade & Business Law Review* 165 (2010).

Anri Engel, 'International domain name disputes: Rules and practice of the UDRP', (2003) 25 *European Intellectual Property Review* 351.

Michael Geist, 'Fair.com?: An examination of the allegations of systemic unfairness in the ICANN UDRP', (2002) 27 *Brooklyn Law School Journal of International Law* 903.

Konstantinos Komaitis, *The Current State of Domain Name Regulation: Domain Names as Second Class Citizens in a Mark-Dominated World*, Routledge, New York, 2010.

Annette Kur, 'UDRP: A study by the Max-Planck Institute for Foreign and International Patent, Copyright and Competition Law, Munich': see Summary and Proposals at p 72. Available at <www.intellecprop.mpg.de/Online-Publikationen/2002/UDRP-study-final-02.pdf>.

---

193 See Spyros M Maniatis, 'Trade mark law and domain name: Back to basics', (2002) 24 *EIPR* 397.
194 *Data Concepts v Digital Consulting Inc. and Network Solutions Inc.* 150 F. 3d 620, 1998 US App. LEXIS 17758 (6th Cir 1998).

Jacqueline Lipton, *Internet Domain Names, Trademarks and Free Speech*, Edward Elgar Publishing, Northhampton, 2010.

Megan Richardson, 'Trade marks and language', (2004) *Sydney Law Review* 9.

Alpana Roy, 'Navigating the landscape of the .au Dispute Resolution Policy as it enters its second decade', (2014) 19 *Media and Arts Law Review* 1.

17

JURISDICTION IN CYBERSPACE

> When a radically new situation is presented to the law it is sometimes neces-
> sary to think outside the square ... this involves a reflection upon the features
> of the Internet that are said to require a new and distinctive legal approach.[1]

Cyberspace is an illusion. There is no such place. Many terrestrial norms do not
and cannot apply to such a fictitious construct. Nevertheless, cyberspace users
perceive metaphorical chat rooms, folders, files, shops, libraries and so forth. They
live digital lives with digital personas in 'places' such as Second Life, Twitter and
Facebook. The reality is that each step of the digital experience is rooted terrestri-
ally. Traditional legal principles are applicable to the majority of electronic commerce disputes. Nevertheless, the operation of electronic commerce in cyberspace
results in new circumstances to which legal jurists cannot readily apply established
legal rules.

The borderless nature of the internet often hides or disguises the origin of
particular websites and corresponding information. Questions sometimes arise as
to the country or state whose courts have jurisdiction to adjudicate on a matter,
and as to which law is to be applied. Courts also have to determine issues such
as where conduct occurs – at the computer, the server, the place of business or
residence or somewhere else? – and thus which time zone applies. This area of law
is referred to as conflict of laws or private international law,[2] and its principles are
well established.

Rules of private international law

It is possible that an Australian court will determine that the law which applies to a
particular situation is that of another country. In this case the Australian court will
apply that other country's law. Typically, the parties to an international contract
will specifically identify the law which applies to the contract. The parties may also
identify which country's courts have jurisdiction to hear disputes arising under the
contract.

Contractually, parties may include an express choice of law clause under the
principle of party autonomy.[3] However, there are exceptions.[4] Where there is no
express choice of law the courts will attempt to find an implication of choice

---

1 *Dow Jones v Gutnick* [2002] HCA 56, para 112, per Kirby J.
2 See Peter Nygh and Martin Davies, *Conflict of laws in Australia,* 7th edn, LexisNexis, Sydney, 2002.
3 See *Vita Food Products Inc. v Unus Shipping Co.* [1939] AC 277, per Lord Wright.
4 See, for example, *Golden Acres Ltd v Queensland Estates Pty Ltd* [1969] Qd R 378, and
   Minnesota v Granite Gate Resorts Inc. 568 NW 2d 715.

from the language of the documents, the prior conduct of the parties, the place of performance and other surrounding circumstances.[5] Where there is no express choice and one cannot be implied, the contract will be governed by the law of the jurisdiction 'most closely connected' to the contract. This may depend upon the subject matter, nationality or domicile of the parties, the place of performance, and other factors.[6] Once the proper law is determined, the rules of that system of law are applied to the contract.

Forum non conveniens

The issue of choice of forum in which to hear an action is known as *forum non conveniens*. Each nation state determines its own laws and procedures. These laws are termed *lex fori* – the law of the forum. Each nation's court system must determine, through its own civil procedure, when and how it should accept jurisdiction. It will take into account numerous factors, such as residence and nationality of the parties, the place or places of business, and the subject matter (when the law suit begins). Often the issue is routine and uncontroversial, but where one or more of the parties reside outside the nation state or the subject matter of harm occurs elsewhere the question of jurisdiction must be settled.

The English approach to determining the forum, recognised by most common law jurisdictions, is the test of 'the clearly more appropriate forum'.[7] The Australian courts have developed a broader test, that of 'the clearly inappropriate forum'. This has resulted in the taking of jurisdiction more often.[8]

The High Court reaffirmed its position in *Regie National des Usines Renault SA v Zhang*:[9] '[a]n Australian court cannot be a clearly inappropriate forum merely by virtue of the circumstance that the choice of law rules which apply in the forum require its courts to apply foreign law as the *lex causae*'. Although superficially the English and Australian tests look similar, an analysis demonstrates that the Australian test will result in the courts taking jurisdiction more often.

Dow Jones v Gutnick

A number of foreign cases have raised novel problems associated with jurisdiction in cyberspace.

---

5 See *Atlantic Underwriting Agencies Ltd v Compagnia di Assicuranzione di Milano SpA* [1979] 2 Lloyds Rep 240.

6 See *Re United Railways of the Havana and Regla Warehouses Ltd* [1960] Ch 52 and *Mendelson-Zeller Co. Inc. v T& C Providores Pty Ltd* [1981] 1 NSWLR 366.

7 See *Spiliada Maritime Corporation Ltd v Cansulex Ltd* [1987] AC 460.

8 See *Oceanic Sun Line Special Shipping Co. v Fay* (1988) 62 ALJR 389; *Voth v Manildra Flour Mills Pty Ltd* (1990) 65 ALJR 83; *Henry v Henry* (1996) 185 CLR 571.

9 [2002] HCA 10.

The application of the internet vis-à-vis jurisdiction and cyberspace was explained in *Dow Jones v Gutnick*.[10] Gleeson CJ, McHugh, Gummow and Hayne JJ explained:

> The World Wide Web is but one particular service available over the Internet. It enables a document to be stored in such a way on one computer connected to the Internet that a person using another computer connected to the Internet can request and receive a copy of the document … the terms conventionally used to refer to the materials that are transmitted in this way are a 'document' or a 'web page' and a collection of web pages is usually referred to as a 'web site'. A computer that makes documents available runs software that is referred to as a 'web server'; a computer that requests and receives documents runs software that is referred to as a 'web browser'.
>
> The originator of a document wishing to make it available on the World Wide Web arranges for it to be placed in a storage area managed by a web server. This process is conventionally referred to as 'uploading'. A person wishing to have access to that document must issue a request to the relevant server nominating the location of the web page identified by its 'uniform resource locator (URL)'. When the server delivers the document in response to the request the process is conventionally referred to as 'downloading'.[11]

Dow Jones v Gutnick[12] is the most significant Australian authority on internet jurisdiction to date. Dow Jones published the *Barrons Magazine* (Barrons), which contained an article entitled 'Unholy Gains' and subheaded 'When stock promoters cross paths with religious charities, investors had better be on guard'. The article alleged, among other things, that Victorian businessman Joseph Gutnick was 'masquerading as a reputable citizen when he was a tax evader who had laundered large amounts of money'.[13] The magazine sold 305 563 hard copies (14 of those in Victoria) and was available on the website wsj.com to some 550,000 subscribers (some 300 of whom were in Victoria). Dow Jones operated in New York and its internet servers were located in New Jersey.

Dow Jones v Gutnick did not involve personal jurisdiction, as the defendant was not within jurisdiction. Personal jurisdiction is typically satisfied where the defendant is physically present in the jurisdiction or has significant contacts with the jurisdiction, such as a branch office or registered interest. The nature of internet interaction will lead to many instances where personal jurisdiction will not arise.

---

10 [2002] HCA 56; (2002) 210 CLR 575.
11 [2002] HCA 56, [15]–[16]; (2002) 210 CLR 597, 598.
12 [2002] HCA 56 ('*Dow Jones* case'); on appeal from *Gutnick v Dow Jones* [2001] VSC 305 and *Dow Jones Company Inc. v Gutnick* [2001] VSCA 249. See, generally, 'A "category-specific" legislative approach to the internet personal jurisdiction problem in US law', (2004) 117 *Harv LR* 1617.
13 [2001] VSC 305, para 3.

The case attracted significant international attention. Media outlets were concerned about the implications for them if nations such as Australia accepted jurisdiction for publications which were ostensibly intended for the domestic US market, but which were sold in part – or peripherally – internationally. The High Court of Australia permits pleadings in appeals by interveners in matters of general public importance if the issue relates to maintaining some particular right, power or immunity which affects the interveners.[14] An intervener has the same rights and obligations as the other parties to the action, including the ability to appeal, tender evidence and participate fully in all aspects of the argument. The interveners included Amazon.com Inc., Associated Press, Cable News Network LP LLLP (CNN), Guardian Newspapers Ltd, The New York Times Company, News Limited, Time, Inc., Tribune Company, The Washington Post Company, Yahoo! Inc. and John Fairfax Holdings Ltd.

The matter came before Hedigan J at first instance. His Honour particularly examined jurisdiction in relation to the internet connection, as this could affect the award of damages.

Geoffrey Robertson QC for Dow Jones made several unsuccessful submissions. Robertson submitted that imposing liability where downloading occurred 'would have a serious "chilling effect" on free speech'. He argued that 'a narrow rule was appropriate for the age of globalisation' and that 'the Internet offer[ed] Australians the greatest hope of overcoming the tyranny of distance'. He submitted that Hedigan J had 'a national duty to decide that there was no jurisdiction in Australia even if [the judge] had a legal view to the contrary, and that it [wa]s [his Honour's] duty publicly to declare that Mr Gutnick's action against Dow Jones take place in New Jersey'. Robertson suggested that downloading is 'self-publishing' and that 'the process is akin to taking a book out of a library in New Jersey and taking it home to Victoria to read'. He 'flirted with the idea' that cyberspace should be a defamation-free zone,[15] and argued that the article was published 'in America for Americans' and that the events constituted 'a tort having an indelibly American complexion'.[16] The plaintiff submitted that publishing occurs when data is made 'intelligible or manifest to a third party' and argued that that has been the law for 400 years in other contexts.

Hedigan J rejected counsel's 'bold assertions', commenting that the unique nature of the internet must not lead to the abandonment of the analysis that the law has traditionally and reasonably followed to reach just conclusions. His Honour expressed concern that Robertson's arguments, 'attractively presented as they were,

---

14 *Australian Railways Union v Victorian Railways Commissioners* (1930) 44 CLR 319 at 33, per Dixon J.
15 See M Kirby, 'Privacy in cyberspace', (1998) *UNSW Law Journal* 47.
16 [2001] VSC 305, paras 15–20.

became enmeshed in pop science language' and degenerated into '"sloganeering" which in the end decides nothing'.[17]

Hedigan J referred to the following authorities to formulate his view. First, his Honour politely questioned the value of the decision in *Macquarie Bank v Berg*,[18] without making any attempt to directly address the issues raised in that case. He then referred to *Digital Equipment Corporation v Alta Vista Technology Inc.*, where to determine jurisdiction the court examined the question of whether the owner and controller of a website can with some degree of certainty 'know' if the content of the site reaches the user. The court, in that case, felt that:

> Using the Internet ... is as much knowingly 'sending'... as is a *telex, mail or telephonic transmission;. ...* ATI 'knows' that its Web-site reaches residents ... who choose to access it, just as surely as it 'knows' any letter or telephone call is likely to reach its destination.[19]

Lee Teck Chee v Merrill Lynch International Bank[20] involved the republication of a Singapore newspaper on the internet. Nathan J, of the High Court of Malaysia, held that publication had not taken place in Malaya because the alleged defamatory words had been published on a Singapore server. However, the judgement is of limited value as there was no evidence presented that any person in Malaya had accessed the website.

In *Kitakufe v Oloya Ltd*,[21] the Canadian court assumed jurisdiction for a defamatory statement made in a Ugandan newspaper republished on the internet. The plaintiff was a medical practitioner born in Uganda, but practising in Canada. The defendant argued that Uganda was a more convenient and natural forum, and that the proceedings had numerous real and significant links to Uganda. These included that the plaintiff had assets in Uganda, and that the defendant's concerns regarding malice, ethnic rivalry and the defence's credibility meant that the case would be better dealt with in Uganda. The defence also expressed concern about the significant expense and inconvenience of calling witnesses based in Uganda to a case run in Canada. Despite this multitude of connections with Uganda, Hume J assumed jurisdiction on the basis of access to the website and downloading, concluding that the court was 'not satisfied that the plaintiff would not be deprived of a legitimate personal and juridical advantage' if the case were run in Uganda. Hedigan J described this case as one where 'a superior court assumed jurisdiction over a defamation suit on the basis of access to the Website and its reception (that is, downloading) in Ontario, Canada'.

---

17 Ibid., paras 70 and 71.
18 [1999] NSWSC 526.
19 960 F. Supp. 456 (D Mass 1997) at 2, emphasis added.
20 [1998] CLJ 188.
21 [1998] OJ No. 2537 QL (Ont Gen Div).

In *Godfrey v Demon Internet Ltd*,[22] Moreland J determined that an internet bulletin board amounted to publishing postings to subscribers. Godfrey was a science lecturer in England and the defendant hosted a news group where users could post contributions to targeted discussions. One posting claimed to be posted by Godfrey, but in fact was written by an imposter. The posting was defamatory. Godfrey requested its removal within 10 days. The defendant did not and it remained online until it expired in the usual time (two weeks later). Moreland J held that the defendant had published the posting whenever a subscriber accessed the news group:

> In my judgment the defendant, whenever it transmits and whenever there is transmitted from the storage of its news server a defamatory posting, publish[es] that posting to any subscriber to its ISP who accesses the newsgroup containing that posting. Thus every time one of the defendant's customers accesses 'soc.culture.thai' and sees that posting defamatory of the plaintiff there is a publication to that customer.

Hedigan J took particular note of the expression 'sees that posting defamatory of the plaintiff': he regarded this as the equivalent of downloading.

Hedigan J cited *Calder v Jones*[23] with approval, referring to the statement of the US Supreme Court that 'jurisdiction may be exercised over a foreign defendant who directs his or her defamatory message at the forum and the plaintiff suffers harm there'.[24]

From these cases Hedigan J concluded that the place of defamation is 'the jurisdiction where the defamatory material was published and received by the plaintiff, rather than where it was spoken or written', and so the Dow Jones article was published in the state of Victoria when downloaded by Dow Jones subscribers who had met Dow Jones's payment conditions and used their passwords. The defendant's argument that it would be unfair for the publisher to have to litigate in the multitude of jurisdictions in which its statements are downloaded and read, he said, 'must be balanced against the world-wide inconvenience caused to litigants, from Outer Mongolia to the Outer Barcoo'. His Honour stated that 'if you do publish a libel justiciable in another country with its own laws … then you may be liable to pay damages for indulging that freedom'.[25]

Hedigan J considered the following additional factors as significant:

- the publication was downloaded in Victoria;
- the plaintiff's residence, business headquarters, family, social and business life are in Victoria;

---

22 [2001] QB 201.
23 465 US 783 (1984).
24 Counsel also referred to *R v Burdett* (1820) 4 B &Ald 115.
25 [2001] VSC 305, para 75.

- the plaintiff seeks to have his Victorian reputation vindicated by the courts of the state in which he lives;
- the plaintiff undertook not to sue in any other place.

His Honour concluded that given these factors 'it would be verging on the extraordinary to suggest that Mr Gutnick's action in respect of that part of the publication on which he sues should be removed for determination to the State of New Jersey'.[26] Dow Jones maintained that the article was 'indelibly American, written by Americans for Americans interested in the stock market and its affairs'. The weakness in this argument, writes Hedigan J, is that 'the aspect sued on by Mr Gutnick is indelibly Victorian, connected with no other place, and that any documentation or evidence concerning the matter will all be found in Victoria'.[27]

Less than one month after the judgement by Hedigan J, the Victorian Court of Appeal quickly – and with little consideration and analysis – dismissed the appeal by Dow Jones.[28] The issue then came before the High Court of Australia.

On 10 December 2002 the High Court of Australia handed down its decision in *Dow Jones v Gutnick*. By 7:0, but in four separate judgements, the High Court dismissed the appeal of Dow Jones. The court determined that publication of a defamatory statement for an online subscription website occurs at the place of downloading. Kirby J flagged the danger in finding otherwise, stating:

> To tell a person uploading potentially defamatory material onto a website ...
> [that that act] will render that person potentially liable to proceedings in
> courts of every legal jurisdiction where the subject enjoys a reputation, may
> have undesirable consequences. Depending on the publisher and the place
> of its assets, it might freeze publication or censor it or try to restrict access
> to it in certain countries so as to comply with the most restrictive defamation
> laws that could apply.[29]

Kirby J dealt with the legal response to the impact of the internet. His Honour described the internet as 'essentially a decentralised, self-maintained telecommunications network' which 'demands a radical reconceptualisation of the applicable common law'.[30] His Honour drew an analogy between the development of such new legal rules and the law merchant (*lex mercatoria*), which arose out of the general custom of the merchants of many nations in Europe.

26 Ibid., para 131.
27 Ibid., para 129.
28 *Dow Jones v Gutnick* [2001] VSCA 249. This judgement was less than two pages.
29 [2002] HCA 56, para 117.
30 Ibid., para 79.

Adventitious and opportunistic

Dow Jones submitted that the applicable law should be that of the place where the web servers were maintained, 'unless that place was merely adventitious or opportunistic'. Dow Jones recognised the argument that publishers could place their servers in jurisdictions most advantageous to them, but argued that it did not 'misuse' this rule, as the location of its servers was not determined for legal or advantageous considerations. Gleeson CJ, McHugh, Gummow and Hayne JJ stated that 'adventitious' and 'opportunistic' are words likely to produce considerable debate, and noted that a publisher may choose the server's location based on a range of factors, including costs of operation, benefits offered for setting up business, security, and continuity of service. They also noted that the publisher may have servers in more than one state or country.

The corollary argument was made that plaintiffs like Gutnick could choose the most favourable jurisdiction to them in which to commence proceedings, bypassing nations with free speech and freedom of expression. Gutnick's response was that whilst that may be so, on this occasion he sued in the jurisdiction of his business, domicile and residence, and sought no adventitious of opportunistic advantage.

The court's attitude towards either the plaintiff or the defendant choosing the most advantageous jurisdiction or the publisher placing its server in a jurisdiction with no defamation law remains untested.

Gleeson CJ, McHugh, Gummow and Hayne JJ suggested that 'reasonableness of the publisher's conduct' might be considered 'necessary or appropriate' as a common law defence where all the publisher's conduct occurred outside the jurisdiction. Their Honours identified relevant circumstances as 'including where that conduct took place, and what rules about defamation applied in that place or those places'. Their Honours drew an analogy with the developing defence of innocent dissemination.[31]

Kirby J described the dismissal of the appeal as 'contrary to intuition', and felt that it did 'not represent a wholly satisfactory outcome'. His Honour seemed to feel that a balance is yet to be determined between the human right of access to information and to free expression, and the human right to protection by law for the reputation and honour of individuals, and that this warrants 'national legislative attention and ... international discussion in a forum as global as the Internet itself'.[32]

The court determined that the place where damage was inflicted was a most significant factor. The place where the defamation was comprehended and the plaintiff's connection with the locality were also important factors.[33]

---

31 Ibid., para 51.
32 Ibid., para 166.
33 Postscript: The High Court of Australia determined that the Supreme Court of Victoria had jurisdiction, but it did not determine liability. The issue of defamation did not reach the court. Dow Jones made an out of court payment of $450,000, but claimed that the payment was not for defamation. Dow Jones claimed it was in the right and that the payment would not cover Gutnick's legal costs. Gutnick claimed vindication.

According to Gleeson CJ, McHugh, Gummow and Hayne JJ, the 'spectre which Dow Jones [seeks] to conjure up' – that a publisher would be forced to consider, for every article it publishes on the internet, 'the defamation laws of every country from Afghanistan to Zimbabwe' – is:

> unreal when it is recalled that in all except the most unusual of cases, identifying the person about whom material is to be published will readily identify the defamation law to which that person may resort.[34]

Effects test

One solution may be the adoption of an effects test. *Calder v Jones*[35] concerned Shirley Jones, an Academy award-winning actress who lived and worked in California. Jones was defamed by an article in the *National Enquirer* which was published in Florida but had a nationwide circulation, including a substantial readership in California. The defendants challenged the jurisdiction of the Californian courts. The US Supreme Court held that California was the 'focal point both of the story and of the harm suffered'. This joint 'target' and 'harm' criteria is often referred to as the 'effects test':

> The allegedly libelous story concerned the California activities of a California resident. It impugned the professionalism of an entertainer whose television career was centered in California. The article was drawn from California sources, and the brunt of the harm, in terms both of respondent's emotional distress and the injury to her professional reputation, was suffered in California. In sum, California is the focal point both of the story and of the harm suffered. Jurisdiction over petitioners is therefore proper in California based on the 'effects' of their Florida conduct in California ... The mere fact that [the defendant] can 'foresee' that the article will be circulated and have an effect in California is not sufficient for an assertion of jurisdiction ... [The defendants] are not charged with mere untargeted negligence. Rather, their intentional, and allegedly tortious, actions were expressly aimed at California. Under the circumstances, petitioners must 'reasonably anticipate being hauled into court there' to answer for the truth of the statements made in their article.[36]

This case did not involve the internet or cyberspace, but its approach has been used and quoted in cyberspace jurisdiction cases.[37] The concept that a person

---

34 [2002] HCA 56, para 54.
35 465 US 783 (1984).
36 465 US 783 (1984), 788–89.
37 For example, by Hedigan J in *Gutnick v Dow Jones* [2001] VSC 305 and *Healthgrades.com v Northwest Healthcare Alliance* No. 01–35648 (9th Cir 2002).

ought to be liable for a deliberate act which targets another jurisdiction and causes harm there clearly can be useful for cyberspace quandaries.

The effects test can be compared to the terminatory theory of criminal law espoused by Professor Glanville Williams[38] and approved by Stephen J in *Ward v R*.[39] It is the place where the physical act took effect on its victim, not where the physical act of perpetrator was done, that determines the locus of the crime and, in turn, which courts have jurisdiction in respect of that act.

In *Dow Jones v Gutnick*, Gleeson CJ, McHugh, Gummow and Hayne JJ endorsed the effects test approach:

> Activities that have effects beyond the jurisdiction in which they are done may properly be the concern of the legal systems in each place. In considering where the tort of defamation occurs it is important to recognise the purposes served by the law regarding the conduct as tortious: purposes that are not confined to regulating publishers.[40]

Australian cases

The first Australian case with an element of internet jurisdiction is *Macquarie Bank v Berg*.[41] Berg was a disgruntled ex-employee of Macquarie Bank who placed defamatory material regarding the bank and its senior employees on a website. Berg had moved to California and the material in question was located on a server there, but could be accessed and viewed in New South Wales. Macquarie Bank sought an *ex parte* interlocutory injunction to restrain publication of the material on the internet. Simpson J, bearing in mind the fact that publication on the internet is continuous, 24 hours a day, for as long as the material remains online, described the difficulties of such a request in the following terms:

> [O]nce published on the Internet, material is transmitted anywhere in the world that has an Internet connection ... to make the order as initially sought, would have the effect of restraining publication of all the material presently contained on the website to any place in the world. Recognising the difficulties associated with orders of such breadth, [counsel] sought to narrow the claim by limiting the order sought to publication or dissemination 'within NSW'. The limitation, however, is ineffective.[42]

---

38 See G Williams, 'Venue and the ambit of criminal law', Part 3, (1965) 81 *Law Quarterly Review* 518.
39 *Ward v R* [1980] HCA 11, para 4 per Stephen J.
40 [2002] HCA 56, para 24.
41 [1999] NSWSC 526.
42 [1999] NSWSC 526, para 12.

Simpson J did not accept jurisdiction and refused to grant the injunction. However, her Honour reasoned thus (spuriously, in my view):

> The difficulties are obvious. An injunction to restrain defamation in NSW is designed to ensure compliance with the laws of NSW, and to protect the rights of plaintiffs, as those rights are defined by the law of NSW. Such an injunction is not designed to superimpose the law of NSW relating to defamation on every other state, territory and country of the world. Yet that would be the effect of an order restraining publication on the Internet. It is not to be assumed that the law of defamation in other countries is coextensive with that of NSW, and indeed, one knows that it is not. It may very well be that, according to the law of the Bahamas, Tazhakistan, or Mongolia, the defendant has an unfettered right to publish the material. To make an order interfering with such a right would exceed the proper limits of the use of the injunctive power of this court.[43]

The mere fact that a website reaches another jurisdiction is not a sufficient ground to grant or assume that jurisdiction. However, Berg clearly had several connections with New South Wales, and the website was dedicated entirely to Macquarie Bank and its senior employees. In terms of an effects test, the target and the harm were entirely in New South Wales, so Berg ought to have expected to be brought before the courts there.

The factors against the grant of jurisdiction included the enforceability of such an order, the undesirability of superimposing the defamation law of New South Wales onto every other state, territory and country of the world, and the interlocutory nature of the application.[44]

The NSW Supreme Court had the opportunity to revisit the *Macquarie Bank Limited v Berg* case in mid-2002.[45] Smart AJ distinguished the *Dow Jones* case, noting, without deciding the issue, that 'Gutnick was not concerned with the World Wide Web because Dow Jones only put its material on for subscribers or trial subscribers.'[46]

Though the *Dow Jones* case caused international concern, its impact has been limited, implicitly if not expressly, to subscription websites. In *Ward Group Pty Ltd v Brodie & Stone Plc*,[47] the Federal Court of Australia distinguished the Dow Jones case:

> As the allegedly defamatory publication was made available to subscribers in Victoria on the Internet, no issue arose about the publication of that material in Victoria. Therefore that case is of no assistance to the Ward Group.[48]

43 Ibid., para 14.
44 Ibid., see paras 14–16.
45 [2002] NSWSC 254.
46 Ibid., para 41.
47 [2005] FCA 471.
48 Ibid., para 42.

However, the Federal Court accepted a test implicitly identical to the effects test in *Calder v Jones*. The court in that case held that the use of a trade mark on the internet, uploaded on a website outside of Australia, without more, is not a use by the website proprietor of the mark in each jurisdiction where the mark is down-loaded. However:

> if there is evidence that the use was specifically intended to be made in, or *directed or targeted at*, a particular jurisdiction then there is likely to be a use in that jurisdiction when the mark is downloaded. Of course, once the website intends to make and makes a specific use of the mark in relation to a particular person or persons in a jurisdiction there will be little difficulty in concluding that the website proprietor used the mark in that jurisdiction when the mark is downloaded.[49]

In what began as an April Fools' Day joke, Dow Jones, through its publication the *Wall Street Journal*, published an article about the floating of shares by Harrods, with the headline 'The Enron of Britain?' Action was commenced by Harrods in England, claiming that the article caused serious damage to the company's reputa-tion. Dow Jones filed suit in the Southern District of New York, seeking to block the action. In the US case Judge Marrero said that Dow Jones was eager to avoid a British trial because Britain's libel laws were far more friendly to plaintiffs.[50] In a declaratory judgement, Judge Marrero expressed concern that any relief granted by the New York court would nevertheless be subject to recognition and enforce-ment in the United Kingdom. Dow Jones argued that a declaratory judgement was appropriate in that it would free them from 'vexatious and oppressive' litigation abroad. In refusing relief, the judge held that granting authority to enjoin foreign lawsuits should be done sparingly and only with care and restraint.

In *Jamieson v Chiropractic Board of Australia*,[51] the Queensland *Limitation of Actions Act 1974* provides for a 12-month limitation period 'after the date of publication'. White JA, with whom the other two justices agreed, commented that legal advice to the Applicant 'regarded this, arguably erroneously, as the date [on which] the statement was uploaded'. Her honour hypothesised that this advice was 'perhaps, due to a mistaken understanding that uploaded material on to an internet website … was akin to the factual inference of publication readily drawn in the case of a widely circulating newspaper or magazine'.[52] The Court of Appeal cited with approval the *Dow Jones* case and *Sands v Channel Seven Adelaide*.[53] In the latter case the South Australian court stated that the action arises at the place

---

49 Ibid., para 43, emphasis added.
50 *Dow Jones & Co. Inc. v Harrods Ltd*, 237 F. Supp. 2d 394 (SD NY 2002).
51 [2011] QCA 56.
52 Ibid., para 13.
53 [2009] SASC 215.

where the material is downloaded, which will also be the place where the tort of defamation is committed.[54]

In *Paramasivam v Sabanathan*:[55]

- Words said in court by the lawyer in Sri Lanka – the place of the tort is Sri Lanka.
- Phone call initiated in Australia received in Sri Lanka – publication is in Sri Lanka (per *Dow Jones & Company Inc v Gutnick*).
- The more pertinent question is whether the court should, in the circumstances, decline to exercise its jurisdiction on the basis that this is a clearly inappropriate forum for the trial of the plaintiff's cause.
- Strong basis for concluding that it was a clearly inappropriate forum.

The NSW Supreme Court denied jurisdiction, concluding that if the relevant words were said in court by the lawyer in Sri Lanka, then the place of the tort is Sri Lanka. If instructions were given by telephone to the lawyer in Sri Lanka, then the publication is also in Sri Lanka, based on the principles in the *Dow Jones* case. However, the court considered that the 'identification of the place of publication' is not the key element in determining jurisdiction. The court regarded whether or not New South Wales was 'a clearly inappropriate forum for the trial of the plaintiff's cause' as the 'more pertinent question'.[56]

In *Jenman v McIntyre*,[57] the NSW Supreme Court held that to take jurisdiction requires proof that the material was downloaded from a website and seen by at least one person.[58] Similarly, the same court, in *Munn v Tunks*, held that jurisdiction arises where the material is downloaded in a form able to be comprehended by a reader, not when it is posted on a website.[59] In *Wells v Commonwealth of Australia*, the NSW Supreme Court stated that the 'determination of the place of the tort requires an assessment of the defendant's conduct, not [of] the plaintiff's damage'.[60]

Early US experience

The early cases emanated from the United States, where disputes arose between parties in different states. Although these US cases involved constitutional factors, more than one common law jurisdiction has been guided by them.[61]

---

54 Ibid., para 389. See also *Al Amoudi v Brisard* [2006] EWHC 1062.
55 [2013] NSWSC 1033.
56 Ibid., paras 19 and 20.
57 [2013] NSWSC 1100.
58 Ibid., paras 3 and 20.
59 [2013] NSWSC 1263, para 22.
60 [2014] NSWSC 148, para 38.
61 For example, see the British Columbia Court of Appeal in *Braintech Inc. v Kostiuk* (1999) 63 BCLR (3d) 156 and the High Court of Delhi in *Yahoo! Inc. v Akash Arora* (1999) PTC (19) 210 (Delhi).

In the United States, to determine personal jurisdiction, it is sufficient if the defendant 'purposefully availed' itself of the jurisdiction (such as by repeatedly conducting business there). US courts are required to use due process under the 14th Amendment to the *US Constitution*. In *International Shoe Co. v Washington*,[62] the US Supreme Court held that due process requires the defendant to have 'minimum contacts' with the plaintiff's jurisdiction and prescribes that the choice of jurisdiction be consistent with 'traditional notions of fair play and substantial justice'.[63]

The 'purposeful availment' requirement ensures that random and fortuitous contacts do not cause a defendant to be improperly brought into a forum. The 'fair play' requirement permits the court to examine whether the defendant's acts or their consequences have sufficient connection with the state to make jurisdiction reasonable.

Early cyberspace cases mistakenly granted jurisdiction merely on the basis that the defendant's website could be accessed in the plaintiff's jurisdiction. In *Inset System Inc. v Instruction Set Inc.*,[64] the court, on hearing evidence that as many as 10,000 residents of the state could access the website, granted jurisdiction over a defendant who maintained a mere passive website. This number of potential users is now ridiculously conservative.

In *Minnesota v Granite Gate Resorts Inc.*,[65] the Minnesota court examined five factors: the quantity of contacts; the quality of contacts; the connection between the cause of action and the contacts; the state's interest; and the convenience of the parties.

The courts later distinguish between passive and active websites. Passive sites merely display information. Active websites may provide for form filling, and for contracting online, or may simply provide an email link. On this basis, in *Zippo Manufacturing Co. v Zippo Dot Com Inc.*,[66] the court formulated a sliding scale approach which has since been generally adopted.

At one end of the scale:

> are situations where a defendant has simply posted information on an Internet Web site which is accessible to users in foreign jurisdictions. A passive Web site that does little more than make information available to those who are interested in it is not grounds for the exercise of personal jurisdiction.[67]

---

62 326 US 310 (1945).
63 Ibid., 316.
64 937 F. Supp. 161 (D Conn 1996). See also *Maritz Inc. v Cybergold Inc.* 947 F. Supp. 1328 (ED Mo 1996).
65 568 NW 2d 715.
66 952 F. Supp. 1119 (WD Pa 1997) ('*Zippo's* case'). See also *Helicopteros Nationales de Columbia SA v Hall* 466 US 408.
67 952 F. Supp. 1119, 1124 (WD Pa 1997).

For example, in *Bensusan Restaurant Corp. v King*,[68] the plaintiff was the owner of the well-known Blue Note jazz nightclub in New York. The defendants advertised their nightclub, which had the same name, in Missouri; it catered mainly for local university students. Notwithstanding evidence that New York residents both accessed and indeed made bookings based on the information from the Missouri website, the Appeals Court held that passive websites do not meet the standard of 'purposeful availment'. There was no element of 'targeting' (see Effects test, above) and accordingly no substantial connection was created.[69]

In *Webber v Jolly Hotels*,[70] the New Jersey-based plaintiff booked a holiday in Italy online. The defendant ran several hotels in Italy and had no connection with the United States. The website provided photographs of hotel rooms, descriptions of hotel facilities, information about numbers of rooms and telephone numbers. The plaintiff was injured whilst on holiday in the defendant's hotel. She commenced proceedings in New Jersey. The court held that it lacked jurisdiction over the defendant. Access to the website alone was held to be insufficient. The court required continuous and substantial contacts with the forum to establish the defendant's personal jurisdiction:

> exercising jurisdiction over a defendant who merely advertises its services or product on the Internet would violate the Due Process Clause of the Fourteenth Amendment [and] would disrespect the principles established by International Shoe.

The defendant's website provided no more than passive advertising information.[71]
At the other end of the scale:

> are situations where a defendant clearly does business over the Internet. If the defendant enters into contracts with residents of a foreign jurisdiction that involve the knowing and repeated transmission of computer files over the Internet, personal jurisdiction is proper.[72]

The Appeals Court in *Zippo's* case cited *Compuserve Inc. v Patterson*[73] as an example: there the defendant had purposefully directed his business activities towards residents of another state and the repeated transmissions showed a substantial

---

68 937 F. Supp. 296 (SD NY 1996).
69 See also *Cybersell Inc. v Cybersell Inc.* 130 F. 3d 414 (9th Cir 1997).
70 977 F. Supp. 327 (D NJ 1997).
71 See also *Casio India Co. Ltd v Ashita Tele Systems Pvt Ltd* (2003 (27) PTC 265 (Del)), where the Delhi High Court held that once a website can be accessed from Delhi, it is enough to invoke the territorial jurisdiction of the court.
72 *Zippo Manufacturing Co. v Zippo Dot Com Inc.* 952 F. Supp. 1119 (WD Pa 1997), 1124.
73 89 F. 3d 1257 (6th Cir 1996).

connection with that state. Acts such as selling goods or services would in all likelihood be sufficient to constitute 'business' on the internet.

In *Playboy Enterprises Inc. v Chuckleberry Publishing Inc.*,[74] the court held that the Italy-based defendant actively solicited US customers to its internet site, and in doing so had distributed its product within the United States in breach of a contempt order. One of defendant's websites was not just a source of passive information, but was a 'pay' site. The defendant knew that US citizens accessed its site and ought to have expected to be held accountable for its breach of the contempt order. Taking jurisdiction was thus appropriate.

The middle ground is occupied by interactive websites where a user can exchange information with the host computer. In these cases, the exercise of jurisdiction is determined by examining the level of interactivity and commercial nature of the exchange of information that occurs on the website.[75]

These initial cases are difficult to reconcile as they are complicated by non-internet factors and by the varying degrees of judicial understanding of the technology involved.[76] First, the defendant must have acted deliberately and purposefully. The courts then determine the defendant's level of cognisance. Next, the defendant must have targeted or singled out a particular forum. If the defendant has repeatedly and knowingly engaged in business with the plaintiff, the grant of jurisdiction is more likely.

Universal rights

Australia and the United States are signatories to the UN *International Covenant on Civil and Political Rights* (ICCPR). In *Dow Jones*, Kirby J argued that the Australian courts must uphold the right to freedom of speech and freedom of expression as enunciated in Article 19 of the ICCPR:

Article 19

1. Everyone shall have the right to hold opinions without interference.
2. Everyone shall have the right to freedom of expression; this right shall include freedom to seek, receive and impart information and ideas of all kinds, regardless of frontiers, either orally, in writing or in print, in the form of art, or through any other media of his choice.

---

74 939 F. Supp. 1032 (SD NY 1996).
75 *Zippo Manufacturing Co. v Zippo Dot Com Inc.* 952 F. Supp. 1119 (WD Pa 1997), 1124.
76 Criticism has been levelled at the minimum contacts test in relation to the internet and as to what level of interactivity is required to trigger jurisdiction. The required level of 'interactivity' can be gleaned from *Compuserve v Patterson* 89 F. 3d 1257 (6th Cir 1996) and *Cybersell Inc. v Cybersell Inc.* 130 F. 3d 414 (9th Cir 1997).

3. The exercise of the rights provided for in paragraph 2 of this article carries with it special duties and responsibilities. It may therefore be subject to certain restrictions, but these shall only be such as are provided by law and are necessary:

    (a) For respect of the rights or reputations of others;

    (b) For the protection of national security or of public order (ordre public), or of public health or morals.

Kirby J was the only High Court Justice to address the effect of this article of the covenant. However, his Honour balanced this with the requirements of Articles 17.1 and 17.2:

Article 17

1. No one shall be subjected to arbitrary or unlawful interference with his privacy, family, home or correspondence, nor to unlawful attacks on his honour and reputation.

2. Everyone has the right to the protection of the law against such interference or attacks.

On the one hand, Kirby J stated that any development of the common law of Australia should be consistent with the ICCPR principles, to the extent that Australian law does not provide effective legal protection for the honour, reputation and personal privacy of individuals: 'Australia, like other nations so obliged, is rendered accountable to the relevant treaty body for such default'[77] pursuant to the first Optional Protocol to the ICCPR.

On the other hand, he foreshadowed Dow Jones' plea, stating the 'the need for a clear and single rule to govern the conduct in question according to pre-established norms'.

In response to the High Court's decision, Dow Jones issued a press release supporting an action by William Alpert, the author of the article in question. In 2003 Alpert stated that he was filing an action with the Human Rights Commission in Geneva, fearing unjustified restrictions on journalists. Alpert stated:

> I am filing this action with the Human Rights Commission in Geneva because I fear restrictions on the ability of financial journalists such as myself to report truthfully to United States investors on the activities of foreigners who are actively engaged in the U.S. markets. I even fear for our ability to report on U.S. corporations and business people, who might see the High Court's decision as an invitation to attack the U.S. press in a remote forum. Given the differences between the laws of Australia and those of other countries in the Commonwealth and beyond, the impact of Australia's law – as laid out by the High Court – could harm journalists throughout the world. Powerful

---

77 *Dow Jones v Gutnick* [2002] HCA 56, para 116.

and sophisticated plaintiffs could search out overseas jurisdictions willing to help stifle news coverage that was only directed at local readers in those journalists' home markets.

Australia has accepted the jurisdiction of the U.N. Human Rights Committee and is obliged to modify Australia's libel laws, should the Committee find that those laws unduly restrict the right of free speech that's protected under Article 19 of the International Convention on Human Rights.

I hope that the Human Rights Committee will recognize the threat to free speech – and an informed public – posed by Australian laws that allow suit against any journalist, anywhere that an article published on the internet can be downloaded. Perhaps the Government of Australia will recognize the need to modify its laws, even before the Human Rights Committee takes up this case.[78]

This foreshadowed action may have been politic, but it seems that it did not in fact proceed.

Council of Europe Cybercrime Convention

The *Convention* is the first international treaty dealing with internet and computer network crimes. It covers issues such as copyright infringement, computer-related fraud, child pornography and network security. It contains significant law enforcement powers and procedures. The *Convention* commenced in 2004 and has been adopted extensively, not only by European nations but also by Australia, the United States, Canada and Japan.

Jurisdiction arises pursuant to the *Convention* where the cybercrime was committed in a member's territory; on board a ship flying the flag of the country; on board an aircraft registered in country; or by one of the country's nationals (if the offence is punishable where it was committed or if the offence is committed outside the territorial jurisdiction of any state).

Single publication rule

Most US states have adopted a single publication rule which treats all sales of a defamatory book or newspaper as a single publication. The time of the single publication (download) is fixed as the time of the first publication. In the United

---

78 Dow Jones press release, April 2003.

Kingdom and Australia each publication gives rise to a separate cause of action. That principle was confirmed by the English Court of Appeal in *Loutchansky v Times Newspapers Ltd (Nos 2–5)*.[79]

Samuels JA's observation in *Australian Broadcasting Corporation v Waterhouse*,[80] that a single publication rule could only be introduced throughout Australia by statute, was approved by Kirby J in *Dow Jones v Gutnick*.[81]

In the same case Gaudron J described the single publication rule as 'a legal fiction which deems a widely disseminated communication … to be a single communication regardless of the number of people to whom, or the number of states in which, it is circulated'.[82] Dow Jones described the Australian position as 'primitive'.[83]

Callinan J rejected Dow Jones' submission that publication occurs at one place, such as the place where the matter is provided, or first published, on the grounds that that view 'cannot withstand any reasonable test of certainty and fairness'. However, he expressed concern that publishers would set up in a 'defamation free jurisdiction' or one in which the defamation laws are tilted towards defendants. Why, he asked, 'would publishers, owing duties to their shareholders to maximise profits, do otherwise?'[84]

Gleeson CJ, McHugh, Gummow and Hayne JJ noted that in *Firth v State of New York*[85] the New York Court of Appeals decided that the one-year statute of limitations in New York runs from the first posting of defamatory matter upon an internet site and that the single publication rule applies to that first posting. The Australian position on the position of the limitation period is yet to be determined.

In *Harrods Limited v Dow Jones & Co. Inc.*,[86] Justice Eady noted the limited amount of publication in England (only 10 copies) of the *Wall Street Journal* and that there were very few English hits on the *Wall Street Journal* website. Nevertheless, jurisdiction was granted to protect a reputation in England. His Honour rejected the single publication rule, which provides that a defendant should only be sued in the place of the first publication of the defamatory material, finding instead that if a target of a publication is based in England, then an online or offline publisher can be brought before the UK courts.

---

79 [2002] QB 783.
80 (1991) 25 NSWLR 519.
81 [2002] HCA 56, para 127.
82 Ibid. See Debra Cohen, 'The single publication rule: One action, not one law', (1966) 62 *Brooklyn Law Review* 921.
83 See also *Leighton v Garnham* [2012] WASC 314, para 48.
84 [2002] HCA 56, para 199.
85 775 NE 2d 463 (2002).
86 [2003] EWHC 1162.

Substantial publication

Jurisdiction was not taken by the English courts in *Jameel v Dow Jones & Co. Inc.*,[87] where Dow Jones published the article 'WAR ON TERROR, List of Early al Qaeda Donors Points to Saudi Elite, Charities' in the *Wall Street Journal,* allegedly defaming Yousef Jameel, a Saudi businessman. Jameel was unable to prove 'substantial harm'. Although there were 6000 online subscribers to the *Wall Street Journal,* technical evidence showed that only five subscribers had actually accessed the article, and that three of those five were associated with Jameel. The other two subscribers had no knowledge of or connection to Jameel. The court ruled that without a 'substantial' publication in England, there could have been no damage to Jameel's reputation.

Uniform defamation legislation – choice of law

From 1 January 2006, in all states and territories in Australia except the Northern Territory, legislation for uniform defamation law commenced:[88]

Choice of law for defamation proceedings
(1) If a matter is published wholly within a particular Australian jurisdictional area, the substantive law that is applicable in that area must be applied in this jurisdiction to determine any cause of action for defamation based on the publication.

(2) If there is a multiple publication of matter in more than one Australian jurisdictional area, the substantive law applicable in the Australian jurisdictional area with which the harm occasioned by the publication as a whole has its closest connection must be applied in this jurisdiction to determine each cause of action for defamation based on the publication.

(3) In determining the Australian jurisdictional area with which the harm occasioned by a publication of matter has its closest connection, a court may take into account:
  (a) the place at the time of publication where the plaintiff was ordinarily resident or, in the case of a corporation that may assert a cause of action for defamation, the place where the corporation had its principal place of business at that time, and
  (b) the extent of publication in each relevant Australian jurisdictional area, and

---

87 [2005] EWCA Civ 75.
88 The Northern Territory's uniform legislation commenced on 26 April 2006. See Chapter 7.

(c)   the extent of harm sustained by the plaintiff in each relevant Australian jurisdictional area, and

(d)   any other matter that the court considers relevant.[89]

Subsection (2) in particular assists in determining jurisdiction within Australia. This
provision is in part a codification of the 'effects test' postulated in the US case
of *Calder v Jones*.[90]

Conclusion

The application of traditional rules has proved appropriate for cases such as
Bensusan and Macquarie Bank. Where the internet is used peripherally – for example, where conduct remains in a single, specific, geographical location – the
mere use of the internet should not complicate the application of the jurisdictional principles.

In the absence of an unusual feature involving the internet as the medium of
choice, courts should apply the usual principles for jurisdictional questions. Quite
often there are a number of factors involved in a given dispute, including the use of
the telephone and mail. Any peripheral effect of the internet should be disregarded
unless it is central to the dispute. Where the internet is central to a dispute, consideration should be given to the effect of non-internet factors. The mere possibility
of access to a website should be insufficient grounds for jurisdiction. Similarly, the
mere viewing of a site, as opposed to engaging in some further interaction, should
be disregarded. The courts should adopt the distinction between passive and active
sites. The greater the degree of interactivity, the greater the likelihood that the site's
owner is engaging, or should be aware that he or she is engaging, in commerce
with the user. Correspondingly, where the site owner purposefully avails himself
or herself of the benefits of commerce from that jurisdiction, he or she should be
more likely to be subject to that jurisdiction. If courts take jurisdiction too broadly
or recklessly there should be legislative intervention to impose a fairness requirement similar to the approach taken in the US cases.[91] The effect of action by the
defendant and its likelihood to result in harm to a known target will also affect the
courts' reasoning in taking jurisdiction.

---

89 *Defamation Act 2005* (NSW) s11, *Defamation Act 2005* (Qld) s11, *Defamation Act 2005* (Tas)
s11, *Defamation Act 2005* (Vic) s11, *Defamation Act 2005* (WA) s11, *Defamation Act 2005*
(SA) s11; *Defamation Act 2006* (NT) s10; and *Civil Law (Wrongs) Act 2002* (ACT) s123.

90 See Effects test, above.

91 In relation to due process and the 14th Amendment, see *International Shoe Co. v Washington*
326 US 310.

The development of the internet permits various uses.[92] Distinctions will continue to be made between the intended, expected and foreseeable consequences of those uses. The typical website is open to the world, and evidence of use and access within a court's jurisdiction is necessary before that court will grant jurisdiction. The same cannot be said of subscription websites, where it is reasonable to assume use and access by subscribers. Discussion forums or bulletin boards may similarly be open or closed. Proof of use and of impact are necessary for jurisdiction to be granted. Electronic mail is less of an issue, as it is typically targeted. Nevertheless, the location of the recipient, the computer and server become complicating factors.

FURTHER READING

Anonymous, 'A "category-specific" legislative approach to the internet personal jurisdiction problem in US law', (2004) 117 *Harvard Law Review* 1617.

Debra Cohen, 'The single publication rule: One action, not one law', (1966) 62 *Brooklyn Law Review* 921.

---

92 For example, *Australian Football League v Age Company Ltd* [2006] VSC 308 involved a discussion forum. The Victorian Supreme Court described the discussion forum as enabling 'opinions, gossip, trivia, rumour and speculation to be published as an assertion of fact by anonymous contributors' (para 55).

18

CYBERCRIME

In the online era, both law-abiding and nefarious kinds of order have emerged. Society has demanded that steps be taken in response to criminal behaviour that involves the internet and other modern tools: steps that are technological, practical and legal.

The advance of information technology and computer technology has led to a corresponding increase in computer crime. There is no accepted definition of computer crime. Computers may be the subject of a crime, such as theft, or a computer may be used to commit a crime.[1] Often, a computer is used, or misused, to elicit or manipulate data or processing. Simple unlawful access to a computer system can be regarded as an offence. Telecommunications may be involved. The result may be a transfer of funds or of confidential information. Sending an email to place a virus can be unlawful. The free flow of information has generated undesirable and abhorrent material. The public has expressed concern about pornography, information on how to make bombs and information about ways to commit suicide. New offences have been created in response to these concerns. Persons gaining unlawful access to computers for these purposes are typically referred to as 'crackers': hackers with malicious intent. Many crimes that are not specifically related to computers can be substantially facilitated by the use of computers. Crimes involving electronic commerce typically involve the use of computers and telecommunications. This area is often referred to as 'cybercrime'.

More than 90 per cent of Australian homes have a computer in them. In addition to home subscriptions to the internet, almost 10 million Australians connect to the internet via their mobile phones and other devices. The Norton Cybercrime Report 2013 stated that the costs to consumers worldwide of cybercrime exceeded $113 billion, reaching more than $1 billion in Australia with more than 5 million victims. The international cost of cybercrime is greater than the global expenditure on marijuana, cocaine and heroin combined. The average direct cost per cybercrime in Australia was $201 in 2013, compared to $306 in 2012. This may be due to cybercriminals having to shift tactics as users become more educated in cyberscams. However, there is much cybercrime that is not reported to authorities, particularly by companies that do not wish to expose their securities issues.[2]

The most common breaches involve viruses (programs or codes that can replicate themselves and 'infect' computers without the owner's consent and often without the owner's knowledge), worms (programs or codes which replicate themselves using a network system, and that are designed to cause damage) and Trojan infections (code incorporated into an existing program which gives the appearance of performing a desirable function but which in fact performs malicious functions).

---

1 The US has many unique examples of computer crime – stealing an ATM with a front-end loader or shooting an ATM with a handgun.

2 Norton Cybercrime Report 2013, see <www.symantec.com>.

Security breaches – viruses, laptop theft and financial fraud, in particular – generated the highest cost to the organisations.

This chapter examines unlawful access, malicious damage, spam, cyberstalking, internet gambling, child pornography and child grooming online and more.

The Commonwealth *Criminal Code* and computer crime

In Australia cybercrime is generally dealt with by federal law, because the *Australian Constitution* includes 'postal, telegraphic, telephonic, and other like services' as legislative powers of the federal Parliament.[3] Although the drafters of the *Constitution* did not envisage the internet, the power has been interpreted as including modern telecommunications.[4] The majority of computer crime is committed using telecommunication networks such as telephone systems and the internet.

Amendments to the *Crimes Act 1914* (Cth) in 1989 introduced a range of computer offences. These have been superseded by amendments to the *Criminal Code 1995* (Cth) by the *Cybercrime Act 2001* (Cth)[5] and by the *Crimes Legislation Amendment (Telecommunications Offences and Other Measures) Act (No. 2) 2004* (Cth). The *Cybercrime Act* was based on the 25th draft of the *Council of Europe Convention on Cybercrime*,[6] released on 22 December 2000.[7] The Council of Europe released the Final Draft in 2001 and the *Convention* became operative in 2004.[8]

The *Cybercrime Act* inserted seven computer offences into the *Criminal Code 1995* (Cth).

It is an offence to access or modify computer data or impair electronic communications to or from a computer without authority, with the intention of committing a serious offence.[9] A 'serious offence' is defined as an offence punishable by five or more years' imprisonment. The maximum penalty for this offence is equal to the maximum penalty for the serious offence. For example, if a person hacked into a bank computer and accessed credit card details with the intention of using the details to obtain money, the maximum penalty would be equivalent to

---

3 *Australian Constitution* s51(v).
4 Geraldine Chin, 'Technological change and the Australian Constitution', (2000) *Melbourne University Law Review* 25. See *R v Brislan; Ex parte Williams* (1935) 54 CLR 262 and *Jones v Commonwealth [No. 2]* (1965) 112 CLR 206.
5 See Second reading speech of Attorney-General Daryl Williams, <www.aph.gov.au/legis.htm>.
6 See Cybercrime Bill 2001 (Cth) Explanatory Memorandum.
7 See Council of Europe: <conventions.coe.int>.
8 Ibid.
9 *Criminal Code 1995* (Cth) s477.1.

that for the fraud offence – 10 years' imprisonment. 'Data' includes 'information in any form ... or any program (or part of a program)'.[10] 'Electronic communication' is defined as 'communication by means of guided or unguided electromagnetic energy or both'.[11]

Proving intent is always problematic. Hackers often experiment with computer code, unsure of the consequences and with no specific intent. It is an offence for a person to cause unauthorised modification of data in a computer where that person is reckless as to whether that modification will impair data. The maximum penalty for this offence is 10 years' imprisonment. The offence covers a range of situations, including a person who obtains unauthorised access to a computer system and impairs data and a person who circulates a disk that contains a computer virus which then infects a Commonwealth computer.[12]

Another offence is causing an unauthorised impairment of electronic communications to or from a computer knowing that such impairment is unauthorised. This prohibits strategies such as 'denial of service attacks', where, for example, a service provider is swamped by useless messages causing the service to be inoperable. This offence recognises the importance of internet communications. The maximum penalty for this offence is, again, 10 years' imprisonment.[13]

It is an offence for an unauthorised person to access or modify data that is protected by a password or some other security feature. This is referred to as 'restricted data'. The offence targets hackers attempting to circumvent password-protected computer systems.[14] 'Restricted data' is defined as '(a) data held in a computer; and (b) to which access is restricted by an access control system associated with a function of the computer'.[15] The maximum penalty for this offence is 2 years' imprisonment.

The *Criminal Code* targets destructive actions such as passing a magnet over a credit card or cutting a computer disk in half. Specifically, it is an offence to cause unauthorised impairment of the reliability, security or operation of any data held on a Commonwealth computer disk or credit card or other device. The maximum penalty for this offence is 2 years' imprisonment.[16]

Finding evidence of these computer offences is problematic. They may be difficult to trace, and have originated within another jurisdiction. In an attempt to address such concerns, the *Criminal Code* also makes it an offence to possess, control or supply data or programs which are intended for use in the commission

10 *Criminal Code 1995* (Cth) Dictionary.
11 *Criminal Code 1995* (Cth) Dictionary.
12 *Criminal Code 1995* (Cth) s477.2.
13 *Criminal Code 1995* (Cth) s477.3.
14 *Criminal Code 1995* (Cth) s478.1.
15 *Criminal Code 1995* (Cth) s478.1.
16 *Criminal Code 1995* (Cth) s478.2.

of a computer offence. The maximum penalty for each of these offences is 3 years' imprisonment. The offences cover persons who possess, create or trade in programs and technology designed to hack or damage other computer systems.[17]

Telecommunications services

The *Criminal Code 1995* (Cth) Part 10.6 contains comprehensive provisions dealing with telecommunications services.[18] Division 473 of Part 10.6 includes a broad list of definitions which are technology-specific. Division 474 contains the substantive provisions dealing with telecommunications offences. These include criminal offences that involve use of the internet and other telecommunications and carriage services: internet child pornography and child abuse and assisting suicide.[19]

Part 10.6 applies to the generic medium of 'carriage service', which includes the internet, email and SMS messages. 'Carriage service' is given the same meaning as in the *Telecommunications Act 1997* (Cth): 'a service for carrying communications by means of guided and/or unguided electromagnetic energy'.[20] Guided electromagnetic energy utilises a physical means such as a wire, cables and optical fibre: unguided electromagnetic energy includes radio and infrared waves.[21] It is a broad definition, intended to cover future technologies.

Division 474 begins with general dishonesty provisions. A person is guilty of an offence if the person does anything with the intention of dishonestly obtaining a gain from, or causing a loss to, a carriage service provider by way of the supply of a carriage service. A person similarly commits an offence for knowingly risking such a loss. Dishonesty is determined by reference to the standards of ordinary people. The maximum penalty is 5 years' imprisonment.[22]

The focus of Division 474 is the misuse of carriage services and telecommunications, including International Mobile Equipment Identity (IMEI) (the actual phone number) and mobile phone Subscriber Identity Module (SIM) card data. The early legislative approach was to simply deal with concepts, such as access and manipulation of computer systems. Division 474 goes beyond this, referring to specific mediums and intent, and in particular covering acts such as possessing, producing, supplying and obtaining. In their attempt to be comprehensive, the

---

17 *Criminal Code 1995* (Cth) ss478.3, 478.4.
18 The *Crimes Legislation Amendment (Telecommunications Offences and Other Measures) Act (No. 2) 2004* (Cth) replaced the previous Part 10.6, which was notable for its brevity and lack of detail.
19 For applicable decisions on the prior legislation see *R v Idolo* [1998] VICSC 57; *DPP (Cth) v Rogers* [1998] VICSC 48; and *R v Stevens* [1999] NSWCCA 69.
20 *Telecommunications Act 1997* (Cth) s7.
21 *Criminal Code 1995* (Cth) Dictionary.
22 See *Criminal Code 1995* (Cth) ss474.1, 474.2.

legislature has created many overlapping offences. A prosecutor will have quite an arsenal.

It is an offence for a person to cause a communication to be received by a person or carriage service other than the person or service to whom it is directed. It is also an offence to tamper with, or interfere with, a carriage service facility.[23] Modifying or interfering with a telecommunications device identifier is an offence. Possessing or controlling data or a device with intent to modify a telecommunications device identifier is an offence, though there is a range of defences: for manufacturers, certain employees, and law enforcement agencies and intelligence and security officers in the course of their duties.[24]

Producing, supplying or obtaining data or a device with intent to modify a telecommunications device identifier is an offence; possessing or controlling such data or devices with the same intent is also an offence.[25] Copying subscription-specific secure data from an existing account or onto a new account identifier is an offence.[26]

Using a telecommunications network with intention to commit a serious offence is an offence.[27] Notably, using a carriage service to make a threat, a hoax threat or to menace, harass or cause offence are offences.[28] Improper use of emergency call service is also an offence.[29]

Child pornography

Prior to 2005, child pornography offences were dealt with by the states and territories; the approaches varied. A federal approach was warranted given the extensive use made of the internet to upload and download child pornography and the use of internet communications, such as email and chat rooms, to contact vulnerable children. The *Criminal Code 1995* (Cth) now provides a consistent nationwide approach.[30] The new offences target online 'grooming' activities by offenders, where adults use the internet to forge relationships with children as a first step in luring them into sexual abuse.

'Child pornography' and 'child abuse' are defined in detail.[31] However, each specific provision concludes with the expression: 'and does this in a way that

23 *Criminal Code 1995* (Cth) ss474.5, 474.6 respectively.
24 *Criminal Code 1995* (Cth) ss474.7, 474.8 respectively.
25 *Criminal Code 1995* (Cth) ss474.9; ss474.09, 474.11 respectively.
26 *Criminal Code 1995* (Cth) s474.10.
27 *Criminal Code 1995* (Cth) s474.14.
28 *Criminal Code 1995* (Cth) ss474.15, 474.16, 474.17.
29 *Criminal Code 1995* (Cth) s474.18.
30 *Criminal Code 1995* (Cth) ss474.19–474.29.
31 *Criminal Code 1995* (Cth) s473.1.

reasonable persons would regard as being, in all the circumstances, offensive'. The term 'offensive' can vary from person to person and community to community. The inability by the US Supreme Court in *Reno v American Civil Liberties Union*[32] to determine a unified standard of 'offensive' within the US community was a significant part of the rationale for invalidating much of the US *Communications Decency Act 1996*.[33] The Criminal Code includes a guide for determining whether or not material is offensive:

473.4 Determining whether material is offensive

The matters to be taken into account in deciding for the purposes of this Part whether reasonable persons would regard particular material, or a particular use of a carriage service, as being, in all the circumstances, offensive, include:

(a) the standards of morality, decency and propriety generally accepted by reasonable adults; and

(b) the literary, artistic or educational merit (if any) of the material; and

(c) the general character of the material (including whether it is of a medical, legal or scientific character).

The expression 'reasonable adult' provides flexibility; it is therefore also imprecise.

A person is guilty of an offence if the person uses a carriage service to: access material; cause material to be transmitted; transmit material; make material available online; or publish or otherwise distribute material, and the material is child pornography or child abuse material.[34] The maximum penalty is 10 years' imprisonment.[35] Possessing, controlling, producing, supplying or obtaining child pornography or child abuse material with the intention that the material is for use through a carriage service is an offence punishable by up to 10 years' imprisonment.[36]

It is a defence to such prosecutions to find that the conduct in question is 'for the public benefit'. Conduct is for the public benefit if, and only if, the conduct is necessary for or of assistance in: enforcing the law; monitoring compliance with, or investigating a contravention of the law; the administration of justice; or conducting scientific, medical or educational research that has been approved by the relevant minister in writing.[37] 'In determining whether the person is ... not criminally responsible for the offence, the question whether the conduct is of public benefit is a question of fact and the person's motives in engaging in the conduct are

---

32 521 US 844 (1997). Janet Reno was the Attorney General during the Clinton Administration.
33 This case permits online pornography under the guise of freedom of speech and freedom of expression and is the foundation of the escalation of online pornography in the modern era.
34 *Criminal Code 1995* (Cth) ss474.19, 474.22.
35 *Criminal Code 1995* (Cth) ss474.19, 474.22.
36 *Criminal Code 1995* (Cth) ss474.20, 474.23.
37 *Criminal Code 1995* (Cth) s474.24.

irrelevant.'[38] Action by law enforcement authorities in accessing and downloading such material in the performance of their duty is not an offence.[39] Acts in good faith for the sole purpose of assisting the Australian Communications Media Authority (ACMA) to detect prohibited content (within the meaning of *Broadcasting Services Act 1992* (Cth) Schedule 7),[40] or to manufacture, develop or update certain content filtering technology (including software), are also exempt.[41]

The term 'grooming' is not defined. It refers to enticing a child with the intent of engaging in sex. A person (the sender) commits an offence if he or she uses a carriage service to transmit a communication to another person (the recipient) and:

(b) the communication includes material that is indecent;

(c) the sender does this with the intention of making it easier to procure the recipient to engage in, or submit to, sexual activity with the sender or another person (the third party);

(d) the recipient is someone who is, or who the sender believes to be, under 16 years of age; and

(e) the sender or the third party is at least 18 years of age.[42]

The maximum penalty is 12 years' imprisonment. 'Indecent' means 'indecent according to the standards of ordinary people', another flexible and imprecise term.[43]

Assisting suicide

The ease with which information can be accessed online has prompted a response by law makers. A person is guilty of an offence if that person uses a carriage service to access, distribute, transmit or make available material (such as on an internet web page) that directly or indirectly counsels or incites suicide. An element of the offence is that the person intended the material to be used for counselling or inciting suicide. It is also an offence to use a carriage service to promote a particular method of committing suicide.[44]

The offence also covers persons who possess, control, produce, supply or obtain suicide-related material for use through a carriage service. A person may be found guilty of an offence even if the suicide is impossible.

---

38 *Criminal Code 1995* (Cth) s474.24.

39 Ibid.

40 Ibid. On the role of ACMA and detecting 'prohibited content', see Chapter 10.

41 *Criminal Code 1995* (Cth) ss474.21, 474.24.

42 *Criminal Code 1995* (Cth) s474.27.

43 *Criminal Code 1995* (Cth) s474.27.

44 *Criminal Code 1995* (Cth) ss474.29A, 474.29B, inserted by *Criminal Code Amendment (Suicide Related Material Offences) 2004* (Cth).

Police and security powers

Law enforcement and security agencies are able to monitor and eavesdrop on suspected terrorists' and criminals' emails, SMS messages and voicemail. In 1979 the Australian Federal Parliament passed problematic telecommunications interception legislation which had been sought by police, regulatory and security agencies to aid investigations.[45]

Authorities are able to apply for search warrants to inspect 'stored communications'.[46] A 'stored communication' is a communication that is held on equipment that is operated by a carrier and cannot be accessed on that equipment by a person who is not a party to the communication without the assistance of an employee of the carrier, but does not pass over a telex system.[47]

Recent amendments substantially improved the original telecommunications interception legislation, which was drafted at a time when telecommunications was largely land-based and involved live telephone conversations.

Investigative powers

The *Cybercrime Act 2001* (Cth) enhanced the criminal investigation powers under the *Crimes Act 1914* (Cth) and the *Customs Act 1901* (Cth) relating to the search, seizure and copying of electronically stored data. Police may analyse the computer on site or seize computer equipment, including data storage disks, and may copy and analyse them elsewhere.

The use of security measures such as encryption and passwords presents particular problems for law enforcement agencies. Encrypted data can be impossible to decipher. A magistrate may order a person with knowledge of a computer system to provide information or assistance.[48] This power extends to the compulsory disclosure of passwords, keys, codes, cryptographic and steganographic methods (the art and science of writing hidden messages in such a way that no one, apart from the sender and intended recipient, suspects the existence of the message – it is a form of security through obscurity) used to protect information 'as is necessary and reasonable':

---

45 *Telecommunications (Interception and Access) Act 1979* (Cth).
46 *Telecommunications (Interception and Access) Act 1979* (Cth) s117.
47 'Carrier' means a carrier and a carriage service provider within the meaning of the *Telecommunications Act 1997* (Cth), such as Internet Service Providers (ISPs).
48 *Crimes Act 1914* (Cth) s3LA.

(1) The executing officer may apply to a magistrate for an order requiring a specified person to provide any information or assistance that is reasonable and necessary to allow the officer to do one or more of the following:

    (a) access data held in, or accessible from, a computer that is on warrant premises;

    (b) copy the data to a data storage device;

    (c) convert the data into documentary form.

(2) The magistrate may grant the order if the magistrate is satisfied that:

    (a) there are reasonable grounds for suspecting that evidential material is held in, or is accessible from, the computer; and

    (b) the specified person is:

        (i) reasonably suspected of having committed the offence stated in the relevant warrant; or

        (ii) the owner or lessee of the computer; or

        (iii) an employee of the owner or lessee of the computer; and

    (c) the specified person has relevant knowledge of:

        (i) the computer or a computer network of which the computer forms a part; or

        (ii) measures applied to protect data held in, or accessible from, the computer.[49]

Failing to comply with the magistrate's order is punishable by up to 6 months' imprisonment.[50] Some commentators have described the new investigative powers as draconian and dangerous. Their argument is that the provision contravenes the privilege against self-incrimination, often colloquially referred to as the 'right to silence'. Supporters of the provision claim that it is a valuable tool to fight organised crime, paedophilia, terrorist activities and any criminal who hides material in an encrypted form. The provision is akin to requiring a person to hand over a key to a filing cabinet. In reality the police can break open a filing cabinet if necessary; but they need the 'key' to access encrypted computer data. In fact, the provision provides law enforcement agencies with a necessary tool to fight crime. There has also been exaggerated criticism of the provisions, which make it offence to possess hacker toolkits, scanners and virus code, on the basis that these are tools of the trade for security vendors.

The *Crimes Act 1914* (Cth) permits both the Defence Signals Directorate, the Australian Security Intelligence Organisation (ASIO) and the Australian Secret Intelligence Service (ASIS) to hack: it is seen as part of their role of providing national security.[51]

---

49 *Cybercrime Act 2001* (Cth) s3LA.

50 Some accused may prefer imprisonment to revealing the contents.

51 See *Crimes Act 1914* (Cth), Part IAA – Search, Information Gathering, Arrest and Related Powers.

Child pornography – international

The International Child Pornography Conference held in Austria in 1999 sought to combat child pornography and exploitation on the internet. Initially the discussion revolved around the existing international obligations and commitments related to the protection of children, including the UN *Convention on the Rights of the Child*. The conference built and acted upon commitments undertaken at the Stockholm World Congress against the Commercial Sexual Exploitation of Children (1996) and ongoing initiatives in many countries and regions.

The UNICEF-sponsored Optional Protocol on the Sale of Children, Child Prostitution and Child Pornography became effective in January 2002. UNICEF estimates that one million children, mainly girls, are forced into the multi-billion dollar commercial sex trade (this includes child pornography) every year. To date there are 169 parties to the Optional Protocol. It requires signatories to criminalise violations of children's rights and calls for increased public awareness and international co-operation.

The UN *Convention on the Rights of the Child*[52] has been ratified by almost all nation states. The Convention recognises child pornography as a violation of children and requires parties to take legislative and practical measures to prevent the exploitative use of children in pornographic materials.

Internet gambling

The *Interactive Gambling Act 2001* (Cth) commenced in January 2002. The regulation of gambling is typically a state and territory matter, but the Federal Parliament has power with regard to internet activities and other communications technologies. The Act is the government's response to the community's concern about the increase in gambling resulting from new technologies.

The problem

Seventy per cent of Australians believe that gambling does more harm than good. Australia has the highest number of poker machines per head worldwide. In 2004–05 Australians lost $15.5 billion in gambling. Some 7000 businesses – including 2888 hotels, 2408 clubs and 13 casinos – provide gambling services. The

---

52 See UNICEF <www.unicef.org/crc>.

Productivity Commission has found that around 290 000 Australians, or 2.1 per cent of the total population, are problem gamblers. It found that problem gamblers comprise 15 per cent of regular gamblers and account for one-third of all gambling expenditure annually. The commission's final report estimated that 1.5 million people are affected through consequential bankruptcy, divorce, suicide and lost time at work.[53]

The public's concern is that increased access to gambling through the internet and similar technologies will exacerbate problem gambling. The Productivity Commission described the new interactive technologies as a quantum leap in the accessibility of gambling. A Department of Family and Community Services survey found that more than two-thirds of Australians support a ban on internet gambling. The Productivity Commission found that 92 per cent did not want any further expansion of poker machines.

Interactive Gambling Act 2001 (Cth)

The *Interactive Gambling Act 2001* (Cth) prohibits the provision of interactive gambling to people located in Australia. The Act defines 'interactive gambling service' as including internet casinos and internet poker machines, online ball-by-ball wagering on sporting events, and online scratch lotteries. The prohibition applies to casino-type gaming, betting on a sporting event after it has commenced and scratch lotteries online. Offences apply to both Australian and overseas interactive gambling service providers. Fines of up to $1.1 million per day apply.

The responsible minister has the power to designate foreign countries that Australian interactive gambling operators will be banned from providing their services to. Countries with similar laws have reciprocal powers, which means they can stop operators based in Australia from providing interactive gambling services to customers located in those countries.

The Act regulates interactive gambling services by:

- prohibiting interactive gambling services from being provided to customers in Australia;
- prohibiting Australian-based interactive gambling services from being provided to customers in designated countries; and
- establishing a complaints-based system to deal with internet gambling services where the relevant content (prohibited internet gambling content) is available for access by customers in Australia.[54]

---

53 The Productivity Commission is the Australian Government's independent research and advisory body on a range of economic, social and environmental issues affecting the welfare of Australians. Its role, expressed simply, is to help governments make better policies that are in the long-term interest of the Australian community: <www.pc.gov.au>.

54 *Interactive Gambling Act 2001* (Cth) ss15, 15A.

A person may complain to the Australian Communications Media Authority (ACMA) about prohibited internet gambling content.[55] If the site on which the content appeared was hosted in Australia and ACMA considers the complaint warranted, it must refer the complaint to the Australian Federal Police (AFP). For content hosted outside Australia, ACMA must also notify internet service providers (ISPs) so that the ISPs can apply the industry standard: this might mean updating internet content-filtering software.

The Act encourages the development of an industry code by ISPs. ACMA can establish an industry standard if there is no industry code or if an industry code is deficient. The industry codes and standards are available at the website of the Internet Industry Association.[56] Regulations provide that civil proceedings do not in every instance lie against a person to recover money alleged to have been won or been paid in connection with an illegal interactive gambling service. The Act also prohibits the advertising of interactive gambling services.

The minister is required to undertake regular reviews of the impact of the Act. The reviews must take into account the growth of interactive gambling services, the social and commercial impact of interactive gambling services, and the effect of the exemptions (there are excluded wagering services, excluded gaming services, services that have a designated broadcasting or datacasting link, and excluded lottery services).

Television broadcasters raised concerns that the legislation may unintentionally apply to certain game shows – such as *Video Hits* or *Classic Catches* – where viewers pay a fee via a 1900 phone call. Late amendments to the Act addressed these concerns (through exclusions). The minister has the power to impose additional conditions.

Comment

In Australia, betting on horse races over the internet remains legal, as do several other forms of online gambling, such as lotteries. However, the Act prohibits poker machine or roulette-style gambling. Senator Richard Alston (Liberal, Victoria) described the Act as 'strong action to combat the tragic economic and social consequences of gambling in this country'.[57] The chief executive of the Internet Industry Association, however, has stated that the legislation 'is technically inept and has no real prospects of protecting those whom it claims to protect'. The latter comment seems to be closer to the mark. Most internet gambling sites are based offshore. The impact of the Act on access to such sites will be minimal. When searching

---

55 *Interactive Gambling Act 2001* (Cth) Part 3.
56 See the website of the Internet Industry Association: <www.iia.net.au>.
57 Senator Alston, press release, 27 March 2001.

for gambling sites, Australians do not look for Australian sites, as there are many 'reputable' sites in other countries, such as the United States. In 2000, before the Act was passed, Australia's leading internet casino – Lasseters, in Alice Springs – turned over $100 million. Lasseters have since closed their internet gambling services in Australia, stating that they would relocate to Vanuatu, resulting in the loss of 45 jobs from Alice Springs (and related expertise in intellectual property and electronic commerce). Nevertheless the Act is a step, albeit a small step, towards management of the problems caused by gambling.

Cyberstalking

Various pieces of state legislation define stalking as 'continued and intentional conduct directed at another person that would cause a reasonable apprehension of violence or detriment to the stalked person or another person'. 'Cyberstalking', or stalking online, is not dealt with directly by legislation in Australia or New Zealand. However, stalking can involve use of the internet, email or other electronic communications to harass or threaten another person. Stalking behaviour includes posting improper messages on bulletin boards, forwarding viruses, sending threatening or offensive emails, and electronic theft.

The Crimes Acts in most jurisdictions describe stalking in general terms, leaving it to the courts to consider specific instances, such as harassment by electronic means.[58] In Victoria and the Northern Territory the offence of stalking specifically includes 'telephoning, sending electronic messages to, or otherwise contacting, the victim or any other person'.[59] In 1999, the Queensland *Criminal Code* was amended to extend stalking to conduct utilising the 'telephone, fax, mail, email or other technology'.[60] In the ACT, stalking includes circumstances where the offender 'telephones, sends electronic messages to or otherwise contacts the stalked person; sends electronic messages about the stalked person to anybody else or makes electronic messages about the stalked person available to anybody else'.[61] However, even if the stalker can be identified, the enforcement of such laws can be problematic, as the offender may not be located within the jurisdiction.

In cyberspace terms, cyberstalking behaviour includes spamming, flaming, posting improper messages on bulletin boards, forwarding viruses, sending threatening or offensive email, and electronic theft. CyberAngels, an organisation assisting

58 *Criminal Law Consolidation Act 1935* (SA) s19AA, *Criminal Code Act 1913* (WA) s338E, *Criminal Code 1924* (Tas) s192, *Crimes Act 1991* (NZ) Part 11.
59 *Crimes Act 1958* (Vic) s21A, *Criminal Code Act 1983* (NT) s189.
60 See *Criminal Code 1899* (Qld) ss359A–359F.
61 *Crimes Act 1900* (ACT) s35(2)(f).

victims of cybercrime, estimates that there are approximately 63 000 internet stalkers and 474 000 victims worldwide. In Los Angeles, 20 per cent of the 600 cases dealt with by the Stalking and Threat Assessment Unit involve email and other electronic communications; in New York, 40 per cent of the work of the City Police Computer Investigations Unit in recent years has involved electronic harassment and threats. ISPs are reporting a marked increase in complaints regarding cyberstalking.

According to CyberAngels, cyberbullies employ a number of methods to threaten and disparage their targets. They include:

- Email messages: While this is the most common form of electronic communication, the use of this method for cyberbullying is less pervasive since most email programs allow the use of filters to block offending emails.
- Instant Messaging: Cyberbullies can and do use IM on computers and cell phones to send harassing and threatening messages to their targets.
- Chat rooms: Chat rooms allow cyberbullies to anonymously enter and write anything they want, mocking and insulting their victims in a forum that potentially has a large audience.
- Websites: Cyberbullies create websites or use social networking sites or blogs to mock, torment and harass the intended victims.
- Voting and Polling booths: Some websites offer users the opportunity to create online polling or voting booths. Cyberbullies use these to vote online for some insulting topics (for example: 'The ugliest, fattest, dumbest, etc, boy or girl at [stated] school').[62]

Cyberspace provides stalkers with new methods to contact victims. Threats can be sent electronically from anywhere in the world. Messages can be sent at random or set intervals automatically. The identity and location of the stalker can be concealed by using anonymous remailers that strip off the message header, making tracing difficult. The ease of the technology may encourage some to make threats. By using chat rooms and bulletin boards, and posting controversial material, stalkers can now enlist others to harass their victim – by impersonating them, or by publicising the victim's name, address and telephone number.

The nature of the internet and electronic communications makes it difficult for people to protect their personal information and privacy. Password-protected mailing lists and personal emails cannot really be regarded as private: communications can be intercepted, and many websites provide personal information such as silent phone numbers, identifying photographs of the victim and of his or her home, home and work addresses, financial data and other sensitive material.[63]

---

62 See <www.cyberangels.org>. CyberAngels is an online safety protection and educational non-profit body. See also Internet Education & Safety Services: <www.iness.com.au>.
63 On stalking generally see *Grosse v Purvis* [2003] QDC 151 and *DPP v Sutcliffe* [2001] VSC 43.

Even without reliable statistics, it would be relatively safe to predict that as users become more cyber-aware, abuses will increase. Legal and policy approaches to the problem have tended to lag behind the technology. Also, the jurisdictional problems of the internet present a real barrier to effective enforcement. Legal recourse will only be available when the law deals with cyberstalking in a meaningful way; until and unless that happens, it will be largely up to consumers to use social and technical tools to prevent and control cyberstalking.

Technical responses available for consumers include the following:

- blocking and filtering software: this can delete email or chat room messages. The criteria used can include the name of the author, certain offensive words and so on;
- sophisticated encryption programs: these can prevent messages being read by unauthorised people;
- digital signatures and certificates: these will authenticate the author;
- gender-neutral names; and
- changing passwords regularly.

International approach to cybercrime

Attacks against commercial websites have drawn international attention to the dangers presented by the internet and other computer networks. Cybercriminals and cyberterrorists can threaten business and government interests and cause vast damage.

The Council of Europe's *Convention on Cybercrime* is the first international instrument to address various types of offending behaviour involving computer systems, networks or data.[64] It aims to harmonise national legislation in this field, facilitate investigations and allow co-operation between the authorities of different nation states. Non-European nations may also join the *Convention* and Australia did so in 2013, after amending its legislation to conform to the *Convention*. Other non-European nations that have joined include the United States, Canada and Japan.

The *Convention* includes provision for the co-ordinated criminalisation of computer hacking and hacking devices, of illegal interception of data and interference with computer systems, and of computer-related fraud and forgery. It prohibits on-line child pornography, including the possession of such material after downloading, as well as the reproduction and distribution of copyright-protected material.

---

64 See Council of Europe, *Convention on Cybercrime*, ETS 185, Open for signature Budapest, 23 November 2001: <www.conventions.coe.int>.

The *Convention* defines offences, addresses questions related to the liability of individual and corporate offenders and determines minimum applicable penalties.

It deals with law enforcement issues including the power to carry out computer searches and seize computer data, to require data-subjects to produce data under their control and to obtain the expeditious preservation of vulnerable data by data-subjects. These computer-specific investigative measures also imply co-operation by telecom operators and ISPs – their assistance is vital in terms of identifying computer criminals and securing evidence of their misdeeds.

Spam

Who could have predicted that Monty Python's use of the word 'Spam' continuously and ludicrously in a comedy skit would result in a new term, meaning 'unsolicited multiple postings of electronic mail', and in due course to federal legislation, the *Spam Act 2003* (Cth)? It is curious that the word 'spam' does not appear in the body of the Act, except for the title section. Prior to the legislation, the possibility of liability for spamming was considered under the *Privacy Act 1988* (Cth), the *Criminal Code 1995* (Cth), the relevant state criminal legislation and at common law. The New Zealand equivalent is the *Unsolicited Electronic Messages Act 2007*.[65]

The problem

All email users have experienced spam. In Australia the reviewing Senate Committee described spam as a cancer. Spam can be offensive, intrusive, misleading and an invasion of privacy. It clogs email boxes and obscures legitimate email. Spam slows email systems and is often illegal or offensive. Minister Peter McGauran states that the legislation was a direct response to the groundswell of business and community anger about the costly and disruptive occurrence of spam.

According to Star Internet, a large ISP in the United Kingdom, the cost in lost productivity is AUD$915 per employee per year. Other studies believe this figure to be conservative. Costs arise through increased download times and lost productivity. An EU study in 2001 estimates that the worldwide cost of spam at approximately AUD$18.4 billion; Ferris Research estimates that the worldwide cost of spam was approximately US$130 billion in 2009. A more conservative estimate by Microsoft and Google places the cost at US$20 billion in 2012.[66]

---

65 See Department of Internal Affairs, 'Anti-spam': <www.dia.govt.nz/diawebsite.nsf/wpg_URL/Services-Anti-Spam-Index>.
66 Justin M Rao and David H Reiley, 'The Economics of Spam', (14 July 2012) <www.davidreiley.com/papers/SpamEconomics.pdf>.

The cost to spammers can be as little as 0.003 cent to send a single email,[67] and only 0.00032 cent to obtain one email address using harvesting software. Even receiving positive responses of less than 1 per cent can be profitable for the spammer.

Spam Act 2003 (Cth)

This Act deals with 'unsolicited commercial electronic messages'. In brief, a person must not send, or cause to be sent, a commercial electronic message unless the recipient has consented to the message being sent.[68] The word 'message' is used to ensure that the legislation extends to other sorts of electronic communications, such as SMS messages.[69]

Sender information

All commercial electronic messages must:

- clearly and accurately identify the person who authorised the sending of the message;
- include accurate information about how the recipient can readily contact the sender;
- comply with the regulations; and
- reasonably be likely to be valid for at least 30 days after the message has been sent.[70]

Unsubscribe function

Section 18 of the Act deals with this area. It states that all commercial electronic messages (solicited and unsolicited) must include the statement that the recipient may unsubscribe by replying using an electronic address set out in the message. The statement 'must be presented in a clear and conspicuous manner' and the electronic address must be 'reasonably likely to be capable of receiving' such a message for 'a period of at least 30 day safter the message is sent'. In addition, the section requires the electronic address to have been 'legitimately obtained'.[71] An unsubscribe message is defined as 'an electronic message to the effect that the relevant electronic account-holder does not want to receive any further commercial electronic messages from the sender'.[72]

---

67 See <www.noie.gov.au/publications/NOIE/spam/final_report/index.htm>.
68 *Spam Act 2003* (Cth) s16.
69 The *Unsolicited Electronic Messages Act 2007* (NZ) became operational in 2007; see below.
70 *Spam Act 2003* (Cth) s17.
71 *Spam Act 2003* (Cth) s18(1).
72 *Spam Act 2003* (Cth) s18(9).

Defences include the fact that the recipient consented, that the message was sent by mistake, or that the message only contained factual information.[73]

Factual information

The greatest weakness in the legislation is the exemption for sending 'factual information'. The Act does not regard email as spam if it contains factual information (with or without directly related comment) and additional peripheral information such as the sender's name, logo and contact details.[74]

'Factual information' is not defined in the Act. However, the explanatory memorandum states that the provision is designed 'to ensure that messages which may be seen to have some form of commercial element, but which are primarily aimed at providing factual information are not covered by the rules'. It gives as examples:

- an electronic message from a private law firm which includes an information sheet outlining the effects of a particular court decision;
- an electronic version of a neighbourhood watch newsletter which is sponsored by the local newsagent;
- an electronic newsletter from the local chamber of commerce which is sponsored by one of its members;
- factual information relating to bird-watching that is sponsored by a commercial entity.

Exemptions

Government bodies, political parties, religious organisations, charities and educational institutions are granted a special exemption from the application of the Act in certain circumstances.[75] Clauses 3 and 4 of Schedule 1 provide:

> 3   Government bodies, political parties and charities
>
> For the purposes of this Act, an electronic message is a *designated commercial electronic message* if:
>
> (a) the sending of the message is authorised by any of the following bodies:
>> (i)   a government body;
>> (ii) a registered political party;
>> (iii) a registered charity; and
>
> (b) the message relates to goods or services; and
>
> (c) the body is the supplier, or prospective supplier, of the goods or services concerned.

---

73 *Spam Act 2003* (Cth) s18(2), (3), (4).
74 *Spam Act 2003* (Cth) Schedule 1, cl 2.
75 *Spam Act 2003* (Cth) Schedule 1, cll 3, 4.

4 Educational institutions

For the purposes of this Act, an electronic message is a *designated commercial electronic message* if:

(a) the sending of the message is authorised by an educational institution; and

(b) either or both of the following subparagraphs applies:

    (i) the relevant electronic account-holder is, or has been, enrolled as a student in that institution;

    (ii) a member or former member of the household of the relevant electronic account-holder is, or has been, enrolled as a student in that institution; and

c) the message relates to goods or services; and

d) the institution is the supplier, or prospective supplier, of the goods or services concerned.

Remedies

The main remedies for breaches of this Act are civil penalties and injunctions. The Act provides a tiered enforcement regime available to ACMA, which includes:

- a formal warning;
- acceptance of an enforceable undertaking;[76]
- the issuing of an infringement notice;[77]
- application to the Federal Court for an injunction;[78] and
- the commencement of proceedings in the Federal Court for breach of a civil penalty provision.[79]

Search and seizure

The *Spam (Consequential Amendments) Act 2003* (Cth) makes amendments to the *Telecommunications Act 1997* (Cth) and the *Australian Communications and Media Authority Act 2005* (Cth) to enable investigation and enforcement of breaches of the *Spam Act*. The amendments would make it legal, in certain circumstances, for inspectors and police to enter homes and search and seize computers and other possessions without a search warrant and without the consent of the person whose home was entered. The wording is such that the same could be done to a recipient of spam.

Nicholson J examined the first application of the legislation in an Australian superior court in *ACMA v Clarity1 Pty Ltd*.[80] ACMA alleged that Clarity1 contravened

---

76 *Spam Act 2003* (Cth) Part 6.
77 *Spam Act 2003* (Cth) Schedule 3.
78 *Spam Act 2003* (Cth) Part 5.
79 *Spam Act 2003* (Cth) Part 4.
80 [2006] 410 FCA.

section 16(1) of the Spam Act: that 'unsolicited commercial electronic messages' must not be sent. Clarity1 had sent or caused to be sent:

- at least 213 443 382 Commercial Electronic Messages (CEM), of which 41 796 754 were successfully sent, to 5 664 939 unique electronic addresses; and
- at least 56 862 092 CEM, of which 33 199 806 were successfully sent, to 2 291 518 unique electronic addresses.[81]

On an analysis of 1 469 820 electronic addresses, 182 actually placed an order with Clarity1 for its materials.

Section 16(5) of the *Spam Act 2003* (Cth) relates to the burden of proof. The sender must prove that the relevant electronic account-holder (the recipient) consented to the sending of the message, or that the sender did not know or had not ascertained with reasonable diligence that the message had an Australian link, or that it was sent by mistake. In other words, it is the sender who is obliged to show (to the civil standard of proof) that there is sufficient evidence to raise an issue as to the existence or non-existence of a fact in issue.[82] An unexplained failure to call witnesses in relation to this burden of proof provision will allow the application of the rule in *Jones v Dunkel*:[83] an inference that the uncalled evidence or missing material would not have assisted the respondent's case. In such a case, 'considerable significance may attach if the absent witness is either the party or a senior executive of a corporate party closely engaged in the transactions in question and present in court during the hearing'.[84]

The term 'send' in section 16(1) includes an attempt to send, so it is immaterial whether or not the respondents had successfully sent the CEMs.

In Clarity1's favour, Nicholson J identified three mitigating facts: each of the CEMs included a functional unsubscribe facility; from March 2001 to the hearing date, some 166 000 requests were made for removal from the defendant's lists, all of which were acted upon; and only 80 complaints were made to Clarity1, none of which related to a failure to remove an electronic address from the database.

Clarity1 raised many defences under the Act, of which a number were highly questionable. For instance, Nicholson J dismissed Clarity1's claims that it acted as a charity or an educational institution. Clarity1 also claimed consent, arguing that:

- as the CEMs contained an unsubscribe facility and the recipients did not use the unsubscribe facility, it is reasonable to infer consent;

81 Para 58.
82 See JD Heydon, *Cross on Evidence*, 6th edn, Butterworths, Sydney, 2000, at [7015].
83 (1959) 101 CLR 298.
84 Heydon, above n 82, [1215], citing *Dilosa v Latec Finance Pty Ltd* (1966) 84 WN (Pt 1) (NSW) 557 at 582.

- consent may be inferred from the business relationship between Clarity1 and the recipients; and
- the recipients published their electronic addresses on the internet.

Other than evidence by eight affidavits by deponents who indicated that they were 'happy' to receive the spam, there was no evidence supporting these arguments, other than by inference. However, neither that evidence nor Clarity1's claims indicate that Clarity1 was aware of such consent prior to dispatch.[85]

Clarity1 placed reliance on the Office of the Federal Privacy Commissioner's publication *Guidelines to the National Privacy Principles*, issued in September 2001, which stated that 'it may be possible to infer consent from the individual's failure to opt out'. However, in another passage the guidelines add:

> It is unlikely that consent to receive marketing material on-line could be implied from a failure to object to it. This is because it is usually difficult to conclude that the message has been read and ... it is commonly considered that there are adverse consequences to an individual from opening or replying to email marketing – such as confirming [that] the individual's address exists.

Nicholson J concluded: 'The mere fact that Clarity1 sent a CEM to an electronic address and did not receive a response from the recipient does not provide a proper foundation for an inference of consent.'[86]

Clause 2 of Schedule 2 of the Act provides that consent may be inferred from a business or other relationship. Nicholson J referred to the government-issued publication *Spam Act 2003: A practical guide for business*, in particular the following passage:

> You may be able to reasonably infer consent after considering both the conduct of the addressee and their relationship with you. For example, if the addressee has an existing relationship with you and has previously provided their address then it would be reasonable to infer that consent has been provided ... as long as it is consistent with the reasonable expectations of the addressee, and their conduct ... initiated by a commercial activity (including provision, for a fee or free of charge, of information, goods, or of services) or other communication between you and potential addressee.[87]

Nicholson J reasoned that 'the receipt of electronic messages without more cannot give rise to the inference of consent because the receipt could be accounted for on many bases other than consent ... There is no relationship when the communication is one sided.'[88] Even though there were 182 recipients who placed orders

---

85 [2006] 410 FCA para 72.
86 Ibid., paras 75–79.
87 [2006] 410 FCA para 89.
88 [2006] 410 FCA para 92.

for materials, ACMA submitted that it does not follow even in these instances that these purchasers gave consent to the receipt of the CEMs. Indeed the Explanatory Memorandum explains that even a pre-existing business transaction may be insufficient to imply consent. Consider a person who anonymously purchases groceries or other goods from Coles, Big W, Target and so forth. There is no consent to spam. Nevertheless, Nicholson J inferred conferred consent in the 'limited instances' of the 182 purchasers.[89]

Spam may be sent to persons who provide their electronic details by way of a 'conspicuous publication': where an 'electronic address has been conspicuously published; and it would be reasonable to assume that the publication occurred with the agreement' of the publisher of the electronic details.[90] However, such publication only constitutes consent if it is not accompanied by a statement to the effect that the electronic account-holder does not want to receive spam. Also, the spam must relate to work-related business, functions or duties. The court referred to the *Macquarie Dictionary* meaning of 'conspicuous': 'easy to be seen … readily attracting … attention'. There were several examples given in evidence of individuals whose email addresses were available from online yellow pages, their personal website and trade directories. However, ACMA countered with the example of an academic whose email address was published on his academic website, and pointed out that the CEMs at issue did not relate to academic activities. Nicholson J held that:

> it may be inferred from the sheer volume of the electronic addresses contained in the Databases and Lists that … the respondents did not consider whether the publication of the electronic address on the internet was done in circumstances that met each of the criteria set out in cl 4 of Sch 2 to the Spam Act.[91]

Clarity1 used address-harvesting software. However, they maintained that the harvesting occurred prior to 10 April 2004, when the *Spam Act* came into operation. Sections 20, 21 and 22 respectively provide that address-harvesting software and harvested address lists must not be 'supplied', 'acquired' or 'used'. The court naturally held that section 22 applied to 'use' after the commencement of the Act of lists acquired at any time, and thus there had been a contravention.

New Zealand response

The *Unsolicited Electronic Messages Act 2007* (NZ) came into effect in September 2007. It is based on the *Spam Act 2003* (Cth). The Act applies to email, instant

---

89 [2006] 410 FCA para 97.
90 *Spam Act 2003* (Cth) Schedule 2, cl4.
91 [2006] 410 FCA para 108.

messaging, SMS and MMS (text and image-based mobile phone messaging) of a commercial nature. It does not cover facsimiles, internet pop-ups or voice telemarketing. The Act prohibits unsolicited commercial electronic messages with a New Zealand link, and provides that commercial electronic messages must include accurate information about the person who authorised the sending of the message and a functional unsubscribe facility to enable the recipient to instruct the sender that no further messages are to be sent to the recipient. Address-harvesting software is prohibited.

The Department of Internal Affairs, which has responsibility for the Act, investigates complaints and enforces the provisions of the Act. The department is also charged with undertaking research into technologies used to send spam and advising the NZ government.

The first prosecution under the Act demonstrates the inadequacies of its penalty provisions. In *Chief Executive Department of Internal Affairs v Atkinson*,[92] the defendant admitted sending more than 2 million contravening emails to NZ computers. Justice French imposed a NZ$100000 penalty (the maximum possible is NZ$200000). However, Atkinson grossed more than NZ$1.6 million. Although acknowledging that 'the deterrent effect of a penalty will be lost if it only marginally increases the cost of the illegal activity',[93] her Honour commented that the penalty should be 'substantially discounted' due to the 'co-operation and candour in an early stage with the authorities'.[94] The penalty amounted to a small percentage of Atkinson's overheads. The NZ legislature may need to review the penalty provisions of the Act.

Criticisms

The *Spam Act 2003* (Cth) bans some email which many would not regard as spam. For example, if you write an article in a magazine, a single unsolicited email to you asking that the article be reprinted elsewhere for a fee would be in contravention of the legislation. No single email should be regarded as spam. The Act also legitimises some email which almost all would agree should be regarded as spam. Using the 'factual information' loophole, car dealers could send bulk emails stating their name and address and that the latest model is now available. This loophole has been described as 'large enough to drive a truck through'.[95] Using the 'conspicuous

---

92 (Unreported, High Court of New Zealand, CIV-2008-409-002391, December 2008.) Available at <www.courtsofnz.govt.nz/from/decisions/judgments.html>.
93 Ibid., para 20.
94 Ibid., para 21. See *Unsolicited Electronic Messages Act 2007* (NZ) ss32, 45. Atkinson and another had previously been fined US$2.2 million in 2005 by the US Federal Trade Commission. Atkinson and his partner had controlled 35 000 computers, sending out more than 10 billion emails a day.
95 See comments by Electronic Frontiers Australia: <www.efa.org.au>.

publication' rule, one may be regarded as consenting to all spam if one's email address appears on a letterhead or business card.

Critics also argue that the search and seizure requirements should be amended to require the authorities to obtain a warrant. Further, the legislation will be ineffective against overseas spam. It is estimated that some 80–90 per cent of all spam comes from overseas.

Identity fraud

Rogues were impersonating others to commit fraud, using fake documents, lies and cunning, long before the advent of technology. In the electronic age, these rogues are using sophisticated means, sometimes not even leaving their computers. The resultant crimes include obtaining goods or services by deception, false voter registration, terrorism, drug trafficking and identity fraud (the terms 'identity fraud' and 'identity theft' tend to be used interchangeably). Rogues may also use such stolen or fictitious identities to avoid tax obligations, obtain government benefits or gain access to services, medical and otherwise.

Recent technology has resulted in a sharp increase in identity fraud: fraudsters are quick to utilise scanners, imaging equipment and colour printers. In 2003 the Australian Transaction Reports and Analysis Centre (AUSTRAC) estimated that identity fraud costs more than $1.1 billion per year in Australia. This figure is likely to be quite conservative, as most studies and commentators agree that many instances of identity fraud are not reported. Many entities are reluctant to admit a failure in their security systems.

Identity theft can range from finding identification cards in garbage bins to using card readers, hacking into computers, stealing and forging documents such as driver's licences and 'phishing'. Phishing is sending an email to a user falsely claiming to be a legitimate enterprise in an attempt to scam the user into surrendering private information (such as bank account usernames and passwords) that will be used for identity theft.[96]

'Shoulder surfing' is where rogues spy on people at ATMs. 'Skimming' is where credit card data is copied from the magnetic strip electronically. Examples include restaurants where the customer hands over the credit card for payment or where a rogue's reader is attached surreptitiously to an ATM and the PIN that is entered is observed via a minute hidden camera.

Australians use the internet for banking and financial transactions that require the provision of credit card or other account details over the internet. Many government agencies have websites that allow for online transactions which involve

---

96 See below.

the giving of personal information. For example, each year the Australian Taxation Office issues several hundred thousand tax file numbers, Centrelink processes 3–4 million new claims or re-grants, and the Department of Foreign Affairs issues more than one million passports. Each is a potential target.

Identity fraud and terrorism

A horrendous case of identity fraud involves the terrorists acts of September 11, 2001. Two of the terrorists bribed a legal secretary to complete and notarise false affidavits and residency certifications which they then used to obtain official identification papers from the US government, allowing them to board the planes which they then hijacked. In the days that followed, lists of the missing were published, allowing rogues to contact government departments claiming replacement identification documents. On obtaining these replacement driver's licences, they then obtained credit cards and purchased hundreds of millions of dollars' worth of goods and services.

Technological response

Possible technological solutions include biometrics such as fingerprint and iris recognition technology, digital signature authentication and encryption.

Governmental response

The Proof of Identity Steering Committee (POISC) is a co-operative effort by government and the financial sector to address these issues. POISC commissioned the Securities Industry Research Centre of Asia-Pacific (SIRCA) to conduct the first comprehensive study of the cost of identity fraud to the Australian community.

There is no Commonwealth legislation making it a criminal offence to merely steal or assume another person's identity, and the only state that has such a law is South Australia.[97] Most relevant laws relate to the effects of the action, not the preparatory action. South Australia has made identity theft a specific offence:

144B – False identity etc

(1) A person who –
   (a) assumes a false identity; or

---

97 *Criminal Law Consolidation Act 1935* (SA) Part 5A.

(b) falsely pretends –

(c) to have particular qualifications; or

(d) to have, or to be entitled to act in, a particular capacity, makes a false pretence to which this section applies.

(2) A person who assumes a false identity makes a false pretence to which this section applies even though the person acts with the consent of the person whose identity is falsely assumed.

(3) A person who makes a false pretence to which this section applies intending, by doing so, to commit, or facilitate the commission of, a serious criminal offence is guilty of an offence and liable to the penalty appropriate to an attempt to commit the serious criminal offence.

144C – Misuse of personal identification information

(1) A person who makes use of another person's personal identification information intending, by doing so, to commit, or facilitate the commission of, a serious criminal offence, is guilty of an offence and liable to the penalty appropriate to an attempt to commit the serious criminal offence.

(2) This section applies irrespective of whether the person whose personal identification information is used –

(a) is living or dead; or

(b) consents to the use of the personal identification information.[98]

Other states rely on offences relating to forgery and dishonesty. The *Privacy Act 1988* (Cth) deals with the collection, storage and use of personal information but not the theft of that information. The *Crimes Legislation Amendment (Telecommunications Offences and Other Measures) Act (No. 2) 2004* (Cth) prohibits credit card skimming and internet banking fraud, including phishing. The *Financial Transaction Reports Act 1988* (Cth) and the *Financial Transaction Reports Regulations 1990* provide that it is an offence to open an account in a false name by tendering a false identification document.

State and territory legislation deals with general offences such as fraud and false pretences. In Queensland, for example, relevant provisions of the *Criminal Code 1899* (Qld) include:

- section 408C(1) fraud;
- section 427(1) false pretences;
- section 441 falsifying records and producing false records;
- section 398 stealing; and
- section 408C misappropriation.

---

98 *Criminal Law Consolidation Act 1935* (SA).

Phishing

Phishing is a form of criminal activity involving attempts to fraudulently acquire sensitive information such as passwords and credit card details by masquerading as a trustworthy person or business. The term 'phishing' was coined because fraudsters used sophisticated lures as bait to catch unsuspecting prey. Phishing dates back to 1996, when hackers phished for credit card numbers. Today phishing is more usually carried out by people masquerading as financial institutions and on-line payment services known to the target.

Initially, fraudsters randomly selected a target in the hope that they would already have an account with the financial institution imitated. However, recent research has indicated that fraudsters gain access to records that list customers of a particular body, and then target those customers. This practice is known as 'spear phishing'.

The damage from phishing includes financial loss, loss of access to email facilities, theft of credit card numbers and social services numbers. The victim's credit rating may be negatively affected. The process is relatively easy for anyone with rudimentary internet skills.

In the United States in 2005, 1.2 million computer users suffered losses caused by phishing, to an estimated value of US$929 million; US businesses lose an estimated US$2 billion every year. The United Kingdom reports similar numbers of incidents. In 2007 the Australian Attorney General, Philip Ruddock, reported that identity fraud costs Australians at least $1 billion a year.

Phishing and other forms of identity fraud are typically dealt with by the relatively recent amendments to the Commonwealth *Criminal Code 1995* (Cth) Part 10.6 – Telecommunications Services.

FURTHER READING

O Akindemowo, *Information Technology Law in Australia*, Law Book Company, Sydney, 1999.

Australian Communications and Media Authority, 'Anti-spam', <www.acma.gov.au/Industry/Marketers/Anti-Spam>.

Australian Institute of Criminology, <www.aic.gov.au>.

Geraldine Chin, 'Technological change and the Australian Constitution', (2000) *Melbourne University Law Review* 25.

Alan Davidson, 'Cybercrime – update and review', (2005) 25 *Proctor* 35.

JD Heydon, *Cross on Evidence*, 6th edn, Butterworths, Sydney, 2000.

Inquiry into Cybersafety for Senior Australians: <www.aphref.aph.gov.au-house-committee-jscc-senior_australians-subs-sub9.pdf>.

Joint Select Committee, Parliament of Australia, *Submission to the Joint Select Committee on Cyber-Safety: Inquiry into Cybersafety for Senior Australians*. Available at <www.aphref.aph.gov.au-house-committee-jscc-senior_australians-subs-sub9.pdf> .

National Plan to Combat Cybercrime (2013): <www.ag.gov.au/CrimeAndCorruption/Cybercrime/Documents/national-plan-to-combat-cybercrime.pdf>.

H Pontell,'"Pleased to meet you ... won't you guess my name?" Identity fraud, cyber-crime and white collar delinquency', (2002) 23(2) *Adelaide Law Review* 305.

19

EVIDENCE OF ELECTRONIC RECORDS

The systemisation of laws and societies' penchant for structure and order reflect the endogenous nature of humanity's development. Each culture develops a principle-based rule set to administer justice. The more complex the society, the richer the system. Rules of evidence are one subset of these developments which provide collective certainty, predictability and justice. Many of these principles have evolved over eons, and now are put the test by changes wrought by the emergence and development of technology. The regulations depend upon the perspective of the players who fashion, mostly unconsciously, community norms. Societies' 'norms and institutions' are necessary for a functioning society; the 'more complex' the society the greater the structure; however, state action can 'undermine or destroy these norms and institutions, with potentially catastrophic effect'.[1]

It is said that a verbal contract is worth the paper it is written on.[2] Although the common law recognises oral contracts, this oxymoron reflects the problems associated with proving not only the terms of a verbal contract, but also its very existence. The law of evidence is central to legal systems. Its restraints, rules and procedures aim to provide certainty and reliability within the criminal and civil justice systems. New and unanticipated problems have emerged when these historic and sometimes antiquated rules of evidence have been applied to electronic documents and records.

This chapter identifies the problems of applying paper-based rules of evidence in the electronic era. It first addresses how electronic information should be retained for the purposes of its potential use as evidence in legal proceedings and examines the relevant case law and statutory provisions. It then tackles the thorny problem of submitting to a court, as evidence, hard 'copies' – typically printouts – of electronic records such as email, particularly in circumstances where the electronic version has been deleted.

Evidence of electronic records

Courts typically establish facts before determining rights and imposing orders. The rules of evidence were developed to ensure a just basis for the making of such determinations. Evidence should be relevant, reliable and the best that is available. Notwithstanding modern statutes on evidence, case law from the 17th and 18th centuries still dictates the form in which evidence must be presented.[3] The rules relating to documentary evidence emerged when the quill and parchment were

---

1 Albert Loan, 'Institutional Bases of the Spontaneous Order: Surety and Assurance', (1991) 7 *Humane Studies Review* 1.
2 This statement is traditionally attributed to movie mogul Samuel Goldwyn.
3 See JD Heydon, *Cross on Evidence*, 7th edn, LexisNexis Butterworths, Sydney, 2004, Chapter 1, and John Forbes, *Evidence Law in Queensland*, 7th edn, Lawbook Co., Sydney, 2008, Chapter 1.

in use – copies of documents were originally made meticulously by hand. The assumption, when these rules were formulated, could only have been that any requirement for 'writing' and 'signature' would be paper-based.

Background

The *Statute of Frauds* in 1677[4] required 'writing' and a 'signature' in specific circumstances in an attempt to prevent or reduce certain frauds which could arise through the use of oral evidence. The reason stated in the statute was for the 'prevention of many fraudulent Practices which are commonly endeavoured to be upheld by Perjury and Subornation of Perjury'.[5] The statute's central provision required:

> Noe Action shall be brought ... unlesse the Agreement upon which such Action shall be brought or some Memorandum or Note thereof shall be in Writeing and signed by the partie to be charged therewith or some other person thereunto by him lawfully authorized.[6]

These provisions are effectively reproduced in modern statutes dealing with such matters as the disposition of land, intellectual property, insurance contracts and consumer protection. Naturally, the 'writing' and 'signature' elements, in 1677, referred to a tangible medium such as paper or parchment.

Where copies of 'originals' were handmade, the law treated such copies circumspectly, appreciating the real possibility of transcription error, or worse, deliberate and undetectable alteration. Modern photocopy machines make copies which are often indistinguishable from the original. Nevertheless, remnants of the pre-electronic era remain in the law of evidence and copies continue to be treated with suspicion: an explanation as to why the original was not tendered as evidence can be required.

The efficiencies of electronics, computerisation and communications have led to streamlining and rationalisation in the preparation of business documents, often with little regard to legal consequences. Chapter 11 discussed the international legislative approach taken to ensure consumer and business confidence in electronic transactions. Electronic documents coming within the purview of the *Electronic Transactions Acts*[7] are regarded as documents, subject to the same rules of evidence as paper documents. The legislature's approach here, as in other areas, has

---

4 *Statute of Frauds* 29 Car 2. c. 5.3.4.
5 Ibid., Preamble.
6 Ibid., s4.
7 *Electronic Transactions Act 1999* (Cth), *Electronic Transactions Act 2000* (NSW), *Electronic Transactions (Queensland) Act 2001* (Qld), *Electronic Transactions Act 2000* (SA), *Electronic Transactions Act 2000* (Tas), *Electronic Transactions (Victoria) Act 2000* (Vic), *Electronic Transactions Act 2011* (WA), *Electronic Transactions Act 2001* (ACT), *Electronic Transactions (Northern Territory) Act 2000* (NT).

been reactive rather than proactive: to provide a means of accepting all forms of evidence, including emails, digital photographs, electronic banking records and logs, word processing documents, instant message histories, electronic accounting files, records of internet use and databases. Subject to appropriate levels of verification and integrity, any electronic record and document can be admitted. This is not new. The courts and the legislature have developed principles under which analogue records such as photographs, sound and filming recordings and facsimiles can be accepted.[8] However, in many circumstances the courts may reject the admission of, or the credibility of, electronic records.

All commercial parties should retain documents in the form in which the documents are issued or presented, electronic or otherwise; not doing this risks admissibility problems should such documents be required as evidence in court. When a commercial dispute arises, the immediate concern is the ability to prove the issues before a court of law. We will now consider the common law principle known as the 'secondary evidence rule' and evidentiary legislation.

Secondary evidence rule

Courts are not free to use all information as evidence.[9] In applying the common law secondary evidence rule, courts are often obliged to disregard otherwise relevant material. The two main exclusionary rules are the rule against hearsay and the rule as to secondary evidence of the contents of a document. The former excludes certain relevant information on the grounds that it cannot be tested and is thus not reliable. Both rules include several exceptions. It is the latter rule which is less than satisfactory when applied to electronic records. The secondary evidence rule is often referred to as the 'best evidence' rule. In 1745, Lord Harwicke, in *Omychund v Barker*,[10] stated that no evidence was admissible unless it was 'the best that the nature of the case will allow'. The general rule is that a secondary evidence document will be inadmissible if the primary document is available.

There are a number of established exceptions. For example, where a party requires a document in the possession of another to be admitted into evidence, that party may issue a Notice to Produce: that is, a subpoena for documents. A copy of the original may be admitted as evidence if the party served with a Notice to Produce fails to produce the original. In the absence of the Notice to Produce, the original document is admissible but the copy is not. Other exceptions include consent, lost documents, where the production of the original is impossible, and certain public documents.

---

8 *Butera v Director of Public Prosecutions for the State of Victoria* (1987) 164 CLR 180 at 186.
9 Heydon, above n 3, 101 and Forbes, above n 3, A.1.
10 (1745) 1 Atk, 21, 49; 26 ER 15 at 33.

The application of this rule to electronic records is fraught with danger. The courts need to determine whether electronic records on such media as videotapes, audiotapes, CDs, DVDs, a computer's hard disk, a floppy disk, and electronic messages, are documents for the purpose of the rule.

In relation to electronic messages, debate rages over which version is the original and which is the copy: a minimum of eight 'copies' of an electronic message come into existence from creation to receipt. The question of which are admissible and which are not has not been resolved. Many argue that the original electronic message is the version created in the sender's computer and that the recipient only acquires a copy. Others would argue that the 'electronic record' as received forms the original, especially where it is changed along the path by, for example, data fluctuations altering a few characters or by the addition of underlying metadata. With paper documents, the recipient is typically in possession of the original.

In 2007 the High Court of Australia, in *Golden Eagle International Trading Pty Ltd v Zhang*,[11] reaffirmed the 'vitality' of the best evidence rule. In considering the applicability of historical versus prospective actuarial tables, the majority judgment stated:

> Despite criticism of it, the 'best evidence rule' has not fallen completely into desuetude. Subject to the exigencies of litigation, the circumstances of the parties, and the other settled and statutory rules of evidence, it has vitality. An aspect of the rule is that courts should act upon the least speculative and most current admissible evidence available. To prefer the prospective rather than the historical life expectancy tables is to do no more than that.[12]

Callinan J subsequently acknowledged the reaffirmation of the best evidence rule, whilst simultaneously taking a modern and practical approach, stating:

> courts must evaluate the evidence having regard to the capacities of the respective parties to adduce it, reflect the necessary pragmatism and experience of the common law with respect to human affairs and evidence about them.[13]

The Supreme Court of Queensland refused to admit secondary evidence of videotaped evidence in circumstances where the police had reused the original tapes to 'conserve resources'. Referring to the High Court's 1987 decision

---

11 [2007] HCA 15.

12 Ibid., para 4 per Gummow, Callinan and Crennan JJ. Also approved impliedly by Kirby and Hayne JJ at para 70. See also *R v Governor of Pentonville Prison, ex p Osman* [1989] 3 All ER 701, 728 (1990) 90 Cr App R 281, 308–9.

13 *Thomas v Mowbray* [2007] HCA 33, para 599. See also *Kajala v Noble* (1982) 75 Cr App R 149, 152, where Ackner LJ stated, 'The only remaining instance of it [the best evidence rule] is that, if an original document is available in one's hands, one must produce it; that one cannot give secondary evidence by producing a copy.'

in *Butera v Director of Public Prosecutions for the State of Victoria*,[14] the court required a 'satisfactory explanation' for the absence of the original evidence before admitting secondary evidence. The police had placed static video cameras in place to gather 'intelligence' for its investigations. The police mistakenly regarded the tapes 'to be of no further use':

> It is clear therefore that a deliberate decision was made to delete the video and reuse the tape. I do not consider that to be a satisfactory explanation. Having made a deliberate decision that the evidence was no longer required I do not consider that it can be resurrected in the way sought by merely saying that the wrong forensic decision was made. *Why should secondary evidence be admitted when a deliberate decision was made to discard the best evidence?*[15]

In the same case, the High Court considered the best evidence rule in the context of copied audiotapes.[16] The majority held that:

> when the tape is available or its absence is not accounted for satisfactorily, there can be no reason to admit the evidence of an out-of-court listener to the tape recording to prove what the tape recorded: it should be proved by the playing over of the tape. *Prudence and convenience combine to support the application of the best evidence rule in such a case* ...[17] A copy of the tape is admissible provided the provenance of the original tape, the accuracy of the copying process and the provenance of the copy tape are satisfactorily proved.[18]

Such a formulation lends itself well to the electronic age. The High Court wrestled with the problematic consequences of a rule formulated as long ago as the 16th century, and decided to sidestep the best evidence rule and instead permit consideration of all the circumstances. In other words, the court gave itself discretion to consider the weight to be attributed to the evidence – something which the original rule was at pains to remove.

Ideally, authenticating an electronic document should be possible within the document itself, as with the signature on a traditional paper document. The header and other additional information in emails and other electronic documents corroborate and authenticate the nature of the document as well as features such as

---

14 [1987] HCA 58, see below.
15 *R v Ainsworth* [2011] QSC 418, para 19, emphasis added.
16 [1987] HCA 58.
17 Ibid., para 9, emphasis added.
18 Ibid., para 11.

the sender, author, date and time.[19] The use of a digital signature or a secure or sophisticated electronic signature can help prove the origin of the document as well as authenticate it and verify its contents.

In *R v Maqsud Ali*,[20] the British court discussed the application of the rule to photographs. The court considered that photographs are admissible 'on proof that they are relevant to the issues involved in the case and that the prints are taken from negatives that are untouched'.[21] The prints are in fact copies reproduced by means of mechanical and chemical devices. The court noted that evidence of things seen through telescopes or binoculars which could not be picked up by the naked eye have been admitted, and now there are devices for picking up, transmitting, and recording conversations. There should be 'no difference in principle between a tape recording and a photograph'.[22] This statement ought not be interpreted to mean that such recordings are admissible whatever the circumstances, but it did appear wrong to that court to deny advantages to the law of evidence available through new techniques and new devices, 'provided the accuracy of the recording can be proved', the voices recorded could be properly identified, the evidence is relevant and otherwise admissible, and the court is satisfied that a tape recording is admissible in evidence. The court added, 'Such evidence should always be regarded with some caution and assessed in light of all the circumstances of each case.'[23]

In *R v Frolchenko*,[24] in the Queensland Court of Appeal, the issue of the signature on a document was briefly canvassed by Williams J. His Honour noted that given modern methods of communication, such as email, many communications in writing will not bear a personal signature, but can still be authenticated by looking at such things as whether the name appears in typescript at the end of the document. The court stated that 'absence of an immediate challenge to the admissibility of the document on the ground that the party to the litigation was not responsible for its contents is material'.[25]

One possible factor that the court could take into account is the implementation and use of an audit trail by the organisation or individual who receives or sends the email message. This would go part of the way towards demonstrating that the output from the system that is audited is what it purports to be.

---

19 C Reed, 'Authenticating electronic mail messages – some evidential problems', (1989) 52 *Modern Law Review* 649.
20 [1966] 1 QB 688.
21 Ibid., at 701.
22 Ibid.
23 [1966] 1 QB 688 at 703.
24 [1998] QCA 43.
25 Ibid., per Williams J.

Evidence legislation

Evidence legislation often provides an extremely complicated mechanism for adducing evidence of electronic records. For example, section 95 of the *Evidence Act 1977* (Qld) provides:

> 95 Admissibility of statements in documents or things produced by processes or devices
>
> (1) In a proceeding where direct oral evidence of a fact would be admissible, a statement contained in a document or thing produced wholly or partly by a device or process and tending to establish that fact is, subject to this part, admissible as evidence of that fact.
>
> (2) A court may presume the process or device produced the document or thing containing the statement if the court considers an inference can reasonably be made that the process or device, if properly used, produces a document or thing of that kind.
>
> (3) In a proceeding, a certificate purporting to be signed by a responsible person for the process or device and stating any of the following matters is evidence of the matter for the purpose of subsection (2)–
>
> (a) that the document or thing was produced wholly or partly by the process or device;
>
> (b) that the document or thing was produced wholly or partly in a particular way by the process or device;
>
> (c) that, if properly used, the process or device produces documents or things of a particular kind;
>
> (d) any particulars relevant to a matter mentioned in paragraph (a), (b) or (c).
>
> (4) A person who signs a certificate mentioned in subsection (3) commits an offence if–
>
> (a) a matter is stated in the certificate that the person knows is false or ought reasonably to know is false; and
>
> (b) the statement of the matter is material in the proceeding.

Similar provisions appear in the statutes of South Australia.[26]

The section has been criticised by many commentators.[27] In *R v Shephard*,[28] the House of Lords considered the then UK equivalent of section 95, stating that oral evidence could be accepted in lieu of a certificate signed by a person with responsibility for the operation of the computer:

---

26 *Evidence Act 1929* (SA) ss34C, 59B. For the NZ approach see *Evidence Act 2006* (NZ) Part 3, subpart 8 – Documentary evidence and evidence produced by machine, device of technical process.

27 For example the Queensland Law Reform Commission *The receipt of evidence by Queensland courts: Electronic records*, Issues Paper WP No. 52, 58 (1998). <www.qlrc.qld.gov.au/wp52. html>.

28 [1993] AC 380.

Proof that the computer is reliable can be provided in two ways. Either by calling oral evidence or by tendering a written certificate in accordance with the terms of paragraph 8 of Schedule 3 (s 95(4) Queensland), subject to the power of the judge to require oral evidence.[29]

The House of Lords held that oral evidence as to the requirements of the section concerning the workings of the computer could be satisfied by 'the oral evidence of a person familiar with the operation of the computer who can give evidence of its reliability and such a person need not be a computer expert'.[30] As a consequence, it is most important for all organisations to consider engaging staff who become sufficiently familiar with the organisation's computer system to be in a position to give evidence of its reliability and of the process of record keeping.

Section 48 of the Evidence Acts of the Commonwealth, New South Wales, Tasmania, Victoria and the ACT provides for proof of the contents of documents. The courts have held that the term 'document' includes electronic documents and records.[31]

48 Proof of contents of documents

(1) A party may adduce evidence of the contents of a document in question by tendering the document in question or by any one or more of the following methods:

(a) adducing evidence of an admission made by another party to the proceeding as to the contents of the document in question;

(b) tendering a document that:

(i) is or purports to be a copy of the document in question; and

(ii) has been produced, or purports to have been produced, by a device that reproduces the contents of documents;

(c) if the document in question is an article or thing by which words are recorded in such a way as to be capable of being reproduced as sound, or in which words are recorded in a code (including shorthand writing) – tendering a document that is or purports to be a transcript of the words;

(d) if the document in question is an article or thing on or in which information is stored in such a way that it cannot be used by the court unless a device is used to retrieve, produce or collate it – tendering a document that was or purports to have been produced by use of the device;

(e) tendering a document that –

(i) forms part of the records of or kept by a business (whether or not the business is still in existence); and

(ii) is or purports to be a copy of, or an extract from or a summary of, the document in question, or is or purports to be a copy of such an extract or summary …

29 Ibid., Lord Griffiths at 386.
30 Ibid., at 387.
31 For example, *Eastman v R* [1997] FCA 548.

The *Evidence Act 1906* (WA) contains a similar provision,[32] but an amendment was inserted to effectively remove the best evidence rule: section 73A provides that reproductions are admissible and the 'best evidence rule [is] modified'. Where a document 'accurately reproduces the contents of another document' it is admissible in evidence before a court 'in the same circumstances, and for the same purposes, as that other document, whether or not that other document still exists':[33]

> In determining whether a particular document accurately reproduces the contents of another, a court is not bound by the rules of evidence and–
>
> **(a)** may rely on its own knowledge of the nature and reliability of the processes by which the reproduction was made; or
> **(b)** may make findings based on a certificate in the prescribed form signed by a person with knowledge and experience of the processes by which the reproduction was made; or
> **(c)** may make findings based on a certificate in the prescribed form signed by a person who has compared the contents of both documents and found them to be identical; or
> **(d)** may act on any other basis it considers appropriate in the circumstances.[34]

The provision expressly applies to a reproduction made:

> **(a)** by an instantaneous process; or
> **(b)** by a process in which the contents of a document are recorded by photographic, electronic or other means, and the reproduction is subsequently produced from that record; or
> **(c)** by a process prescribed for the purposes of this section; or
> **(d)** in any other way.[35]

Legislation abolishing the 'original document' rule

In the early 1990s an attempt was made to unify all Australian federal, state and territory Evidence Acts. Today, the Evidence Acts of the Commonwealth, New South Wales, Tasmania, Victoria and the ACT are effectively identical.[36] In each of these jurisdictions the best evidence rule has been abolished. Section 51 of each of the Acts, entitled 'Original document rule abolished', provides:

---

32 *Evidence Act 1906* (WA) s79C.
33 *Evidence Act 1906* (WA) s73A(1).
34 *Evidence Act 1906* (WA) s73A(2).
35 *Evidence Act 1906* (WA) s73A(3).
36 *Evidence Act 1995* (Cth), *Evidence Act 1995* (NSW), *Evidence Act 2001* (Tas), *Evidence Act 2008* (Vic) and *Evidence Act 2011* (ACT).

> The principles and rules of the common law that relate to the means of proving the contents of documents are abolished.

Additionally, the Acts make no reference to 'original'. The Acts define 'document' by reference to the contents rather than the medium. Reference to a document adduced into evidence is a reference to the contents of that document. Reference to a copy of a document adduced into evidence 'includes a reference to a document that is not an exact copy of the document in question but that is otherwise identical to the document in question in all *relevant* respects'.[37] This definition explains the rationale of the legislation. This approach, on its own, would be sufficient to impliedly abolish the best evidence rule.

However, the following provisions elaborate. In addition to adducing evidence of the contents of a document by tendering the original, and by adducing evidence of an admission made by another party to the proceeding with respect to the contents of the documents, specific provisions permit a variety of copies to be adduced.

A party may tender a document that is, or purports to be, a copy of the document in question which has been produced, or purports to have been produced, by a device that reproduces the contents of documents. Second, if the document in question is an article or thing by which words are recorded in such a way as to be capable of being reproduced as sound, or in which words are recorded in a code, including shorthand writing, the evidence may be adduced by tendering a document that is, or purports to be, a transcript of the words. Third, if the document in question is an article or thing on or in which information is stored in such a way that it cannot be used by the court unless a device is used to retrieve, produce or collate it, evidence may be adduced by tendering a document that has been produced by use of the device. Fourth, evidence may be adduced by tendering a document that forms part of business records which purports to be a copy of or an extract from or a summary of, the document.[38]

As a result, all documents, including electronic documents and copies, are now admissible in those jurisdictions. However, most importantly it is left to the courts to determine the weight given to them.

In the High Court of Australia, in *Butera v DPP*,[39] Dawson J stated that 'some modes of proof are better than others, but that … goes to weight rather than admissibility'.[40] As with oral evidence given by witnesses, the fact that certain evidence is admissible does not mean that it will be accepted by the court, or even be given the same weight throughout.

---

37 Evidence Acts of the Commonwealth, New South Wales, Victoria, Tasmania and the ACT, s47, emphasis added.
38 Evidence Acts of the Commonwealth, New South Wales, Tasmania, Victoria and the ACT, s48(1).
39 (1987) 164 CLR 180 (*Butera's* case').
40 (1987) 164 CLR 180 at 195.

In *Eastman v R*,[41] the Federal Court of Australia considered the application of section 48 in relation to the admission into evidence of an audiotape:

> The definition of '*document*' includes a record of information from which sounds can be reproduced. As the transcripts were admissible under s.48(1)(c) as evidence of the contents of the tapes, the procedure followed by the trial judge could not affect the admissibility of the tape recordings. As it was, the transcripts were received into evidence as an aide-memoire, and the jury was instructed to treat the transcripts only as an aid. Where, on the evidence adduced in a particular case, there is doubt or disagreement whether the transcript, or part of it, accurately deciphers the sounds captured on the tape, it seems to us that this should be the role of the transcript, notwithstanding the provisions of s.48(1)(c) of the Evidence Act. In the present case, the transcript[s] … were admissible for the purpose of assisting the jury.[42]

Section 48 applies equally to electronic records. This section permits copies or printouts to be tendered as evidence in these four jurisdictions. The expression 'device' is used to include a computer system, and correspondingly, 'tendering a document that was or purports to have been produced by use of the device' is satisfactory. In *Wade (a pseudonym) v The Queen*,[43] the Victorian Court of Appeal, in applying the Victorian equivalent of section 48, stated that the section 'is manifestly not discretionary in any sense other than enabling a litigant who satisfied its conditions to choose to prove the contents of a document by secondary evidence'.

International perspective

The UN Commission on International Trade Law (UNCITRAL) *Model Law on Electronic Commerce 1996* ('Model Law')[44] includes a provision dealing with 'Admissibility and evidential weight of data messages'. The expression 'data messages' is defined to include:

> information generated, sent, received or stored by electronic, optical or similar means, including, but not limited to, electronic data interchange (EDI), electronic mail, telegram, telex or telecopy.[45]

Article 9 provides that the rules of evidence must not deny the admissibility of a data message in evidence on the sole ground that it is a data message, nor, where the data message is the best evidence reasonably available, on the grounds that it

---

41 [1997] FCA 548.
42 [1997] FCA 548, Ground 11.
43 [2014] VSCA 13, para 39 per Nettle JA.
44 UNCITRAL website: <www.uncitral.org/pdf/english/texts/electcom/05–89450_Ebook.pdf>.
45 UNCITRAL, above n 44, art 2.

is not in its original form. Especially, sub-article 9(2) states, 'Information in the form of a data message shall be given due evidential weight.'

In a manner reminiscent of *Butera's* case, the Model Law provides that in assessing the evidential weight of a data message:

> regard shall be had to the reliability of the manner in which the data message was generated, stored or communicated, to the reliability of the manner in which the integrity of the information was maintained, to the manner in which its originator was identified, and to any other relevant factor.[46]

Although the Model Law has been used as a template in more than 50 jurisdictions internationally,[47] this particular provision was omitted from the Australian and New Zealand Electronic Transactions Acts, because it was thought that such a provision is best placed in a jurisdiction's evidence legislation and not in its electronic commerce legislation. For example, in Australia, the Model Law was the basis for the Electronic Transactions Acts in all nine jurisdictions;[48] however, this provision was omitted from the initial *Electronic Transactions Act 1999* (Cth) because the *Evidence Act 1995* (Cth) had a few years earlier abolished the best evidence rule, making an additional provision obsolete. The remaining eight Australian jurisdictions followed the lead of the Commonwealth, even though there was no similar redundancy in most jurisdictions' legislation at the time.

The *Electronic Transactions Act 2002* (NZ) also did not include this provision. The *Evidence Act 2006* (NZ) provides that where a party offers evidence that was produced 'wholly or partly by a machine, device, or technical process' (for example, scanning) and the machine, device, or technical process is 'of a kind that ordinarily does what a party asserts it to have done', it is presumed, in the absence of evidence to the contrary, 'that on a particular occasion the machine, device, or technical process did what that party asserts it to have done'.[49] Where the information is stored so that it cannot be accessed by the court unless the relevant 'machine, device, or technical process' is used, then 'a party may offer a document that was or purports to have been displayed, retrieved, or collated by use of the machine, device, or technical process'.[50]

The *Civil Evidence Act 1995* (UK) also effectively abolishes the best evidence rule. The substantive provision permits the admission of copies of any degree of remoteness from the original. A statement contained in a document may be proved either '(a) by the production of that document, or (b) whether or not that document is still in existence, by the production of a copy of that document or of the material

---

46 UNCITRAL, above n 44, sub-art 9(2).
47 See Chapter 11.
48 The Commonwealth, six states and two territories; and New Zealand.
49 *Evidence Act 2006* (NZ) s137(1).
50 *Evidence Act 2006* (NZ) s137(2).

part of it, authenticated in such manner as the court may approve'.[51] It is immaterial 'how many removes there are between a copy and the original'.[52] Section 13 encompasses electronic documents by providing that a 'document' means anything in which information of any description is recorded, and 'copy', in relation to a document, means anything onto which information recorded in the document has been copied, by whatever means and whether directly or indirectly.

In the United States, federal courts follow the Federal Uniform Rules of Evidence, while state courts generally follow state legislature rules. At the federal level, the best evidence rule has been retained and is largely codified in the *Federal Uniform Rules of Evidence*.[53] To prove 'the content of a writing, recording, or photograph, the original writing, recording, or photograph is required, except as otherwise provided in these rules or by Act of Congress'.[54] Duplicates are admissible 'to the same extent as an original' unless a genuine question is raised as to the authenticity of the original or in circumstances in which it would be unfair to admit the duplicate in lieu of the original.[55] The official notes to this provision explain that when the only concern is 'with getting the words or other contents before the court with accuracy and precision, then a counterpart serves equally as well as the original'.[56] A 'duplicate' is defined as 'a counterpart produced by the same impression as the original, or from the same matrix, or by means of photography, including enlargements and miniatures, or by mechanical or electronic re-recording, or by chemical reproduction, or by other equivalent techniques which accurately reproduce the original'.[57]

Writings and recordings include not only 'handwriting, typewriting, printing, photostating, photographing', but also electronic forms such as a 'magnetic impulse, mechanical or electronic recording, or other form of data compilation'.[58] Photographs include still photographs, x-rays, videotapes and motion pictures.[59]

The *Indian Evidence Act 1872* (India) codifies the secondary evidence rule providing that the contents of documents 'may be proved either by primary or by secondary evidence';[60] '[d]ocuments must be proved by primary evidence'[61] subject to the customary exceptions.[62] Section 65 provides:

---

51 *Civil Evidence Act 1995* (UK) s8.
52 *Civil Evidence Act 1995* (UK) s8.
53 Several US states (such as California) follow this federal approach.
54 *Federal Uniform Rules of Evidence*, art X, rule 1002.
55 *Federal Uniform Rules of Evidence*, art X, rule 1003.
56 *Federal Uniform Rules of Evidence*, art X, Official Note to rule 1003.
57 *Federal Uniform Rules of Evidence*, art X, rule 1003.
58 *Federal Uniform Rules of Evidence*, art X, rule 1001.
59 *Federal Uniform Rules of Evidence*, art X.
60 *Indian Evidence Act 1872* (India) s61.
61 *Indian Evidence Act 1872* (India) s64; see also s22.
62 *Indian Evidence Act 1872* (India) s65.

65 Cases in which secondary evidence relating to documents may be given

Secondary evidence may be given of the existence, condition or contents of a document in the following cases:

(a)   When the original is shown or appears to be in the possession or power of the person against whom the document is sought to be proved, or of any person out of reach of, or not subject to, the process of the Court, or of any person legally bound to produce it, and when, after the notice mentioned in Section 66, such person does not produce it;

(b)   when the existence, condition or contents of the original have been proved to be admitted in writing by the person against whom it is proved or by his representative in interest;

(c)   when the original has been destroyed or lost, or when the party offering evidence of its contents cannot, for any other reason not arising from his own default or neglect, produce it in reasonable time;

(d)   When the original is of such a nature as not to be easily movable;

(e)   when the original is a public document within the meaning of Section 74;

(f)   when the original is a document of which a certified copy is permitted by this Act, or by any other law in force in India to be given in evidence;

(g)   when the originals consist of numerous accounts or other documents which cannot conveniently be examined in Court, and the fact to be proved is the general result of the whole collection.

In cases (a), (c) and (d), any secondary evidence of the contents of the documents is admissible. In case (b), the written admission is admissible. In case (e) or (f), a certified copy of the document, but no other kind of secondary evidence, is admissible. In case (g), evidence may be given as to the general result of the documents by any person who has examined them, and who is skilled in the examination of such documents.

Primary evidence is defined as 'the document itself produced for the inspection of the Court'.[63] Secondary evidence is defined as:

(1)   certified copies as given under the provisions hereinafter contained;

(2)   copies made from the original by mechanical processes which in themselves ensure the accuracy of the copy, and copies compared with such copies;

(3)   copies made from or compared with the original;

(4)   counterparts of documents as against the parties who did not execute them;

(5)   oral accounts of the contents of a document given by some person who has himself seen it.[64]

---

63 *Indian Evidence Act 1872* (India) s62.
64 *Indian Evidence Act 1872* (India) s63. The Act includes specific examples, referred to as 'illustrations'.

Hard copies of electronic records as evidence

Where the original document is electronic, a question sometimes arises as to whether a hard copy, such as a printout of the electronic document, is admissible as evidence in a court of law if strictly applying the secondary evidence rule. For example, many organisations print out a hard copy of important emails as a 'permanent' record, and then delete the electronic version. These organisations risk a ruling that the printout is inadmissible, thus jeopardising their opportunity to provide relevant evidence before the court. Law firms that adopt this practice would be professionally negligent. The printouts are inferior copies of the electronic documents.

This practice is an unnecessary hangover from the early days of computers being used for commercial purposes, the 1970s and 1980s, when computer space was expensive and computer specialists urged and advised users to 'clean out' the computer space for premium efficiency. In the 21st century computer space is cheap and plentiful, and there are many electronic methods of archiving and storing such records, documents and communications.

The US case of *Armstrong v Executive of the President*[65] involved the status of a printout of an email. The court concluded that the printed version of the email contained less information than the electronic version. The missing information included the date of the transmission, the date of receipt, the detailed list of recipients and linkages between messages sent and replies received.

Should such a document be called into question, it is clear that, in jurisdictions where the secondary evidence rule has been abolished, greater weight would and should be given to the electronic document. Also, it may be reasonable for the court to question why the 'original' document was destroyed, particularly if it is thought that the electronic version contained information which would have assisted the court in substantiating the document's originality and accuracy. The requirement for documents to be kept for set periods of time under statutes of limitation applies equally to electronic documents.[66]

This issue has connections to the role of President Reagan in the Iran-Contra affair in the 1980s. In 1986 Oliver North and national security adviser John Poindexter erased thousands of their email messages on their way out of the National Security Council (NSC). However, the system's backup tapes allowed investigators

---

65 810 F. Supp. 335 (1993).
66 See Catherine E Pasterczyk, 'E-Federal e-mail management: A records manager's view of *Armstrong v Executive Office of the President* and its aftermath', (1998) 32–2 *ARMA Records Management* 10–22.

to recover these messages and use them as evidence in court proceedings. Journalist Scott Armstrong and others sought the NSC records. The Executive Office of the President argued that the entire NSC was exempt from otherwise applicable US Freedom of Information legislation. The subsequent lawsuit, *Armstrong v Executive Office of the President*,[67] was brought to prevent the backup records from being erased. Researchers were using the records to piece together the controversial arms sales to Iran and the funding of Nicaraguan rebels.

The Reagan Administration planned to delete the backups. Court rulings established that the archives and records laws for the retention of documents apply to email. The Bush Administration[68] then staged a midnight raid, on Inauguration Eve in January 1993, to put the tapes beyond the law.

Judge Richey pointed out the problems with paper copies of electronic material:

> paper and the computer versions of these electronic records are different ...
> A note distributed over these computer system[s] includes information that is
> not reproduced on the paper copy regarding who has received the informa-
> tion and when the information was received, neither of which is reproduced
> on the paper copy ... Material must be saved in a way that includes all the
> pertinent information contained therein ... paper copies of these materials do
> not include all of the relevant information.[69]

There are no cases in Australia or New Zealand decided on this evidentiary issue, but the potential remains. As long as legal systems require standards for the quality of evidence, secondary evidence will be rejected or, in appropriate cases, given less weight in judicial determinations.

Originals and copies – envelopes and attachments

The secondary evidence rule is less than satisfactory when applied to electronic records. Who has the original when an email is sent? This is a complicated question and one which has not been adequately dealt with by the courts. There are a number of complicating factors.

First, there are multiple copies of the email created and copied. The sender has a copy in the space for Random Access Memory (RAM), temporary space and permanent space. On sending, the email is copied to the internet service provider

(ISP), several routers on the internet, the recipient's ISP and finally the recipient's RAM space, temporary space and permanent space. The recipient may copy the email electronically to storage folders or archives.

Second, the recipient actually receives a different document from that sent. Hidden from the reader is additional information. This was identified in *Armstrong's* case (see above). Some of this information is not part of the email at the time it is sent – the final email that is copied differs from the one that was sent.

Third, there is a requirement to consider the intention of the sender. Did the sender intend that the entire electronic record form the communication, or only the 'text' of the main message? This is not an entirely new problem. When a traditional letter is sent by post, to what extent does the sender intend including the envelope, postmark and stamps as part of the communication? The envelope and postmark can be evidence of sending, receipt and timing. The dilemma is the difference between the intended use of the sender and the actual use made by the recipient: it is not clear if the recipient's understanding and use should be seen as dependent on the intention of the sender. Should a dispute arise, both parties would be in a much stronger position if they retained the full electronic version of, for example, the email, as recognised in *Armstrong's* case. Intention and use may both be gleaned from the format and structure used by the sender.

Many organisations, businesses and individuals prefer their communications to be more formal than emails. Some prepare a formal electronic letter, with the organisation's letterhead and even a digitised traditional signature, and attach it to the electronic communication, which may simply state that the 'document' is attached. It has been argued that the email would now operate in the same manner as an envelope, perhaps merely corroborating the time and place of the communication, but not forming part of the message. This practice raises several questions. Should the attachment be kept in its original electronic form or can it be printed out? It may appear that the sender simply prefers the appearance of a formal hardcopy letter. However, assuming that the attachment was a simple Microsoft Word file, there are several complicating factors.[70] Microsoft Word files contain a significant amount of statistical information in addition to the text: the date the file was created, the number of revisions, the date and times of revisions and in some cases prior drafts. This additional information could corroborate claims made by one party regarding a particular statement of affairs. The nature and extent of other formats can exacerbate such considerations. A printout of the attachment and deletion of the electronic file removes this potential corroborative evidence.

Fourth, the courts – and much of the public discussion – have failed to recognise the distinction between analogue and digital data. Data recorded onto audio and videotapes is typically analogue. Every time analogue data is copied the data

---

70 These factors arise with many similar word processing programs.

is degraded. The picture may be less clear and the sound may have decreased quality and increased background noise. Photocopies typically scan the original and attempt to recreate it. Some modern photocopiers are excellent, but colours may be marginally copied or turned to black, white or grey; and a light pencil notation may become invisible on the copy. The reproduction is clearly inferior and less reliable. Digital copying, for example of DVDs and computer data, involves recording by the duplication of bits and bytes precisely. When the process operates correctly the copy is identical to the original. Copies of analogue data ought to be regarded with greater suspicion than digital copies, putting aside the question of tampering. *Butera's* case involved an analogue copy. The court ultimately required information on the provenance of the original tape, the accuracy of the copying process and the provenance of the copy tape. Despite the difference in the process and the result, the same approach is appropriate for digital copies. It is vital that organisations set up processes which record all steps, are secure, and are capable of presentation as evidence when required.

Conclusion

As a general principle, in jurisdictions applying the secondary evidence rule, courts must dictate that the printout is an inadmissible copy. There are well-established exceptions to this rule, such as lost or destroyed documents, public documents, and the application of a Notice to Produce. However, courts ought not admit evidence where the loss or destruction was a deliberate act of the party relying on the copy.[71] The probity of the inferior copy must in appropriate cases be questioned.

In jurisdictions where the secondary evidence rule has been abolished, greater weight should be given to the electronic document. Destroying the electronic record in preference to a printed hard copy risks the 'document' being inadmissible or being given less weight. It is reasonable for the court to question why 'original' electronic documents have been destroyed, as they contain information which would assist the court in substantiating originality and accuracy.

In legal proceedings, most parties, as a matter of practice and convenience, admit undisputed documents into evidence. Nevertheless, where the legitimate interests of the client would be furthered by challenging a hard copy of an electronic record, it is incumbent on the lawyer to do so and for the court to consider, if it remains appropriate, the principle of the secondary evidence rule.

---

71 See RA Brown, *Documentary Evidence in Australia*, 2nd edn, LBC Information Services, Sydney, 1996, 128–29.

All parties should retain documents in the form in which they were issued or presented. Attempting to change the medium may have undesirable, if not unpredictable, consequences.

FURTHER READING

Alan Davidson, 'Armstrong's case 10 years on', (2003) 23 *Proctor* 34.

John Gregory, 'The Uniform Electronic Evidence Act Revisited (By Archivists)', *Slaw*: <www.slaw.ca>.

Catherine E Pasterczyk, 'E-Federal e-mail management: A records manager's view of *Armstrong v Executive Office of the President* and its aftermath', (1998) 32–2 *ARMA Records Management* 10–22.

Queensland Law Reform Commission, *The receipt of evidence by Queensland courts: Electronic records*, Issues Paper WP No. 52, (1998) 58; <www.qlrc.qld.gov.au/wp52.html>.

C Reed, 'Authenticating electronic mail messages – some evidential problems', (1989) 52 *Modern Law Review* 649.

PART

4

CONCLUSION

20

REFLECTIONS AND CONCLUSIONS

Social media and electronic commerce have evolved with unprecedented speed and energy. As with *lex mercatori*, where merchants and commercial parties embraced new methods and opportunities with a cavalier attitude to the law, so do participants in the online world. The law makers have the job of reacting to and providing an appropriate response to this ever-changing landscape. In the majority of circumstances, traditional legal principles will apply. This book reflects on the jurisprudential underpinnings, and at how they absorb and assimilate changing circumstances and create new structures and new rules.

The lawyer is trained not to know all the laws but to master the ability to research current law. The lawyer must carve a path through a labyrinth of regulations, primary and secondary sources, rulings, practice notes, periodicals and databases. No single law firm or department can physically store all the materials that may be called upon, but the internet can now deliver this avalanche of material, with only two preconditions. First, the authors and handlers of the material must be willing to permit public access, and second, the lawyer must be aware of its presence.

Australian lawyers and commercial parties need to monitor the changing Australian and international legal environment to ensure that their social, legal and commercial risk is controlled and minimised. Governments and courts must remain vigilant to keep abreast of social media issues and electronic commerce developments. Regulations in cyberspace must evolve in a way that maintains the global community's commitments to fundamental human rights and to national governance, and that reflects the range of global values and human diversity. The application of the rule of law, and of human rights law, must move into cyberspace. There are 'profound consequences for the future of the rule of law in cyberspace',[1] which has developed into its own unique notion: 'the rule of cyberspace'. This rule of cyberspace is but another step in the path of social and jurisprudential development.

The hypothesis of this book was that order is endogenous. Each chapter and instance discussed and examined has demonstrated how such law and order has been built, from both large and small changes. The emergence of structures to facilitate personal communications, short texts, images and videos, sites for daily journals and experiences, mass and global communications, as well as the development of domain names, intellectual property concerns, jurisdiction and contract formation, reveal the 'invisible hand' of Adam Smith and the 'spontaneous order' of Friedrich Hayek. The 'Electronic Renaissance' has woven its way into the fabric of society. The rule of cyberspace is the rule of law emerging in an Aristotelian manner, with the commercial growth achieved through individual self-interest, as predicted by Adam Ferguson. The progression of the law of social media and electronic commerce demonstrates that human existence tends towards structure, and that order therefore always emerges endogenously.

---

1 M Kirby, 'Privacy in Cyberspace' [1998] *UNSW Law Journal* 47.

Appendix A *Electronic Transactions (Victoria) Act 2000*

No. 20 of 2000
Version as at 1 January 2015

Part 1 – Preliminary

1 Purposes

The purposes of this Act are –

(a) to recognise that transactions effected electronically are not by that reason alone invalid;

(b) to provide for the meeting of certain legal requirements as to writing and signatures by electronic communication;

(c) to permit documents to be produced to another person by electronic communication;

(d) to permit the recording and retention of information and documents in electronic form;

(e) to provide for the determination of time and place of dispatch and receipt of electronic communications;

(f) to stipulate when an electronic communication will bind its purported originator.

2 Commencement

This Act comes into operation on 1 September 2000.

3 Definitions

(1) In this Act –

addressee of an electronic communication means a person who is intended by the originator to receive the electronic communication, but does not include a person acting as an intermediary with respect to the electronic communication;

automated message system means a computer program or an electronic or other automated means used to initiate an action or respond to data messages in whole or in part, without review or intervention by a natural person each time an action is initiated or a response is generated by the system;

consent includes consent that can reasonably be inferred from the conduct of the person concerned, but does not include consent given subject to conditions unless the conditions are complied with;

data includes the whole or part of a computer program within the meaning of the Copyright Act 1968 of the Commonwealth;

data storage device means any article or material (for example, a disk) from which information is capable of being reproduced, with or without the aid of any other article or device;

electronic communication means –

(a) a communication of information in the form of data, text or images by means of guided or unguided electromagnetic energy, or both; or

(b) a communication of information in the form of sound by means of guided or unguided electromagnetic energy, or both, where the sound is processed at its destination by an automated voice recognition system;

information means information in the form of data, text, images or sound;

information system means a system for generating, sending, receiving, storing or otherwise processing electronic communications;

information technology requirements includes software requirements;

law of this jurisdiction means any law in force in this jurisdiction, whether written or unwritten, but does not include a law of the Commonwealth;

non-profit body means a body that is not carried on for the purposes of profit or gain to its individual members and is, by the terms of the body's constitution, prohibited from making any distribution, whether in money, property or otherwise, to its members;

originator of an electronic communication means a person by whom, or on whose behalf, the electronic communication has been sent or generated before storage, if any, but does not include a person acting as an intermediary with respect to the electronic communication;

performance of a contract includes non-performance of the contract;

place of business means –

(a) in relation to a person, other than an entity referred to in paragraph (b) – a place where the person maintains a non-transitory establishment to pursue an economic activity other than the temporary provision of goods or services out of a specific location; or

(b) in relation to a government, an authority of a government or a non-profit body – a place where any operations or activities are carried out by that government, authority or body;this jurisdiction means Victoria;

transaction includes –

(a) any transaction in the nature of a contract, agreement or other arrangement; and

(b) any statement, declaration, demand, notice or request, including an offer and the acceptance of an offer, that the parties are required to make or choose to make in connection with the formation or performance of a contract, agreement or other arrangement; and

(c) any transaction of a non-commercial nature.

(d) Notes do not form part of this Act.

4 Object

The object of this Act is to provide a regulatory framework that –

(a) recognises the importance of the information economy to the future economic and social prosperity of Australia; and

(b) facilitates the use of electronic transactions; and

(c) promotes business and community confidence in the use of electronic transactions; and

(d) enables business and the community to use electronic communications in their dealings with government.

5 Outline of Act

(1) The following is an outline of this Act –

(a) for the purposes of a law of this jurisdiction, a transaction is not invalid because it took place by means of one or more electronic communications;

(b) the following requirements imposed under a law of this jurisdiction can generally be met in electronic form –

    (i) a requirement to give information in writing;

    (ii) a requirement to provide a signature;

    (iii) a requirement to produce a document;

    (iv) a requirement to record information;

    (v) a requirement to retain a document;

(c)   for the purposes of a law of this jurisdiction, provision is made for determining the time and place of the dispatch and receipt of an electronic communication;

(d)   the purported originator of an electronic communication is bound by it for the purposes of a law of this jurisdiction only if the communication was sent by the purported originator or with the authority of the purported originator.

(1A) Part 2A contains provisions applying to contracts involving electronic communications, including provisions (relating to the Internet in particular) for the following –

(a)   an unaddressed proposal to form a contract is to be regarded as an invitation to make offers, rather than as an offer that if accepted would result in a contract;

(b)   a contract formed automatically is not invalid, void or unenforceable because there was no human review or intervention;

(c)   a portion of an electronic communication containing an input error can be withdrawn in certain circumstances;

(d)   the application of certain provisions of Part 2 to the extent they do not apply of their own force.

(2)   Subsections (1) and (1A) are intended only as a guide to the general scheme and effect of this Act.

6 Crown to be bound

This Act binds the Crown in right of Victoria and, in so far as the legislative power of Parliament permits, the Crown in all its other capacities.

6A Exemptions

(1)   The regulations may provide that all or specified provisions of this Act do not apply –

(a)   to transactions, requirements, permissions, electronic communications or other matters specified, or of classes specified, in the regulations for the purposes of this section; or (b) in circumstances specified, or of classes specified, in the regulations for the purposes of this section.

(2)   The regulations may provide that all or specified provisions of this Act do not apply to specified laws of this jurisdiction.

Part 2 – Application of Legal Requirements to Electronic Communications

Division 1 – General rule about validity of transactions for the purposes of laws of this jurisdiction

7 Validity of electronic transactions

(1) For the purposes of a law of this jurisdiction, a transaction is not invalid because it took place wholly or partly by means of one or more electronic communications.

(2) The general rule in subsection (1) does not apply in relation to the validity of a transaction to the extent to which another, more specific, provision of this Part deals with the validity of the transaction.

Division 2 – Requirements under laws of this jurisdiction

8 Writing

(1) If, by or under a law of this jurisdiction, a person is required to give information in writing, that requirement is taken to have been met if the person gives the information by means of an electronic communication, where –

    (a) at the time the information was given, it was reasonable to expect that the information would be readily accessible so as to be useable for subsequent reference; and

    (b) the person to whom the information is required to be given consents to the information being given by means of an electronic communication.

(2) If, by or under a law of this jurisdiction, a person is permitted to give information in writing, the person may give the information by means of an electronic communication, where –

    (a) at the time the information was given, it was reasonable to expect that the information would be readily accessible so as to be useable for subsequent reference; and

(b) the person to whom the information is permitted to be given consents to the information being given by means of an electronic communication.

(3) This section does not affect the operation of any other law of this jurisdiction that makes provision for or in relation to requiring or permitting information to be given, in accordance with particular information technology requirements –

(a) on a particular kind of data storage device; or

(b) by means of a particular kind of electronic communication.

(4) This section applies to a requirement or permission to give information, whether the expression 'give', 'send' or 'serve', or any other expression, is used.

(5) For the purposes of this section, *giving information* includes, but is not limited to, the following –

(a) making an application;

(b) making or lodging a claim;

(c) giving, sending or serving a notification;

(d) lodging a return;

(e) making a request;

(f) making a declaration;

(g) lodging or issuing a certificate;

(h) making, varying or cancelling an election;

(i) lodging an objection;

(j) giving a statement of reasons.

9 Signatures

(1) If, by or under a law of this jurisdiction, the signature of a person is required, that requirement is taken to have been met in relation to an electronic communication if –

(a) a method is used to identify the person and to indicate the person's intention in respect of the information communicated; and

(b) the method used was either –

(i) as reliable as appropriate for the purpose for which the electronic communication was generated or communicated, in the light of all the circumstances, including any relevant agreement; or

(ii) proven in fact to have fulfilled the functions described in paragraph (a), by itself or together with further evidence; and

(c) the person to whom the signature is required to be given consents to that requirement being met by way of the use of the method mentioned in paragraph (a).

(2)　This section does not affect the operation of any other law of this jurisdiction that makes provision for or in relation to requiring –

(a)　an electronic communication to contain an electronic signature (however described); or

(b)　an electronic communication to contain a unique identification in an electronic form; or

(c)　a particular method to be used in relation to an electronic communication to identify the originator of the communication and to indicate the originator's intention in respect of the information communicated.

(3)　The reference in subsection (1) to a law that requires a signature includes a reference to a law that provides consequences for the absence of a signature.

10 Production of document

(1)　If, by or under a law of this jurisdiction, a person is required to produce a document that is in the form of paper, an article or other material, that requirement is taken to have been met if the person produces, by means of an electronic communication, an electronic form of the document, where –

(a)　having regard to all the relevant circumstances at the time the communication was sent, the method of generating the electronic form of the document provided a reliable means of assuring the maintenance of the integrity of the information contained in the document; and

(b)　at the time the communication was sent, it was reasonable to expect that the information contained in the electronic form of the document would be readily accessible so as to be useable for subsequent reference; and

(c)　the person to whom the document is required to be produced consents to the production, by means of an electronic communication, of an electronic form of the document.

(2)　If, by or under a law of this jurisdiction, a person is permitted to produce a document that is in the form of paper, an article or other material, then, instead of producing the document in that form, the person may produce, by means of an electronic communication, an electronic form of the document, where –

(a)　having regard to all the relevant circumstances at the time the communication was sent, the method of generating the electronic form of the document provided a reliable means of assuring the maintenance of the integrity of the information contained in the document; and

(b)   at the time the communication was sent, it was reasonable to expect that the information contained in the electronic form of the document would be readily accessible so as to be useable for subsequent reference; and

(c)   the person to whom the document is permitted to be produced consents to the production, by means of an electronic communication, of an electronic form of the document.

(3)   For the purposes of this section, the integrity of information contained in a document is maintained if, and only if, the information has remained complete and unaltered, apart from –

(a)   the addition of any endorsement; or

(b)   any immaterial change –

which arises in the normal course of communication, storage or display.

(4)   This section does not affect the operation of any other law of this jurisdiction that makes provision for or in relation to requiring or permitting electronic forms of documents to be produced, in accordance with particular information technology requirements –

(a)   on a particular kind of data storage device; or

(b)   by means of a particular kind of electronic communication.

11 Retention of information and documents

(1)   If, by or under a law of this jurisdiction, a person is required to record information in writing, that requirement is taken to have been met if the person records the information in electronic form, where –

(a)   at the time of the recording of the information, it was reasonable to expect that the information would be readily accessible so as to be useable for subsequent reference; and

(b)   if the regulations require that the information be recorded on a particular kind of data storage device, that requirement has been met.

(2)   If, by or under a law of this jurisdiction, a person is required to retain, for a particular period, a document that is in the form of paper, an article or other material, that requirement is taken to have been met if the person retains, or causes another person to retain, an electronic form of the document throughout that period, where –

(a)   having regard to all the relevant circumstances at the time of the generation of the electronic form of the document, the method of generating the electronic form of the document provided a reliable means of assuring the maintenance of the integrity of the information contained in the document; and

(b)   at the time of the generation of the electronic form of the document, it was reasonable to expect that the information contained in the electronic form of the document would be readily accessible so as to be useable for subsequent reference; and

(c)   if the regulations require that the electronic form of the document be retained on a particular kind of data storage device, that requirement has been met throughout that period.

(3)   For the purposes of subsection (2), the integrity of information contained in a document is maintained if, and only if, the information has remained complete and unaltered, apart from –

(a)   the addition of any endorsement; or

(b)   any immaterial change – which arises in the normal course of communication, storage or display.

(4)   If, by or under a law of this jurisdiction, a person (**the first person**) is required to retain, for a particular period, information that was the subject of an electronic communication, that requirement is taken to have been met if the first person retains, or causes another person to retain, in electronic form, the information throughout that period, where –

(a)   at the time of commencement of the retention of the information, it was reasonable to expect that the information would be readily accessible so as to be useable for subsequent reference; and

(b)   having regard to all the relevant circumstances at the time of commencement of the retention of the information, the method of retaining the information in electronic form provided a reliable means of assuring the maintenance of the integrity of the information contained in the electronic communication; and

(c)   throughout that period, the first person also retains, or causes the other person to retain, in electronic form, such additional information obtained by the first person as is sufficient to enable the identification of the following –

   (i)   the origin of the electronic communication;

   (ii)   the destination of the electronic communication;

   (iii)   the time when the electronic communication was sent;

   (iv)   the time when the electronic communication was received; and

(d)   at the time of commencement of the retention of the additional information covered by paragraph (c), it was reasonable to expect that the additional information would be readily accessible so as to be useable for subsequent reference; and

(e)   if the regulations require that the information be retained on a particular kind of data storage device, that requirement has been met throughout that period.

(5)   For the purposes of subsection (4), the integrity of information that was the subject of an electronic communication is maintained if, and only if, the information has remained complete and unaltered, apart from –

(a)   the addition of any endorsement; or

(b)   any immaterial change –

which arises in the normal course of communication, storage or display.

Division 3 – Other provisions relating to laws of this jurisdiction

13 Time of dispatch

(1)   For the purposes of a law of this jurisdiction, unless otherwise agreed between the originator and the addressee of an electronic communication, the time of dispatch of the electronic communication is –

(a)   the time when the electronic communication leaves an information system under the control of the originator or of the party who sent it on behalf of the originator; or

(b)   if the electronic communication has not left an information system under the control of the originator or of the party who sent it on behalf of the originator – the time when the electronic communication is received by the addressee.

Note – Paragraph (b) would apply to a case where the parties exchange electronic communications through the same information system.

(2)   Subsection (1) applies even though the place where the information system supporting an electronic address is located may be different from the place where the electronic communication is taken to have been dispatched under section 13B.

13A Time of receipt

(1)   For the purposes of a law of this jurisdiction, unless otherwise agreed between the originator and the addressee of an electronic communication –

(a)   the time of receipt of the electronic communication is the time when the electronic communication becomes capable of being retrieved by the addressee at an electronic address designated by the addressee; or

(b)   the time of receipt of the electronic communication at another electronic address of the addressee is the time when both –

      (i)   the electronic communication has become capable of being re-trieved by the addressee at that address; and

     (ii) the addressee has become aware that the electronic communica-tion has been sent to that address.

(2)   For the purposes of subsection (1), unless otherwise agreed between the originator and the addressee of the electronic communication, it is to be as-sumed that the electronic communication is capable of being retrieved by the addressee when it reaches the addressee's electronic address.

(3)   Subsection (1) applies even though the place where the information system supporting an electronic address is located may be different from the place where the electronic communication is taken to have been received under section 13B.

13B Place of dispatch and place of receipt

(1)   For the purposes of a law of this jurisdiction, unless otherwise agreed be-tween the originator and the addressee of an electronic communication –

    (a)   the electronic communication is taken to have been dispatched at the place where the originator has its place of business; and

    (b)   the electronic communication is taken to have been received at the place where the addressee has its place of business.

(2)   For the purposes of the application of subsection (1) to an electronic com-munication –

    (a)   a party's place of business is assumed to be the location indicated by that party, unless another party demonstrates that the party making the indication does not have a place of business at that location; and

    (b)   if a party has not indicated a place of business and has only one place of business, it is to be assumed that that place is the party's place of business; and

    (c)   if a party has not indicated a place of business and has more than one place of business, the place of business is that which has the closest relationship to the underlying transaction, having regard to the circum-stances known to or contemplated by the parties at any time before or at the conclusion of the transaction; and

    (d)   if a party has not indicated a place of business and has more than one place of business, but paragraph (c) does not apply – it is to be assumed that the party's principal place of business is the party's only place of business; and

    (e)   if a party is a natural person and does not have a place of business – it is to be assumed that the party's place of business is the place of the party's habitual residence.

(3) A location is not a place of business merely because that is –

    (a) where equipment and technology supporting an information system used by a party are located; or

    (b) where the information system may be accessed by other parties.

(4) The sole fact that a party makes use of a domain name or electronic mail address connected to a specific country does not create a presumption that its place of business is located in that country.

14 Attribution of electronic communications

(1) For the purposes of a law of this jurisdiction, unless otherwise agreed between the purported originator and the addressee of an electronic communication, the purported originator of the electronic communication is bound by that communication only if the communication was sent by the purported originator or with the authority of the purported originator.

(2) Subsection (1) does not affect the operation of a law of this jurisdiction that makes provision for –

    (a) conduct engaged in by a person within the scope of the person's actual or apparent authority to be attributed to another person; or

    (b) a person to be bound by conduct engaged in by another person within the scope of the other person's actual or apparent authority.

Part 2A – Additional Provisions Applying to Contracts Involving Electronic Communications

14A Application and operation of this Part

This Part applies to the use of electronic communications in connection with the formation or performance of a contract between parties where the proper law of the contract is (or would on its formation be) the law of this jurisdiction, and so applies –

(a) whether some or all of the parties are located within Australia or elsewhere; and

(b) whether the contract is for business purposes, for personal, family or household purposes, or for other purposes.

14B Invitation to treat regarding contracts

(1) A proposal to form a contract made through one or more electronic communications that –

    a.   is not addressed to one or more specific parties; and

    b.   is generally accessible to parties making use of information systems – is to be considered as an invitation to make offers, unless it clearly indicates the intention of the party making the proposal to be bound in case of acceptance.

(2) Subsection (1) extends to proposals that make use of interactive applications for the placement of orders through information systems.

14C Use of automated message systems for contract formation – non intervention of natural person

A contract formed by –

(a) the interaction of an automated message system and a natural person; or

(b) the interaction of automated message systems –

is not invalid, void or unenforceable on the sole ground that no natural person reviewed or intervened in each of the individual actions carried out by the automated message systems or the resulting contract.

14D Error in electronic communications regarding contracts

(1) This section applies in relation to a statement, declaration, demand, notice or request, including an offer and the acceptance of an offer, that the parties are required to make or choose to make in connection with the formation or performance of a contract.

(2) If –

    (a) a natural person makes an input error in an electronic communication exchanged with the automated message system of another party; and

    (b) the automated message system does not provide the person with an opportunity to correct the error –

the person, or the party on whose behalf the person was acting, has the right to withdraw the portion of the electronic communication in which the input error was made if –

    (c) the person, or the party on whose behalf the person was acting, notifies the other party of the error as soon as possible after having learned of the error and indicates that he or she made an error in the electronic communication; and

(d)   the person, or the party on whose behalf the person was acting, has not used or received any material benefit or value from the goods or services, if any, received from the other party.

(3)   The right of withdrawal of a portion of an electronic communication under this section is not of itself a right to rescind or otherwise terminate a contract.

(4)   The consequences (if any) of the exercise of the right of withdrawal of a portion of an electronic communication under this section are to be determined in accordance with any applicable rule of law.

Note – In some circumstances the withdrawal of a portion of an electronic communication may invalidate the entire communication or render it ineffective for the purposes of contract formation (see paragraph 241 of the UNCITRAL explanatory note for the United Nations Convention on the Use of Electronic Communications in International Contracts).

14E Application of Act in relation to contracts

(1)   Subject to subsection (2), the provisions of sections 7, 13, 13A and 13B apply to –

(a)   a transaction constituted by or relating to a contract; or

(b)   an electronic communication relating to the formation or performance of a contract –

in the same way as they apply to a transaction or electronic communication referred to in those sections, and so apply as if the words "For the purposes of a law of this jurisdiction" were omitted.

(2)   However, this Part (including subsection (1)) does not apply to or in relation to a contract to the extent that –

(a)   Part 2 would of its own force have the same effect as this Part if this Part applied; or

(b)   a law of another State or Territory (that is in substantially the same terms as Part 2) would of its own force have the same effect as this Part if this Part applied.

Note – This section applies provisions of Part 2 to contracts or proposed contracts to the extent (if any) that those provisions do not apply merely because they are expressed to apply in relation to a law of this jurisdiction. This section also disapplies the provisions of Part 2A to the extent that Part 2 would apply of its own force. An example where Part 2 may not apply of its own force is where a contract is being negotiated in a State or Territory from a supplier located overseas.

Part 3 – Miscellaneous

15 Regulations

The Governor in Council may make regulations for or with respect to any matter or thing required or permitted by this Act to be prescribed or necessary to be prescribed to give effect to this Act.

16 Transitional provisions – Electronic Transactions (Victoria) Amendment Act 2011

(1) Regulations made under this Act before the commencement of section 6A (as inserted by section 6 of the **Electronic Transactions (Victoria) Amendment Act 2011**) and in force immediately before that commencement have effect as if section 6A had been in force when they were made and, on and from that commencement, are taken to have been made under section 6A and may be amended or revoked accordingly.

Note – See section 16 of the **Interpretation of Legislation Act 1984**.

(2) Subject to subsection (3) –

(a) section 14B extends to proposals made before the commencement date; and

(b) section 14C extends to actions carried out before the commencement date; and

(c) section 14D extends to statements, declarations, demands, notices or requests, including offers and the acceptance of offers, made or given before the commencement date.

(3) Subsection (2) and Part 2A do not apply in relation to contracts formed before the commencement date.

(4) In subsections (2) and (3), *commencement date* means the date of commencement of Part 2A, as inserted by section 12 of the *Electronic Transactions (Victoria) Amendment Act* **2011**.

Appendix B Australian Privacy Principles

The Australian Privacy Principles are to be found in Schedule 1 of the *Privacy Act 1988* (Cth).

Part 1 sets out principles that require APP entities to consider the privacy of personal information, including ensuring that APP entities manage personal information in an open and transparent way.

Part 2 sets out principles that deal with the collection of personal information including unsolicited personal information.

Part 3 sets out principles about how APP entities deal with personal information and government related identifiers. The Part includes principles about the use and disclosure of personal information and those identifiers.

Part 4 sets out principles about the integrity of personal information. The Part includes principles about the quality and security of personal information.

Part 5 sets out principles that deal with requests for access to, and the correction of, personal information.

The Australian Privacy Principles are:

Australian Privacy Principle 1 – open and transparent management of personal information

Australian Privacy Principle 2 – anonymity and pseudonymity

Australian Privacy Principle 3 – collection of solicited personal information

Australian Privacy Principle 4 – dealing with unsolicited personal information

Australian Privacy Principle 5 – notification of the collection of personal information

Australian Privacy Principle 6 – use or disclosure of personal information

Australian Privacy Principle 7 – direct marketing

Australian Privacy Principle 8 – cross-border disclosure of personal information

Australian Privacy Principle 9 – adoption, use or disclosure of government related identifiers

Australian Privacy Principle 10 – quality of personal information

Australian Privacy Principle 11 – security of personal information

Australian Privacy Principle 12 – access to personal information

Australian Privacy Principle 13 – correction of personal information

Part 1 – Consideration of personal information privacy

1 Australian Privacy Principle 1 – open and transparent management of personal information

1.1   The object of this principle is to ensure that APP entities manage personal information in an open and transparent way.

Compliance with the Australian Privacy Principles etc.

1.2   An APP entity must take such steps as are reasonable in the circumstances to implement practices, procedures and systems relating to the entity's functions or activities that:

(a)   will ensure that the entity complies with the Australian Privacy Principles and a registered APP code (if any) that binds the entity; and

(b)   will enable the entity to deal with inquiries or complaints from individuals about the entity's compliance with the Australian Privacy Principles or such a code.

APP Privacy policy

1.3   An APP entity must have a clearly expressed and up-to-date policy (the *APP privacy policy*) about the management of personal information by the entity.

1.4   Without limiting subclause 1.3, the APP privacy policy of the APP entity must contain the following information:

(a)   the kinds of personal information that the entity collects and holds;

(b)   how the entity collects and holds personal information;

(c)   the purposes for which the entity collects, holds, uses and discloses personal information;

(d)   how an individual may access personal information about the individual that is held by the entity and seek the correction of such information;

(e)   how an individual may complain about a breach of the Australian Privacy Principles, or a registered APP code (if any) that binds the entity, and how the entity will deal with such a complaint;

(f)   whether the entity is likely to disclose personal information to overseas recipients;

(g)   if the entity is likely to disclose personal information to overseas recipients – the countries in which such recipients are likely to be located if it is practicable to specify those countries in the policy.

Availability of APP privacy policy etc.

1.5 An APP entity must take such steps as are reasonable in the circumstances to make its APP privacy policy available:

(a) free of charge; and

(b) in such form as is appropriate. **Note:** An APP entity will usually make its APP privacy policy available on the entity's website.

1.6 If a person or body requests a copy of the APP privacy policy of an APP entity in a particular form, the entity must take such steps as are reasonable in the circumstances to give the person or body a copy in that form.

2 Australian Privacy Principle 2 – anonymity and pseudonymity

2.1 Individuals must have the option of not identifying themselves, or of using a pseudonym, when dealing with an APP entity in relation to a particular matter.

2.2 Subclause 2.1 does not apply if, in relation to that matter:

(a) the APP entity is required or authorised by or under an Australian law, or a court/tribunal order, to deal with individuals who have identified themselves; or

(b) it is impracticable for the APP entity to deal with individuals who have not identified themselves or who have used a pseudonym.

Part 2 – Collection of personal information

3 Australian Privacy Principle 3 – collection of solicited personal information

Personal information other than sensitive information

3.1 If an APP entity is an agency, the entity must not collect personal information (other than sensitive information) unless the information is reasonably necessary for, or directly related to, one or more of the entity's functions or activities.

3.2 If an APP entity is an organisation, the entity must not collect personal information (other than sensitive information) unless the information is reasonably necessary for one or more of the entity's functions or activities.

Sensitive information

3.3   An APP entity must not collect sensitive information about an individual unless:

(a)   the individual consents to the collection of the information and:

(i)   if the entity is an agency – the information is reasonably necessary for, or directly related to, one or more of the entity's functions or activities; or

(ii)   if the entity is an organisation – the information is reasonably necessary for one or more of the entity's functions or activities; or

(b)   subclause 3.4 applies in relation to the information.

3.4   This subclause applies in relation to sensitive information about an individual if:

(a)   the collection of the information is required or authorised by or under an Australian law or a court/tribunal order; or

(b)   a permitted general situation exists in relation to the collection of the information by the APP entity; or

(c)   the APP entity is an organisation and a permitted health situation exists in relation to the collection of the information by the entity; or

(d)   the APP entity is an enforcement body and the entity reasonably believes that:

(i)   if the entity is the Immigration Department – the collection of the information is reasonably necessary for, or directly related to, one or more enforcement related activities conducted by, or on behalf of, the entity; or

(ii)   otherwise – the collection of the information is reasonably necessary for, or directly related to, one or more of the entity's functions or activities; or

(e)   the APP entity is a non-profit organisation and both of the following apply:

(i)   the information relates to the activities of the organisation;

(ii)   the information relates solely to the members of the organisation, or to individuals who have regular contact with the organisation in connection with its activities.

Note: For permitted general situation, see section 16A. For permitted health situation, see section 16B.

Means of collection

3.5   An APP entity must collect personal information only by lawful and fair means.

3.6   An APP entity must collect personal information about an individual only from the individual unless:

   (a)   if the entity is an agency:

      (i)   the individual consents to the collection of the information from someone other than the individual; or

      (ii)   the entity is required or authorised by or under an Australian law, or a court/tribunal order, to collect the information from someone other than the individual; or

   (b)   it is unreasonable or impracticable to do so.

Solicited personal information

3.7   This principle applies to the collection of personal information that is solicited by an APP entity.

4 Australian Privacy Principle 4 – dealing with unsolicited personal information

4.1   If:

   (a)   an APP entity receives personal information; and

   (b)   the entity did not solicit the information; the entity must, within a reasonable period after receiving the information, determine whether or not the entity could have collected the information under Australian Privacy Principle 3 if the entity had solicited the information.

4.2   The APP entity may use or disclose the personal information for the purposes of making the determination under subclause 4.1.

4.3   If:

   (a)   the APP entity determines that the entity could not have collected the personal information; and

   (b)   the information is not contained in a Commonwealth record;

      the entity must, as soon as practicable but only if it is lawful and reasonable to do so, destroy the information or ensure that the information is de-identified.

4.4   If subclause 4.3 does not apply in relation to the personal information, Australian Privacy Principles 5 to 13 apply in relation to the information as if the entity had collected the information under Australian Privacy Principle 3.

5 Australian Privacy Principle 5 – notification of the collection of personal information

5.1   At or before the time or, if that is not practicable, as soon as practicable after, an APP entity collects personal information about an individual, the entity must take such steps (if any) as are reasonable in the circumstances:

(a)   to notify the individual of such matters referred to in subclause 5.2 as are reasonable in the circumstances; or

(b)   to otherwise ensure that the individual is aware of any such matters.

5.2   The matters for the purposes of subclause 5.1 are as follows:

(a)   the identity and contact details of the APP entity;

(b)   if:

(i)   the APP entity collects the personal information from someone other than the individual; or

(ii)   the individual may not be aware that the APP entity has collected the personal information;

the fact that the entity so collects, or has collected, the information and the circumstances of that collection;

(c)   if the collection of the personal information is required or authorised by or under an Australian law or a court/tribunal order – the fact that the collection is so required or authorised (including the name of the Australian law, or details of the court/tribunal order, that requires or authorises the collection);

(d)   the purposes for which the APP entity collects the personal information;

(e)   the main consequences (if any) for the individual if all or some of the personal information is not collected by the APP entity;

(f)   any other APP entity, body or person, or the types of any other APP entities, bodies or persons, to which the APP entity usually discloses personal information of the kind collected by the entity;

(g)   that the APP privacy policy of the APP entity contains information about how the individual may access the personal information about the individual that is held by the entity and seek the correction of such information;

(h)   that the APP privacy policy of the APP entity contains information about how the individual may complain about a breach of the Australian Privacy Principles, or a registered APP code (if any) that binds the entity, and how the entity will deal with such a complaint;

(i)   whether the APP entity is likely to disclose the personal information to overseas recipients;

(j)   if the APP entity is likely to disclose the personal information to over-seas recipients – the countries in which such recipients are likely to be located if it is practicable to specify those countries in the notification or to otherwise make the individual aware of them.

Part 3 – Dealing with personal information

6 Australian Privacy Principle 6 – use or disclosure of personal information

Use or disclosure

6.1   If an APP entity holds personal information about an individual that was col-lected for a particular purpose (the *primary purpose*), the entity must not use or disclose the information for another purpose (the *secondary purpose*) un-less:

(a)   the individual has consented to the use or disclosure of the information; or

(b)   subclause 6.2 or 6.3 applies in relation to the use or disclosure of the information.

Note: Australian Privacy Principle 8 sets out requirements for the disclosure of personal information to a person who is not in Australia or an external Territory.

6.2   This subclause applies in relation to the use or disclosure of personal infor-mation about an individual if:

(a)   the individual would reasonably expect the APP entity to use or disclose the information for the secondary purpose and the secondary purpose is:

(i)   if the information is sensitive information – directly related to the primary purpose; or

(ii)   if the information is not sensitive information – related to the pri-mary purpose; or

(b)   the use or disclosure of the information is required or authorised by or under an Australian law or a court/tribunal order; or

(c)   a permitted general situation exists in relation to the use or disclosure of the information by the APP entity; or

(d)   the APP entity is an organisation and a permitted health situation exists in relation to the use or disclosure of the information by the entity; or

(e) the APP entity reasonably believes that the use or disclosure of the in-
     formation is reasonably necessary for one or more enforcement related
     activities conducted by, or on behalf of, an enforcement body.

Note: For permitted general situation, see section 16A. For permitted health
situation, see section 16B.

6.3 This subclause applies in relation to the disclosure of personal information
     about an individual by an APP entity that is an agency if:

(a) the agency is not an enforcement body; and

(b) the information is biometric information or biometric templates; and

(c) the recipient of the information is an enforcement body; and

(d) the disclosure is conducted in accordance with the guidelines made by
     the Commissioner for the purposes of this paragraph.

6.4 If:

(a) the APP entity is an organisation; and

(b) subsection 16B(2) applied in relation to the collection of the personal
     information by the entity;

the entity must take such steps as are reasonable in the circumstances to
ensure that the information is de-identified before the entity discloses it in
accordance with subclause 6.1 or 6.2.

Written note of use or disclosure

6.5 If an APP entity uses or discloses personal information in accordance with
     paragraph 6.2(e), the entity must make a written note of the use or disclosure.

Related bodies corporate

6.6 If:

(a) an APP entity is a body corporate; and

(b) the entity collects personal information from a related body corporate;

this principle applies as if the entity's primary purpose for the collection of
the information were the primary purpose for which the related body corporate collected the information.

Exceptions

6.7 This principle does not apply to the use or disclosure by an organisation of:

(a) personal information for the purpose of direct marketing; or

(b) government related identifiers.

7 Australian Privacy Principle 7 – direct marketing

Direct marketing

7.1   If an organisation holds personal information about an individual, the organisation must not use or disclose the information for the purpose of direct marketing.

Note: An act or practice of an agency may be treated as an act or practice of an organisation, see section 7A.

Exceptions – personal information other than sensitive information

7.2   Despite subclause 7.1, an organisation may use or disclose personal information (other than sensitive information) about an individual for the purpose of direct marketing if:

(a)   the organisation collected the information from the individual; and

(b)   the individual would reasonably expect the organisation to use or disclose the information for that purpose; and

(c)   the organisation provides a simple means by which the individual may easily request not to receive direct marketing communications from the organisation; and

(d)   the individual has not made such a request to the organisation.

7.3   Despite subclause 7.1, an organisation may use or disclose personal information (other than sensitive information) about an individual for the purpose of direct marketing if:

(a)   the organisation collected the information from:

    (i)   the individual and the individual would not reasonably expect the organisation to use or disclose the information for that purpose; or

    (ii)   someone other than the individual; and

(b)   either:

    (i)   the individual has consented to the use or disclosure of the information for that purpose; or

    (ii)   it is impracticable to obtain that consent; and

(c)   the organisation provides a simple means by which the individual may easily request not to receive direct marketing communications from the organisation; and

(d)   in each direct marketing communication with the individual:

    (i)   the organisation includes a prominent statement that the individual may make such a request; or

    (ii)   the organisation otherwise draws the individual's attention to the fact that the individual may make such a request; and

(e)   the individual has not made such a request to the organisation.

Exception – sensitive information

7.4 Despite subclause 7.1, an organisation may use or disclose sensitive information about an individual for the purpose of direct marketing if the individual
has consented to the use or disclosure of the information for that purpose.

Exception – contracted service providers

7.5 Despite subclause 7.1, an organisation may use or disclose personal information for the purpose of direct marketing if:

(a) the organisation is a contracted service provider for a Commonwealth
contract; and

(b) the organisation collected the information for the purpose of meeting
(directly or indirectly) an obligation under the contract; and

(c) the use or disclosure is necessary to meet (directly or indirectly) such an
obligation.

Individual may request not to receive direct marketing communications etc.

7.6 If an organisation (the *first organisation*) uses or discloses personal information about an individual:

(a) for the purpose of direct marketing by the first organisation; or

(b) for the purpose of facilitating direct marketing by other organisations;
the individual may:

(c) if paragraph (a) applies – request not to receive direct marketing communications from the first organisation; and

(d) if paragraph (b) applies – request the organisation not to use or disclose
the information for the purpose referred to in that paragraph; and

(e) request the first organisation to provide its source of the
information.

7.7 If an individual makes a request under subclause 7.6, the first organisation
must not charge the individual for the making of, or to give effect to, the
request and:

(a) if the request is of a kind referred to in paragraph 7.6(c) or (d) – the first
organisation must give effect to the request within a reasonable period
after the request is made; and

(b) if the request is of a kind referred to in paragraph 7.6(e) – the organisation must, within a reasonable period after the request is made, notify
the individual of its source unless it is impracticable or unreasonable to
do so.

Interaction with other legislation

7.8   This principle does not apply to the extent that any of the following apply:

(a)   the Do Not Call Register Act 2006;

(b)   the Spam Act 2003;

(c)   any other Act of the Commonwealth, or a Norfolk Island enactment, prescribed by the regulations.

8 Australian Privacy Principle 8 – cross-border disclosure of personal information

8.1   Before an APP entity discloses personal information about an individual to a person (the *overseas recipient*):

(a)   who is not in Australia or an external Territory; and

(b)   who is not the entity or the individual; the entity must take such steps as are reasonable in the circumstances to ensure that the overseas recipient does not breach the Australian Privacy Principles (other than Australian Privacy Principle 1) in relation to the information.

Note: In certain circumstances, an act done, or a practice engaged in, by the overseas recipient is taken, under section 16C, to have been done, or engaged in, by the APP entity and to be a breach of the Australian Privacy Principles.

8.2   Subclause 8.1 does not apply to the disclosure of personal information about an individual by an APP entity to the overseas recipient if:

(a)   the entity reasonably believes that:

(i)   the recipient of the information is subject to a law, or binding scheme, that has the effect of protecting the information in a way that, overall, is at least substantially similar to the way in which the Australian Privacy Principles protect the information; and

(ii)   there are mechanisms that the individual can access to take action to enforce that protection of the law or binding scheme; or

(b)   both of the following apply:

(i)   the entity expressly informs the individual that if he or she consents to the disclosure of the information, subclause 8.1 will not apply to the disclosure;

(ii)   after being so informed, the individual consents to the disclosure; or

(c)   the disclosure of the information is required or authorised by or under an Australian law or a court/tribunal order; or

(d)   a permitted general situation (other than the situation referred to in item 4 or 5 of the table in subsection 16A(1)) exists in relation to the disclosure of the information by the APP entity; or

(e)   the entity is an agency and the disclosure of the information is required or authorised by or under an international agreement relating to information sharing to which Australia is a party; or

(f)   the entity is an agency and both of the following apply:

   (i)   the entity reasonably believes that the disclosure of the information is reasonably necessary for one or more enforcement related activities conducted by, or on behalf of, an enforcement body;

   (ii)   the recipient is a body that performs functions, or exercises powers, that are similar to those performed or exercised by an enforcement body.

Note: For *permitted general situation*, see section 16A.

9 Australian Privacy Principle 9 – adoption, use or disclosure of government related identifiers

Adoption of government related identifiers

9.1   An organisation must not adopt a government related identifier of an individual as its own identifier of the individual unless:

(a)   the adoption of the government related identifier is required or authorised by or under an Australian law or a court/tribunal order; or

(b)   subclause 9.3 applies in relation to the adoption.

Note: An act or practice of an agency may be treated as an act or practice of an organisation, see section 7A.

Use or disclosure of government related identifiers

9.2   An organisation must not use or disclose a government related identifier of an individual unless:

(a)   the use or disclosure of the identifier is reasonably necessary for the organisation to verify the identity of the individual for the purposes of the organisation's activities or functions; or

(b)   the use or disclosure of the identifier is reasonably necessary for the organisation to fulfil its obligations to an agency or a State or Territory authority; or

(c)   the use or disclosure of the identifier is required or authorised by or under an Australian law or a court/tribunal order; or

(d) a permitted general situation (other than the situation referred to in item 4 or 5 of the table in subsection 16A(1)) exists in relation to the use or disclosure of the identifier; or

(e) the organisation reasonably believes that the use or disclosure of the identifier is reasonably necessary for one or more enforcement related activities conducted by, or on behalf of, an enforcement body; or

(f) subclause 9.3 applies in relation to the use or disclosure.

Note 1: An act or practice of an agency may be treated as an act or practice of an organisation, see section 7A.

Note 2: For *permitted general situation*, see section 16A.

Regulations about adoption, use or disclosure

9.3 This subclause applies in relation to the adoption, use or disclosure by an organisation of a government related identifier of an individual if:

(a) the identifier is prescribed by the regulations; and

(b) the organisation is prescribed by the regulations, or is included in a class of organisations prescribed by the regulations; and

(c) the adoption, use or disclosure occurs in the circumstances prescribed by the regulations.

Note: There are prerequisites that must be satisfied before the matters mentioned in this subclause are prescribed, see subsections 100(2) and (3).

Part 4 – Integrity of personal information

10 Australian Privacy Principle 10 – quality of personal information

10.1 An APP entity must take such steps (if any) as are reasonable in the circumstances to ensure that the personal information that the entity collects is accurate, up-to-date and complete.

10.2 An APP entity must take such steps (if any) as are reasonable in the circumstances to ensure that the personal information that the entity uses or discloses is, having regard to the purpose of the use or disclosure, accurate, up-to-date, complete and relevant.

11 Australian Privacy Principle 11 – security of personal information

11.1 If an APP entity holds personal information, the entity must take such steps as are reasonable in the circumstances to protect the information:

(a)   from misuse, interference and loss; and

(b)   from unauthorised access, modification or disclosure.

11.2 If:

(a)   an APP entity holds personal information about an individual; and

(b)   the entity no longer needs the information for any purpose for which the information may be used or disclosed by the entity under this Schedule; and

(c)   the information is not contained in a Commonwealth record; and

(d)   the entity is not required by or under an Australian law, or a court/tribunal order, to retain the information; the entity must take such steps as are reasonable in the circumstances to destroy the information or to ensure that the information is de-identified.

Part 5 – Access to, and correction of, personal information

12 Australian Privacy Principle 12 – access to personal information

Access

12.1 If an APP entity holds personal information about an individual, the entity must, on request by the individual, give the individual access to the information.

Exception to access – agency

12.2 If:

(a)   the APP entity is an agency; and

(b)   the entity is required or authorised to refuse to give the individual access to the personal information by or under:

(i) the Freedom of Information Act; or

(ii) any other Act of the Commonwealth, or a Norfolk Island enact-ment, that provides for access by persons to documents;

then, despite subclause 12.1, the entity is not required to give access to the extent that the entity is required or authorised to refuse to give access.

Exception to access – organisation

12.3 If the APP entity is an organisation then, despite subclause 12.1, the entity is not required to give the individual access to the personal information to the extent that:

(a) the entity reasonably believes that giving access would pose a serious threat to the life, health or safety of any individual, or to public health or public safety; or

(b) giving access would have an unreasonable impact on the privacy of other individuals; or

(c) the request for access is frivolous or vexatious; or

(d) the information relates to existing or anticipated legal proceedings be-tween the entity and the individual, and would not be accessible by the process of discovery in those proceedings; or

(e) giving access would reveal the intentions of the entity in relation to negotiations with the individual in such a way as to prejudice those negotiations; or

(f) giving access would be unlawful; or

(g) denying access is required or authorised by or under an Australian law or a court/tribunal order; or

(h) both of the following apply:

(i) the entity has reason to suspect that unlawful activity, or miscon-duct of a serious nature, that relates to the entity's functions or activities has been, is being or may be engaged in;

(ii) giving access would be likely to prejudice the taking of appropri-ate action in relation to the matter; or

(i) giving access would be likely to prejudice one or more enforcement related activities conducted by, or on behalf of, an enforcement body; or

(j) giving access would reveal evaluative information generated within the entity in connection with a commercially sensitive decision-making process.

Dealing with requests for access

12.4 The APP entity must:

(a) respond to the request for access to the personal information:

    (i) if the entity is an agency – within 30 days after the request is made; or

    (ii) if the entity is an organisation – within a reasonable period after the request is made; and

(b) give access to the information in the manner requested by the individual, if it is reasonable and practicable to do so.

Other means of access

12.5 If the APP entity refuses:

(a) to give access to the personal information because of subclause 12.2 or 12.3; or

(b) to give access in the manner requested by the individual;

    the entity must take such steps (if any) as are reasonable in the circumstances to give access in a way that meets the needs of the entity and the individual.

12.6 Without limiting subclause 12.5, access may be given through the use of a mutually agreed intermediary.

Access charges

12.7 If the APP entity is an agency, the entity must not charge the individual for the making of the request or for giving access to the personal information.

12.8 If:

(a) the APP entity is an organisation; and

(b) the entity charges the individual for giving access to the personal information;

    the charge must not be excessive and must not apply to the making of the request.

Refusal to give access

12.9 If the APP entity refuses to give access to the personal information because of subclause 12.2 or 12.3, or to give access in the manner requested by the individual, the entity must give the individual a written notice that sets out:

(a) the reasons for the refusal except to the extent that, having regard to the grounds for the refusal, it would be unreasonable to do so; and

(b) the mechanisms available to complain about the refusal; and

(c) any other matter prescribed by the regulations.

12.10   If the APP entity refuses to give access to the personal information because of paragraph 12.3(j), the reasons for the refusal may include an explanation for the commercially sensitive decision.

13 Australian Privacy Principle 13 – correction of personal information

Correction

13.1 If:

(a)   an APP entity holds personal information about an individual; and

(b)   either:

(i)   the entity is satisfied that, having regard to a purpose for which the information is held, the information is inaccurate, out-of-date, incomplete, irrelevant or misleading; or

(ii)   the individual requests the entity to correct the information;

the entity must take such steps (if any) as are reasonable in the circumstances to correct that information to ensure that, having regard to the purpose for which it is held, the information is accurate, up-to-date, complete, relevant and not misleading.

Notification of correction to third parties

13.2 If:

(a)   the APP entity corrects personal information about an individual that the entity previously disclosed to another APP entity; and

(b)   the individual requests the entity to notify the other APP entity of the correction;

the entity must take such steps (if any) as are reasonable in the circumstances to give that notification unless it is impracticable or unlawful to do so.

Refusal to correct information

13.3 If the APP entity refuses to correct the personal information as requested by the individual, the entity must give the individual a written notice that sets out:

(a)   the reasons for the refusal except to the extent that it would be unreasonable to do so; and

(b)   the mechanisms available to complain about the refusal; and

(c)   any other matter prescribed by the regulations.

Request to associate a statement

13.4 If:

(a)   the APP entity refuses to correct the personal information as requested by the individual; and

(b)   the individual requests the entity to associate with the information a statement that the information is inaccurate, out-of-date, incomplete, irrelevant or misleading;

the entity must take such steps as are reasonable in the circumstances to associate the statement in such a way that will make the statement apparent to users of the information.

Dealing with requests

13.5 If a request is made under subclause 13.1 or 13.4, the APP entity:

(a)   must respond to the request:

(i)   if the entity is an agency – within 30 days after the request is made; or

(ii) if the entity is an organisation – within a reasonable period after the request is made; and

(b)   must not charge the individual for the making of the request, for correcting the personal information or for associating the statement with the personal information (as the case may be).

INDEX

Printed in the United States
By Bookmasters